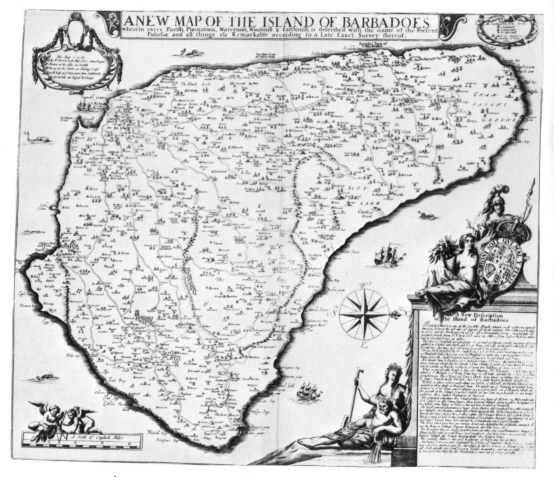

RICHARD FORD'S MAP OF BARBADOS, ca. 1675. COURTESY OF THE JOHN CARTER BROWN LIBRARY, BROWN UNIVERSITY.

A Guide to Source Materials

for the Study of

BARBADOS HISTORY

1627 - 1834

By Jerome S. Handler

Southern Illinois University Press   *Carbondale and Edwardsville*

Feffer & Simons, Inc.   *London and Amsterdam*

COPYRIGHT © *1971*
by SOUTHERN ILLINOIS UNIVERSITY PRESS
All rights reserved
Printed in the United States of America
Designed by Andor Braun
ISBN 0-8093-0436-8
Library of Congress Catalog Card Number 79-93882

CONTENTS

PREFACE   vii

CODE TO LIBRARIES   xv

1   Printed Books, Pamphlets, Broadsheets

        1630–1699   1
        1700–1749   17
        1750–1799   34
        1800–1839   59
        1840–1968   94

2   Parliamentary Papers   106

3   Newspapers   116

4   Prints   119

5   Manuscripts

        Barbados   121
        West Indies (*other than Barbados*)   123
        England   126
        Ireland   160
        Scotland   163
        Europe (*other than England, Ireland, and Scotland*)   165
        United States   168

INDEX   183

An overview of Barbadian history can provide a contextual basis for discussing the background to this *Guide* and the procedures followed in compiling it.

The first non-Amerindian settlement in this southeastern Caribbean island was established in 1627 when a handful of Englishmen and a small group of Africans, captured during the voyage, arrived directly from England. In the early years, the island's cash economy rested upon the production of tobacco, cotton, and indigo, largely grown on small holdings by both free and indentured Europeans. By the 1640s it was the first of Britain's possessions in the Caribbean to produce sugar on a commercial basis. As the plantation system expanded, thousands of Europeans left the island in search of land and other opportunities elsewhere, and many thousands more of Africans were imported to take their place. In the 1650s, the plantation system based upon slave labor was firmly entrenched, and the island's flourishing economy made it the richest of Britain's Caribbean possessions. Although the zenith of prosperity was reached by the 1660s and 1670s, throughout the remainder of the seventeenth century (until later surpassed by Jamaica) the wealth of the island and its planters became legendary.

The status of Barbados sugar was subjected to many pressures over the eighteenth and early nineteenth centuries, and despite sometimes marked fluctuations in the island's economy, the traffic in African slaves continued. In 1807, the trade was abolished; the slaves were nominally freed in 1834, and, after an abortive "apprenticeship" period, in 1838 they were formally emancipated.

However, fundamental patterns, developed during the slave period, persisted. The plantation, as a social and economic institution, dominated island polity and society, and a rigid stratification system, based to a considerable degree on racial origins, perpetuated the low status and limited opportunities for most of the island's population. Also, the process of creolization, wherein African and European cultural patterns were modified and transformed and new cultural traits evolved, had already started within the context of the slave society. Today, the island's culture, despite the prominence of English-derived national institutions, is fundamentally of the New World, a variant of wider West Indian culture.

By the late nineteenth century, Barbados had slipped into the backwater of the British colonial empire, far removed from its position in earlier days, and of limited concern to colonial policy. Despite vicissitudes and threats to its external market, sugar continued its domination of the island's economy, as it does to the present day, and basic political patterns, established in early colonial history, continued.

In the early years of Barbados's colonization, proprietary rights were granted by the Crown. But, by the 1650s, the home government had assumed direct control and appointed its own governor who, in turn, selected a council, usually composed of leading planters and merchants. Somewhat earlier, a House of Assembly had emerged whose members, elected on a narrow franchise based on property and race, were largely concerned with protecting their own political and economic interests. Barbados's political history was frequently marked by conflict between these local interests and the governor or even the British Parliament itself, and the island was the only British Caribbean possession to have two legislative chambers throughout most of its colonial history.

Although absentee plantation owners were not uncommon in Barbados, the island had many locally-based planters, and throughout most of its history a larger proportion of whites than other West Indian territories. This population, although a numerical minority, dominated and controlled the society's major internal political and economic institutions until fairly recent times.

The basic social, economic, and political patterns delineated above, continued until the late 1930s when the system's inequities, aggravated by the depression, unleashed demonstrations with more urgent pleas for social reform. The reform movement was to some extent heeded by the Imperial government, and ameliorative measures were instituted. By the 1940s, the trade unions which had emerged earlier, formed the basis for mass political parties. Suffrage qualifications were modified, and more members of the island's non-white population took their places in the legislature. With the establishment of universal adult suffrage in 1950, Barbados moved toward the first popular government in over three hundred years of its elected House of Assembly.

The island, by now with a great measure of internal self-government, became a member of the ill-fated West Indies Federation (1958–62), and in the early 1960s its government decided for complete independence. In November 1966, after close to three hundred and forty years of continuous and uninterrupted British rule, Barbados became a politically independent member of the British Commonwealth.

In its major outlines, Barbadian history does not differ to any considerable degree from the experiences and forces that helped shape other West Indian societies. In recent years, historical studies of these societies appear to reflect a trend where less emphasis is placed on the history of the colonial powers and their agents in the area, and

more on the development and nature of the societies themselves. Although traditional emphases upon political and economic history are still very apparent, scholars in a variety of fields and of various nationalities, are showing a greater concern with broader socio-cultural topics and issues. Such interests are to be greatly encouraged. Among other legacies, the colonial heritage has often left a distorted view of West Indian society and culture, the historical roots from which they sprang, and the processes by which they developed. The period of the slave society is of special significance for an understanding of such developments; Edward Brathwaite makes the point succinctly when he writes: "In the same way that West Indian culture must be defined in terms of the process of creolization, so too must this creolization be understood against its background of slavery."[1]

The position of Barbados in the West Indies during the days of slavery needs no extensive documentation here. As noted above, the sugar plantation system based upon slave labor was flourishing by the mid-seventeenth century, and the social and cultural patterns which developed over the years were to leave an indelible imprint on the island in the postemancipation period. Barbados in turn provides materials for a wider perspective on the slave society of the British Caribbean as a whole.

Despite contributions to an understanding of this period in Barbados, such as the work of J. Harry Bennett[2] and the volume of articles edited by Frank J. Klingberg,[3] major studies of slavery and the slave society of Barbados are lacking. Important and intensively

---

[1] "Caribbean Critics," *New World Quarterly,* 5 (1969), 7.

[2] *Bondsmen and Bishops: Slavery and Apprenticeship on the Codrington Plantations of Barbados, 1710–1838.* University of California Publications in History, vol. 62 (Berkeley and Los Angeles, 1958).

[3] *Codrington Chronicle: An Experiment in Anglican Altruism on a Barbados Plantation, 1710–1834.* University of California Publications in History, vol. 37 (Berkeley and Los Angeles, 1949).

researched contributions to a study of slavery in the British West Indies have been published in recent years for Jamaica[4] and the Leeward Islands,[5] but it is still generally true that relatively more is known about the structure and institutional organization of the slave society itself, than about the life of the slaves from a cultural and social perspective.[6]

Such considerations prompted me to start, during the summer of 1965, a research project designed to provide an intensive case study of the social and cultural life of Africans and their descendants in Barbados during the seventeenth, eighteenth, and early nineteenth centuries. It is hoped that this study, when completed, will yield an ethnographic picture of a slave population, and insights into the ways in which Africans contributed to the development of Barbadian society and the formation of a creole culture; it is further hoped that this study will be able to isolate some of the forces which contributed to the growth and development of British West Indian societies and cultures in general.[7]

The bibliographic guide presented in the following pages focuses on the period 1627–1834, and is a by-product of this research project; it is offered for the benefit of other scholars who might be concerned with Barbadian and West Indian history.

As far as I know, there are three reasonably comprehensive Caribbean bibliographies which contain items published in the time period considered here.[8] But each of these has limitations in terms of its utility for one engaged in intensive research on early Barbadian social and cultural history. In the earliest of these bibliographies, compiled by Frank Cundall,[9] the section dealing with Barbados lacks annotation, many important items are missing, and there are some misleading citations. Furthermore, items containing important materials on Barbados are not all found under the Barbados section of the bibliography, and this can easily cause the researcher focusing on the island to overlook them. Although J. Graham Cruickshank's bibliography[10] builds upon Cundall's and is specifically concerned with Barbados, it too lacks many items and contains errors. In addition, neither author makes any comprehensive effort to locate items, and both fail to treat manuscript sources which are integral to any full-range study of Barbadian history. Despite such limitations, both bibliographies are useful compilations of a number of printed sources dealing with the slave and postemancipation periods. The most comprehensive biblio-

---

4 Orlando Patterson, *The Sociology of Slavery: An Analysis of the Origins, Development, and Structure of Negro Slave Society in Jamaica* (London, 1967).

5 Elsa V. Goveia, *Slave Society in the British Leeward Islands at the End of the Eighteenth Century* (New Haven, 1965).

6 See, for example, Sidney W. Mintz, rev. of *Slavery*, by Stanley M. Elkins, *American Anthropologist*, 63 (1961), *579–87*; Arnold A. Sio, "Society, Slavery, and the Slave," *Social and Economic Studies*, 16 (1967), *330–44*; Edward Brathwaite, "Jamaican Slave Society, A Review," *Race*, 9 (1968), *331–42*.

7 This project is described more fully in Jerome S. Handler, "African Immigrants and Their Descendants in Barbados: The Social and Cultural Life of a West Indies Slave Population, 1640–1834," *American Philosophical Society, Yearbook, 1969* (Philadelphia, 1970), *pp. 384–86*.

8 In addition, two libraries have catalogs specifically devoted to their Barbados holdings: *Bibliotheca Barbadiensis: A Catalog of Materials Relating to Barbados 1650–1860 in the Boston Public Library* (Boston, 1968), lists forty-one published works and twenty manuscripts relating to the preemancipation period, but is incomplete on the library's printed holdings and contains some minor errors; *Barbadiana: A List of Works Pertaining to the History of the Island of Barbados* (Bridgetown, 1966), lists works contained in the Barbados Public Library, most of which were published in the post-1834 period, and some of which do not specifically relate to Barbados.

9 *Bibliography of the West Indies, Excluding Jamaica* (Kingston, 1909).

10 "A Bibliography of Barbados," *Journal of the Barbados Museum and Historical Society*, 2 (1935), *155–65, 220–25*; 3 (1935), *20–25*.

graphy available for the British Caribbean is the now classic work by Lowell
J. Ragatz[11] after which my own *Guide*
is admittedly modeled. Ragatz's work,
however, covers a much shorter time
period than is dealt with here. In
addition, he does not locate sources (see
below) and although two brief sections
of his *Guide* are specifically devoted to
Barbados, its general West Indies
coverage sometimes makes it difficult,
despite frequent annotations, topical
organization, and comprehensive index,
to discover those entries which refer to
the island, and to discern the types of
information contained within them.
Also, Ragatz's primary concern with
political and economic history often
leads him to underemphasize or mini-
mize sources which contain potentially
useful information on Barbadian social
life and customs.

The present work owes a considerable
debt to the above three authors as
many of the printed items cited in this
Guide were initially discovered through
use of these sources. Others were un-
covered through a variety of means,
mainly by searching library catalogs,
including the National Union Catalog
at the Library of Congress, and, when
possible, the shelves of libraries which
had specialized West Indian collections.
I have also made extensive use of Joseph
Sabin's bibliography,[12] and the bibliographies compiled by L. W. Hanson[13]
and Donald Wing.[14] In the following
pages, these bibliographies and the ones
by Cruickshank, Cundall, and Ragatz
are generally only referred to by the
author's last name and the item or page
number which refers to a particular
title. Other bibliographic sources, including those utilized for the location
and/or description of manuscript materials, are cited and discussed in various
pages of the following sections and
chapters.

This *Guide* cannot include all of the
items I have consulted over a number
of years of research.[15] For the intensive
researcher, a considerable amount of
time could be saved by knowing which
items dealing with the West Indies
contain no specific treatment of Barbados, but space limitations make such
inclusions impractical. Although some
of the literature that treats the West
Indies in general would have bearing
on Barbados history, I have generally
tried to confine my citations to those
items that mention Barbados in their
titles or treat the island in their contents; included as well, even if they
do not meet these criteria, are titles
published in Barbados and those authored by persons known to be Barbadians
or long-term island residents. In addition, to provide some assistance in
judging the contents of sources, I have
included a number of items which,
by their titles or subtitles, imply that
they contain primary or firsthand
observational information on the island,
but which, in reality, are merely paraphrases or outright plagiarisms of other
sources.[16] Such items, and at least
some of the sources upon which they
are based, are briefly described in the
annotations.

In annotating an item, I have tried,
at the minimum, to indicate its major
emphasis, and the types of materials
contained within it. Because of space

---

[11] *A Guide for the Study of British Caribbean
History, 1763–1834* (Washington, D.C.,
1932).

[12] *Bibliotheca Americana: A Dictionary of Books
Relating to America From Its Discovery to the
Present Time*, 29 vols. (New York, 1868–
1936).

[13] *Contemporary Printed Sources for British and
Irish Economic History, 1701–1750* (Cambridge, Eng., 1963).

[14] *Short-Title Catalogue of Books Printed in
England, Scotland, Ireland, Wales, and British
America and of English Books Printed in Other
Countries, 1641–1700*, 3 vols. (New York,
1945–51).

[15] Although I have examined a great deal of
the voluminous literature relating to the
emancipation controversy, I cannot pre-
tend that my coverage was exhaustive.
Both Ragatz and Cundall cite a number of
works I have not seen, and there are
undoubtedly many more they do not list.
Some of these may contain materials
specifically treating Bardados.

[16] Excluding published transcripts of manuscripts, *Parliamentary Papers*, newspapers,
various editions of printed works, etc., this
Guide lists approximately 654 printed titles.

limitations, it is sometimes necessary to simply give an overall assessment. This applies especially to travelers' accounts and manuscript collections in which materials on a variety of topics are presented.

Generally speaking, many of the works cited appear to offer sparse and cursory information; yet, they could be useful to those seeking specialized data. As a guiding principle, then, I fully agree with the sentiments expressed by H. I. Hogbin who, referring to a bibliography of the Pacific, notes, "Some of the minor publications, it may be thought, would have been decently left in oblivion. But . . . subsequent generations may well discover significant material in the most unlikely places."[17]

As indicated above, the period covered in this *Guide* is from 1627 to 1834; the vast majority of the sources cited were written or published within this period, but some later items (especially those relating to the Apprenticeship period) have been included because they contain firsthand information which could easily be applicable to preemancipation society and culture.

I have generally avoided citing late nineteenth and twentieth-century works unless they include transcripts or reproductions of earlier items. This is particularly so in the case of the *Journal of the Barbados Museum and Historical Society*[18] whose volumes, since the *Journal*'s inception in 1933, contain numerous articles of interest to the scholar concerned with the island's history. I have, however, frequently cited those articles that help illuminate the primary sources by, for example, providing biographical materials on the author or background to his work. In general, for a useful introduction to secondary twentieth-century materials that deal with the preemancipation period, the reader is referred to the recent West Indies bibliography compiled by Lambros Comitas.[19]

Many of the printed works in this *Guide* are found in very few libraries;[20] not even the largest depositories such as the Library of Congress and the British Museum contain all of them. Because of this, one of the great difficulties in using Ragatz's *Guide* is its failure to list at least one location for each of the items cited. Ragatz informs his readers that the *Guide* "is based on material in 69 repositories, both public and private, in seven countries."[21] Although he lists these repositories, he makes no attempt to correlate them with items in his bibliography. Thus, the researcher who uses his *Guide* is often faced with a veritable "treasure hunt," and a great deal of time can be consumed in tracing the location of source materials.

In the present work I have tried to overcome this difficulty by placing in brackets, at the end of each citation, at least one repository in which the item is known to be located.[22] This repository may be the one in which the item was consulted and/or it may be the one in which an authoritative source has given its location. I made no attempt to survey the holdings in each of the libraries visited, and thus do not offer a census of locations; it is to be understood, then, that the repository cited for a published item may not be the only one in which it is located. In most cases, some effort to locate was made even if I had no opportunity to personally

---

17 Quoted in Lambros Comitas, *Caribbeana 1900–1965: A Topical Bibliography* (Seattle, 1968), *pp. viii–ix.*

18 Abbreviated throughout this *Guide* as *Jl. BMHS*. Complete runs of the *Jl. BMHS* are located in various libraries including the British Museum, New York Public Library, American Museum of Natural History, Smithsonian Institution, University of the West Indies (Mona), Institute of Jamaica, Barbados Public Library, Barbados Museum and Historical Society, and the Barbados Department of Archives.

19 Comitas, *Caribbeana 1900–1965.*

20 In general, published materials which, as a group, have been consistently the most difficult to locate were those published in Barbados during the eighteenth (printing was first established on the island in 1730) and nineteenth centuries.

21 *Caribbeana 1900–1965, p. iii.*

22 Libraries most frequently referred to in the section on printed works have been assigned a letter-symbol. See Code to Libraries, *p. xv* of this volume.

examine the item. In other cases, which are commented on in the annotations, fairly intensive search failed to yield a copy. Many of the items I cite, both printed and manuscript, were not personally examined, for a variety of reasons, including not being able to ascertain their location or discovering the item when I no longer had access to the repository in which it is located. In all such cases, I have identified the source for my citation, whether it be a bibliography, article, library catalog, and so forth. Printed materials I have not examined are marked with an asterisk (*) preceding the author or title of the work, and manuscripts in this category are clearly specified as well.

Each published entry is comprised of the author's name, if known, title, place and date of publication, the number of volumes or pages. Library locations appear either in code in the entry or in full in the annotation. If the author's name, date or place of publication, etc., is not published in the work itself, such information, if known, is given in brackets. I have tried to indicate my reasons or sources for ascribing authorship to anonymous works, and have often relied upon sources such as Hanson, Wing, and Sabin for assigning dates to undated works. In some cases, I have been forced to assign provisional dates myself; I did this with some trepidation, being somewhat aware of the manifold difficulties involved in assigning precise dates, especially to early works.

A number of printed works, such as medical dissertations in Latin, have been cited by short title, but I have tried to insure that the title entry is of sufficient length to permit easy identification of the item. Cross-referencing to printed works is usually done by simply citing the author or short title, and the year of publication.

I have indicated the number of volumes or pages in printed items to give the reader some idea of the physical size of the work, although the number of pages may not be precise in terms of technical bibliographic criteria. In addition, I have tried to give information, where available, on various editions of a given work, although I use the term edition loosely to mean any printing of an item. In some cases I have compared editions and indicate the similarities and differences in content, if any, between them, but in most cases I have not done this.

For a variety of reasons, many researchers will not have direct access to repositories which contain a majority of the items they may wish to consult. And because of restrictive loan policies and the rarity and fragility of many of the books, journals, and manuscripts, interlibrary loans will, in many cases, prove to be impractical or impossible. Yet, a number of repositories will be in a position to provide reproductions of sections of books, or even manuscripts, in their possession. To facilitate inquiries and ordering procedures in these circumstances, I have indicated for many items the pages which specifically refer to Barbados.

As a final word, I should like to emphasize that many of the citations and much of the information in this *Guide* were not originally compiled for publication. They derive from a bibliography I developed as an aid to my own researches, and the decision to publish came much later, when the work was well under way. One consequence of this is that the completeness of citations and the depth of annotations are of variable quality and some may not satisfy the standards of professional archivists and bibliographers. It is my hope, however, that this *Guide* will not only be of assistance to historians, but to other scholars who, like myself, were not trained in the use of source materials, but whose interests have carried them into historical research.

This *Guide* could not have been compiled without the assistance of scores of persons on the staffs of the libraries and archival depositories in which I worked and with which I have corresponded. With rare exceptions, I have encountered nothing but courtesy and a willingness to help from such persons, many of whose names I did not learn, and the debt that I owe them is considerable. Certain individuals have consistently gone out of their way to provide assistance, and the amiable way in which they have done so greatly contributed to the pleasure of this project. Michael Chandler, Barbados Government Archivist, and Neville Connell, Director of the Barbados Museum, both friends of many years' standing, have shown a keen interest in this project from its inception and have yielded to many impositions I have placed on their time and knowledge of Barbadian source materials. Others who have been exceptionally kind in helping the research along are Father Brendan Connolly, Director of the Boston College Library, Alan Cohn and Dr. John Clifford, of the Morris Library at Southern Illinois University, Miss Joan Gibbs, Archivist at the University of London, and Samuel J. Hough and Christopher Klein, of The John Carter Brown Library. Dr. David Watts helped in the identification of source materials at the start of the research, and Kenneth E. Ingram, Deputy Librarian at the Mona campus of the University of the West Indies, provided generous assistance in locating manuscripts in the United States and United Kingdom.

I am grateful to Michael Chandler and Dr. Edward Brathwaite, who read the final draft of this manuscript, and to Professors Carl Bridenbaugh, Elsa Goveia, Jack Greene, Robert Manners, and Carroll L. Riley who read portions of earlier drafts. All of them offered suggestions for improvement, but they, of course, are in no way responsible for my not having always followed their suggestions. I am also indebted to Thomas R. Adams, Director of The John Carter Brown Library, whose thoughtful and critical comments were very helpful and to whom I must apologize for having deviated from the rigorous bibliographic standards to which he adheres.

Research assistance over the years was given by Eugenia Handler, Sharon Hunt, Michael Spence, and, especially, John Strawn who helped get this project under way; Adrienne Hahn typed, often under frustrating conditions, various drafts of the manuscript. Dr. Matthew Kelley provided translations of materials in Latin, and Alexander Gunkel of those in German.

The expenses involved in this project have been largely met with research grants from the National Institutes of Health (MH 11434–01), the National Science Foundation (GS-1154), and the American Philosophical Society (Johnson Fund, number 750). Southern Illinois University's Graduate School (program in Cooperative Research in Cultural Anthropology) and College of Liberal Arts and Sciences have, periodically, also provided assistance. The *Guide* was completed while I was a Visiting Research Fellow at the University of the West Indies (Mona) under a Younger Scholar Fellowship from the National Endowment for the Humanities (H69–1–138). Funds to aid in preparing the *Guide* for publication were provided by the Research Institute for the Study of Man, Dr. Vera Rubin, Director, and the Southern Illinois University Office of Research and Projects, Dr. Ronald Hanson, Coordinator.

J.S.H.

Kingston, Jamaica
June 1970

CODE TO LIBRARIES

BC   Boston College
(Chestnut Hill, Boston, Mass.)

BM   British Museum
(Great Russell Street, London, W.C. *1)*

BMHS   Barbados Museum and Historical Society
(St. Ann's Garrison, St. Michael)

BOS   Boston Public Library
(Copley Square, Boston, Mass.)

BPL   Barbados Public Library
(Bridgetown, St. Michael)

E   University of Edinburgh
(Edinburgh, Scotland)

F   Society of Friends
(Euston Road, London, N.W. *1)*

H   Harvard University
(Cambridge, Mass.)

IJ   Institute of Jamaica (West India Reference Library)
(East Street, Kingston)

JCB   The John Carter Brown Library
(Brown University, Providence, R.I.)

LCP   The Library Company of Philadelphia
(1314 Locust Street, Philadelphia, Pa.)

LC   Library of Congress
(Washington, D.C.)

NYPL   New York Public Library
(Fifth Avenue and 42nd Street, New York, N.Y.)

RCS   Royal Commonwealth Society
            (*Northumberland Avenue, London,* w.c. *2*)

SIU   Southern Illinois University
            (*Carbondale, Ill.*)

UL   University of London (Senate House)
            (*Malet Street, London,* w.c. *1*)

USPG   United Society for the Propagation of the Gospel
            (*15 Tufton Street, London,* s.w. *1*)

WIC   West India Committee
            (*18 Grosvenor Street, London,* w. *1*)

A Guide to Source Materials

for the Study of

BARBADOS HISTORY,

1627–1834

Printed Books, Pamphlets, Broadsheets

1630–1699

SMITH, CAPTAIN JOHN
*The true travels, adventures, and observa-
tions of Captain John Smith . . . from . . .
1593 to 1629.*
London, 1630. *60 pp.* [BM]
Smith's brief comments on Barbados's
geography, economy, population, history, etc. (*pp. 55–56*), are largely, if not
entirely, based on information provided
by two of the island's settlers, John
White and Charles Wolverston, the
latter the island's governor in 1628.
For an extended discussion of this and
other editions see Sabin (82851–852).

COLT, HENRY
The voyage . . . [in 1631].
See Colt (1925).

*A relation of the successful beginnings of
the Lord Baltemore's plantation in Maryland. Being an extract of certaine letters
written from thence.*
[London], 1634. *14 pp.* [JCB, BM]
It is noted (*p. 1*) that the party arrived
in Barbados in early 1634 and stayed
for about twenty days, but nothing is
said about the island. Father Andrew
White (1874) was a member of this
group, and "authorship has been
attributed to" him (Sabin 69291).
Reprinted at Albany, N.Y. (1865, *23 pp.*
[LC]).

WHITE, FATHER ANDREW
Narrative of a voyage . . . [1634].
See White (1874).

THURLOE, JOHN
A collection of state papers . . . [1638–

1660].
See Thomas Birch (1742).

VERNEY, THOMAS
[Letter from Barbados, 1638.]
See John Bruce (1853).

DERING, JAMES
A letter from Barbados in 1640.
See Dering (1960).

LAET, JEAN [JOHANNES] DE
*Histoire du nouveau monde, ou description
des Indes occidentales.*
Leyden, 1640. *632 pp.* [BM]
On page 26 there is a brief paragraph
describing Barbados. This volume is
apparently a translation of the second
Dutch edition (Leyden, 1630) or the
1633 Latin edition *Novus Orbis . . .*; *see*
G. W. Asher (*A Bibliographical and
Historical Essay on the Dutch Books and
Pamphlets Relating to New Netherland,*
Amsterdam, 1854–67; reprinted
Amsterdam, 1960) and Sabin (38554 ff.)
for various editions.

HIRBEC, DANIEL LE
*Voyages . . . aux Antilles . . . 1642–
1644.*
See E. Moreau (1890).

*A true state of the case between the heires
and assignes of Sir William Courteen,
Knight, deceased, and the late Earl of
Carlisle, and planters in the island of
Barbadoes, annexed to the petition of
William Courteen . . . and others, exhibi-
ted in Parliament.*
[London, ca. 1644.] [BM]

A broadsheet which reviews the history of the conflict between Carlisle and Courteen for proprietary rights to the island — in so doing, events in the island's early political history and settlement are recapitulated. A copy of this item is bound into a volume of manuscripts in the BM (Egerton Mss. 2395, *fol. 602*).

Die Sabbathi 23 Januari 1646. Whereas the several plantations in Virginia, Bermudas, Barbados, and other places of America have been much beneficiall to this kingdome by the increase of navigation.
London, 1646.   [JCB]
Broadsheet; a proclamation by the British parliament dealing with the export of commodities and the transport of indentured servants to the colonies.

CARLISLE, JAMES HAY
A declaration by James, Earl of Carlile, Lord of the Caribee Islands . . . Manifesting his care of, and affection to, the good and welfare of the inhabitants of the island of Barbados, and of all other people under his government.
London, 1647.   [NYPL, LC, BM]
A broadsheet of thirty-two printed lines. In it Carlisle remarks on the plight of indentured servants and others who went to Bardados with the hope of acquiring land of their own upon completion of their labor service. But, with the expansion of the sugar plantation system, he notes that "land is now so taken up as there is not any to be had but at great rates too high for the purchase of poor servants . . ." He thus declares "that each freeman who is unprovided of land, and shall therefore desire to go off from the Barbados shall have a portion of land allotted to him in my islands of Nevis, Antigua, or any other island under my command . . ." The declaration also promises investigations into complaints against various governors of the islands and assures that supply ships will be sent more regularly to the West Indies.
The photostat of this declaration in the NYPL and LC was made in 1926 from a copy located in the British Museum (see *Photostat Americana, no. 174*, Massachusetts Historical Society, Boston, Nov. 1926).

PLANTAGENET, BEAUCHAMP
A description of the Province of New Albion.
[London], 1648. *32 pp.*   [BM]
In 1648, the author briefly visited Barbados. Page 5 includes a twenty-two-line description of the island which makes note of its commercial crops, staple foods, domestic animals, a plague, runaway slaves, lack of empty lands, high prices, and external trade.
An "extremely rare tract. . . . The second edition [London, 1650] is even more rare than the first" (Sabin 63310–11). Reprinted in Peter Force, ed., *Tracts and Other Papers*, vol. 2, tract 7 (Washington, 1838) [BM].

FOSTER, NICHOLAS
A briefe relation of the late horrid rebellion acted in the island Barbadas, in the West Indies. Wherein is contained their inhumane acts and actions, in fining and banishing the well-affected to the Parliament of England. . . . Acted by the Waldronds and their abettors, anno 1650.
London, 1650. *112 pp.*   [BM, BOS]
Deals with the repercussions in Barbados of the English Civil War, and is a useful source for the island's early political history. Reprinted in London in 1927 [BMHS]; Cruickshank (2a) cites an 1879 Barbados reprint.

Beschrijvinghe van Virginia, Nieuw Nederlandt, Nieuw Engelandt, en d'eylanden Bermudes, Berbados, en St. Christoffel. Dienstelijck voor elck een derwaerts handelende, en all voortplanters van nieuw colonien. Met kopere figuren verciert.
Amsterdam, 1651. *88 pp.*   [NYPL]
Contains a twenty-six-line (*p. 84*) description of Barbados economy, geography, etc.; taken from J. de Laet's second edition, published in 1630 (*see* G. M. Asher, *A Bibliographical and Historical Essay on the Dutch Books and Pamphlets Relating to New Netherland*, Amsterdam, 1854–67; reprinted 1960, *p. 2*).

A declaration set forth by the Lord Lieutenant General and the gentlemen of the councell and assembly [of Barbados] occasioned from the view of a printed paper, entitled, An Act Prohibiting Trade with the Barbados, Virginea, Bermudes and Antegoe.

Hagh, 1651. *8 pp.*   [BM]

An interesting appeal for the political and commercial autonomy of the island in defiance of the Cromwell government. The declaration adamantly opposes the Act's prohibition on Barbados's trade with "foreigners" and points out the island's indebtedness to the Dutch in particular, viz., "Whereas all the old planters well know how much they have been beholding to the Dutch for their subsistence, and how difficult it would have been (without their assistance) ever to have settled this place and even to this day we are sensible what necessary comforts they bring us and how much cheaper they sell their commodities to us than our own nation . . . we do declare that we will never be so ungrateful to the Dutch for former helps as to deny them or any other nation the freedom of our ports and protection of our laws."

GARDYNER, GEORGE
A description of the new world; or, America islands and Continent.
London, 1651. *187 pp.*   [BM]
The author apparently never visited Barbados; he offers a brief and superficial general description of the island (*pp. 77–79*).

AISENE, GEORGES
"Journal de ce qui s'est passé en la navigation de la flote du Parlement d'Angleterre vers l'isle des Barbades . . . envoyé a Londres par le Chevalier Georges Aisene [Ayscue?], et traduit de l'original Anglois."
Gazette de France, Supplement, Paris, June 7, 1652, *pp. 543–52.*   [LC]
A description of the military activities by which Parliament's expedition subdued and gained control of Barbados's Royalist government in early 1652.

Articles of agreements, made, and concluded the 11th day of January, 1651. By and between the commissioners of the right honourable, the Lord Willoughby of Parrham, on the one part; and the commissioners in the behalfe of the Commonwealth of England, on the other part. Being in order to the rendition of the island of Barbadoes, etc.

London, 1652. *8 pp.*   [JCB]
Otherwise known as the Charter of Barbados, the articles contain twenty-three provisions under which the island's Royalists relinquished the government to Cromwell's representatives. These articles, important to early Barbadian history, include provisions such as the following: "that a liberty of conscience in matters of religion be allowed to all, excepting to such whose tenents are inconsistent to a civil government"; "that the courts of justice shall still continue, and all judgements and orders therein be valid, until they be reversed by due form of laws"; "that no taxes, customs, imposts, loans, or excise shall be laid, nor levies made on any the inhabitants . . . without their free consent in a general assembly"; "that no man shall be imprisoned or put out of his possession of lands and tenements . . . without due proceedings according to the known and common laws of England and statutes and customs of this island."

The articles are also reproduced in Schomburgk (1848, *pp. 280–83*) and J. Jennings (1654, 1656).

Bloudy newes from the Barbadaes, being a true relation of a great and terrible fight between the Parliaments Navie, commanded by Sir George Ayscue; and the King of Scots forces under the conduct and command of the Lord Willoughby. With the particulars of the fight; the storming of the island; the manner how the Parliaments forces were repulsed, and beaten off from Carlisle Bay, and the Blockhouse; and the number killed and wounded.

London, 1652. *8 pp.*   [BM]
Only one-half page of this newsletter is directed to the events indicated in the title, the remaining pages having nothing to do with Barbados or the West Indies.

"From aboard the Rainbow in Carlisle Bay, before the island of Barbados, 19 October 1651."
Mercurius Politicus, no. 90, London, 1652, *pp. 1429–31.*   [BM]
An account of the military and naval actions by which Ayscue captured Barbados from the island's Royalists.

A brief relation of the beginning and ending of the troubles of the Barbadoes, with the true causes thereof, set forth by A. B., a diligent observer of the times.
London, 1653. *10 pp.* [BM]
Treats the political aspects of the Cavalier–Roundhead struggles. The BM copy is bound into a volume of manuscripts (Egerton Mss. 2395, *fols. 48–53*).

[JENNINGS, JOHN]
Acts and Statutes of the island of Barbados. Made and enacted since the reducement of the same, unto the authority of the Commonwealth of England, and set forth the seventh day of September, in the year of our Lord God 1652.
London [1654]. *176 pp.*
[LCP, BM, BOS]
Compiled by the clerk of the Barbados Assembly (*see* Schomburgk, 1848, *p. 203*), this is the earliest publication of Barbadian laws; one hundred and two are reproduced. A second edition, identical in content to the first, was published in London in 1656 [LCP].

N., N.
America; or, an exact description of the West Indies: more especially of those provinces which are under the dominion of the King of Spain.
London, 1655. *484 pp.* [WIC]
The author does not appear to have visited Barbados; his brief description of the island (*pp. 470–71*) is largely concerned with agricultural products and physical geography.

S., I.
A brief and perfect journal of the late proceedings and success of the English Army in the West-Indies, continued until June the 24th 1655. . . . by I. S. an eyewitness.
London, 1655. *27 pp.* [BM]
The author was a member of the Penn and Venables expedition sent against the Spanish in the West Indies. He remained in Barbados for about two months; although his journal offers no descriptive materials on the islands, he details the manner in which the expedition was provisioned and the preparations undertaken prior to leaving for the northern islands. Many Barbadian settlers joined this military

venture, and of them the author comments: ". . . certainly these islanders must be the very scum of scums, and meer dreggs of corruption, and such upon whose endeavors, it was impossible to expect a blessing," an assessment shared by Henry Whistler (BM, Sloane Mss. 3926).

ROUS, JOHN
A warning to the inhabitants of Barbadoes, who live in pride, drunkennesse, covetousnesse, oppression, and deceitful dealings.
[London], 1656. *8 pp.* [F]
Written by a Quaker in Barbados this short tract (six hundred copies of which were distributed on the island) is a diatribe against the morality and religious life of Barbados' white inhabitants. Wing (R2043, R2044) cites, by the same author, *New England a Degenerate Plant* [London], 1659 [F]; *The Sins of a Gainsaying and Rebellious People* [London], 1659 [F].

LIGON, RICHARD
A true and exact history of the iland of Barbados.
London, 1657. *122 pp.* [BMHS, BM]
A classic and indispensable source for any study of Barbadian social history and early sugar production; a considerable part of the work is devoted to the island's flora and fauna. Includes the earliest known detailed map of the island (reproduced in Tony Campbell, 1965). Based upon the author's residence from 1647–50. A second edition, with the same contents, was published in London in 1673 [NYPL, BOS]; this edition has been reprinted by Frank Cass & Company (London, 1970).

[ROCHEFORT, CHARLES DE]
Histoire naturelle et morale des iles Antilles de l'Amerique.
Rotterdam, 1658. *527 pp.* [BM]
Pages 11–12 provide a general description of Barbados in the mid 1640s (the last date mentioned is 1646) when sugar production was well under way.

Later editions of this well-known work are cited by Sabin (72315–322) who also provides an extensive discussion of its authorship.

RIVERS, MARCELLUS AND FOYLE, OXEN-BRIDGE

England's slavery, or Barbados merchandize. Represented in a petition to the high and honorable court of Parliament, by Marcellus Rivers and Oxenbridge Foyle, Gentlemen, on behalf of themselves and three-score and ten more of freeborn Englishmen, sold (uncondemned) into slavery.

London, 1659. *7 pp.* [BM]

The authors claim that they had been falsely accused of participating in the Royalists' 1655 "Salisbury uprising," otherwise known as "Penruddock's rising." After a year's imprisonment in England, they were shipped to Barbados where they were indentured. In this petition they complain about their "inhuman treatment" in Barbados, ask Parliament to alleviate their suffering, and to prevent others from coming to "this place of torment." Appended to the petition are letters from four other persons involuntarily indentured in Barbados whose complaints run in a similar vein to those in the petition itself. The petition and the proceedings in Parliament relating to it are reproduced in L. F. Stock (1924–41, vol. 1, *pp. 247–66*).

FOX, GEORGE

The promise of God proclaimed; . . . by his servants and messengers sent forth since for Barbadoes, New-England, Virginia.

London, 1660. [BOS]

A broadsheet, entirely religious in nature; contains no information on Barbados.

*PINDER, RICHARD

A loving invitation (to repentance and amendment of life) unto all the inhabitants of the island Barbados. Before the Lords sore judgements come upon them, which is seen to be nigh, and which they cannot escape . . . with something more particularly to the heads and owners of the several plantations.

London, 1660. [BM]

"Written at Barbados the 10th day of the 8th month, 1660" (Sabin 62920); the author was a Quaker "minister" on a visit to the island (Manuscripts, Society of Friends, Portfolios, vol. 17, no. 2).

HICKERINGILL, EDMUND

Jamaica viewed . . . with several other collateral observations and reflections upon the island.

London, 1661. *87 pp.* [BM]

Offers no information on Barbados, but in discussing the advantages of settling in Jamaica, because of its land resources, he notes (*pp. 16–17*) ". . . whereas in St. Kitts, Barbadoes, etc. you cannot turn a horse out but he presently trespasseth upon his neighbor, if not upon your own canes. The most barren rocks (even in the Scotland of Barbadoes) owning a proprieter, and the whole island pestered with a supernumerary glut of inhabitants; too small a hive for such a swarm of people."

BIET, ANTOINE

Voyage de la France Equinoxiale en l'isle de Cayenne, entrepris par les François en l'Annee M.DC.LII.

Paris, 1664. *432 pp.* [BM, LC]

Biet, a French priest, spent close to three months in Barbados in early 1654. His little known account of the island, pages 268–95, offers a variety of details on social life and customs and can be a useful source complementing other contemporary accounts. The chapters treating the author's visit to Barbados have been translated and annotated in my article "Father Antoine Biet's Visit to Barbados in 1654" (*Jl. BMHS*, 32, 1967, 56–76).

*[BYAM, WILLIAM]

An exact relation of the most execrable, attempts by John Allin, committed on the person of His Excellency Francis Lord Willoughby of Parham, Captain General of the Continent of Guiana, and of all the Caribby-Island, and our Lord Proprietor.

London, 1665. *12 pp.* [LC, BM]

Cited by Sabin (9704). The author, a former Barbados planter, had been forced to leave the island in 1652 with other Royalists (see Jerome S. Handler, "Father Antoine Biet's Visit to Barbados in 1654." *Jl. BMHS*, 32, 1967). A related item (Sabin 76501) is Robert Sanford, *Surinam Justice . . . set forth under that title by William Byam . . . Governor of that colony* (London, 1662).

EYNDHOVEN, JAN VANS

Journael, ofte Dagh-register, over de reyse,

*gedagen door de Heer Luytenant Admirael
M. A. de Ruyter. In de West Indies. Door
A. F.* [*Journal or Diary about the trip
done by Lt. Admiral M. A. de Ruyter in
the West Indies. By A. F.*]
Amsterdam, 1665. *8 pp.* [NYPL, LC]
Contains a copy of a letter which describes de Ruyter's unsuccessful attack
on Barbados in late 1664. The account
is signed at the end by the author who
participated in the campaign. "A.F.,"
who presumably brought this account
into print, has not been identified.

DAVIES, J.
*The history of Barbados, St. Christophers,
Mevis, . . . and the rest of the Caribby-
Islands.*
London, 1666. *351 pp.*   [BPL, BC]
A "translation of the anonymous French
edition of 1658" by Charles de Roche-
fort (Sabin 72322); Barbados is treated
on pages 8 and 9. Sabin cites the title as
*The History of the Caribby-Islands, viz.,
Barbados, St. Christophers.*

[FOX, GEORGE]
*To friends in Barbadoes, Virginia,
Maryland, New England, and elsewhere.*
[London, 1666?]. *3 pp.*   [BM]
A religious epistle written from London,
this provides no information on the
island's Quaker community; signed
"G.F."

SANFORD, PELEG
The Letter Book . . . 1666–1668.
See P. Sanford (1928).

UCHTERITZ, HEINRICH VON
*Kurtze Reise-Beschreibung Hrrn. Hein-
rich von Uchteritz, Lieutenants, erbsassen
auf Modelwitz in Meissen, und worinnen
vermeldet was er auf derselben für
unglück und glück gehabt sonderlich wie
er gefangen nach West-Indien geführet zur
sclaverey verkaufft und auf der insul
Barbados.*
Schlesswig, 1666. *28 pp.*   [JCB]
Von Uchteritz, a German nobleman,
fought for the Royalists during the
English Civil War; captured at the
Battle of Worcester in 1651, he was
shipped to Barbados where he spent
approximately four and a half months
as an indentured servant in early 1652.
Only pages 3–16 of this pamphlet

record his adventures, but close to three-
fourths of these describe how he acquired his freedom through the intervention of German merchants visiting
Barbados. The remaining pages offer
very brief descriptive passages on the
treatment and life of indentured servants and slaves, house construction,
sugar and cotton production, currency,
the consumption of cassava and potatoes and the manufacture of beverages
from these plants, clothing, and religion.

This rare pamphlet (only one other
copy of this edition is known to exist) is
one of two known published accounts
in which persons indentured by Cromwell relate their experiences in Barbados
(see also M. Rivers and O. Foyle, 1659).
It was republished in 1705 and 1712 in
Weissenfels; more details on these
editions and their locations as well as a
translation of von Uchteritz's account
are given in A. Gunkel and J. Handler,
"A German Indentured Servant in
Barbados in 1652: The Account of
Heinrich von Uchteritz" (*Jl. BMHS*,
33, 1970, *91–100*).

RICH, ROBERT
*Love without dissimulation: or, the letter
and directions of Robert Rich to Mr. John
Raynes. For the distributing his benevo-
lence to the seven churches in London.*
[London, 1667?] *7 pp.*   [BM]
In 1654 Rich, a Barbados planter,
became a Quaker, but in 1656 he broke
with that group. Some of his published
works touch on his altercation with the
Barbados Quaker community, but most
are largely concerned with theological
issues and are valueless sources for
information on the island.

In the above work, Rich describes
how he heard of the "Great London
Fire," while in Barbados, and his
religious reasons for sending money to
be distributed among various church
groups. His gift to the Quakers was
refused because of their criticisms of
his behavior. His reactions to this refusal are described, but are treated
more fully in his pamphlet *Mr. Robert
Rich, His Second Letters from Barbadoes*
(London, 1669, *18 pp.* [BM]). In these
letters, written in 1668, he also notes
that he had recently attended three
Quaker meetings in Barbados, but

"how much contrary to the spirit of love and truth, they have appeared in all their dealings with me" (rebutted in a pamphlet by John Bolton, *Judas His Thirty Pieces Not Received*, London, 1670 [BM]).

Other items by Rich include: *The Hidden Things Brought to Light* (London, 1678 [BM]), a criticism of Quakers (rebutted in *Something in Answer to a Book Printed in 1678*, London, 1679 [BM]); the posthumously published *The Epistles of Mr. Robert Rich to the Seven Churches* (London, 1680 [BM]) which contains a brief biography of Rich by "J.W.," reprints of some items on Rich's theological views, and a summary of his altercations with the Quakers; *Abstracts of Some Letters Written by Mr. Robert Rich, Treating Mostly Spiritual Matters* (London, 1680 [BM]) includes materials written from the 1650s to 1670s and focuses upon theological issues and the stance of the Quakers.

For items by Rich, *see* Sabin (70892–897) and Wing (R1355–R1364). *See also* Ogilby, 1671.

TERTRE, JEAN BAPTISTE DU
Histoire Générale des Antilles habitées par les François.
Paris, 1667–71. 4 vols.   [BM]
In volume 3, Du Tertre continues his political history of the French islands. Anglo-French relations are discussed and Barbados and Governor Willough-by are frequently mentioned. Some useful insights are provided into French views of the relationship between Bardados, as an English colony, and the French islands, e.g., in the discussion of attacks on St. Lucia, launched from Barbados in the 1660s.

Du Tertre admits to never having been in Barbados. For this reason, he reproduces (*pp. 294–96*) a description of the island, "Remarques faites par Monsieur [Gordelier] du Blanc dans l'isle de la Barbade, ou Barboude." Du Blanc had spent a week in Barbados in early 1666 while on a mission (described by Du Tertre on *pp. 282–93*) to discuss Anglo-French relations. His brief account largely records observations on the island's military organization and fortifications, but also offers minor comments on Bridgetown, house

construction, etc.

An earlier, shorter edition of Du Tertre's work (Paris, 1654 [BM]) does not treat Barbados.

[BUSHEL, JOHN AND BOND, FRANCIS]
A true and perfect narrative of the late dreadful fire which happened at Bridge-Town in the Barbadoes, April 18, 1668. As the same was communicated in two letters from Mr. John Bushnel and Mr. Francis Bond, two eminent merchants there, to Mr. Edward Bushel, citizen and merchant of London.
London [1668]. *6 pp.*   [NYPL, BM]
The letter extracts, dated Bridgetown April 20 and 27, 1668, describe the origins and damage caused by a devastating fire which "in the space of two or three hours time burnt and consumed almost all the whole buildings . . . no less then 800 houses [were] consumed in this terrific conflagration, with a very great value of goods . . ." The editor of this pamphlet adds, in a postscript, that the fire caused a loss that "amounted to above £400,000."

STUBBES, DR. [HENRY?]
"*Observations made by a curious and learned person, sailing from England to the Caribe-Islands.*"
Philosophical Transactions of the Royal Society, vol. 2, no. 27, London, 1668, *pp. 493–500*; vol. 3, no. 36, 1669, *pp. 699–709.*   [NYPL]
The author (identified by last name on *p. 699*) visited Barbados, but he only makes a few very brief and superficial references to the island's weather and flora. His account is reprinted in the *Philosophical Transactions and Collections to the End of the Year [1700] Abridged* (vol. 3, 5th ed., London, 1749, *p. 546*) under the title "Observations Made in a Voyage from England to the Caribbee Islands."

CLARKE, SAMUEL
A true and faithful account of the four chiefest plantations of the English in America. To wit, Virginia, New England, Bermudus, Barbados.
London, 1670. *85 pp.*   [LC]
The description of Barbados (*pp. 60–85*) is an abridgement and rephrasing of Richard Ligon (1657); this is also

included in Clarke's *Geographical Description of all the Countries in the Knowne Worlde*, London, 1670–71 (Sabin 13444).

*Case stated between the East India Company of the United Netherlands and the assigns of W. Courteen.
[London?], 1671.
A "folio" listed by Sabin (17179) who notes "This celebrated case relates to the island of Barbados."

FORTESCUE, WILLIAM, *et al.*
A short relation concerning the life and death of that man of God, and faithful minister of Jesus Christ, William Simpson, who laid down his body in the island of Barbados, the eighth day of the twelfth month [1670].
[London], 1671. *15 pp.*   [BOS]
Simpson, a Quaker, had come to Barbados to preach. This brief tract is comprised of five eulogies; two written by William Fortescue and the others by Oliver Hooton, George Fox, and Elizabeth Hooton. Most are valueless for information on the Barbados Quaker community. The possible exception is Fortescue's account of Simpson's death (*pp. 3–8*) which mentions the names of a few Quakers on the island and notes that Simpson "was buried in a garden belonging to Richard Forstal, being honourably accompanied thither with several hundreds of Friends." Each eulogy is signed by its respective author.

OGILBY, JOHN
America: being the latest and most accurate description of the new world.
London, 1671. *674 pp.*   [BM]
Ogilby's treatment of Barbados (*pp. 377–80*) is primarily of interest because of the verbatim publication of a lengthy letter, dated May 31, 1670, he received from Robert Rich. Rich, a prominent planter and former Quaker, had lived on Barbados for more than twenty years; he objects to Peter Heylyn's account of the island (which appeared in his 1666 edition; see P. Heylyn, 1674), and offers a systematic description of its geography, economy, population, government, etc.
The first edition was published in London in 1670; see Sabin (50088–89)

for comments on this and other editions, and a challenge to Ogilby's authorship.

BLOME, RICHARD
A description of the island of Jamaica; with the other isles and territories in America, to which the English are related, viz. Barbadoes, St. Christophers, Nievis.
London, 1672. *192 pp.*
            [BM, JCB, LC, H]
Brief synopses of geography, demography, etc., based upon a variety of papers the author received from friends who had visited the colonies. His account of Barbados (*pp. 65–96*) seems to be largely a paraphrasing of Richard Ligon (1657). A second edition, under the same title, was published in London in 1678 [BC, JCB]; the pagination differs from the first, but the contents are identical. Another edition was published in London in 1687 under the title *The Present State of His Majesties Isles and Territories in America . . .* [BM], but it contains no important substantive changes although there has been some rewriting of the materials.

FOX, GEORGE
To the ministers, teachers, and priests (so called, and so stileing your selves) in Barbadoes.
[London], 1672. *79 pp.*   [BM, F]
Pages 3–47 contain Fox's impassioned attack on the Anglican clergymen of Barbados which accuses them of hypocrisy, ineffectiveness, mendacity, and slander (rebutted in Morgan Godwyn, 1680). The pamphlet also contains a copy of a petition given to the President and Council of Barbados in 1671 by the Anglican ministers, requesting the Council to pass restrictive legislation on the Quakers (*pp. 48–49*); a declaration by Barbados Quakers (*pp. 65–70*), dated 1671, which specifically rebuts accusations made against them and delineates their belief system — this includes some interesting passages stating their position on slavery (also printed in J. L. Nickalls, 1952, *pp. 602–6*); and miscellaneous items dealing with the controversy between Quakers and the established church in Barbados.

HUGHES, WILLIAM
The American physitian; or a treatise of

the roots, plants, trees, shrubs, fruit, herbs, etc. growing in the English plantations in America.
London, 1672. *159 pp.* [BM]
The author, a doctor in the Royal Navy, made a number of shore visits to most of the British West Indian islands, including Barbados. Various plants are described, their popular names given, and information is presented on the localities in which they are grown, their methods of cultivation, and the use to which they are put.

B., E.
A letter sent from Barbados to a friend in London. Being a true relation of the surrender of the island of Tobago. By Peter Constant, Governour of the island for the Dutch, unto Sir Tobias Bridge, who was sent against it by the . . . Lord Willoughby, Governour of Barbados.
London, 1673. *6 pp.* [JCB]
Pages 1–5 reproduce a few brief notes between Constant and Bridge, relative to the surrender of Tobago, in late 1672, to a military force which came from Barbados. On page 6, E.B. publishes a letter he wrote from Barbados on January 31, 1673, which offers a few more details on the expedition to Tobago, and adds a brief comment on a fire in Bridgetown during January which "burnt down about 30 houses in the street called New-England Row."

HEYLYN, PETER
Cosmography in four books. Containing the chorography and history of the whole world.
London, 1674. [BM]
A revised and enlarged version of earlier editions (*see* Sabin 31655). It is noted that Barbados "is said to be worth all the rest [of the plantations] which are made by the English" (pt. 2, 4th bk.), but the author had no firsthand knowledge of the island and his very brief descriptive statement is of no value.

Recueil de divers voyages faits en Afrique et en l'Amerique, qui n'ont point esté encore publiez.
Paris, 1674. [BM, JCB]
Includes translations of Richard Ligon (1657) and the Barbados chapter in

Richard Blome's book (1672) – the latter under the title "Relation de l'isle des Barbades."

[FORD, RICHARD]
A new map of the island of Barbadoes.
[London, ca. 1675.] [JCB]
This extremely detailed map is the first one based upon a systematic survey of the island; it identifies the names of over eight hundred plantations and shows the sugar mills attached to each. Another edition, with some modifications, was published ca. 1678. Tony Campbell (1965) discusses both editions and reproduces the first whose date of publication he tentatively gives as 1681. The second edition is reproduced, and both editions are discussed, in Jeannette D. Black, ed. *The Blathwayt Atlas: A Collection of Forty-eight Manuscript and Printed Maps of the Seventeenth Century . . . brought together circa 1685 . . . by William Blathwayt* (Providence, Brown University Press, 1970). The map is also discussed in detail, and reproduced, in Richard S. Dunn, "The Barbados Census of 1680: Profile of the Richest Colony in English America," *William and Mary Quarterly*, 26, 1969, *3–30.*

A continuation of the state of New-England; being a farther account of the Indian warr. . . . together with an account of the intended rebellion of the Negroes in the Barbadoes.
London, 1676. *20 pp.* [BM]
In this newstract, the section on Barbados (signed by G.W. and dated November 30, 1675) is only one and one-half pages (*pp. 19–20*). About one page describes how the Speightstown area was affected by an August hurricane, and a few additional sentences relate the manner in which a 1675 slave plot was discovered.
Cruickshank (15, 15a) cites a 1678 London edition and one published in 1833 in Boston.

FELL, LYDIA
A testimony and warning given forth in the love of truth, and is for the governour, magistrates, and people inhabiting on the island of Barbadoes; which is a call to turn to the Lord.
[London? 1676.] *7 pp.* [JCB]

The author's name is signed on the last page. Lydia Fell, a Quaker, visited Barbados in 1676 (Manuscripts, Society of Friends, Portfolios, vol. 17, no. 2) and lived in Bridgetown "when the last great fire was in town." Her religious diatribe was apparently a reaction against the persecutions of the Quakers.

FOX, GEORGE
Gospel family-order, being a short discourse concerning the ordering of families, both of whites, blacks, and Indians.
[London], 1676. *22 pp.*   [F, BM]
"The following discourse is as it was taken from the mouth of George Fox at a mens meeting at Tho. Rous his house in Barbadoes in the year 1671." This is a concise and unequivocal statement of Fox's position on slavery and the treat- ment of slaves in which he prescribes the obligations masters should have and stresses that slaves should be instructed in Christianity.
Sabin (25351) cites this item as hav- ing been published in 1674 and re- printed in Philadelphia in 1701; he locates a copy at the LCP and adds: "A tract of great rarity. Translated into French in 1684."

Great newes from the Barbadoes. Or, a true and faithful account of the grand conspiracy of the Negroes against the English. And the happy discovery of the same with the number of those that were buried alive, beheaded, and otherwise executed for their horrid crimes. With a short description of that plantation.
London, 1676. *14 pp.*   [BM]
The author visited Barbados which he finds "to be the finest and worthiest island in the world"; his brief descrip- tion refers to Richard Ligon (1657), but notes the changes which have occurred since Ligon's time. He provides informa- tion on Barbados flora, and gives a brief, but useful, secondhand account (*pp. 9–13*) of the 1675 slave plot which was discovered before plans could be activated.

SPEED, JOHN
A prospect of the most famous parts of the world.
London, 1676.   [WIC]
The "Description of Barbados" (*p. 48*)

contains brief information on topics such as physical geography, flora and fauna, towns, government, etc., most of which is apparently based on sources such as Ligon (1657) and Ogilby (1671). A map of Barbados is also included, but, according to Tony Campbell (in whose work the map is reproduced) "the island's outline is copied from Ogilby but the interior is dotted with trees and hills that owe little to Ligon or geographical accuracy" (1965, *p. 10*). For other editions *see* Sabin (89228).

TOWNS, DR. THOMAS
"An extract of a letter of Mr. Listers containing some observations made at the Barbado's."
Philosophical Transactions of the Royal Society, vol. 10, London, 1676, *pp. 399–400.*   [NYPL]
Dated Barbados, March 26, 1675, the letter contains brief paragraphs on the consumption of imported wines, climate, "purslane" and other plants, springs and ponds as sources of water, house construction and the use of limestone, and a commentary on the observation that "the blood of Negro's is almost as black as their skin." A useful abridgement of this item, under the title "Observations made at the Barba- does" is in the *Philosophical Transactions and Collections to the End of the Year [1700], Abridged* (vol. 3, 5th ed., London, 1749, *pp. 560–61*).

Address of the executors of Sir William Courteen and Sir Paul Pyndar; or a hue and cry after their goods and chattels.
[London], 1677.   [BM]
Cited by Cundall (9a) as published in 1679, this broadsheet has nothing to do with the West Indies, and may have been confused with *A Brief Narrative and Deduction of the Several Remarkable Cases* (1679).

Quaker Records [*1677–1679*].
See "Quaker Records" (1956–67).

SPÖRRI, FELIX CHRISTIAN
Americanische Reiss-Beschreibung nach den Caribes Insslen, und Neu Engelland. Verichtet und aufgesezt durch Felix- Christian Spori, schnitt-und wund-artzet von Zurich.

Zurich, 1677. *90 pp.*
[BM, BOS, H, JCB, LC, NYPL]
The author, a Swiss medical doctor, voyaged on merchant ships trading in the West Indies. He visited Barbados at least three times during the early 1660s and ultimately spent a total of approximately fourteen weeks on the island. His description (*pp. 10–29*) includes brief comments on topics such as trade, towns, diseases, slave life, beverages, and fauna; approximately half the pages are devoted to the island's commercial and noncommercial plants. He describes these plants and sometimes includes information on how they are cultivated and used, e.g., sugar-cane planting and processing.

Spörri's account is translated in A. Gunkel and J. Handler, "A Swiss Medical Doctor's Description of Barbados in 1661: The Account of Felix Christian Spörri (*Jl. BMHS*, 33, 1969, 3–13).

A brief narrative and deduction of the several remarkable cases of Sir William Courteen and Sir Paul Pyndar, Knights; and William Courteen, late of London. . . . Faithfully presented to both houses of Parliament. . . . Recollected out of the original writings and records.
London, 1679. *12 pp.* [JCB]
Barbados is dealt with on pages 1–3 wherein are sympathetically reviewed the history of William Courteen's claims against Carlisle, the efforts made by Courteen's descendants to regain Barbados, and the requests for compensation by his heirs for losses suffered.

ALLARD, CAREL
Orbis Habitabilis Oppida et Vestitus.
Amsterdam [1680?]. [BM, LC, NYPL]
Contains a copper engraving, number 88, entitled *Engelse Quakers en Tabak Planters aende Barbados.* The print shows two large costumed figures, a European male and female, in the foreground, with slaves and shipping in a bay, in the background.

The print is apparently based upon an earlier engraving depicting New Amsterdam in which the foreground

figures have been retained, but the background has been altered. The LC tentatively dates its copy of Allard at 1698 and the BM at 1680. The NYPL has a copy with the print in color. For more details on Allard's work, problems of dating it, the Barbados print and other editions of it, see Clara E. LeGear, *A List of Geographical Atlases in the Library of Congress* (Washington, D.C., 1958, vol. 5, title 5385 [a continuation of P. L. Phillips's volumes]), I. N. Phelps Stokes, *Iconography of Manhattan* (New York, 1915, vol. 1, *pp. 140–42*), Stokes and Haskell, *American Historical Prints* (New York, 1932, *p. 9*).[1]

CURWEN, ALICE
A relation of the labour, travail and sufferings of that faithful servant of the Lord Alice Curwen.
London, 1680. *75 pp.* [F]
The author, a Quaker, arrived at Barbados in late 1676 and stayed for about seven months. Most of this pamphlet is devoted to pious accounts of her religious activities, the meetings she attended in Barbados, and epistles written to Quakers in other areas. Included within these are occasional references to Quaker attitudes on slaves and slavery.

GODWYN, MORGAN
The Negro's and Indians Advocate, suing for their admission into the Church: or a persuasive to the instructing and baptizing of the Negroes and Indians in our plantations.
London, 1680. *174 pp.* [BM]
The author, an Anglican minister, offers this tract as a direct rebuttal to George Fox's (1672) attack on the Anglican ministers of Barbados. Godwyn gives no indication as to how long he lived in Barbados but he was there sometime between 1672 and 1680 and his tract is directly related to his experiences on the island. In it he argues for the humanity of the Negro and develops an elaborate case for the necessity of instructing him in Christianity. Godwyn argues for neither the abolition of the slave trade nor for the emancipation of the slaves, but his position is a liberal one for the period. The work, however, contains relatively sparse

---

[1] Christopher Klein, of The John Carter Brown Library, provided these references.

information on the behavior and social life of the slaves themselves.

GODWYN, MORGAN
A Supplement to the Negro's and Indians Advocate: or, some further considerations and proposals for the effectual and speedy carrying on of the Negro's Christianity in our Plantations.
London, 1681. *12 pp.*　　　[BM]
Adds virtually nothing on Barbados to the author's 1680 work.

[LODDINGTON, WILLIAM]
Plantation work, the work of this generation.
London, 1682. *18 pp.*　　　[BM]
Written by a Quaker who is trying to encourage settlers to the northern colonies; contains a brief excerpt from a letter by "Lewis Morris late of Barbadoes . . . June 1681" which says he is pleased to be in New York. Signed "W.L."; author cited in BM catalog.

[TAYLOR, JOHN]
A loving and friendly invitation to all sinners to repent. . . . with a brief account of the latter part of the life of John Perrot . . . also a testimony against Robt. Rich and John Perrot, their filthy books lately printed against God's people in scorn called Quakers.
London, 1683. *20 pp.*　　　[JCB]
On the title page of the JCB copy there is a manuscript inscription "by John Taylor." Taylor had visited Barbados at least in 1659, 1662, 1666 (*see* Manuscripts, Society of Friends, Portfolios, vol. 17, no. 2). His tract, of little value for a study of the island's Quaker community, criticizes two former Quakers who had lived in Barbados.
　　Taylor's *An Account of Some of the Labours, Excercises, Travels. . . . By Way of Journal* (London, 1710 [BM]) "contains accounts of his travels in New England and the West Indies" (Sabin 94478).

*"To His Most Excellent Majesty, the humble address of the grand jury for the body of the island of Barbados, at a general sessions holden for the said island on Monday, the 2nd of April, 1683, before the honourable Lieutenant General Henry Waldrond etc. with another humble address to His Majesties Council and General Assembly at Barbados."
London Gazette, nos. 1824 and 1843. [1683–84?]
Cited by Bishop White Kennett, *Bibliothecae Americanae Primordia* (London, 1715, *p. 141* [NYPL]).

AYRES, PHILIP (ed.)
The voyages and adventures of Capt. Barth. Sharp and others in the South Sea. Being a journal of the same. . . . published by P.A., Esq.
London, 1684. *172 pp.*
　　　　　　　　[NYPL, BM, LC]
Bartholomew Sharp, an adventurer, arrived at Barbados on January 28, 1682. Fearing that his ship would be taken as a prize, he left soon after arrival, without having gone ashore, and his journal (*pp. 113–14*) records no observations on the island. His account is also published in William Hacke's *A Collection of Original Voyages* (London, 1699 [BM, LC]).

HANSON, SAMUEL
The Case of Samuel Hanson, merchant and planter in Barbados, humbly offer'd and submitted to the Kings most excellent majesty's consideration, and royal determination in Council.
[London, 1684.] *19 pp.*　　[JCB, BM]
This complicated case, of interest for a study of the island's legal and judicial machinery and the role of the governor, took place during the late 1670s and early 1680s. Hanson, a long-time resident of Barbados, had been accused of fraudulently acquiring and selling guns belonging to a Jewish merchant, Anthony Rodriguez. He was found guilty and his ". . . several applications to Sir Richard [Dutton], praying favor to be heard, in order to the vindication of his reputation, not in the least regarding the fine, but only to preserve his credit . . ." were refused. His appeal to the King was forwarded to the Lords of Trade who then asked for more details from Governor Dutton. The affair snowballed, Dutton became angered and Hanson was imprisoned; he escaped to England and continued his appeals.

SELLER, JOHN
Barbados Almanack for XXX Yeares, shewing the days of the month, the suns place. . . . Also the moveable Feasts and other Useful Remarks calculated for the meridian of that Famous island.
London [1684]. [BM]
Contains standard almanac information.

[TRYON, THOMAS]
Friendly advice to gentlemen planters of East and West Indies.
[London], 1684. *222 pp.* [RCS]
Tryon, a London merchant and prolific writer on various subjects, had spent about five years in Barbados in the 1660s. Some of his experiences are reflected in this book which is divided into three parts: part 1 (*pp. 1–73*), "A Brief Treatise of the Principal Fruits and Herbs that Grow in Barbadoes, Jamaica, and other Plantations in the West Indies," is not particularly informative, and about half of its pages are devoted to advice on how to live and eat so as to preserve one's health; part 2 (*pp. 75–145*) "The Negroes Complaint of Their Hard Servitude . . ." makes a strong plea for milder and more humane treatment of slaves. Barbados is not specifically mentioned in this section, but Tryon's comments seem to be based upon his observations in the island; part 3 (*pp. 146–222*) "A Discourse in way of Dialogue between an Ethiopean . . . and a Christian, that was his Master in America" is an interesting satire on the subjects of Christianity, white supremacy and slavery, in which the slave points out various contradictions between Christian belief and practice. In all, the book is of very little value as a source of information on Barbados. Despite Tryon's lengthy residence in Barbados, his posthumously published autobiography (*Some Memoirs of the Life of Mr. Thomas Tryon*, London, 1705 [BM]) contains no information about the island.

B[URTON], R[ICHARD]
The English Empire in America, or a prospect of His Majesties Dominions in the West Indies.
London, 1685. *209 pp.* [BM]
The description of Barbados (*pp. 198–*

203) is virtually a plagiarism of Richard Ligon (1657). Author cited by BM catalog which notes his name is a pseudonym for Nathaniel Crouch; Sabin (9499) cites the author as R[ichard] B[urton]. See Sabin and BM catalog for later editions.

HAYNE, SAMUEL
An abstract of all the statutes made concerning aliens trading in England . . . also of all the laws made for securing our plantation trade to ourselves. With observations thereon, proving that the Jews . . . break them all.
[London], 1685. *38 pp.* [BM]
A polemic against Jewish merchants and traders in general, with some references to Barbados trade and the island's Jewish community.

SCAMLER, ROBERT
Several Sermons; some preached in England, and some in the island of Barbadoes in America upon several occasions.
[London], 1685. *80 pp.* [BOS]
None of these sermons provides any information on Barbados.

"The solemnity and order of proclaiming James King of England, Scotland, etc. in the island of Barbados, by Sir Richard Dutton, His Majesties Governor."
London Gazette, no. 2051 [1685].
Cited in Bishop White Kennett, *Bibliothecae Americanae Primordia* (London, 1713, *p. 144* [NYPL]).

[LITTLETON, EDWARD]
The Groans of the Plantations; or a true account of their grievous and extreme sufferings by the heavy impositions upon sugar and other hardships relating more particularly to the island of Barbados.
London, 1689. *35 pp.* [BM, BOS]
Examines the economic plight of the planter from a planter's perspective; it provides useful materials on plantation economics, the business aspects of sugar production, and the costs of plantation maintenance. Reprinted in London in 1698 [BM, BOS, BMHS]. The author is identified in the BM catalog.

PITMAN, HENRY
A relation of the great sufferings and strange adventures of Henry Pitman,

chirurgeon to the late Duke of Monmouth.
London, 1689. *37 pp.*   [NYPL]
After the defeat of Monmouth's army in 1685, Pitman was imprisoned in England and was subsequently shipped to Barbados as an indentured servant. Only a few pages of his account are devoted to his approximately sixteen-month stay on the island and the harsh treatment he received while there, but he relates in considerable detail the manner in which he clandestinely procured a boat and escaped in the company of seven other servants.

The "Monmouth rebels" were considered a special category of indentured servant, and reproduced in this work is the stringent law of early 1686, passed to regulate their behavior and prevent their removal from Barbados before their ten-year period of indenture expired. Richard Hall (1764, *p. 455*) only reproduces the title of this law, "An act for the governing and retaining within this island, all such rebels convict . . ." and comments on it, in a footnote: ". . . the condition of these rebels was by this act, made as bad as, if not worse, than the Negroes; but King William III was pleased to release them from servitude, and this act was repealed, March 17, 1690."

Pitman's account is reproduced in Edward Arber's *An English Garner, Stuart Tracts 1603–1693* (vol. 8, Westminster, 1903, *pp. 431–76*). "A very rare tract" (Sabin 63047).

*Relation [of an earthquake in Barbados in 1690].
Bridgetown, 1690.
The above title and imprint are taken from the following passage in *Dissertation Upon Earthquakes, Their Causes and Consequences* (London, 1750, *p. 42* [NYPL]): "We shall . . . proceed to another Relation . . . printed by Authority at *Bridgetown*, in *Barbadoes* and bearing date April 23d 1690. 'About [quoting from the *Relation*] three weeks since there were felt most violent earthquakes in the Leeward islands of Montserrat, Nevis, Antigua; in the first two no considerable hurt was done, most of their buildings being of timber. . . . This earthquake was felt in some places of this island [Barbados?] but

did no manner of hurt to men or cattle . . . it happening in the daytime. It is reported to have been more violent in Martinico, and other French islands . . .'"

I have come across no other reference to this *Relation*, have been able to find no trace of an earthquake on the island in 1690 (cf. Schomburgk, 1848, *pp. 68–69*), and, from all evidence, nothing was published in Barbados until 1730.

THOMAS, DALBY
An historical account of the rise and growth of the West India colonies, and of the great advantages they are to England in respect to trade.
London, 1690. *53 pp.*   [BM, NYPL]
Highly sympathetic to the West Indian planters, this book tries to convince Parliament of the economic importance of the West Indian colonies to Great Britain. It is not certain if Thomas ever visited Barbados, but he shows a relatively intimate acquaintance with the island's economy and agricultural practices, and details on these are frequently used as illustrative of West Indian conditions in general.

Reprinted in the *Jl. BMHS* (25, 1957–58, *172–86*; 26, 1958–59, *33–47*, *138–43*), and the *Harleian Miscellany* vol. 9 (London, 1810, *pp. 403–45*).

A true and faithful account of an intire and absolute victory over the French fleet in the West-Indies, by two East-India ships, and other vessels, at Barbadoes, made into men of war.
London, 1690.   [BOS, NYPL]
This London newsletter (a broadside printed on two sides) reports a story which came from the West Indies via a ship at Bristol. The story describes how two merchantmen, hearing of the war between England and France and fearing to return to London without a convoy, made for Barbados. The island's Assembly convinced the ships' captains to unload their cargoes and convert their ships to men-of-war. Thus converted, the two ships, joined by seven other "smaller vessels," and twenty-three hundred men sailed for St. Kitts where, after capturing some French vessels and destroying others,

they landed, plundering and destroying various French settlements. After this venture "... this victorious fleet of Barbadians, to the great honor and reputation of the island, [were] flushed with success" and wanted to continue their campaign against the French elsewhere. A copy of this item is also located in the LC (Manuscript Division, "Papers Relating to Barbados, 1663–1762").

BURNYEAT, JOHN
The truth exalted in the writings of that eminent and faithful servant of Christ John Burnyeat, collected into this ensuing volume as a memorial to his faithful labours in and for the truth.
London, 1691. *264 pp.* [BM]
I have not examined the above edition, but a reprinting of it: *Journal of the Life and Gospel Labours of John Burnyeat. . . .* (London, 1839 [RCS, BM]). Burnyeat, a Quaker who died in 1691, visited various of the American colonies, and spent a total of approximately fifteen months in Barbados during three visits made in 1664, 1667, and 1670/71. His account of these visits (*pp. 186–87, 190, 194–95*) is extremely sparse, and is largely devoted to comments on the Quaker community.

SPENCER, THOMAS
A true and faithful relation of the proceedings of the forces of their majesties, K. William and Q. Mary, in their expedition against the French, in the Carriby islands in the West Indies: under the conduct of . . . Christopher Codrington . . . in the years 1689 and 1690.
London, 1691. *12 pp.* [BM]
Very briefly describes how Barbados raised a regiment of seven hundred men to participate in a military venture against the French in St. Kitts.

[PEACHIE, JOHN]
Some observations made upon the Barbados seeds, shewing their admirable virtue in curing dropsies.
London, 1694. *7 pp.* [BM]
Written by an English physician, this tract has nothing to do with Barbados. The author is identified by Wing (P928).

PHILLIPS, THOMAS
A journal of a voyage . . . 1693, 1694.
See Thomas Phillips (1746).

A brief account of the present declining state of the West Indies: in reference to its trade, and in particular, that of Barbadoes. By a West India Merchant.
London, 1695. *8 pp.* [BM, IJ]
This item is solely concerned with matters of trade and economics. It deals with the "many and great advantages that England receives from the West Indies," points to the shipping difficulties of West Indian producers in getting their products to market, and makes an appeal, while offering a plan, for easing the commercial pressures on West Indian planters.

COPENS, SAMUEL
A Prospect of Bridge Town in Barbados.
[London?], 1695. [BM, BMHS]
An engraved panorama, showing shipping in Carlisle Bay, and the town, forts, windmills, etc., in the background. A foldout photographic reproduction is in *The West India Committee Circular* (vol. 28, no. 381, 1913, *between pp. 196 and 197*).

A discourse of the duties on merchandize, more particularly of that on sugars, occasionally offer'd, in answer to a pamphlet, intitled, The Groans of the Plantations, etc. exposing the weakness of the said pamphlet. . . . By a merchant.
London, 1695. *32 pp.* [BM]
A detailed rebuttal to Edward Littleton (1689) which, in turn, is criticized in *A State of the Present Condition of the Island of Barbadoes* (1696).

The irregular and disorderly state of the plantation-trade discuss'd, and humbly offered to the consideration of the Right Honorable the Lords and Commons in Parliament assembled.
[London, ca. 1695.] *4 pp.* [BM]
The author tries to make a case against allowing the West Indian islands, Barbados in particular, to refine their own sugar before export, and discusses the general economic dangers to England of permitting the colonies to transform their raw products into finished ones.

A letter to S[ir] C.M., a member of Parliament, from an inhabitant of the island of Barbados.
[London, ca. 1695.] *8 pp.* [JCB]
The author complains about the island's economic plight, but spends most of his time in arguing against the power and prerogatives of the governor and in discussing the inadequacies of the island's defense system. He argues that Barbados cannot afford to maintain its own military defenses because public funds are inadequate and that the 4½ percent export duty makes it difficult for Barbados planters to contribute more to the public treasury. Things might work out, he suggests, if the money raised from the 4½ percent duty could be used for internal needs, "but when they raise money in the colonies for their own defence, and for their own use, to have that transmitted from them to England, seems to be very hard, and altogether repugnant to the freedom that every Englishman is born to." A clue to the publication date of this item is offered by the author's comment that "above thirty years ago" the act imposing the 4½ percent duty was passed by the island's assembly; the act was passed in September 1663.

POYNTZ, JOHN
The present prospect of the famous and fertile island of Tobago, to the southward of the island of Barbadoes.
London, 1695. *50 pp.* [JCB]
The author, who appears to have been well acquainted with Barbados, makes an occasional very brief comment on the island: viz., the use of corn stalks as fuel in the boiling houses (*p. 4*); mobby, made from potatoes, "is the universal drink" (*p. 12*); "cedar wood" from Tobago is shipped to Barbados (*p. 29*); the "bully-tree" is used in mill rollers, "but principally for coggs, spindles, and shafts in their windmills, besides several other uses" (*p. 31*); comment on the use of "manjack" or "tarr" (*p. 38*); the value that "pieces of eight" in Tobago have in Barbados currency (*pp. 33, 46*).
The first edition was published in London in 1683 (Sabin 64857).

The present case of a Barbados planter,

and reasons against laying a further duty on sugar.
[London, 1695?] *3 pp.* [BM]
In presenting his case against export duties, the author provides information on economic conditions and plantation operations.

Reasons humbly offered (in behalf of the island of Barbados) to the Honorable House of Commons against laying a further duty on sugar.
[London, ca. 1695.] *3 pp.* [BM]
Designed to convey the planters' economic plight.

The Association Oath Rolls ... 1696.
See W. Gandy (1922).

A short account of the manifest hand of God that hath fallen upon several Marshals and their Deputies, Who have made Great Spoil and Havock of the Goods of the People of God called Quakers in the Island of Barbadoes.
London, 1696. *23 pp.* [BM]
For a variety of reasons such as failing to participate in the island's militia and permitting Negroes to attend their meetings, the Quakers were often legally persecuted. Written by a Quaker, this pamphlet recounts misfortunes which befell marshalls who carried out court orders in confiscating Quaker property (the confiscated property is itemized) or who informed on or prosecuted Quakers for having Negroes in their house meetings.
Reproduced in J. Besse (1753, vol. 2, *pp. 344–51*).

A state of the present condition of the island Barbadoes: with some reasons why there ought not to be any more duties or imports laid on sugars than what already are; shewing, that they pay full as much as they can bear, and that they who make that manufactory, pay more in proportion, than any other of His Majesty's subjects. By a merchant, trading to the West Indies.
London [ca. 1696]. *4 pp.* [BM]
Deals solely with trade and economics, and is a specific rebuttal to *A Discourse of the Duties on Merchandize* (1695).

WALKER, WILLIAM
Victorious Love: A Tragedy.
London, 1698. [BM]

Written by a Barbadian, this play and *Marry or Do Worse: A Comedy* (London, 1704 [BM, BOS]) contain no information on the island.

GREY, RALPH
A Proclamation. April 13, 1699.
[JCB, NYPL]
Issued by the governor to prohibit persons in Barbados from dealing in any way with members of the Company of Scotland, should such persons arrive at the island. The original proclamation may never have been published; this copy, published in Edinburgh in 1699, is printed on the same page as a similar proclamation issued in another territory.

MAKEMIE, FRANCIS
Truths in a true light. Or, a pastoral letter to the Reformed Protestants, in Barbados, vindicating the Non-Conformists, from the misrepresentations, commonly made of them in that island, and in other places.
Edinburgh, 1699. *38 pp.*　　[H]
Written by a Presbyterian minister; signed by the author (as Mackemie) and dated Barbados, December 28, 1697 (*p. 24*). Pages 1–24 elaborate on two central themes: *1*] "that we are Protestant brethren . . . and therefore deserve not to be treated, as many ignorantly do, and particularly in this

island"; *2*] "that of all Protestants that differ from them, we differ in the least and smallest matters . . ." Although the author does not mention Barbadian conditions per se, it is clear that he is addressing the tract to the Anglican ministers of Barbados. A "post-script" (*pp. 25–38*) also deals with the "misrepresentations of the principles and practices of the Presbyterians in this island."
Sabin (44082) comments that "this is a very rare piece"; he locates a copy at the American Antiquarian Society.

RAWLIN, WILLIAM
The Laws of Barbados, collected in one volume.
London, 1699. *239 pp.*　[BM, BMHS]
Prepared by the clerk of the Barbados Assembly; full texts of laws in force (the earliest passed in 1648 or 1649) and an extensive list of the titles of laws which had become obsolete and/or had expired.

TRYON, THOMAS
England's grandeur and way to get wealth: or, promotion of trade made easy.
London, 1699. *26 pp.*　　[BM]
A general discussion of trade and commerce; contains an occasional superficial reference to Barbados where the author had resided in the 1660s.

1700–1749

*ZOUCH, [ARTHUR?]
A Catalogue of books, to be sold by Mr. Zouch, in the town of St. Michael, alias the Bridgetown . . . where gentlemen and others may be supplyed with great variety of books not contained in this catalogue.
[London? 17–]. *35 pp.*　　[LC]
This rare item forms part of the Rosenwald collection which is to be presented to the LC at a later date; at present the collection is located in Jenkintown, Pennsylvania. Arthur Zouch was clerk of the Barbados Assembly from at least 1712 to 1714.

TRYON, THOMAS
Tryon's letters, domestick and foreign, to

several persons of quality.
London, 1700. *240 pp.*　　[BM, UL]
An alternate title is *Tryon's Letters, Upon Several Occasions.* . . . The author resided in Barbados for about five years in the 1660s. Letter 33 (*pp. 187–94*) "To a Gentleman in Barbadoes," argues that the planter should reduce his acreage in sugar and devote more attention to the production of food crops; letter 35 (*pp. 200–221*) "Of the Making of Sugar" describes in considerable detail the processing of sugar cane, distillation, etc., and offers occasional specific references to Barbadian practices. These letters are reproduced in a 1701 edition published in London under the title

The Merchant, Citizen, and Countryman's Instructor [JCB, UL].

A few brief reflections upon a paper, stiled, some considerations offer'd to both houses of Parliament, concerning the sugar-colonies, and chiefly the island of Barbadoes.
[London, 1701.] *7 pp.*   [BM]
A bitter and direct rebuttal to *Some Considerations Humbly Offered to Both Houses of Parliament* (1701) in the controversy over the $4\frac{1}{2}$ percent export duty on sugar and its effects on the Barbadian economy.

[HODGES, THOMAS]
Plantation Justice. Shewing the constitution of their courts, and what sort of judges they have in them. By which merchants may see the occasions of their great losses and sufferings in the plantation trade.
London, 1701. *12 pp.*   [JCB]
A brief, but interesting, commentary entirely devoted to the Barbadian legal and judicial system, offering a critique of it, and showing how the legal machinery affects investments and trade on the island.

The author's name is given in the BM catalog. A second edition was published in London in 1702 [BM].

SOCIETY FOR THE PROPAGATION OF THE GOSPEL IN FOREIGN PARTS
Annual Reports.
London, 1701–1839. 19 vols.
          [USPG]
Alternate titles to this series are *An Abstract of the Proceedings of the Society for the Propagation of the Gospel in Foreign Parts*, or *Proceedings of the Society for the Propagation of the Gospel in Foreign Parts*. Materials on Barbados start in the report for 1710 (vol. 1) when the S.P.G. assumed control of the Codrington plantations.

The entries relating to Barbados for the first three decades or so are usually very brief, a few lines at most, and relate largely to Codrington College itself, e.g., its construction, staffing, and to general progress made in the religious instruction of the slaves; occasionally one finds comments on the state of the plantations. Every year, however, there is appended to each report a summation

of the plantations' finances showing expenditures, receipts, and profits. These reports, although lacking in detail, permit a useful overview of the development of the college and plantations.

Beginning in the mid-1740s, entries on Barbados become lengthier, and more details, especially relating to the college, are offered. By the late 1760s and through the next decade, reports dealing with Barbados are sporadic, appearing every few years, although the annual financial statement of the plantations is continuously published. The reports start again in the early 1780s and deal with financial and economic problems of the plantations, the progress in paying off debts, etc., but they continue to be erratic, and by 1800 cease again. Recommencing in 1823, the Barbados reports become more elaborate than ever before, and often contain transcripts and lengthy extracts of letters written from Barbados, reporting on conditions of the plantations, especially with respect to the slaves and the provisions and progress made in their religious instruction. Reports for the 1830s are extremely detailed and a great deal of information is also provided on the college itself, its academic affairs, curricula, etc.

A complete set of these reports is located in the USPG Archives.

Some considerations humbly offered to both houses of Parliament concerning the sugar colonies, and chiefly the island of Barbadoes.
London, 1701. *11 pp.*   [BM, IJ]
The author outlines the ways in which he feels Barbados is economically important to England, discusses the need for building up the island's fortifications to insure its remaining in English hands, and argues that Parliament, and not the islanders, should bear the expense of such fortifications.

**An act to encourage privateers in case of war . . . past by the Council and Assembly and consented to by His Excellency the Governor [November 18, 1701].*
[Boston, 1702.]   [NYPL]
The NYPL copy is a photostat of a broadside printed on both sides; accord-

ing to the library catalog, the last paragraph of the act states "That this act be forthwith sent to New England or some other convenient place to be printed."

A brief representation of My Lord Dupplin's title and right to the payment of one thousand pound per annum, and what is due unto him by way of arrears, out of the four and a half percent charged on all commodities exported from Barbadoes: humbly laid before . . . the House of Commons.
[London, 1702.] *4 pp.* [BM]
Written in reaction to *Some Considerations Humbly Offered* (1701), this primarily relates to the controversy between the heirs of the Earl of Carlisle and his creditors.

A copy of the articles exhibited by Mr. [William] Freeman to the House of Commons against Colonel Codrington: and some observations and remarks in answer to the same.
[London], 1702. *36 pp.* [BM]
This item has nothing to do with Barbados *per se.*

A copy of the petition of William Freeman, Esq., in behalf of himself and others, against Col. Christopher Codrington, Governour of the Leeward Islands, presented to the House of Commons the 19th of February, 1701. With some remarks thereon.
[London], 1702. *13 pp.* [BM]
Complaints against the "misgovernments and illegal proceedings" of Codrington which resulted in the loss of estates in the Leewards.

*"The humble address of the President and Council administering the government of Her Majesty's [Queen Anne] island of Barbados; together with the principal officers and inhabitants thereof, now assembled in the chief town of the said island, to proclaim Her Majesty. Dated, Bridgetown, May 18, 1702."
London Gazette, no. 3829. [1702–3.]
Cited by Bishop White Kennett, *Bibliothecae Americanae Primordia* (London, 1713, *p. 185* [NYPL]).

*DUDLEY, JOSEPH
A proclamation for an embargo on ships and vessels bound to Barbados, and the Careby Leeward Islands.
Boston, 1705. [NYPL]
According to the NYPL catalog, this is a broadside issued by the Governor of Massachusetts and dated October 30, 1705. The NYPL copy is a photostat of the original located in the Public Record Office, London.

SLOANE, HANS
A voyage to the islands Madera, Barbados, Nievis, S. Christophers and Jamaica, with the natural history of the herbs and trees . . . etc. of the last of those islands.
London, 1707–25. 2 vols. [BC]
Sloane spent ten days in Barbados in late 1687; his description (vol. 1, *pp. 32–41*) is largely concerned with plant life.

Also based on his visit to the West Indies is his plant list: *Catalogus Plantarum Quae in Insula Jamaica Sponte Proveniunt . . . cum Earundem Synonymis & Locis Natalibus; Adjectis Aliis Quibusdam Quae in Insulis Maderae, Barbados, Nieves,* London, 1696 (Sabin 76501).

OLDMIXON, JOHN
The British Empire in America, containing the history of the discovery, settlement, progress, and present state of all the British colonies, on the continent and islands of America.
London, 1708. 2 vols. [BM, IJ]
Pages 1–196 of volume 2 are devoted to Barbados. In nine chapters, the author deals with the island's political history, geography, military establishment, agriculture, flora and fauna, population, government, sugar production, etc. The author never visited the West Indies, and relies upon Ligon (1657) to a considerable degree, but he also uses other published sources and information provided by residents and former residents. The result is that his acquaintance with Barbados appears to be much more intimate than that of many other writers who never visited the island. He frequently attempts to update Ligon, and sometimes offers useful comparative materials to assess social change since the time of Ligon's writing.

A second, two-volume edition, "corrected and amended," was published in London in 1741 [BM, IJ, BMHS]. The Barbados section (vol. 2, *pp. 1–171*) contains few significant differences in content from the first edition. In the first edition, chapter 1 takes the island's political history up to 1708 and the administration of Governor Mitford Crowe; the second edition continues the history through 1739 and the administration of Robert Byng. The remaining chapters are identical in the two editions, except that the last three paragraphs of the final chapter in the first edition are omitted in the second one. The dedication page is signed J. Oldmixon in the 1708 edition.

A voyage to the new island of Fonseca, near Barbadoes. With some observations made in a criuze among the Leeward Islands. In letters from two captains of Turkish men of war, driven thither in the year 1707. Translated out of Turkish and French.

London, 1708. *44 pp.*   [LC]

This item has nothing to do with Barbados.

A NOTE ON FONSECA[2] — "The nonexistent island of Fonseca is to be found located northeast of Trinidad on numerous maps of the seventeenth and eighteenth centuries. The earliest use of the name seems to have been in Jan Huyghen van Linschoten's *Itinerario* (Amsterdam, 1596) on the map of South America compiled for him by Peter Plancius from Portuguese sources. On this map the island is called 'I. da Fonçequa al: de S. Barnaldo.' Possibly the name refers to João Vicente da Fonseca, Archbishop of Goa (d. 1587), who had been Linschoten's patron during the years he spent in India. On earlier sixteenth-century maps, including those of Ortelius and Mercator, the island appears in the same location with the name of St. Bernard or St. Bartholomew, spelled in various ways. In some cases (for instance a manuscript atlas by Vaz Dourado of 1580), the name appears as 'São Brandão', suggesting that it may have been originally intended to represent one of the many imaginary islands to which, according to legend, the Irish monk St. Brendan voyaged in the sixth century.

The extreme durability of this ancient cartographical tradition is evidenced by the inclusion of 'I. Fonseca very doubtful' on *A Chart of North and South America*, published in London as late as 1753 by Thomas Jefferys and compiled by the very capable geographer who worked under the name of John Green."

An account of the number of Negroes delivered in to the islands of Barbados, Jamaica, and Antego, from the year 1698 to 1708, since the trade was opened, taken from the accounts sent from the respective governours of those islands to the Lords Commissioners of Trade.

[London, 1709.] *2 pp.*   [BM, UL]

Contains statistics which are employed to demonstrate that since the cessation of the Royal Africa Company's monopoly of the slave trade, the trade has increased considerably.

A letter from the most considerable proprietors of the island of Barbados, to the several persons in Great Britain interested in the said island, requesting their application to the . . . House of Commons, for establishing the African trade by a joint stock.

[London], 1709. *3 pp.*   [BM, BOS]

An alternate title is, "A Joint-Letter from the most Considerable Proprietors of the Island of Barbadoes, to Colonel Richard Scot, Colonel Robert Stewart, Richard Bate, Patrick Mein, and Thomas Fullerton, Esqs., and other Friends in England having Estates or Interests in the said Island; touching the Petition which they lately transmitted to be given into the Honourable House of Commons, for having the Trade to Africa carried on by a Company of a Sufficient Joint-Stock; together with their Reasons subjoin'd."

The 77 signatories to this petition claim to own two-thirds of all the land and slaves in Barbados, offer some valuable information on the island's trading activities, and vigorously defend a reassertion of the Royal African Company's monopoly, while complain-

---

[2] Furnished by Jeannette D. Black, Curator of Maps, The John Carter Brown Library, August 20, 1969. For other items on Fonseca, see Sabin 20248, 74617.

ing that private traders have been destructive to the slave trade.

Hanson (1035) cites a 1713 edition.

GORDON, WILLIAM
A sermon preached at the funeral of the Honourable Colonel Christopher Codrington . . . who departed this life at his seat in Barbadoes, on . . . 7th of April, 1710, and was interred the day following in the Parish of St. Michael.
London, 1710. *24 pp.* [BM, BOS]
Contains a brief (*pp. 19–23*) highly laudatory account of Codrington's life by the rector of St. James parish church.

An Ode Pindarick on Barbadoes.
[London? 1710?] *2 pp.* [BM]
A poem of four stanzas extolling the island's virtues.

To the Queen's Most Excellent Majesty, the humble petition of several planters, and others, the inhabitants of Your Majesty's island of Barbadoes.
[London, 1710.] [BM]
Broadsheet printed on both sides. Eighty-eight persons signed "The Barbadoes Petition" which complains that the price of slaves is too high, and argues that when the Royal African Company formerly monopolized the slave trade Barbados was more regularly supplied with slaves at lower prices.

Atlas Geographicus: or A Compleat System of Geography (Ancient and Modern) for America.
London, 1711–17. 5 vols. [BM]
The section on Barbados (vol. 5, *pp. 477–98*) is based upon sources such as Ligon (1657), Davies (1666), Thomas (1690), Littleton (1689), and Rawlin (1699). It contains a conventional description of topography, soils, climate, fauna, agriculture, "the inhabitants, their manners, and customs," government, trade, etc. Also included (*between pp. 476–77*) is Herman Moll's detailed map of the island (for a reproduction of this map and comments on it see Tony Campbell, 1965, *pp. 15, 16–18*).

SPANN, JONATHAN
The remarkable occurrences, accidents, and proceedings of Her Majesty's ship Rupert:
and the squadron under the command of Capt. Jonathan Spann. . . . In a late expedition to the West-Indies, commencing the 6th of Feb. 1709/10.
[London], 1711. *27 pp.* [NYPL]
A journal in which the author notes (*p. 7*) that on April 2, 1710, after a twenty-five-day passage from Madeira, his ship stopped at Barbados for four days to "wine and water"; nothing, however, is said about this visit.

[STEELE, RICHARD]
"Inkle and Yariko."
The Spectator, no. 11, London, March 13, 1711. [BM]
Based on Richard Ligon's (1657, *p. 55*) account of Yarico, an Amerindian woman who had been duped and sold into slavery in Barbados. "This story was taken by Richard Steele . . . and, after considerable sentimental embellishment, including the addition of the name of Thomas Inkle of London, to the hero (?), was published in the Spectator . . ." (Sabin, no item number, *see* vol. 29, *p. 209*). For a detailed discussion of the literary influence of Steele's story see Wylie Sypher, *Guinea's Captive Kings* (Chapel Hill, 1942, *pp. 122–37*).

Steele had inherited a plantation from his wife, but he never visited the island (for details, *see* George A. Aitken, *The Life of Richard Steele*, London, 1889, vol. 1).

SHARPE, WILLIAM
The case of William Sharpe, Esq.
London, 1712. *50 pp.* [RCS, BM]
Concerns the altercation between Governor Mitford Crowe and William Sharpe. The latter was removed as President of the Barbados Council when Crowe arrived in 1707. The case was precipitated by the legislature's decision to introduce a paper currency in the island, a decision in which Sharpe had been instrumental and for which he was accused of corruption. This item contains a petition sent to the King by Sharpe in which he explains why a paper currency was established and defends his actions. It also reproduces (*pp. 17–50*) a variety of documents relating to the case, such as letters and petitions supportive of Sharpe and

signed by clergymen, merchants and planters.

[CLELAND, WILLIAM]
The present state of the sugar plantations consider'd; but especially that of the island of Barbadoes.
London, 1713. *30 pp.* [BM, UL, IJ]
Written by a Barbados merchant and planter, this pamphlet contains descriptions of various island institutions (as well as a critique of their inadequacies) such as the church, governor's office, civilian administration, organization of the militia and military fortifications, and agriculture. The largest section deals with the island's trade and commerce, with a few pages devoted to the slave trade. The author's name is inscribed in manuscript in one of the BM's copies and on the dedication page of a 1714 edition [UL].

[CLELAND, WILLIAM]
Some observations shewing the danger of losing the trade of the sugar colonies. Humbly offer'd to the consideration of the Parliament. By a Planter.
London, 1714. *15 pp.* [UL]
This pamphlet is, in effect, an argument for the establishment of a monopoly trade in slaves by a British joint-stock company. It stresses that slaves cost more since the Royal African Company lost its monopoly, discusses a variety of economic factors which "clearly demonstrate how near the desolation of the sugar islands is at hand," and offers a solution which rests upon Parliament's "securing as much as possible the whole trade to Africa, in the hands of the subjects of Great Britain." Although concerned with the West Indies in general, there are frequent specific references to Barbados.
Hanson (2016) cites the author; he is also provisionally identified in the UL catalog.

EDMUNDSON, WILLIAM
A journal of the life, travels, sufferings, and labour of love in the work of the ministry, of that worthy elder, and faithful servant of Jesus Christ, William Edmundson, who departed this life, the 31st of the 6th month, 1712.
Dublin, 1715. *419 pp.* [NYPL]

Edmundson, a Quaker, made five visits to Barbados. Two were in 1671 (the first of these in the company of George Fox, Thomas Briggs, John Stubbs, James Lancaster, Robert Widder, "and several others"); one in 1675; and two in 1683–84. In all, he must have spent close to a year on the island, but his account of these visits (*pp. 53, 55, 70–76, 109, 110*) is superficial and concentrates upon his own religious activities, the meetings he attended, and some of the local Quakers he encountered. Of interest is a brief discussion of his altercation in 1675 with the Anglican minister (Gilbert?) Ramsey, their public debate on theological issues, and his dialogue with Governor Atkins concerning the Quakers' preaching to slaves. Three letters Edmundson wrote from Barbados are also reproduced. One (*pp. 295–99*), written in 1675 and addressed to Friends in Ireland, mentions the names of some Barbados Quakers; the other two (*pp. 303–7*) were written in 1684 to his wife and are primarily religious epistles.
The first edition was published in London in 1713; the last in 1829 (Sabin 21873).

GORDON, WILLIAM
A sermon preach'd before the Governor, Council, and General Assembly of the island of Barbadoes, in the parish-church of St. Michael, on Friday the 18th of August, 1716.
London, 1718. *61 pp.* [BM]
A forty-three page preface contains Gordon's version of his political and personal altercations with Governor Lowther.

[GORDON, WILLIAM]
A representation of the miserable state of Barbadoes under the arbitrary and corrupt administration of His Excellency Robert Lowther, Esq., offer'd to the consideration of His Majesty and the . . . Lords of . . . Privy Council.
London, [1719]. *44 pp.* [BM, JCB]
Written in Barbados in July 1718, and endorsed by a number of prominent persons, this is a useful item for eighteenth-century political history. Aside from the "representation" (*pp. 15–36*), there are other documents and state-

ments dealing with Governor Lowther, especially his seizure of the cargo of a Portuguese ship which had landed at Barbados. The author is cited by Hanson (2526).

The Barbadoes Packet; containing several original papers: giving an account of the most material transactions that have lately happened in a certain part of the West Indies. In a letter from a gentleman of the said island to his friend in London.
London, 1720. *68 pp.*
[BM, LC, JCB, IJ, BOS]
The thrust of this item is an exposure of the arbitrary, corrupt, and slanderous behavior of Governor Robert Lowther. "The G[overnor] partly out of a pique against some particular men, and more out of his own natural arbitrary temper, has carry'd things with so high a hand, as to occasion uneasiness in all, and to incur the dislike of everyone, except the hated few who are his creatures and dependents." Reviewed are the Governor's altercations with the Reverend William Gordon "whose character was privately traduc'd in an unparalled manner to the Bishop of London"; his relationship with Jonathan Blenman, a lawyer; his extortion and legal manipulation in the case of a Portuguese ship that had put into the island; his criticisms of John Smalridge, the manager of the Codrington plantations (whose reply to Lowther's charges, reproduced in this tract, offers some information on the productivity of the plantations); and cases of other individuals who had trouble with Lowther — these are offered as other "flagrant instance[s] in the abandon'd accuser of good men." A useful and interesting work for a study of the relationship between the islanders and the governor.

A Letter From An Apothecary in the West-Indies to the author of the High-German Doctor in England. Occasioned by the late departure of a noted quack from those parts. With a preface.
London, 1720. *41 pp.* [LC]
In the LC, this item is bound into the same volume containing *The Barbadoes Packet* . . . (1720) and *The Self-Flatterer* . . . (1720), but it has its own title page, imprint, and collation. As with these

items, *A Letter From An Apothecary*, is also an attack upon Governor Robert Lowther, but it has the least specific informational value of the three.

The Self-Flatterer: or, the act of complimenting one's self, discovered in some serious animadversions on a merry paper printed in the daily post of the pretender's birthday, and entitled, The Humble Address of the Grand Inquest for the Body of the Island of Barbadoes, etc.
London, 1720. *38 pp.* [LC]
In the LC, this item is bound into the same volume containing *The Barbadoes Packet* (1720); it has its own title page, imprint, and collation. A strong and often sarcastic attack on Governor Robert Lowther, it offers less detail than *The Barbadoes Packet* but more than another companion piece, *A Letter From An Apothecary* (1720).

Acts of Assembly, passed in the island of Barbadoes, from 1648 to 1718.
London: Printed by John Baskett, 1721. *346 pp.* [LC, IJ]
Reference to 616 laws; the full texts of those in force, and the titles of those repealed, expired, etc. Another edition was published in 1732 (see *Acts of Assembly*). *See* Richard Hall (1764) for a comment on these editions (by [Arthur] Zouch?).

LABAT, JEAN BAPTISTE
Nouveau voyage aux isles de l'Amerique.
Paris, 1722. 6 vols. [BM]
In September 1700, Father Labat passed about eight or nine days in Barbados, mostly on the leeward coast. His observations on the island (vol. 4, *pp. 386–417*) contain a miscellany of useful information on social life, customs, slaves, sugar-making, etc. These pages have been translated by N. Connell (*Jl. BMHS*, 24, 1957, *160–74*), Capadose (1845), and John Eaden (*The Memoirs of Pere Labat, 1693–1705, Translated and Abridged*. London, 1931, *pp. 117–30*). For other editions see Sabin (38409 ff.).

*MAYO, WILLIAM
A new and exact map of the island of Barbadoes in America according to an actual and accurate survey made in the

years 1717 to 1721 approved by the Royal Society.
London, 1722. *4 sheets.* [BM]
A portion of this map is reproduced by Tony Campell (1965) who notes that it "was the second systematic, [cf. Richard Ford, ca. 1675] and first large-scale, survey of the island and it was on this that the legal bounds of the parishes were fixed. Schomburgk [1848] . . . suggested that the outdated boundaries should be revised, but it was not until the Admiralty survey of 1873 that Mayo's map ceased to be the standard representation of Barbados." The map also contains an inset plan of Bridgetown and view of Codrington College. Campbell also cites a 1756 London edition, *A New and Accurate Map of the Island of Barbadoes, with some late improvement.*

SEWEL, WILLIAM
The history of the rise, increase, and progress of the Christan people called Quakers . . . written originally in Low-Dutch by W. Sewel, and by himself translated into English.
London, 1722. *723 pp.* [BM]
Contains some brief references (*pp. 345, 555, 627*) relating to Quakers in Barbados. Originally published in Amsterdam in 1717; subsequent editions are listed by Sabin (79603–615).

TROTT, NICHOLAS
The laws of the British plantations in America, relating to the church and clergy, religion and learning.
London, 1725. *435 pp.* [NYPL]
Ten of the eleven Barbadian laws reproduced (*pp. 353–70*) were extracted from William Rawlin (1699); the eleventh, "An act for the better encouragement of the clergy," passed in 1705, was received in manuscript from the island's secretary.
First printed in London in 1721 (Sabin 97056).

[URING, NATHANIEL]
A relation of the late intended settlement of the islands of St. Lucia and St. Vincent in America, in right of the Duke of Montagu . . . in the year 1722.
London, 1725. *135 pp.* [RCS, UL]
Much of this account relates the trials

and tribulations English settlers had with the French; the St. Lucian settlers requested Barbadian aid, and interwoven through this account are materials which shed light on how the Barbadian Governor and Council viewed the island's self-interests and "international" commitments.
The author is identified by Sabin (98127).

ROBERTS, CAPTAIN GEORGE
The four years voyages of Captain George Roberts; being a series of uncommon events which befell him on a voyage to the islands of the Canaries, Cape de Verde, and Barbadoes, from whence he was bound to the coast of Guiney.
London, 1726. *458 pp.* [BMHS, BM]
The author spent about eight or nine months in Barbados during the course of trading expeditions in 1722 and 1724; his few comments on these visits (*pp. 11, 15, 383, 384*) largely relate to his difficulties in acquiring a ship and the nature of his cargoes.

TOWNE, RICHARD
A treatise of the diseases most frequent in the West Indies, and herein more particularly of those which occur in Barbadoes.
London, 1726. *192 pp.* [BM, RCS]
The author, a physician, had apparently lived in Barbados for about seven years at the time of his book's publication. Most of his discussion is devoted to the symptoms and nature of various illnesses, and the remedies he has personally found most effective; little attention is given to types of local cures, the use of plants in the preparation of curatives, etc. In a letter to Hans Sloane, written from Barbados on April 30, 1732 (BM, Sloane Mss. 4052, *fol. 105*), Towne wrote that he was preparing a "second edition of my treatise on the diseases in these parts. It has cost me a good deal of pains and observation and . . . it will be much larger and more complete than the former [edition]." I have been unable to trace this edition, and assume it was either never completed or never published.

URING, CAPTAIN NATHANIEL
A history of the voyages and travels of Capt. Nathaniel Uring.
London, 1726. *384 pp.* [RCS]

The author was engaged in the triangular trade between England, the West Indies, and New England. Although he visited Barbados a few times in the early eighteenth century (*pp. 7, 84*) nothing is recorded of these visits.

Other editions appeared in 1727, 1745, 1749 (Sabin 98124–126).

*CHALKLEY, THOMAS
  Youth persuaded to obedience, gratitude, and honour to God, and their parents. . . . written at sea . . . September, 1730.
  Barbadoes: Printed by David Harry, 1730.
Cited by Sabin (11753). This would appear to be one of the earliest items published in Barbados by the island's first printer. Of interest is D. C. McMurtrie's comment: "There is no scrap of printed matter extant that I know of to testify to David Harry's operation of a press at Bridgetown" (*Early Printing in Barbados*, London, 1933, *p. 6*). For biographical notes on Chalkley, *see* Cadbury reference in T. Chalkley, 1749.

  **Extracts from the votes and proceedings of the honourable the Assembly for the island of Barbados. At a meeting of the General Assembly on Friday the eighteenth day of December, 1730.*
  N.p. [1730?]. *8 pp.*
Listed by the National Union Catalog which locates only one copy, at the Massachusetts Historical Society (Boston).

  The votes and proceedings of the honourable the Assembly for the island of Barbados. At a meeting of the General Assembly at the house of Robert Warren, Esq., in the town of St. Michael, on Saturday the 13th of February, 1730 . . . [and] . . . at the house of Willoughby Duffey . . . on the 15th day of February, 1730.
  Barbados [1730]. *7 pp.*   [LCP]
Contains the report of a house committee appointed to prepare a representation to the crown of grievances against the island's governor; also complaints about the general economic condition of Barbados.
  The imprint reads "Printed and sold by David Harry."

  **Votes and proceedings of the House of Assembly for the island of Barbados at a meeting at Great Pilgrim on 17 November 1730. Printed and sold by David Harry near Broad Street.*
  [Barbados, 1730.]
Cited by E. M. Shilstone ("Some Notes on Early Printing Presses and Newspapers in Barbados," *Jl. BMHS*, 26, 1958–59, *21*). Copies of this item and the *Votes and Proceedings* of subsequent dates to February 13, 1731 (*31 pp. in all*) all printed by David Harry, are located in the Public Record Office, London, c.o. 31/20 (Michael Chandler, personal communication).

[ASHLEY, JOHN]
  The present state of the British sugar colonies consider'd; in a letter from a Gentleman of Barbadoes to his friend in London.
  London, 1731. *28 pp.*   [BM, UL]
The first in a series of three "letters" by the same author (*see* 1733 for authorship), a Barbadian planter who is concerned with the island's economic plight, its losses in the sugar trade, and the competitive advantage of French-produced sugar. In a detailed discussion, he uses Barbadian trade and production figures to illustrate his argument, concludes that the island has suffered economically as a result of a number of impositions on West Indian trade, and offers remedies to ameliorate this situation. A useful source for information on the island's commerce and economy.

  The Gentleman's Magazine and the Historical Chronicle.
  London, 1731–1818. 88 vols.   [BM]
A monthly in which the articles relating to Barbados are mainly short news items largely dealing with political events or natural calamities. Occasionally extracts from letters sent from Barbados are included, but, generally speaking, the articles do not provide rich sources of information on social history. A cumulative index compiled by Samuel Ayscough (London, 1789) covers the period 1731–86, and another by John Nichols (London, 1821) treats 1787–1818.
  Some of the items relating to Bar-

bados are separately referenced in this *Guide* – others, cited by volume number, year of publication, and the beginning page of article, include: brief notation of political events (vol. 1, 1731, *pp. 87, 218*); size of militia (vol. 10, 1740, *p. 241*); extract from a 1740 letter dealing with the House of Assembly and Governor's salary (vol. 11, 1741, *p. 55*); address by Council to Governor (vol. 17, 1747, *pp. 557, 588*); extract from a letter from Barbados dealing with hostilities with the French in the Caribbean (vol. 19, 1749, *p. 166*); 1756 Bridgetown fire (vol. 26, 1756, *pp. 205, 307*); 1766 Bridgetown fire (vol. 36, 1766, *pp. 338, 492, 549*); another fire in Bridgetown (vol. 37, 1767, *p. 140*); news items (vol. 46, 1776, *pp. 430, 453*); petition from planters to House of Commons requesting relief for damages from the 1780 hurricane (vol. 51, 1781, *p. 43*); hurricane of September, 1786 (vol. 56, 1786, *p. 987*); Governor Parry (vol. 60, 1790, *p. 564*); letters from Barbados relating to naval encounters with French (vol. 65, 1795, *p. 690*); reports of heavy rains in Bridgetown and arrival of troops on island prior to General Abercrombie (vol. 66, 1796, *pp. 70, 429*); the Barbados penny of 1788 and 1792 (vol. 70, 1800, *p. 230*); fall of volcanic ash from St. Vincent (vol. 82, 1812, pt. 1, *p. 580*); extract from letter describing poor economic conditions (vol. 82, 1812, pt. 2, *p. 486*).

[HALL, FAYRER]
The importance of the British plantations in America to this kingdom; with the state of their trade, and methods for improving it; as also a description of the several colonies there.
London, 1731. *114 pp.*   [IJ, UL]
In his preface, the author notes "I have traded to most of the places which I give any account of, and have occasionally been at them all." Pages 1–26 generally emphasize that colonial trade, with all its ancillary activities, produces great profits for the mother country. Pages 26–28 specifically treat Barbados and give an overview, with some statistics, of Barbados–Great Britain trade, the value of which, the author estimates, is "above . . . 95,000 [pounds] sterling per annum, over and above the

employment of so many sailors and shipping, and the vast number of all sorts of artificers employed at home in fitting, repairing and building those ships, etc., besides those for the manufacturers."
The author is identified by Hanson (4230) and Sabin (29766).

[HALL, FAYRER]
Remarks upon a book entitled "The Present State of the Sugar Colonies Considered," wherein some of the consequences and effects of restraining our trade are examined.
London, 1731. *34 pp.*   [UL, BM]
A discussion of J. Ashley (1731) which concentrates upon trade (other than in slaves) and commerce, with primary reference to Barbados.
The author is identified by Hanson (4235).

The importance of the sugar colonies to Great Britain stated, and some objections against the sugar colony bill answer'd. In a letter to a member of the House of Commons.
London, 1731. *40 pp.*   [BM, UL]
Argues for the economic importance of the West Indies, and stresses that planters must receive beneficial legislation so they can compete with French sugars on foreign markets – occasionally includes specific references to Barbados.

Observations on the case of the northern colonies.
London, 1731. *31 pp.* [BOS, JCB, UL]
A manuscript inscription on the title page of the BOS copy says this is "By the Barbados Managers," but the item itself only contains two minor references (*pp. 29–30*) to Barbadian trade with New England.

Acts of Assembly passed in the island of Barbados from 1648 to 1718.
London: Printed by John Baskett, 1732. *318 pp.*   [BPL, LC, BM]
Another edition of *Acts of Assembly* (1721). It appears in a separate volume or bound in with *Acts of Assembly* (London, 1739).

[ASHLEY, JOHN]
The British Empire in America, con-

sider'd. In a second letter from a Gentleman of Barbadoes, to his friend in London.
London, 1732. *29 pp.* [UL, LC]
Dated September 30, 1731, this item continues a discussion of trade and economic matters started in the author's first letter (1731). Tax and trade restrictions placed upon West Indian sugar and the competitive strength of sugar produced by the French are dealt with.

A comparison between the British sugar colonies and New England, as they relate to the interest of Great Britain . . . to which is added a letter to a member of Parliament.
London, 1732. *43 pp.* [BM, UL, H]
Argues that the trade of the sugar colonies is economically more important to Great Britain than that of New England; the latter's position will decline as it develops and increases its self-sufficiency. Includes occasional specific, but superficial, references to Barbados.

[ROBERTSON, ROBERT]
A detection of the state and situation of the present sugar planters, of Barbadoes and the Leward Islands; with an answer to this query, why does not England, or her sugar islands, or both, make and settle more sugar colonies in the West Indies? Written in the month of December 1731, by an inhabitant of one of His Majesty's Leward Caribbee Islands.
London, 1732. *99 pp.* [BM, UL, IJ]
Deals with economic matters, but the author appears to have had no direct firsthand experience with Barbados, and for his information on the island he relies almost entirely upon John Ashley (1731) and F. Hall (1731). Hanson (4366) cites the author.

[ASHLEY, JOHN]
Proposals offered for the sugar planters' redress, and for reviving the British sugar commerce. In a further letter from a Gentleman of Barbadoes, to his friend in London.
London, 1733. *35 pp.*
[UL, BM, LC, H]
This third letter (see Ashley 1732) devoted to topics of commerce and trade offers three proposals for "keeping the

sugar trade in our hands; or at least, to the preventing it from being altogether lost to the British nation."
It also deals with the internal economic problems of the planter and provides details on his production costs, etc. The UL catalog identifies the author.

Representation of the Board of Trade relating to the laws made, manufactures set up, and trade carried on, in His Majesty's plantations in America.
[London], 1733. *20 pp.* [BM]
Includes extremely brief comments on recent laws and the trade of Barbados. A copy of this pamphlet is bound in with manuscripts in the DM (Additional Mss. 35907, *fols. 50–59*).

[ROBERTSON, ROBERT]
An enquiry into the methods that are said to be now proposed in England, to retrieve the sugar trade. By the author of the Detection of the State and Situation of the Present Sugar Planters of Barbados and the Leeward Islands . . . written about the middle of April, 1733.
London, 1733. *31 pp.* [JCB]
Treats trade problems in general with occasional specific, but very brief, references to Barbados based upon the writings of others. For authorship, *see* R. Robertson (1732).

[ROBERTSON, ROBERT]
A supplement to the Detection of the State and Situation of the Present Sugar Planters of Barbadoes and the Leeward Islands: shewing . . . that the surest way for England to command the sugar-market abroad, is to contract rather than inlarge her sugar colonies. In a letter from an inhabitant of one of His Majesty's Leeward Islands.
London, 1733. *92 pp.* [BM]
An extensive discussion of trade relationships and the business of trade in the West Indies. Hanson (4529) cites the author.

ASHLEY, JOHN
The sugar trade, with the incumberances thereon, laid open. By a Barbadoes Planter.
London, 1734. *22 pp.*
[BM, JCB, BOS, UL, H]
The dedication page is signed and dated

Barbados, October 2, 1733. This tract deals solely with commercial matters. It argues for the importance of the sugar colonies to the mother country and against duties, etc. which weaken their economic position. Barbados is occasionally used to illustrate a specific point.

BENNETT, JOHN
A memorial of the difficulties, hardships, and perplexities, under which Mr. Bennet hath, and doth still labour under. Humbly submitted to the consideration of the honourable court of directors of the South-Sea Company. To which is added an appendix, containing, Numb. 1. A petition to His Most Excellent Majesty from the General Assembly of Barbados, passed [August 21, 1733] . . . Numb. 2. A state of the case . . . Numb. 3. A state of the licensees case, who are sufferers by Spanish seizures and confiscations.
London, 1734. *40 pp.*   [H]
A complex case in which the author became legally entangled. The South Sea company (the Royal Assiento Company of Great Britain) pursued claims for outstanding debts on slaves sold in Barbados and the Leewards by its former agent in Barbados, Dudley Woodbridge. The dedicatory page is signed and dated London, January 18, 1733/34.

Representation from the commissioners for trade and plantations, to the . . . Lords . . . in Parliament . . . In pursuance of their Lordships addresses to His Majesty . . . , relating to the state of the British islands in America.
London, 1734. *19 pp.*   [BM]
An alternate title is, *Representation of the Board of Trade Relating to the State of the British Islands in America, with Regard to Their Strength, Their Trade, and Fortifications.*
Includes brief comments on Barbadian trade and military fortifications. A copy of this pamphlet is bound in with manuscripts in the BM (Additional Mss. 35907, *fols. 60–69*).

[ASHLEY, JOHN]
Some observations on a direct exportation of sugar, from the British islands. With answers to Mr. [Nathaniel] Toriano's objections to it. In a letter from a Gentle-

man in Barbados to his friend in London.
London, 1735. *23 pp.*   [BM, LC, H]
A detailed argument on trade in which the author makes a strong plea (as in his 1734 work) "towards obtaining an act of Parliament for permitting our sugar to be carried directly from our sugar colonies in ships navigated according to law, to any foreign port in Europe." The author is identified in Sabin (2195) and the BM catalog.

ATKINS, JOHN
A voyage to Guinea, Brazil, and the West Indies, in His Majesty's ships, the Swallow and Weymouth, describing the several islands and settlements, viz. Madeira, the Canaries. . . . Cabo Corso and others on the Guinea coast; Barbados, Jamaica, etc. in the West Indies.
London, 1735. *265 pp.*   [BC, BM, H]
The author, a surgeon in the Royal Navy, spent a little over a week in Barbados in August 1722 while his ship was being provisioned. His general description of the island (*pp. 205–20*) seems to be based as well upon the commentaries of others. A second edition was published in London in 1737 [BM]; "this is the [same as the] previous work, with merely a new title" (Sabin 2275).

*CHALKLEY, THOMAS
Free thoughts communicated to free thinkers. . . . written at sea.
Barbados, 1735. *16 pp.*
Cited by Sabin (11748). A second edition was published in 1735 in Philadelphia [BM].

A pattern for Governours: exemplify'd in the character of Scroop Late Lord Viscount Howe, Baron of Clonawly; and Governour of Barbados. As gratefully attempted by several of the most ingenious pens of that island, and transmitted to be published here in honor of his Lordship's memory.
London, 1735. *18 pp.*   [JCB]
Howe died in Barbados at the age of 37. This pamphlet is largely a reprint of three eulogies which first appeared in the newspaper, *Barbados Gazette* (March 29, April 9, and April 12, 1735). The first gives an account of his death and funeral, and mentions his survivors; in

general terms, the second extols his virtues as a man and his behavior as governor; the third covers the same ground, but with more specifics on the political events during his administration. Also included (*pp. 16–18*) are extracts from a speech in the House of Assembly, April 26, 1735, in which the passage of an act awarding £2500 to Howe's widow is urged, and the final pages reproduce the act itself.

*BENNETT, JOHN
Essay for regulating and improving the trade and plantations of Great Britain.
London, 1736.
Sabin (4730) suggests that this may be the first edition of the author's 1738 work.

BENNETT, JOHN
The national merchant; or, discourses on commerce and colonies; being an essay for regulating and improving the trade and plantations of Great Britain.
London, 1736. *143 pp.*   [H]
Emanuel Bowen (1747, *p. 751*) refers "to the report of the author of the *National Merchant* who lived on [Barbados] many years, and well knew the trade for Negroes," but this book contains few specific references to the West Indies and none, as far as I could see, to Barbados. Bennett's name is signed on the dedicatory page.

Yarico to Inkle. An Epistle.
London, 1736. *16 pp.*   [BOS, BM]
A highly romanticized fantasy based upon Ligon's (1657) celebrated story and the account that appeared in the *Spectator* (Richard Steele, 1711). Sabin lists the following editions with the "same text": (105978) *The Epistle of Yarico to Inkle. A Poem* (Glasgow, 1750 [BM, H, NYPL]); (105981) *Yarico to Inkle, An Epistle* ... (Springfield, 1784 [LC]); (105982) *Yarico to Inkle, An Epistle* ... (Hartford, 1792 [LC, H]); (105983) *An Epistle from Yarico to Inkle, Together with their Characters, as Related in the Spectator* ... (Salem, 1792 [H, NYPL]). In the last item, it is noted, "the text is that of the 1736 edition, with the last 30 lines replaced by the last 28 lines of the entirely different *London*, 1776, poem [by E. Jerningham, 1766]."

BENNETT, JOHN
Two letters and several calculations on the sugar colonies and trade; addressed to two committees nominated by the West India Merchants.
London, 1738. *104 pp.*   [JCB, H]
The author, former agent in the West Indies, notes: "These papers were wrote on several occasions, to shew the value and importance of the British sugar colonies; the difficulties they lie under, the dangers to which they are exposed, and the measures proper to encourage and preserve them. ... There is one general principle diffused through these writings, and it is this ... I have not ... proposed one single advantage for the British sugar colonies, that will be a detriment to Great Britain." The book is concerned with economics and trade in the West Indies in general, but there are occasional specific references to Barbados including tables giving estimates of the value of land, stock, and equipment in 1730 and 1731, estimates of the island's "yearly produce and expences," and a detailed table estimating the income and expenditures on a one thousand acre sugar plantation.
Hanson (5189) cites another edition, also published in 1738 [UL].

[SEYMOUR, FRANCES]
The story of Inkle and Yarico. A most moving tale from the Spectator. Attempted in verse.
London, 1738. *16 pp.*   [BM]
Based upon Richard Steele's (1711) elaboration of Ligon (1657). Included (*pp. 13–16*), with own title page, is *An Epistle from Yarrico to Inkle, After He Had Left Her in Slavery* (London, 1738). Author identified in the BM catalog.

Acts of Assembly passed in the island of Barbadoes, from 1717–18 to 1738, inclusive. Part II.
London: Printed by John Baskett, 1739.   [BM, LC]
Bound in with *Acts of Assembly* (1732). Each part has its own title page and imprint, but their pagination is continuous. *See* Richard Hall (1764) for a comment on this volume (by Mr. Salmon?).

The Jews in Barbados in 1739.
See S. Oppenheim (1914).

ASHLEY, JOHN
Memoirs and considerations concerning the trade and revenues of the British colonies in America.
London, 1740–43. 2 pts.   [BM, H]
Ashley was a member of the Barbados Council and Deputy-Surveyor and Auditor General "of all of his Majesty's revenues arising in Barbados and the Windward Caribbean Islands." In a 1744 testimony before a House of Commons committee, he noted that he had "lived [in Barbados] at different times [for] twenty eight years" (*Reports from Committees of the House of Commons, reprinted by order of the House. Vol. 2, Miscellaneous Subjects: 1738–65.* London, 1803, *p. 72*). Although this work is more extensive than the author's 1734 and 1735 tracts, it deals with the same economic issues. It argues that the sugar colonies are of considerable economic importance to Great Britain and that there are unfair economic burdens imposed upon them. A plan for alleviating such burdens is offered. The book is not concerned with Barbados *per se*, but aspects of its commercial and economic life are frequently noted to illustrate the author's argument.

BAXTER, THOMAS
A letter from a Gentleman at Barbadoes to his friend now in London, concerning the administration of the late Gov. B-----g.
London, 1740. *44 pp.*
          [BMHS, IJ, BOS, BM]
This letter, signed by Baxter and dated Barbados, December 27, 1740, is addressed to Jonathan Blenman in London; it attempts to vindicate Governor Robert Byng of Barbados against character accusations made by the speaker and others of the Assembly.

PERRIN, WILLIAM
The present state of the British and French sugar colonies, and our own northern colonies, considered. Together with some remarks on the decay of our trade.
London, 1740. *63 pp.*   [BM, UL]
A general treatise which occasionally makes specific reference to Barbados.

*[BELL, JOHN]
An epistle to friends in Maryland, Virginia, Barbadoes, and the other colonies, and islands in the West-Indies, where any friends are.
[London, 1741.]   [NYPL]
Sabin (4454) describes this as a "folio, 1 sheet." Bell does not appear to have visited Barbados (Manuscripts, Society of Friends, Portfolios, vol. 17, no. 2).

[DUKE, WILLIAM]
Some memoirs of the first settlement of the island of Barbados, and other of the Carribbee Islands, with the succession of the Governours and Commanders in Chief of Barbados to the year 1741. Extracted from antient records, papers and accounts taken from Mr. William Arnold, Mr. Samuel Bulkly, and Mr. John Summers, some of the first settlers . . . also some remarks on the laws and Constitution of Barbados.
Barbados, 1741. *100 pp.*
          [BM, LC, BOS]
Written by the clerk of the House of Assembly. This book is largely a chronological sketch of the island's political history, focusing upon the succession of governors and occasionally mentioning the more significant legislation passed during their terms of office. According to V. T. Harlow (*The History of Barbados*, London, 1926, *p. xvi*), the *Memoirs* "contain some serious chronological mistakes [but] they are based on original documents which are now lost." I have been able to find record of some legislative acts which are not located in sources such as William Rawlin (1699) and Richard Hall (1764).
This edition is also in the *Photostat Americana* (2nd ser., Massachusetts Historical Society, Boston, 1936), having been photographed from the original in the Massachusetts Historical Society. This copy is inscribed in manuscript on the title page "By William Duke, Esqr." (*See also* Cruickshank 57, and Sabin 3290, for author identification.) A second edition was published in London in 1743 under the title *Memoirs of the first settlement . . . to the Year 1742* [BM], and reprinted in Barbados in 1891 [BMHS].

[KEIMER, SAMUEL]
   Caribbeana: containing letters and dissertations, together with political essays on various subjects and occasions.
   London, 1741. 2 vols.
          [BPL, IJ, BM, BOS]
These lengthy and informative volumes are comprised of items that first appeared in the *Barbados Gazette* from November 30, 1731 to December 16, 1738. "A good part . . . of this work," the editor notes, "does more nearly affect the people of [Barbados] for whose benefit indeed it was principally undertaken. . . . But 'tis apprehended that our European readers will find their account in the perusal of even of this part of our collection, as it may give them an idea of the customs, manners, humours, morals, and politicks of a small subordinate Government, and shew how near it resembles those that are independent . . . and more renowned in story. Here, indeed, they may see Great Britain itself in miniature, observe the direful effects of the same unruly passions, discover the same springs of action, the same inclination to parties and factions, kept up too by the same motives, all centering in self-interest, which alike governs throughout the world."

Both volumes contain subject and name indexes, and a lengthy appendix to volume 2 (*pp. 297–358*) reproduces eight papers "referr'd to in the book, but several others relating to the affairs of Barbados, some whereof were never printed before" — these items, written between 1728 and 1732, largely relate to legal and political issues.

The value of this collection is greatly enhanced because of the rarity of early issues of the *Barbados Gazette.*

Keimer is cited as editor of *Caribbeana* by Sabin (37174) and in the BM catalog. He was the first editor and publisher of the *Barbados Gazette* and was responsible for its publication "until the latter part of 1738" (D. C. McMurtrie, *Early Printing in Barbados,* London, 1933, *p. 12*). Keimer died on August 20, 1742 (not 1738 as stated in the *Dictionary of National Biography*) "and was buried at the Parish church of St. Michael. The record of his burial appears in the Church Register" (E.

M. Shilstone, "Some Notes on Early Printing Presses and Newspapers in Barbados," *Jl. BMHS,* 26, 1958–59, 22).

WARREN, HENRY
   A treatise concerning the malignant fever in Barbados and the neighboring islands: with an account of the seasons there, from the year 1734 to 1738.
   London, 1741. 75 *pp.*   [BPL]
A lengthy description of the symptoms and treatment of yellow fever, with additional comments on other diseases and cures. Also included are meteorological data.

First published in 1740 (Sabin 101466).

BIRCH, THOMAS
   A collection of state papers of John Thurloe . . . [1638–60] to which is prefixed the life of Mr. Thurloe . . . by Thomas Birch.
   London, 1742. 7 vols.   [BM]
Thurloe was Secretary to Oliver and Richard Cromwell. These copious volumes occasionally contain letters from Barbados largely relating to political and legal matters. The index to each volume offers a useful guide to its contents.

[BLENMAN, JONATHAN]
   Remarks on several Acts of Parliament relating more especially to the colonies abroad; as also on diverse acts of assemblies there. . . . Wherein is likewise contain'd, a discourse concerning the 4½ per cent duty paid in Barbados, and the Leeward Islands.
   London, 2nd ed. 1742. *125 pp.*
          [H, JCB, LC, BM]
The first edition was also published in London in 1742 (Sabin 6012). The author is obviously knowledgeable about Barbados and his examination of the effectiveness and rationale behind various of Parliament's laws is often done with particular respect to the island. His discussion thus ranges over a variety of topics in which Barbadian conditions are specified, e.g., trade with Great Britain, the French and Dutch West Indies, and North America; laws governing exports and their implications for island trade; the island's

legal and judicial system with respect to real estate and debts; London merchants and their representatives in Barbados; the island's credit system; general comments on the operation of the island's judicial and legal system and the relationship between local conditions and laws passed in England. Also presented is a detailed history of the 4½ percent export duty and its effects on the Barbadian economy.

On the title page of the JCB copy, "Jonathan Blenman, Esq., Attorney General for Barbados," is inscribed in manuscript. A manuscript *ex libris* in the copy at the Houghton Library (Harvard) notes that the book was given in 1743 to G. Dowding by Jonathan Blenman, Attorney General for Barbados, but a manuscript inscription by a different hand on the title page of the same copy reads "by Jonathan Blumeau, esq." — perhaps taken from Sabin's erroneous attribution (6012); see also Hanson (5638) for authorship.

Incle and Yarico: A Tragedy, of Three Acts. As it was intended to have been performed at the Theatre-Royal, in Covent-Garden.
London, 1742.   [LC]
See Sabin (105986) for possible authorship and a German translation.

SMITH, JOHN
[*Account of Barbados in 1742.*]
See H. Cadbury (1942).

*ASHLEY, JOHN
A supplement to the second part of the memoirs of the trade and revenues of the British colonies in America.
[London], 1744.   [UL]
Title cited by Sabin (2194); referred to by Hanson (5455).

*INGRAM, [DALE?]
Essay on the nature of dysenteries.
Barbados, 1744.
D. McMurtrie (*Early Printing in Barbados*, London, 1933, *p. 13*) refers to this work in the following sentence: "[William] Beeby's [one of the island's early printers] imprint also appeared in 1744 on *Ingram's Essay on the Nature of Dysenteries*, of which no extant copy is known to me." McMurtrie does not

specify the source for his identification of this title. I have been unable to find any trace of the item.

CASTLE, WILLIAM
"*A short discovery of the coast and continent of America, from the equinoctial northward, and of the adjacent isles . . . [1644].*"
In *Harleian Collection of Voyages and Travels.* vol. 2. London, 1745.
     [RCS]
The presence of Barbados is noted, but nothing is said about the island.

PHILLIPS, THOMAS
"*A journal of a voyage made in the Hannibal of London, ann. 1693, 1694, from England, to Cape Monseradoe, in Africa; and thence along the coast of Guiney to Whidaw, the island of St. Thomas, and so forward to Barbadoes.*"
In A. Churchill, ed., *A Collection of Voyages and Travels.* vol. 6. London, 1746.   [BM, BMHS]
This work, one of the classics in the literature on slaving, offers virtually no information on Barbados *per se*, but it does contain an extremely detailed account of a slaving voyage which resulted in the introduction of 372 Africans (out of an original complement of 700) to the island.

*TRAIL, JOHN
A map of the fortified part of the island of Barbados drawn by John Trail, engineer, Feb. 9, 1746, with a list of the forts and batteries in the island.
Bridgetown, 1746.
Cited, but not reproduced, by Tony Campbell (1965, *p. 18*) who notes this is "the first map published in Barbados. The only recorded copy is in the Colonial Office, London." The Colonial Office copy is now in the Public Record Office, London (c.o. 700 Barb/7 MR 769; Michael Chandler, personal communication).

Addresses of the Grand Jury of Barbados to their Governor Sir Thomas Robinson; also of the Council Board to the King, and to their said Governor; and a letter from the Jews settled in Barbados to the said Sir Thomas Robinson; all in justification of his conduct, and subsequent to the

complaints signed against him by twelve
gentlemen of the Assembly on the 10th of
September, 1745.
[Barbados? 1747.] 8 pp. [JCB, LC]
The publication date of this item is
sometimes given as 1745, but the latest
date mentioned in the tract itself (in "a
letter from the Jews") is 1747.

BOWEN, EMANUEL
A complete system of geography. Being a
description of . . . the known world.
London, 1747. 2 vols. [BM]
A detailed and competent description
(vol. 2, pp. 745–54) of Barbados's
physical geography, political history,
economy, civil and legal structure, etc.,
which is based upon a number of
standard published works including
those of Ligon (1657), Labat (1722),
and Oldmixon (1708). Also contains a
very detailed map of the island (reproduced in Tony Campbell, 1965).

*HUGHES, GRIFFITH
"Concerning a zoophyton, somewhat re-
sembling the flower of the marigold . . .
read November 10, 1743."
The Philosophical Transactions . . . of
the Royal Society, Abridged, vol. 9.
London, 1747, pp. 110–11.
From a letter Hughes wrote from Bar-
bados concerning the fauna in the
Animal-flower cave; cited by F. J.
Dallett (p. 15 — see reference in Hughes,
1750).

[HUGHES, GRIFFITH]
Nearly compleated, and to be publish'd by
subscription by the Reverend Griffith
Hughes, Rector of St. Lucy's in Barbados.
The natural history of the island of
Barbados in eleven books.
Barbados, 1747. 2 pp. [BOS]
Simply provides a chapter-by-chapter
overview of the author's Natural History
(1750), then in preparation. Discussed
by Dallett (pp. 17–19 — see reference in
Hughes, 1750) who notes that BOS holds
"the only known copy of this pros-
pectus"; I have come across no other.

STORY, THOMAS
A journal of the life of Thomas Story:
containing, an account of his remarkable
convincement of, and embracing the
principles of truth, as held by the people

called Quakers; and also, of his travels
and labours in the service of the Gospel.
Newcastle upon Tyne, 1747. 768 pp.
[BM, F]
Story spent from three to four months
in Barbados in 1708–9, and about five
months in 1714, but his journal entries
relating to the island (pp. 433–41, 457–
62) contain little more than an itemization of the "meetings" he attended and
the names of the Quakers he encountered.

*CHALKLEY, THOMAS
A collection of the works of Thomas
Chalkley.
Philadelphia, 1749. 590 pp. [DM]
Chalkley, a Quaker merchant, paid
visits to Barbados in at least 1701, 1707,
1718, 1727, 1729, and 1731 (Manuscripts, Society of Friends, Portfolios,
vol. 17, no. 2). The following comments
on the above work are based upon an
article by Henry J. Cadbury, "A Quaker
Account of Barbados in 1718" (Jl.
BMHS, 10, 1942–43, 118–24). Cadbury
provides biographical data on Chalkley
and information on how the volume,
published posthumously, came into
print. He notes that some passages from
the manuscript journal were omitted in
the published volume, and his transcription of Chalkley's 1718 visit to
Barbados is from the original located in
the Historical Society of Pennsylvania.
In his account, Chalkley gives some
information on the island's Quaker
community, makes a brief comment on
the treatment of slaves, and reports on a
visit to "Oliver's Cave" (the Animal-
flower cave?). Cadbury simply summarizes Chalkley's other visits to
Barbados. Sabin (11746–747) cites later
editions.

The royal African: or, memoirs of the
young prince of Annamaboe.
London [1749]. 53 pp. [UL, BM]
The adventures of the "Young Prince"
apparently aroused considerable interest
in England. The author of this account,
"not being perfectly satisfied with the
narrative in the newspapers. . . . it
appeared to me worth employing a few
leisure hours, in reducing what I have
learned into some kind of order . . . this
gave rise to the following Memoirs."

The *Memoirs* detail how "John Corrente," a Fanti (Gold Coast) chief and active slave trader, was encouraged by a privateering captain to send his son to England. Instead, the son was taken to Barbados and sold as a slave; he was ultimately freed through the intervention of the Royal African Company which wanted to stabilize its business relationships with the father in Africa. The account is largely devoted to the intricacies of slaving operations on the African coast; other than briefly recording the son's reactions upon discovering he was enslaved in Barbados (*pp. 40–42*), no information is provided about the island.

The caption on a 1749 mezzotint portrait provides the name of the "Young Prince" and chronological details not given in the *Memoirs*: "William Unsah Sessarakoo, son of John Bannishee Corrantee, Ohinee of Annamaboe, and of Eukobah, daughter of Ansah Sessarakoo, King of Aquamboo, Niece to Quishadoo, King of Akroan. He was sold at Barbadoes as a slave in the year 1744, redeemed at the earnest request of his father in the year 1748 and brought to England." The engraving, done by John Faber, the younger, after a portrait by Gabriel Mathias, is reproduced, with notes, in the *Jl. BMHS* (27, 1959–60, *1–2*).

The UL dates its copies of the *Memoirs* at 1749, Sabin (73755) at 1750?, and the BM catalog at 1720, the latter being much too early. Sabin and the BM catalog also list a second, undated, London edition of fifty-five pages.

1750–1799

HUGHES, GRIFFITH
The natural history of Barbados.
London, 1750. *333 pp.*
[BMHS, BM, BOS]
Although most of this well-known work is devoted to descriptions of the island's flora and fauna, these often contain information on plant use for medicinal, dietary, etc., purposes, and ancillary comments applicable to wider cultural practices. There are also some valuable descriptive passages on the island's human population, agricultural practices, and sugar making.

Hughes first arrived at Barbados in late 1735 and assumed the rectorship of St. Lucy's parish, a post he formally held, with intermittent residences in Pennsylvania and England, until 1754; during this period he lived on the island for about eleven years. For background to his book, biographical details, and references to his correspondence, see F. J. Dallett's informative and intensively researched article "Griffith Hughes Dissected" (*Jl. BMHS*, 23, 1955–56, *3–29*).

Papers laid before the honourable House of Commons by the commissioners for trade and plantations, pursuant to an address of the House of Lords to His Majesty, the 8th of June 1749. For the better securing, improving, and extending, the [slave] trade to Africa.
London, 1750. *53 pp.*   [BM]
Contains seven "papers," some of which make occasional specific references to Barbados.

GREW, THEOPHILUS
The Barbados Almanack, for the year of Our Lord 1752: being Bissextile, or Leap Year.
Philadelphia [1751].   [LCP]
A broadsheet, printed on one side, giving standard almanac information as well as the names of the island's Assembly and Council members and judges of the courts.

BESSE, JOSEPH
A collection of the sufferings of the people called Quakers . . . from . . . 1650 to the . . . Act of Toleration granted to Protestant dissenters . . . in . . . 1689. Taken from the original records and other authentic accounts.
London, 1753. 2 vols.   [BM]
Materials on Barbados are contained in volume 2 (*pp. 278–351*). Besse's own comments tie together a variety of

documents relating to the persecutions and tribulations of Quakers on the island; these documents often contain useful information on various aspects of Barbadian society and material culture.

To Henry Grenville, Esq. Governor and Commander in Chief, of this, and other the King's Carribee Islands, to Windward of Guadeloupe, etc. The respectful address of the people, called, Quakers, in the said island . . . [upon Grenville's retirement and departure] to which address His Excellency was pleas'd to make the following answer.
[Bridgetown, 1753.]
The National Union Catalog lists this as a one-page photostatic copy of a page from the *Barbados Gazette* (May 30, 1753, no. 1052); located at Haverford College, Haverford, Pennsylvania.

*HILLARY, WILLIAM
Observations on the changes of the air and the concomitant epidemical diseases in the island of Barbadoes, and other West India islands.
London, 1754.
Taken from Sabin (31876) who also cites a 1759 London reprint; Cundall (30a) cites a 1752 publication — all apparently the first edition of the author's 1766 work.

ROTHERAM, REVEREND JOHN
A sketch of the one great argument, formed from the several concurring evidences for the truth of Christianity.
Oxford, 1754. *68 pp.* [BM]
The author wrote this purely theological tract while at Codrington College.

WEEKES [NATHANIEL]
Barbados. A poem. To Sir Thomas Robinson, Bart.
London, 1754. *63 pp.* [IJ, BM]
"Fir'd with a sense of filial gratitude," the author notes, ". . . for that industrious, venerable isle, which gave me birth and rear'd me up to life," his "blank verse" extols the island's geography, animal and plant life (occasionally providing information on the cultivation and local use of plants), and white population — a sample: "Industrious are thy sons / and by their toil, made healthy, strong and brave. True to their King, and generous to strangers / a chearful welcome smiles in ev'ry face (the index of their hearts) and hospitality crowns all their boards. Thy daughters too, are blest with ev'ry virtue / prudent, and chaste, and modest, and discreet / in person fair, in shape most delicate."

BELGROVE, WILLIAM
A treatise upon husbandry or planting.
Boston, 1755. *86 pp.* [BM, BOS, H]
The author, identifying himself as a "regular bred, and long experienced planter of . . . Barbados," devotes about fifty pages of this useful pamphlet to a detailed exposition of management, planting, care, cost-accounting, sugar making, etc., on a five-hundred acre sugar plantation. Appended to Belgrove's work (*pp. 51–86*) is Henry Drax's "Instructions for the management of Drax–Hall and the Irish–Hope plantations: to Archibald Johnson." These "Instructions," Belgrove notes, were "given many years ago . . ." but he does not date the manuscript nor relate how he acquired it. On the basis of internal evidence and Drax family history, I would guess the "Instructions" date from the late seventeenth or early eighteenth century; they afford a valuable source of information about plantation operations, especially with respect to agricultural practices and sugar making.

DOUGLASS, WILLIAM
A Summary, historical and political, of the first planting, progressive improvements, and present state of the British settlements in North America.
London, 1755. 2 vols. [RCS]
Dr. Douglass visited Barbados in 1717. His brief chapter specifically dealing with the island (vol. 1, *pp. 130–36*) is largely a chronological history, based on unspecified sources, with some commentary on government, commerce, etc. More useful information, on topics such as plant use, manufacture and cultivation of sugar cane, and slaves, is interspersed throughout his more general chapter "The British Island Settlements" (vol. 1, *pp. 115–30*).
Hanson (6074) notes this was first

published in Boston and issued in parts between 1747 and 1753 [BM]; he cites other issues in Boston (1749, 1758 [LC]), and another London edition in 1760 [BM]. *See also* Sabin (20726–728).

HALL, RICHARD
A general account of . . . Barbados, written in . . . 1755.
See R. Hall (1924).

[BURKE, EDMUND]
An account of the european settlements in America.
London, 1757. 2 vols.   [BM]
Volume 2 (*pp. 81–88*) contains a superficial historical account of Barbados and a brief delineation of its commercial state. Sabin (9282, 9283) cites a number of later editions.

BELLIN, JACQUES NICOLAS
Description geographique des isles Antilles possédées par les Anglois.
Paris, 1758. *171 pp.*   [BM, H]
A competent, but standard description (*pp. 51–87*) of Barbados's physical geography, people, towns, military fortifications, government, commerce, etc., based upon various published works. Contains a map of the island which shows towns and forts (reproduced in Tony Campbell, 1965).

[BUTEL-DUMONT, GEORGE MARIE]
Histoire et commerce des Antilles Angloises.
[Paris], 1758. *284 pp.*   [BM, LC, H]
The section on Barbados (*pp. 3–42*), which includes materials on history, geography, etc., focuses on the island's commerce and economy; it is based on various published sources. Sabin (9601) cites the author.

GARDINER, RICHARD
An account of the expedition to the West Indies, against Martinico, Guadeloupe, and other the Leeward Islands, subject to the French King.
London, 1759. *75 pp.*   [BM]
A captain of the marines very briefly records (*pp. 9–10*) his stay in Barbados while the English fleet was being provisioned and attempts were made to acquire volunteers to join the expedition. Other editions were published in London in 1760 and 1762 (Sabin 26627, 26628).

[ALLEYNE, JOHN G.]
A defence of the conduct of Barbadoes during the late expedition to Martinique and Guadeloupe, in a letter to the Right Hon. Gen. Barrington. By a native, resident in the island.
London, 1760. *88 pp.*   [BM, LC, H]
This work, "attributed to Sir J. G. Alleyne" (Cruickshank 63) a prominent Barbadian planter, focuses upon the problems of raising a Barbadian volunteer force to participate in an expedition against the French. Some useful commentary on the island's militia is provided, but this is specifically written as rebuttal to charges made against Barbadians by Richard Gardiner (1759).

ELLIS, JOHN
"An account of an encrinus, or starfish, with a jointed stem, taken on the coast of Barbados, December 17, 1761."
Philosophical Transactions of the Royal Society, vol. 52, pt. 1, London, 1761, *pp. 357–62.*   [BM]
Simply, as noted in the title, a zoological description.

[CAMPBELL, DR. JOHN]
Candid and impartial considerations on the nature of the sugar trade, the comparative importance of the British and French islands in the West Indies.
London, 1763. *228 pp.*
                         [BM, WIC, BOS, H]
An elaborate treatise on the present and potential value of the sugar islands to Great Britain with references to Barbados, mainly relating to its political and commercial history, scattered throughout. These references contribute to an understanding of the island's trading and political relations with other Caribbean territories. The author is cited by Ragatz (*p. 284*).

*DOLLAND, JOHN
An Almanac for the island of Barbados for the year . . . 1764 being Bissextile or Leap Year.
London [1763].   [BMHS]
Cited by E. M. Shilstone ("Book and Pocket Almanacs." *Jl. BMHS,* 28,

1960–61, *78–79*), who notes "From an advertisement which appeared in the *Barbados Mercury* of Dec. 4, 1784, it would seem that publication of this almanac began with the year 1755. 'Arrived from London and now on sale Matthias Holst's Barbados Almanac for 1785 being the 31st year of continued publication in sheet and books.' A later advertisement in the *Mercury* for Nov. 29, 1788 announces the arrival of the almanac for 1789 being the 35th year of continued publication."

Shilstone's citation permits a delineation of some of the information contained in the 1764 almanac: "districts of the several precincts . . . the time the [mail] pacquets are to sail from Europe for these islands. An exact list of His Majesty's justices of the peace. A table of the holidays observed at the Customs House. Also the times of meeting of the several Lodges of Free and Accepted Masons in this island etc."

Almanacs in this series are rare; *see* Shilstone's article for biographical notes on Holst.

DOLLAND, JOHN
An Almanack for the island of Barbados, for the year . . . 1765; being the first year after Bissextile or Leap-Year.
London [1764]. *84 pp.*   [JCB]
This item was printed for Matthias Holst, a Bridgetown "jeweller, goldsmith, and toyman" who, in the "advertisement," offers an elaborate inventory of his talents and capabilities. The almanac itself provides standard information and includes the names of the members of the Barbados Council, the judges of the island's courts, and other officials. There is also a list of about one-hundred-seventy-five Barbadians "of the Commission of the Peace appointed by His Excellency Charles Pinfold, esq. and published November 10, 1761"; a list of the holidays observed at the customhouse in Barbados for 1765; and the weekly schedule of meetings of the Barbados Mason's Lodge.

The copy of this volume located in the JCB library has eighty-four pages, but only twenty-four of these are printed — many of the remaining ones contain handwritten notes, by the almanac's apparent owner, which largely record business transactions and other personal matters.

HALL, RICHARD
Acts, passed in the island of Barbados. From 1643, to 1762, inclusive . . . by the late Richard Hall, Esquire . . . and since his death, continued by his son, Richard Hall.
London, 1764. *526 pp.*
[BM, JCB, BOS]
An invaluable source, reproducing about two-hundred-thirty of Barbados's laws in force, with occasional marginal commentary by Richard Hall, Sr., who was a long-time member of the Barbados House of Assembly and a Justice of the Peace for almost thirty years. Also contains the titles of over eight-hundred laws which had become obsolete or had been repealed.

In the preface, Richard Hall, Jr., comments on earlier published editions of Barbados laws: "Mr. Rawlin's [1699] edition, which on proper examination with the records will be found to be very imperfect, commenced in 1648, and ended in 1698. Mr. [Arthur] Zouch [*Acts of Assembly*, 1721] also began his compilement in 1648 and continued it to 1717, but he copies the errors of the first edition, introduced many others, and was likewise guilty of great omissions. Mr. Salmon [*Acts of Assembly*, 1739] collected the laws from 1717 to 1738, and his compilement, in conjunction with Mr. Zouch's are the only editions that have been used for many years past . . . Mr. Salmon's is the most correct of these several publications, though by no means accurate: He was particularly careless with respect to dates, not one act in his own collection being dated."

HALL, RICHARD JR.
An abridgement of the Acts, in force, in the island of Barbados. From 1643 to 1762, inclusive. Digested under alphabetical heads.
London, 1764. *84 pp.*
[BM, JCB, BOS]
Having a separate title page, imprint, and pagination, this item is bound in with the volume of Hall's *Acts* (1764);

it provides useful summaries of these acts, arranged under major subject headings.

MASON, ABRAHAM
"*Extract of a letter to the Rev. Thomas Birch . . . from Mr. Abraham Mason of Barbados, relating to an extraordinary agitation of the sea there, 31st of March, 1761, and an epidemical disorder in that island.*"
Philosophical Transactions of the Royal Society, vol. 52, London, 1764, pp. 477–78.   [UL]
Contents as noted in title.

*By the King's authority . . . [begin], January 19, 1765.
[Bridgetown, 1765.]
A separately published proclamation listed by Ragatz (*p. 45*) which gives "the terms on which the crown lands in the ceded colonies were to be disposed of."

FENNING, DANIEL; COLLYER, J., *et al.*
A new system of geography: or, a general description of the world.
London, 1765–66. 2 vols.   [BM]
Volume 1 (*pp. 697–702*) provides a synopsis of Barbados's physical geography, flora and fauna, government, trade, population, etc., although the information is derived from published works, to a large extent G. Hughes (1750).

MARTIN, SAMUEL
An essay upon plantership . . . the fourth edition with many additions.
Antigua and London, 1765. 62 pp.
                              [BM, UL, RCS]
A detailed work, by an Antiguan planter, on how to treat slaves, care for livestock, organize labor, cultivate the land, manufacture sugar, make rum, etc. Although the primary referent in discussion is Antigua, the author's wide knowledge of practices in the West Indies often leads him to bring in comparative materials on plantation practices from the other territories, including Barbados; e.g., "In Barbados, by contrast, they do this. . . ."
Sabin (44920) does not cite the first edition; the second edition was published in Antigua in 1750 (Hanson 6466).

MASKELYNE, NEVIL
Astronomical observations made at the island of Barbados; at Willoughby's Fort; and at the Observatory on Constitution Hill . . . read at the Royal Society, December 20, 1764.
London, 1765.   [BM, BC]
Contents as noted in the title; also published in the *Philosophical Transactions of the Royal Society* (vol. 54, London, 1764, pp. 389–92).

*"Address to the publick, in favour of the sufferers at Bridgetown."
The Gentleman's Magazine, vol. 36, London, 1766, p. 425.   [BM]
Listed by Ragatz (*p. 181*) who notes: "A total of 440 houses in the capital city had been destroyed by fire on May 17, 1766."

Candid observations on two pamphlets lately published, viz. "An address to the Committee of Correspondence in Barbadoes, by a North American" and "An essay towards the vindication of the Committee of Correspondence. By a Barbadian." By a native of Barbados.
Barbados, 1766. 37 pp.   [LCP]
A controversy over colonial responses to the Stamp Act was generated by the publication of *A Letter from the Committee of Correspondence in Barbados to their Agent in London* (1766). In J. Dickinson (1766) the letter was sharply criticized, and in K. Morrison (1766) it was defended. In the present tract, the author points out that an unauthorized and "surreptitious" edition of the original letter was published in Barbados and it was this edition, containing some alterations in wording from the original, that found its way to North America. The object of this tract is to clarify misunderstandings as well as to elaborate on the position of Barbados with respect to the Stamp Act because "it is to the interest of both [the North American colonies and Barbados] ever to preserve a harmony and good understanding." The author also points out that his tract was written before he had seen *A letter to the North-American* (1766).

[DICKINSON, JOHN]
An address to the Committee of Correspondence in Barbados. Occasioned by a

late letter from them to their agent in
London. By a North-American.
Philadelphia, 1766. *18 pp.*

[BM, LC, LCP, BOS]
The author (*see* Sabin 20037) offers a
sharp rebuttal to *A Letter from the
Committee of Correspondence in Barbados to
their Agent in London* (1766). He notes
that the letter "casts unmerited censure
on my countrymen," and tells Barbadians that they themselves have
proved in their letter that the Stamp
Act ". . . is destructive of our [colonial]
property, our freedom, our happiness:
that it is inconsistent with reason and
justice; and subversive of those sacred
rights which God himself . . . has bes-
towed upon mankind. Yet . . . you
[Barbadians] term the opposition made
by my countrymen to the execution of
this . . . act rebellious." Dickinson is
not only incensed at the Barbadians,
but he also challenges the right of the
King to impose taxes of this kind and
presents an elaborate argument for
colonial "freedom" and private property rights. For Barbadian responses
see *A Letter to the North-American* (1766),
*Candid Observations on Two Pamphlets
Lately Published* (1766), and K. Morrison
(1766).

"*Extracts of [eight] letters received from
Barbadoes, since the dreadful fire, May 14,
1766.*"
The Gentleman's Magazine, vol. 36,
London, 1766, *pp. 425–26.* [BM]
Describes the damage caused in Bridgetown by a fire which was estimated to
have destroyed between one-half to
two-thirds of the town's buildings.

*For the unfortunate inhabitants of Bridge-
town, Barbados.*
[London, 1766.] *4 pp.* [BOS]
This item solicits funds for the aid of
persons whose property was destroyed
or damaged during the Bridgetown fire
of May 1766. On one page there are
brief extracts from eleven letters "received from Barbados since the dreadful
fire," which describe the damage, and
often mention the streets, buildings,
and goods destroyed.

GIBSON, J.
"*Plan of Bridgetown, Barbados.*"

Gentleman's Magazine, vol. 36, London, 1766, *p. 425.* [BM]
A street map of the city in which only
the major streets are named, but which
also shows the sections destroyed by the
fire of May 1766. This map is also
reproduced in Tony Campbell (1965).

HILLARY, WILLIAM
*Observations on the changes of the air
and the concomitant epidemical diseases in
the island of Barbadoes. To which is
added a treatise on the putrid bilious fever,
commonly called the yellow fever; and
such other diseases as are indigenous
or endemial in the West India islands or
in the torrid zone.*
London, 2nd ed. 1766. *360 pp.*

[BM, LC]
The author, a medical doctor, lived
more than six years in Barbados during
the late 1740s and 1750s. The first
part of his book gives a detailed monthly
record of climate and a description of
the ailments commonly associated with
each month. The second, and lengthier,
part discusses diseases found in the
West Indies in general. Relatively little
material is presented on Barbadian
attitudes and beliefs concerning illness
and disease, and local curing practices.
A later edition, "with notes by Benjamin Rush of Philadelphia," was published in Philadelphia in 1811 [BM].
Hillary's *A Practical Essay on the Small
Pox* (London, 1740 [BM]) does not deal
with the West Indies.

[JERNINGHAM, EDWARD]
*Yarico to Inkle, an epistle by the author of
the elegy written among the ruins of an
abbey.*
London, 1766. *19 pp.* [BOS, BM]
One of a number of romanticized ver-
sions, ultimately based on Ligon's
(1657) original story. The author is
identified in the BM catalog and by
Sabin (105979).

*LASHLEY, THOMAS
*Dissertatio medica inauguralis de colica
pictonum.*
Edinburgh, 1766. [E]
Medical dissertation by a Barbadian.

*A letter from the Committee of Correspond-
ence in Barbados, to their agent in London.*
Barbados, 1766. [LCP]

The committee represented the Assembly and Council of Barbados. The letter complains about the "hardships which this community labours under by the imposition of the stamp duties, lately put in force amongst us," and notes that Barbadians are paying these duties not because they want to, but rather "from a principle of loyalty to our King and Mother Country," adding that the North American colonies, by their opposition to the Stamp Act, are in "rebellious opposition to authority."

The letter, according to Kenneth Morrison (1766), was first published in the newspaper, *Barbados Mercury*, on April 19, 1766 (the only copy of this issue that I was able to locate is in the LCP) and this was its only authorized publication. In *Candid Observations on Two Pamphlets Lately Published* (1766), it is pointed out that after publication in the *Barbados Mercury*, "surreptitious copies" of the letter, containing some unauthorized alterations in wording, were published and were sent to the mainland colonies. One of these "surreptitious copies" was obtained by John Dickinson who reproduced the letter (1766, *pp. ii–vi*) and sharply criticized it.

A letter to the North-American, on occasion of his address to the Committee of Correspondence in Barbados. By a native of the island.
Barbados, 1766. *47 pp.*
[LCP, LC, NYPL]
A rebuttal to John Dickinson (1766) which attempts to explain how the Barbadian plantocracy feels toward the British Parliament in general and the Stamp Act in particular; also it compares the economic and political position of the island with the mainland colonies.

[MORRISON, KENNETH]
An essay towards the vindication of the Committee of Correspondence in Barbados, from the aspersions and calumnies thrown upon them, in an anonymous piece, printed in Philadelphia, under the title of an address to them, occasioned by their letter to their agent in London. In a letter to a friend. By a Barbadian.
Barbados, 1766. *26 pp.*
[JCB, LCP, LC]

On the title page of the JCB copy, under "By a Barbadian," "The Rev. Mr. [Kenneth] Morrison" is inscribed in manuscript. See W. Dickson (1789, *p. 45*) for biographical notes on Morrison.

This pamphlet, a rebuttal to John Dickinson (1766), points out that the Barbadians "dutifully remonstrate against the oppression of the Stamp Act and the hardship of being taxed internally . . . yet they did not . . . presume expressly to deny [the British Parliament] the right of taxing." The author's criticism of Dickinson's tract is, in effect, a statement of his own political philosophy which stresses the belief ". . . that a dutiful submission to lawful authority, even when its hand lies heavy upon us, will never be thought, by sober-minded men, to indicate any inclination to slavery."

WARBURTON, WILLIAM
A sermon preached before the Incorporated Society for the Propagation of the Gospel in Foreign Parts; at their meeting in the parish church of St. Mary-le-Bow, on Friday, February 21, 1766.
London, 1766. *32 pp.* [BM]
The Bishop of Gloucester devotes one-third of this pamphlet to a discussion of the Church's obligations in the conversion of "the heathen," and the remainder to the problems involved in missionary work among Amerindians and Negro slaves. He indicts the slave trade, but does not consider the subject of emancipation, and very briefly suggests that the Codrington plantations should set an example for the enlightened treatment of slaves.

SINGLETON, JOHN
A general description of the West Indian islands, as far as relates to the British, Dutch, and Danish governments, from Barbados to Saint Croix. Attempted in blank verse.
Barbados, 1767. *159 pp.*
[NYPL, BPL, BM]
The author spent some time in Barbados, but his "blank verse" description of various aspects of island life and geography (*pp. 111–159*) is cumbersome and of limited value. Other editions of this work were published in 1776; one in Dublin with the same title as

the Barbados original, and the other in London under the title *A Description of the West Indies. A Poem, in four books. By Mr. Singleton. During his excursions among those islands.* Both 1776 editions [NYPL] are identical with the first in content, but differ in pagination. Sabin (81425) cites a second London edition, published in 1777.

[ALLEYNE, SIR JOHN GAY]
    Remarks upon a book, intitled, A Short History of Barbados: in which the partial and unfair representations, of the author upon the subjects of his history in general, and upon that of the demand of privileges in particular, are detected and exposed.
    Barbados, 1768. *88 pp.*   [JCB]
The author, who is identified by John Poyer (*The History of Barbados, From the Discovery of the Island,* 1808, *pp. 338–40*), offers a barbed polemic against Frere (1768). For the early years of Barbadian history, Alleyne accuses Frere of having plagiarized from the works of persons such as Oldmixon (1708) and Ligon (1657), and challenges his account and interpretations of the administrations of various eighteenth-century governors. The effect of Frere's work, he notes, is "to inculcate a doctrine of the most abject and undistinguishing submission to our governors, by discouraging every effort of liberty, if it takes the form of opposition, in the representatives of the people." Most of the critique is devoted to events of the mid-eighteenth century, and the book can be useful to one concerned with the politics of this period.
    Frere, though he saw this criticism of his work, chose not to rebut it in his second edition (*see* Frere, 1768), but Poyer points out that "This produced a duel between the two gentlemen; and though it ended without bloodshed, the dispute laid the foundation of an enmity which had a visible influence on the politics of the literary antagonists during their lives."
    The Barbados edition of the *Remarks* is rare; a reprint was published in London in 1768 [H, IJ].

[FRERE, HENRY]
    A short history of Barbados from its first discovery and settlement to the end of the year 1767.
    London, 1768. *129 pp.*
             [BMHS, IJ, BOS, BM]
A well-known local history designed to show that "Barbados hath always preserved a uniform and steady attachment to Great Britain, and therefore is intitled to the affection and indulgence of the mother country." The early historical sections rely on a variety of sources such as the island's laws, and there is some useful information on eighteenth-century administrative structure, economy, trade, etc.
    To a criticism of his history (*see* J. G. Alleyne, 1768), Frere, in the second edition (*A Short History of Barbados from its First Discovery and Settlement to the Present Time,* London, 1768 [E, BM, IJ]) replied: "When this edition was preparing for the press, the author was favoured with a sight of some remarks, published in Barbados, upon the first edition of this work. These remarks contain some assertions that are false, many confutable, and all of them uncandid and ungenerous. They are written with the peevishness of a child whose playthings have been disturbed. ... The remarker will not be indulged with a reply, because a reply would be food for his distempered appetite.... For the present, the writer of the remarks who is well known ... will be permitted to ride his hobbyhorse full speed, uninterrupted."
    Although all sources agree that Frere authored the *Short History,* his first name is cited variously as Henry or George. For example, Poyer (1808, *p. 340*), Sabin (3289), and Ragatz (*p. 182*) cite him only as H. Frere. Poyer (1808, *p. 226*) notes that the "author of the Short History" was the grandson of John Frere, President of the Barbados Council in 1720, and this person is identified as Henry Frere in the *Jl. BMHS* (*17,* 1949–50, *4*). Henry Frere, by at least the 1780s, was a member of the Council and was its President in 1790–93 (Schomburgk, 1848, *pp. 341, 685*).
    George Frere is cited as the author by Cundall (35), Cruickshank (69), and in the catalogs of the BM and LC, among other libraries.

An account of the donations for the relief of the sufferers by fire, at Bridge Town in the island of Barbadoes, in May and December 1766, and of the application of the same.

London [1769].

"Issued for the information of those who had contributed to the relief fund" (Ragatz, *p. 181*); Sabin (3257).

[BLENMAN, JONATHAN]
Remarks on [John Peter] Zenger's tryal, taken out of the Barbados Gazette's; for the benefit of the students in law, and others in North America.

New York, 1770. *60 pp.*   [LC]

The title page is inscribed in manuscript "By Jonathan Blenman, esq. Kings Attorney in Barbados"; pages 7 and 36 are dated June 24 and July 20, 1737. The *Remarks*, first printed in numbers 439, 440, 441, and 442 of the *Barbados Gazette*, concern a famous libel suit against a New York printer. They have nothing to do with Barbados *per se*, but reflect the legal thinking of the island's attorney general. Read in the Readex Microprint edition, published by the American Antiquarian Society.

DOYLE, WILLAM
Some account of the British Dominions beyond the Atlantic.

London [1770]. Pt. 1. *87 pp.*
[BM, LC]

The author visited the West Indies. He implies that the islands will be treated at greater length in part 2 of his work, but this, according to the LC catalog, was never published. In part 1 (*p. 39*) he offers a brief paragraph on Barbados in which he notes "[I] heard many of the inhabitants say they went more [to church] to see and be seen than out of devotion."

RAMBLE, JAMES
The life and adventures of James Ramble, Esq.

London, 1770. 2 vols.   [BM]

Ramble notes (*pp. 216–17*) that he visited Barbados, but no information on his stay is offered other than the remark that he was "entertained with magnificence by the settlers [who are] a vain, shewey, but good natured set of people."

The first edition was published in London in 1755 (Sabin 67615).

WYNNE, JOHN HUDDLESTONE
A general history of the British Empire in America . . . including all the countries in North America and the West Indies ceded to Great Britain at the Peace of Paris.

London, 1770. 2 vols.   [BM, BC]

The short history and description of Barbados (vol. 2, *pp. 500–505*) is based on uncited sources. For other editions see Sabin (105682).

SANDIFORD, WILLIAM
An account of a late epidemical distemper, extracted from a letter addressed to Gedney Clarke, Esq. by William Sandiford, M.D. of Barbados.

Barbados, 1771. *16 pp.*   [LCP]

The epidemic in Barbados raged for three months in 1770 and affected "many patients, white as well as black, young as well as old, and of both sexes. . . . [and particularly those persons who lived] in the lowest and moist-situations . . . fishermen and such as were most exposed to the cold and moistness." The symptoms of the disease and the curative devices Sandiford found most effective in treating it are described in detail.

SENHOUSE, WILLIAM
The autobiographical manuscript [ca. 1771–1790.]

See W. Senhouse (1934–35).

ZIMMERMAN, PETER KARL
Reise nach ost-und West-Indien.

Hamburg, 1771. *40 pp.*   [H]

The author, a cook aboard a Dutch(?) slaver, landed at Barbados in late 1734 where he spent a short time, at best a month or so. He says little about his stay (*pp. 28–30*) other than noting how pleasing the island looked and how heavily populated and planted it was. Not wanting to go to Virginia with his ship, he worked as a blacksmith in Barbados until shipping out as a cook on a vessel bound for St. Eustatius. The account is signed at the end and dated 1743.

[ESTWICK, SAMUEL]
Considerations on the Negroe cause com-

monly so-called. *Addressed to the Right Honourable Lord Mansfield, Lord Chief Justice of the Court of the King's Bench etc., By a West Indian.*
London, 1772. *46 pp.* [BM]
"The author was assistant colonial agent for Barbados and later [in 1777] became agent" (Ragatz, *p. 501*). This tract, addressed to the question of slavery in England and the Somersett Case, has nothing to do with Barbados *per se.* A second edition was published in London in 1773 [BM] and Sabin (23077) cites a third, published in 1788.

*GOULDINO, SAMUEL
   Dissertatio medica inauguralis de caloris in corpore humano effectibus quibusdam.
   Edinburgh, 1772. [E, BM]
Medical dissertation by a Barbadian.

RAYNAL, [ABBÉ] GUILLAUME THOMAS
   Histoire philosophique et politique des etablissemens et du commerce des Européens dans les deux Indes.
   Amsterdam, 1773. 6 vols. [IJ]
Volume 5 (*pp. 198–203*) contains a superficial and sometimes distorted overview of Barbados's early colonization, economy, sugar production, slaving, trade, etc., based on unspecified sources, at least one of these apparently being Ligon (1657). One of the later revised editions which was read in one of its English translations (*A Philosophical and Political History of the Settlements and Trade . . . Newly Translated by J. O. Justamond,* London, 1788, vol. 6, *pp. 291–98* [IJ]), omits some details and adds others. Sabin (68080–095) cites a variety of editions, the first French one having been published in four volumes (Amsterdam, 1770).

*[ANKETELL, JOHN]
   Yarico to Inkle. A Poem. By a young gentleman of Trinity College, Dublin.
   Dublin, 1774.
Cited by Sabin (105980); *see also* Sabin (105985) for more details on this and another version by the same author (*Poems on Several Subjects . . . To Which are Added, the Epistle of Yarico to Inkle.* Boston, 1795).

ENTICK, JOHN *et al.*
   The present state of the British Empire,

containing a description of the [*territories*] *under the British Crown in Europe, Asia, Africa, and America.*
London, 1774. 4 vols. [BM]
Offers a brief overview (vol. 4, *pp. 480–83*) of the island's geography, history, government, etc. A lengthy footnote describes the fires which occurred in Bridgetown in 1756 and 1766. *See also* Sabin (22668, 22670).

HENDY, JAMES
   Tentamen physiologicum inaugurale, de secretione glandulari.
   Edinburgh, 1774. *63 pp.*
                              [BM, LC, E]
Medical dissertation by a Barbadian. *See also* author, 1784.

*BRUCE, ALEXANDER
   Dissertatio medica inauguralis de hydrophobia.
   Edinburgh, 1775. *56 pp.* [E, BM]
Medical dissertation by a Barbadian.

HENDY, JAMES
   An essay on glandular secretion; containing an experimental enquiry into the formation of pus.
   London, 1775. *90 pp.* [H, E]
Sometimes confused with Hendy's dissertation (1774), this item has nothing to do with Barbados.

JEFFERYS, THOMAS
   The West-India Atlas; or, a compendious description of the West Indies.
   London, 1775. [WIC]
Contains a conventional delineation (*p. 20*) of Barbados's geography, history, economy, etc. The main value of this work is that it contains a large and extremely detailed map of Barbados based upon a survey conducted by William Mayo (1722; reproduced and discussed by Tony Campbell, 1965). Sabin (35970) cites other editions.

   The substance of the evidence on the petition presented by the West-India planters and merchants, to the hon. House of Commons, as it was introduced at the bar, and summ'd up by Mr. Glover, on Thursday the 16th of March, 1775.
   New York, 1775. *75 pp.* [JCB]
Pages 3–6 reproduce the petition which complains that the North American

colonies have threatened to cease imports from and exports to the West Indies; the petitioners ask the House to remedy various North American grievances so as to "preserve intercourse between the West-India islands and the northern colonies." Glover, a London merchant and agent for the West India committee, calls two witnesses to elaborate upon points raised in the petition. One of them is George Walker who had lived in Barbados "a great many years and [has] been their agent ever since I left the country." Walker's testimony (*pp. 39–66*) is an elaborate and very informative discussion of Barbados trade in which he deals with a variety of specific problems relating to its dependence upon North America, e.g. for subsistence goods (he notes that if the northern colonies "withhold their supplies . . . nothing will save Barbados and the Leeward islands from the dreadful consequences of absolute famine"), lumber, and other supplies; he also considers the internal economic situation in Barbados which he feels is the cause of this dependence. Pages 66–75 include a similar testimony, but with specific reference to Jamaica. Glover's summation (*pp. 7–38*) is a more general treatise on West Indian trade problems, and has little of the specific informational value of Walker's testimony. A reprint appeared in New York in 1778 (Sabin 27610).

The first edition of these New York reprintings was published in London in 1775 (Sabin 27610); this was not consulted, but according to the Kress Room (Baker Library, Harvard) catalog this omits Walker's testimony.

Another edition of the *Substance*, published under the title *The Evidence Delivered on the Petition Presented by the West India Planters* (no imprint, but Sabin, 27606, brackets London, 1775 [BOS]) has a different pagination and ordering of materials from the 1775 New York edition, but the contents, including Walker's testimony, are the same.

[YOUNG, ARTHUR?]
American husbandry. Containing an account of the soil, climate, production, and agriculture of the British colonies in

North America and the West Indies . . . By an American.
London, 1775. 2 vols. [BM]
A chapter on Barbados (vol. 2, *pp. 151–62*) deals with "climate, soil, productions, exports, [and] observations on the culture of sugar," but it is apparently not based on the author's firsthand observations. *See* Sabin (106062) for authorship.

*ESTWICK, SAMUEL
A letter to the Reverend Josiah Tucker, D.D. Dean of Gloucester, in answer to his humble address and earnest appeal, etc. With a postscript in which the present war against America is shewn to be the effect, not of the causes assigned by him and others, but of a fixed plan of administration.
London, 1776. [NYPL, LC, BM]
Written by the "assistant agent for the Island of Barbadoes." In 1777 Estwick was appointed agent.

The North-American and the West Indian Gazetteer.
London, 1776. [BM]
Of no particular value, this item includes a brief general account of Barbados's geography, population, economics, etc., based on other published sources. A second edition (London, 1778 [BM]) is identical.

WHITWORTH, SIR CHARLES
State of the trade of Great Britain in its imports and exports, progressively from the year 1697.
London, 1776. [BM]
Compiled from official returns, this is a valuable source for statistics on Barbadian trade with England from 1697 to 1773. The tables are arranged on a yearly basis by country and include totals under four headings: value of imports, value of exports, import excess, and export excess.

Remarks on the evidence delivered on the petition presented by the West-India planters and merchants to the hon. the House of Commons, on the 16th of March, 1775, as it was introduced at the bar and summed up by Mr. Glover, so far as the same respects Barbados and the Leeward Islands. In a letter to a member of Parliament. By a West-India Planter.

London, 1777. *50 pp.* [H, JCB, LC]
Dated October 10, 1776, this tract is a
direct rebuttal to *The Substance of the
Evidence on the Petition Presented by the
West-India Planters* (1775). The author
does not deny, as argued in that work,
that the West Indies depend upon
North America, but emphatically dis-
agrees that they could not subsist without food importations from the northern
colonies. The author appears to be well
acquainted with Barbados and most
of his argument is devoted to a critique
of Walker's testimony in the *Substance*;
he feels Walker is naïve about problems
relating to the feeding of slaves and
argues that, if need be, the Leewards
could increase food production and
supply Barbados. His interesting and
informative discussion ranges over a
variety of problems related to food production, e.g. climate and soil conditions,
agricultural practices, nature of foods
produced, and island trade.

*The English Pilot: the fourth book.
Describing the West-India navigation,
from Hudson's Bay to the River Amazones
. . . with all the islands therein, as
Jamaica, Cuba, Hispaniola, Barbadoes
. . . and the rest of the Caribbee Islands.*
London, 1778. *66 pp.* plus maps.
[IJ]
Barbados is treated on pages 26–27,
wherein are briefly presented data of
use to vessels approaching the island.
The first edition appeared in 1689, and
Sabin (22616–619) cites a number of
subsequent editions. From the 1689
edition Tony Campbell (1965) has
reproduced the map of Barbados
(essentially the same as that in the 1778
edition) which shows coastal features.

*LEMAN, JOHN
Disputatio medica inauguralis de cholera.
Edinburgh, 1778.   [E, BM]
Medical dissertation by a Barbadian.

*The present state of the West-Indies.
Containing an accurate description of
what parts are possessed by the several
powers in Europe. . . . The materials for
which were collected on the spot during
the last war by some of the officers of
His Majesty's forces.*
London, 1778. *95 pp.*   [BMHS, BM]

Contains an overview (*pp. 64–66*) of
Barbados's history, geography, commerce, etc.

*LOVELL, ROBERT
*Tentamen medicum inaugurale quaedam
de hepate collegens.*
Edinburgh, 1779.   [E, BM]
Medical dissertation by a Barbadian.

*"Brief account of the desolation made in
several of the West India Islands by the
late hurricanes . . . the following is the
journal of what passed at Barbadoes from
the 9th of October until the 16th.*
The Gentleman's Magazine,* vol. 50,
London, 1780, *pp. 621–22.*   [BM]
A vivid eyewitness account of the
especially destructive 1780 hurricane,
by an army officer, with a miscellany of
details on how James Cunninghame,
Governor of Barbados, and his family
behaved during it.

**Dreadful effects of a hurricane which
happened at Barbadoes in 1780.*
London [1780?].
"The island was laid desolate by one
of the worst storms in its history.
Parliament voted £80,000 relief money,
and a considerable sum was collected
by private subscriptions" (Ragatz, *p.
181*).

*ESTWICK, SAMUEL
*To the Right Hon. Lord George Germain,
His Majesty's Principal Secretary of
State for the Colonies, etc. The humble
memorial of Samuel Estwick, agent for
the Colony of Barbados.*
[London], 1781.
"Praying for the removal of Governor
Major General Cunninghame, charged
with collecting illegal fees. He was sub-
sequently recalled" (Ragatz, *p. 137*).

*For the benefit of the West-India sufferers.
An History of Jamaica and Barbadoes,
with an authentic account of the lives lost,
and the damages sustained in each island,
by the late hurricanes. To which is prefixed
a sermon preached on the melancholy
occasion, at St. Clements, Lombard Street.*
London, 1781. *49 pp.*   [JCB]
This item was published in order to
raise funds for the stricken islands.
Pages 2–36 comprise the sermon, which

is of no informational value on Barbados, and pages 42–44 offer a very superficial and useless account of the island's political history. Ragatz (*p. 153*) comments, "There was no such church [St. Clements] . . . and this leads to questioning as to whether the compiler's motives were as disinterested as he professes them to have been."

FOWLER [JOHN?]
A general account of the calamities occasioned by the late tremendous hurricanes and earthquakes in the West-India Islands, foreign as well as domestic: with the petitions to, and resolutions of, the House of Commons, in behalf of the sufferers at Jamaica and Barbados; also a list of the Committee appointed to manage the subscriptions of the benevolent public, towards their further relief. Carefully collated from authentic papers, by Mr. Fowler.
London, 1781. *87 pp.*　　[NYPL, JCB]
This book was designed to convey to the general public the horrors caused by the massive hurricane of October 1780. The section dealing with Barbados (*pp. 30–42*) reproduces eyewitness accounts from Major-General Vaughan, the Commander in Chief of British Forces in the Leewards and Barbados, Governor Cunninghame, and two anonymous persons; in addition, there is an address to the King, delivered by Samuel Estwick, describing the destruction and requesting aid for the island.
The NYPL catalog gives the author's first name as John; Sabin (25313) notes "Allibone attributes this to William Fowle, M.D." and adds that "some copies are dated 1791."

*ROLLO, JOHN
Observations on the diseases which appeared in the army on St. Lucia, in 1778 and 1779. . . . With an appendix, containing a short address to military gentlemen, on the means of preserving health in the West-Indies.
London, 1781. *160 pp.*　　[H]
"Signed at the end: John Rollo, Barbadoes, January 26, 1781" (Sabin 72869). The BM catalog cites a shorter edition, published in Barbados in 1780. *See also* Rollo (1783).

*ESTWICK, SAMUEL
Considerations on the present decline of the sugar trade; and on the means which are proposed by the refiners of London for re-instating it.
[London], 1782. *58 pp.*
Cited by Sabin (23078); written by the agent for Barbados.

*HALL, HARPER
Dissertatio medica inauguralis de melaena.
Edinburgh, 1782.　　[E, BM]
Medical dissertation by a Barbadian.

*HUNT, REVEREND ISSAC
Discourse delivered at St. Paul's Church, Shadwell, for the benefit of the West Indian sufferers of the islands of Jamaica and Barbados.
[London?], 1782.
Sabin (33863) gives no place of publication; Cruickshank (76) cites London, and comments that "The Rev. Issac Hunt was descended from one of the oldest settlers in Barbados." I assume this item relates to the 1780 hurricane, but I was unable to locate a copy of it.

KEMEYS, JOHN GARDNER
Free and candid recollections occasioned by the late additional duties on sugars and on rum.
London, 1783. *152 pp.*　　[BM]
The author, a Jamaican planter, is primarily concerned with economic issues on that island, but makes occasional comparative reference to Barbados. Sabin (37333) cites a 1785 Dublin edition.

ROLLO, JOHN
Observations on the means of preserving and restoring health in the West Indies.
London, 1783. *162 pp.*　　[RCS, JCB]
The author was an army medical doctor stationed in Barbados. His book is designed, in general, to advise British soldiers in the West Indies on how to take care of themselves, and there are occasional brief references to medical and health conditions in Barbados.

STOKES, ANTHONY
A view of the Constitution of the British colonies in North America and the West Indies, at the time the Civil War broke out on the continent of America.

London, 1783. *555 pp.* [BM]
The author claims that he had resided "in different islands in the West Indies," but it is difficult to say if he ever visited Barbados. However, his elaborate treatise does contain an occasional specific reference to the island's legal and judicial system.

HENDY, JAMES
A treatise on the glandular disease of Barbadoes; proving it to be seated in the lymphatic system.
London, 1784. *140 pp.* [JCB, E]
The author was "physician to His Majesty's naval hospital at Barbadoes and physician general to the militia of the island." For technical reasons, he feels that "the glandular disease," characterized by "enormous swellings of the extremities," should not be called elephantiasis; thus disagreeing with the writings of Richard Towne (1726) and William Hillary (1754, 1766) on the subject. Part 1 of the book, which is apparently a reprinting of his 1774 doctoral thesis, describes the symptoms of the disease, its distribution on the island, causes, and ways of treating it. Occasionally, there are some more specific types of information on medical and social conditions. Part 2 (*pp. 95–140*) presents twenty-six case histories of patients in Barbados who were afflicted with the "glandular disease."
Ragatz (*p. 374*) lists an edition published in 1794 with "no imprint."

RAMSAY, REVEREND JAMES
An essay on the treatment and conversion of African slaves in the British sugar colonies.
London, 1784. *298 pp.* [BPL, BC]
The author spent some twenty years in the West Indies, especially St. Kitts. In this classic work he notes, "I shall assert the claim of the Negroes to attention from us, by explaining their natural capacity and proving them to be on a footing of equality in respect of the reception of mental improvement, with the natives of any other country." Lack of references to specific islands detracts from the utility of this work as a source for Barbadian history, but William Dickson, who knew Barbados well, remarks that "those who wish full information on this subject [i.e., slavery] must consult an essay [by] the Rev. J. Ramsay. That performance, some local circumstances excepted, will apply very well to the island of Barbadoes" (1789, *p. 7*).
For other works by Ramsay, *see* Sabin (67714–718).

SOCIETY FOR THE ENCOURAGEMENT OF ARTS, MANUFACTURES AND COMMERCE IN BARBADOS
Institution and first proceedings of the Society . . . established in Barbados, 1781.
Barbados [1784]. *98 pp.* [BM]
Records the Society's minutes, activities, papers read, etc., from its first meeting on July 5, 1781 to August 30, 1784. The organization, modeled after the London Society and founded at the instigation of Joshua Steele who became its first president, was formed "for the purposes of discovering the useful qualities of the native productions, animal, vegetable, and fossil of Barbados; and to consider of, and to devise the means of encouraging such useful arts, as may excite industry among the lower classes of the white and free inhabitants; and in general to deliberate, and to promote, as far as they can, whatever they judge will contribute to the advancement of the arts, manufactures, and commerce of this island."
The Society's interests ranged over a variety of problems, e.g. development of dyes from native plants, establishment of workhouses "where the poor may be employed in carding, spinning, knitting, and weaving the several materials of this island," importation of silkworms from England in order to stimulate a local industry, production of native salt, how to "tan and dress leather in various ways." The Society also concerned itself with matters such as the systematic collection of information on fossils and climate, and encouraged the making of accurate maps and the dissemination of information on animal husbandry techniques. The *Proceedings* also contain information on wider societal issues, from agricultural and labor productivity to considerations of the status of poor whites and the island's slaves. Throughout the *Proceedings* a theme constantly stressed is

that Barbados must make greater use of its human and natural resources in order to provide work for its lower-class population and to produce locally the goods which were being imported.

A useful complementary source is D. G. C. Allan's article, "Joshua Steele and the Royal Society of Arts" (*Jl. BMHS*, 22, 1954–55, *84–104*), which reproduces nine letters (the originals are in the archives of the Society of Arts in London) written by Joshua Steele from Barbados over the period July 14, 1781–September 10, 1786; these letters relate to the Society's affairs, experiments in utilizing local plants and introducing new ones, and sometimes contain comments on the island's poor white population, and how laws governing slaves affect productivity.

Ragatz (*p. 243*) cites a publication date of 1781 for the *Proceedings*, and comments in two of Steele's letters also indicate that parts of the volume were published separately at earlier dates; in a letter dated June 5, 1782, Steele writes "I send . . . twelve copies of the Institution and First Proceedings of the Barbados Society," and in another, June 13, 1783, he suggests that a critic of the Society's efforts be shown "the printed proceedings of our Society."

*ROLLO, JOHN
  Remarks on the disease lately described by Dr. Hendy under the appelation of the Glandular Disease of Barbados.
  London, 1785.
Cited by E. M. Shilstone ("Dr. James Hendy," *Jl. BMHS*, 28, 1960–61, *64–66*) who notes that this is a criticism of J. Hendy (1784).

*SOCIETY FOR THE ENCOURAGEMENT OF ARTS, MANUFACTURES AND COMMERCE IN BARBADOS
  The abridged minutes of the Society continued.
  Barbados, 1785.
Cited by John Davy (1854, *pp. 70–71*) who took the title and imprint "from the catalogue of the library of the Royal Society of London." In a letter to the Society in London, dated Barbados, May 24, 1785, Joshua Steele wrote: "You'll also find in this packet 12 copies

of the Continuation of our Abridged Minutes . . . in which you'll see the honest endeavors of our Society towards correcting the morals of our people, by showing the necessity for an amendment of those wretched and shameful laws which have been more ruinous to the Colony than all the droughts, blasts, etc. so loudly complained of. For it has been the thorough corruption of the morals of overseers and other white servants, that have made the estates of absentees afford such bad returns for many years past . . ." (in D. G. C. Allan, "Joshua Steele and the Royal Society of Arts," *Jl. BMHS*, 22, 1954–55, *94*). Copies of these minutes are apparently rare.

*SOCIETY FOR THE ENCOURAGEMENT OF ARTS, MANUFACTURES AND COMMERCE IN BARBADOS
  Premium for standards to ascertain tastes and smells.
  Barbados, 1785.
In a letter to the Society in London, dated Barbados, September 10, 1786, Joshua Steele wrote: "We have published some new premiums; that for a discovery of a scale to distinguish and describe intelligibly and accurately, the genera and species of tastes and smells, I sent you last year" (in D. G. C. Allan, "Joshua Steele and the Royal Society of Arts," *Jl. BMHS*, 22, 1954–55, *97*). This premium, according to Ragatz (*pp. 257–58, 291*), is published in *The Scots Magazine* (Edinburgh, August 1787) and *The Gentleman's Magazine* (London, July 1787, *p. 564*); for *The Gentleman's Magazine* citation Ragatz names Samuel Dent as the author. Reverend Dent was, in fact, the secretary of the Society; in 1786 he received the Society's Gold Medal "for the discovery of a dye from a material native of this island" (Steele's letter, in Allan, *p. 98*).

  Instructions for the management of a plantation in Barbadoes. And for the treatment of Negroes, etc. etc. etc.
  [Privately Printed] London, 1786. 64 pp.   [BMHS]
An apparently rare work sometimes confused with a similarly titled item published in the same year (*see* Gibbes, 1786).

On the unnumbered page, following the title page, is printed: "The Following Instructions are Offered to the Consideration of Proprietors and Managers of Plantations in Barbadoes, by Edwin Lascelles, James Colleton, Edward Drax, Francis Ford, John Brathwaite, John Walter, Wm. Thorpe Holder, James Holder, Philip Gibbes." Added to this list in the copy examined is the name John Barney, inscribed in manuscript.

Instructions was originally written by a planter, with "long experience" in Barbados, presumably to his manager and with particular reference to his two-hundred-sixty acre plantation. The pamphlet's emphasis is expressed in the introduction (*p. 2*): "The system I recommend is . . . that a proprietor of a plantation should put it under such a course of management, that the nett profits should more depend upon the smallness of the annual expence than upon the largeness of the crops. To effect this, I propose, that he should proportion the crop of canes to the number of Negroes, not to the quantity of land belonging to the plantation. . . . his first attention should be paid to the preservation of the Negroes and stock. If Negroes are fed plentifully, worked moderately, and treated kindly, they will encrease in most places. . . . The increase is the only test of the care with which they are treated."

The pamphlet is divided into sections: "Instructions for the Management of a Plantation" (*pp. 5–18*) reviews agricultural practices and procedures to be employed at each phase of the agricultural cycle; "Instructions to the Manager" (*pp. 19–20*) deals with what should be the proper behavior of the manager and his white apprentices; "Instructions for the Treatment of Negroes" (*pp. 21–31*) discusses disciplinary measures, gang divisions, work schedules and labor demands, treatment of pregnant women, child and infant care, gardens, food allotments, clothing and medical provisions, houses and households (this section is

reprinted in its entirety in the *Jl. BMHS*, 2, 1934, *24–28*); following are sections on the care, treatment, and use of cattle (*pp. 32–38*), horses (*pp. 39–42*), sheep (*pp. 43–44*), and hogs (*p. 45*); problems associated with sugar and rum manufacture (*pp. 47–50*); "Terms of Agreement with a Manager" (*pp. 51–52*) discusses his salary and various economic and social prerogatives of his position; the final section (*pp. 53–63*) reprints "The Instructions of Henry Drax, Esq. for the Management of Drax–Hall, and the Irish-Hope Plantations. To Archibald Johnson, the Manager" (*see* W. Belgrove, 1755).

The only copy of this item I could locate is in Barbados; it is not listed in the National Union Catalog nor in the catalogs of libraries visited in the United Kingdom. It is cited in Sabin (3272) and by Ragatz (*p. 432*), but the latter's claim that it was later reprinted is incorrect (*see* Gibbes, 1786).

[GIBBES, PHILIP]
Instructions for the treatment of Negroes, etc. etc. etc.
London. Printed for Shepperson and Reynolds, 1786. *37 pp.*

An apparently rare work (the only copy I could locate is at the Western Reserve Historical Society in Cleveland, Ohio),[3] which is always cited as anonymously authored (my authorship identification is discussed under Gibbes, 1797), and which is sometimes confused with a similarly titled item published in the same year (see *Instructions for the Management of a Plantation in Barbadoes*, 1786).

On the unnumbered page following the title page, is the dedication: "To the Society for Propagating the Gospel in Foreign Parts, the Following Instructions . . . are Humbly Inscribed," dated Wimpole Street, May 16, 1786.

The pamphlet is designed to show that Barbadian slaves are not cruelly treated and that plantation owners are concerned about their welfare. The author notes that the "instructions" were originally written "in the course of a correspondence, which began twenty years ago; and were thrown into the present form a long time before this matter [i.e., the abolition of the

---

[3] I am grateful to Kermit J. Pike, Chief Librarian, for making a copy of this available to me.

slave trade] became a subject of controversy."

The pamphlet contains four sections: *1*] "Instructions for the treatment of newly-purchased African slaves. Dated October, 1771" (*pp. 5–8*) reviews housing conditions, diets, work schedules and tasks; *2*] "Instructions for the treatment of Negroes in general" (*pp. 9–23*) is exactly the same, save for two or three minor differences in wording, as pp. 21–31 of the pamphlet *Instructions for the Management of a Plantation in Barbadoes* (1786); *3*] this section (*pp. 24–30*) is untitled and contains extracts from four letters written to Jacob Lewis, the manager of Spring-Head (and Taitts) plantation over the period 1771–75 — these letters comment on, and instruct the manager in, matters such as sanitary water supplies and housing conditions for slaves, their food provisions and general welfare; *4*] "Extract from additional instructions to the manager" (*pp. 31–37*) is dated Barbadoes, June *1787* (the publication date of the pamphlet, it is to be noted, is *1786*) and reviews a variety of particulars on the treatment of slaves.

The dates Sabin (34856) gives for this item's initial publication (1788) and later reprinting (1799) appear to be in error. It was this item that was later reprinted (*see* Gibbes, 1797) and not *Instructions for the Management of a Plantation in Barbadoes* (1786) as stated by Ragatz (*p. 433*); the only resemblance between the two is, as indicated above, in the section entitled "Instructions for the treatment of Negroes in general."

SOCIETY FOR THE ENCOURAGEMENT OF ARTS, MANUFACTURES AND COMMERCE IN BARBADOS
Premiums for cultivation of coffee and chocolate trees in Barbados.
Barbados, 1786.
The first prize, a gold medal, is offered to any Barbados planter who can produce ". . . the greatest quantity of COFFEE, properly cured, being to be the growth of the year 1789, not less than 4000 lb. weight. . . . [and/or] the greatest quantity of COCOA or CHOCOLATE NUTS, properly cured, being to be the growth of the year 1793,

not less than 2000 lb. weight." Signed at the end by the Society's secretary, Samuel Dent.

Reproduced by D. G. C. Allan ("Joshua Steele and the Royal Society of Arts," *Jl. BMHS*, 22, 1954–55, *103–4*), this item was enclosed with a letter sent by Joshua Steele to the Society of Arts in London (both the letter and premium are located in the Society's archives); in this letter, dated Barbados, September 10, 1786, Steele comments that coffee and cocoa ". . . both grow as well here as can be wished for; yet by depending on a precarious supply from the neighboring French islands, the price fluctuates from a shilling to 3/6 a pound; while if it was sufficiently cultivated in the colony it would probably never exceed a bit per pound. . . . we have at least 40,000 people, black, and white, who use coffee and chocolate, morning, or night, or both, as a principal part of their diet. . . we might easily raise enough to supply ourselves and export as much more to Europe" (in Allan, *p. 97*).

[Barbados Almanack for 1788.]
[London, 1787.]
An advertisement in the *Barbados Gazette*, December 8–12, 1787, reads: "Arrived from London, and now on sale, Matthias Holst's Barbados Almanack, for 1788. Being the thirty-fourth year of continued publication in sheet and books" (quoted in E. M. Shilstone, "Some Notes on Early Printing Presses and Newspapers in Barbados," *Jl. BMHS*, 26, 1958–59, *24*).

*CORNCOB, JONATHAN
Adventures of Jonathan Corncob, loyal american refugee. Written by himself.
London, 1787. *213 pp.*   [BM]
W. Sypher (*Guinea's Captive Kings*, Chapel Hill, 1942, *pp. 278–80*) discusses this anti-slavery novel, whose action centers in Barbados, and comments that its "Smollett-like realism and Sternian whimsy make *Jonathan Corncob* unique in anti-slavery fiction." Corncob is a pseudonym (Sabin 477, *see also* vol. 4, *p. 540*).

HAYNES, ROBERT
The Barbadian Diary . . . [1787–1836].
See E. M. W. Cracknell (1934).

MOSELEY, DR. BENJAMIN
A treatise on tropical diseases; on military operations; and on the climate of the West Indies.
London, 1787. *544 pp.* [JCB]
The author did not visit Barbados, and his occasional references to the island are based upon G. Hughes (1750), W. Hillary (1754, 1766), R. Towne (1726), R. Ligon (1657), and other sources. Sabin (51050) cites later editions.

NICHOLLS, REVEREND ROBERT B.
A letter to the Treasurer of the Society Instituted for the Purpose of Effecting the Abolition of the Slave Trade.
London, 1787. *16 pp.* [BM]
At the time of his writing, the author was Dean of Middleham (Yorkshire), but he was born in Barbados, and lived there during his youth; after being educated in England, he returned to the island and for two years (1768–70) lived on a plantation (*see* his testimony in *Parliamentary Papers, Accounts and Papers,* vol. 30, 1790, *pp. 325–60*). This letter, which occasionally refers to specific practices on the island, argues that the planters would suffer no dire economic consequences with abolition of the slave trade, for it would compel them to better care for their slaves; if more humanely treated the slave population would naturally increase and this would provide sufficient numbers for cultivating the islands.
The second edition was published in 1788 (Sabin 55238).

Orderson's Barbados Almanac [1788].
[Barbados, 1787.]
Cited by E. M. Shilstone ("Book and Pocket Almanacs," *Jl. BMHS,* 28, 1960–61, *79*): "John Orderson and Co., editors and proprietors of *The Barbados Mercury,* were the printers and publishers of ORDERSON'S BARBADOS ALMANAC. An advertisement of the forthcoming publication for the year 1788 appeared in the *Mercury* of 5 Dec. 1787, which states that the almanac was 'calculated by Mr. Thomas Donohue, teacher of the mathematics in Bridgetown' (no copy known)."

Perch's sheet and pocket Almanac for the

Year of Our Lord, 1788.
[Barbados, 1787.]
Cited by E. M. Shilstone ("Book and Pocket Almanacs," *Jl. BMHS,* 28, 1960–61, *79*): "The following advertisement appeared in the [*Barbados*] *Gazette* [*or General Intelligencer*] of 8–12 Dec. 1787. 'Perch's sheet and Pocket Almanac . . . will be ready for delivery on Monday next, the 17th inst. This publication is calculated by Mr. Thomas Donohue, teacher of the Mathematics in Bridge-Town and the reputation for which he calculates for 17 years have been received by the public, has rendered doubtless the correctness of the work . . .' (no copy known)."
T. W. Perch was "editor and proprietor of the *Barbados Gazette and General Intelligencer.*"

BEARDMORE, J.
A narrative of facts; with animadversions on the conduct of certain persons.
London, 1788. *126 pp.* [JCB]
A very detailed account of what the author claims were business swindles perpetuated against him. Some of the events described in the 1780s transpired in Barbados. He accuses the Gosling brothers, John Asgill and Hanbury, partners in a London merchant house who, with James Allen, also had a merchant house in Barbados. Signed at the end by the author and dated London, May 8, 1788.

COLMAN, GEORGE, JR.
Inkle and Yarico, an Opera. In Three Acts. As performed at the Theatre-Royal in the Haymarket, on Saturday, August 11th, 1787.
Dublin, 1788. *72 pp.* [BOS]
Based upon the story that appeared in the *Spectator* (Richard Steele, 1711). Republished in London in 1808 "with remarks by Mrs. [Elizabeth] Inchbald" [BM, NYPL]. Sabin (14526) notes the first edition was published in London in 1787, and cites various other editions (no item number, *see* vol. 29, *pp. 211–12*).

*HENDY, JAMES AND ROLLO, JOHN
Über die drüsenkrankheit in Barbados oder über Wilhelm Hillary's elephantiasis aus

*dem Englischen übersetzt von D A F A D.
in G.*
Frankfurt am Main, 1788. *254 pp.*
A translation, presumably of James
Hendy (1784) and John Rollo (1785).
The National Union Catalog locates
copies at the New York Academy of
Medicine, the United States National
Library of Medicine, and the John
Crerar Library (Chicago).

HOLDER, HENRY EVANS
*A short essay on the subject of Negro
slavery, with particular reference to the
island of Barbados.*
London, 1788. *45 pp.*
[BM, JCB, IJ]
Holder, an Anglican minister born in
Barbados, was a defender of the
planter cause and his essay argues for a
continuation of the slave trade and
slave system. He elaborates on the
following points: *1]* Slavery is a result
of God's ordering of the universe and is
supported by the Bible and Mosaic
law; *2]* Negroes were slaves in Africa
so that the slave trade does not fundamentally alter their position, but offers
them greater opportunities by placing
them within a "civilized" society; *3]*
Slaves in Barbados are better treated
than they were twenty years before,
and enjoy a material security unknown
to the free poor of European countries;
4] There are fundamental moral weak-
nesses in slaves which impede their conversion to Christianity, but they should
be converted and such a conversion
would make them better slaves; *5]*
Manumussion, by depriving the slave
of his material security, would not only
be a grave injustice to him but also to
the white who would be deprived of his
private property. In sum, a useful source
for a widely held ideological rationaliza-
tion of slavery.
See also Holder (1791–92, 1792,
1816).

*Abridgement of the minutes of the evidence
taken before a committee of the whole
House, to whom it was referred to consider of the slave trade.*
[London], 1789–91. 4 pts.   [BC]
Testimonies specifically relating to
Barbadian conditions are included in
numbers 2, 3, 4; compiled from *Parliamentary Papers (Accounts and Papers,* vol.
29, 1790; vol. 30, 1790; vol. 34, 1791).

BRYDGES, GEORGE [LORD RODNEY]
*Letters from Sir George Brydges, now
Lord Rodney, to His Majesty's Ministers,
etc. etc. relative to the capture of St.
Eustatius, and its dependencies.*
London, 1789. *180 pp.*   [BOS]
Contains a number of letters written
from Barbados in 1781 relating to
Rodney's campaigns against the French
and Dutch. Included is the set of
fourteen orders issued to his fleet while
it was in Carlisle Bay preparing for the
campaigns to the north. For related
items *see* Sabin (40525, 51314, 66002).

COKE, THOMAS
*Some account of the late missionaries to the
West Indies; in two letters from the Rev.
Dr. Coke to the Rev. J. Wesley.*
London, 1789. *12 pp.*   [JCB]
One of these letters (*pp. 3–8*), dated
Barbados, December 9, 1788, describes Coke's first six-day visit to the
island; he was in the company of a
Mr. Pearce, who remained as a missionary. The letter briefly describes various
religious meetings they attended, the
response received from various quarters,
and notes the individuals they met and
stayed with. It is also pointed out that
the owners of two plantations agreed
to let the Methodists preach to their
slaves.

DICKSON, WILLIAM
*Letters on slavery, to which are added
addresses to the whites and to the free
Negroes of Barbados; and accounts of
some Negroes eminent for their virtues and
abilities.*
London, 1789. *190 pp.*   [BC, BOS]
The author, a former secretary to
Barbados's governor, Edward Hay,
arrived on the island in 1772 and lived
there for about thirteen years. This book
does not provide a wealth of ethnographic information on the slaves themselves, but Dickson is one of the most
useful and intelligent observers on the
institution of slavery in Barbados and
he makes many shrewd sociological
assessments on the working of the slave
system and its effect upon the slaves.
Although definitely partisan on the

slavery issue, he is, relative to the times, dispassionate in his treatment. He argues for the cessation of the slave trade, but cannot consider immediate emancipation. In sum, his position represents that of the enlightened liberal of the day, and the book can be considered an important one for a study of Barbados social history.

EQUIANO, OLAUDAH
   The interesting narrative of the life of Olaudah Equiano, or Gustavas Vassa, the African, written by himself.
   London, 1789. 2 vols.   [BM]
The author, a Nigerian Ibo by origin, wrote this while in his mid-forties to "excite . . . [in Parliament] a sense of compassion for the miseries which the slave-trade has entailed on my unfortunate countrymen." Captured in his natal village, he made the middle-passage to Barbados in 1757, at the age of about eleven or twelve. Not being saleable, he remained on the island "for a few days . . . not . . . above a fortnight." The few pages devoted to his stay (vol. 1, *pp. 83–87*) offer a unique account of the manner in which newly arrived Africans were approached on shipboard and sold. Equiano's book also has a special historical value because it is the only known instance of an African who was shipped to Barbados detailing his experiences on the middle-passage and his life in West Africa. Many of Equiano's countrymen on the same ship which brought him to the island were sold, and the book can thus be taken as a testimony of their experiences in coming to the New World. As a freeman and sailor, Equiano returned to Barbados in 1771 (*p. 96*), but records nothing about this visit.
   At least eight subsequent editions of this volume were published in the eighteenth and early nineteenth centuries [BM]. The Barbados section is kept intact in a recent edition, edited by Paul Edwards, published under the title *Equiano's Travels* (London, 1967).

*[HENDY, JAMES]
   A vindication of the opinions and facts, contained in a treatise of the Glandular Disease of Barbadoes.

London, 1789. *155 pp.*
Listed by Sabin (31335); this is probably a rebuttal to John Rollo (1785). The National Union Catalog locates only one copy, at the College of Physicians of Philadelphia.

*NICHOLLS, F.
   Sable Victims. A Barbadoes narration, inscribed to the promoters of the slave trade and addressed to J. Hargrave, Esq.
   London, 1789.
"Violently anti-slave, with gross exaggerations. An illustration shows a runaway Negro being roasted alive. Reviewed in the Gent[leman's] Mag[azine], September, 1789, p. 827" (Ragatz, *p. 534*). I was unable to locate a copy of this.

*STEELE, JOSHUA
   "History of the Mango Tree."
   Transactions of the Society for the Encouragement of Arts, Manufactures and Commerce, vol. 4, London, 1789.
Cited by D. G. C. Allan ("Joshua Steele and the Royal Society of Arts," *Jl. BMHS*, 22, 1954–55, *93*), the article deals with the history of the tree in Barbados — "the original tree [Steele writes in a 1785 letter] and its immediate descendants, which altogether form a group or grove, are in a plantation called, in Mayo's map, Ball's."

[STEELE, JOSHUA]
   Letters of Philo-Xylon, first published in the Barbados Gazettes, during the years 1787 and 1788. Containing the substance of several conversations, at sundry times, for seven years past, on the subject of Negro laws and Negro government on plantations in Barbadoes.
   Barbados, 1789. *49 pp.*   [LC]
Steele had come to Barbados in the late 1770s to assume control of three plantations he had owned for about thirty years. A rare individual and innovator in Barbadian society, he was instrumental in founding the island's Society for the Encouragement of Arts, became a member of Council, introduced some innovative liberal measures in slave management on his plantations, and originated a unique, and highly controversial, "copyhold system" in his plantations' organization. Critical

of the ways in which slaves were treated and the nature and economic implications of some of the slave codes, in these letters he points out some of the defects in these laws and discusses the administrative measures he was experimenting with on his plantations.

William Dickson (1814, *p. 65*) identifies Steele as Philo-Xylon, comments "that only ninety copies of these letters were printed . . . as a pamphlet," and reproduces the pamphlet as well as other writings by Steele. John Newman's article, "The Enigma of Joshua Steele" (*Jl. BMHS*, 19, 1951–52, *6–20*), provides biographical materials on Steele's life prior to his arrival in Barbados, and his contributions to "English prosody [and] British and American elocution and speech education."

To the equity and policy of a great nation. Barbados, August 10. From a real colonist. Barbados Gazette, September 2, 1789.
[Barbados, 1789.]   [LC]
A broadsheet reprint from the *Barbados Gazette* newspaper which is bound into the LC's copy of Joshua Steele's *Letters of Philo-Xylon* (1789); it is not unlikely that he was the author. Ragatz (*p. 274*) lists the title as *To the equity and policy of Great Britain*.

This item focuses on the slave trade and slavery, and considers the following issues: the status of Africans in Africa; whether the mortality rates in the slave trade can be reduced through legislation; can the slaves be better "governed" in the West Indies (in this is discussed the effects of absenteeism on the treatment of slaves and agricultural productivity); and finally whether slavery can be regulated by moral principles alone or do these have to be reinforced by new laws. The author concludes, ". . . it is not merely humanity, or piety in the hearts of the planters, which are wanting to rectify what is amiss; but it is, a total alteration of the local laws, agreeable to the dictates of humanity and piety which must make the conditions of the slaves more happy and at the same time encrease the fortunes and comforts of their masters, besides giving a commer-cial credit to the colonies, better than they have ever yet had in this century."

WILLOCK, JOHN
Voyages to various parts of the world, and remarks on different countries in Europe, Africa, and America, with the customs and manners of the inhabitants.
Penrith [1789]. *327 pp.*   [JCB]
As a young sailor of about twelve years of age, the author arrived at Barbados aboard a merchantman in 1781 and spent about eight or nine days on the island. His account (*pp. 14–16*) briefly describes how some of his fellow crew members were pressed into the British Navy, and offers a conventional and valueless short paragraph on the island's geography, climate, produce, Carlisle Bay, etc. For other editions *see* Sabin (*104534*).

*"Account of the Number of Negroes Imported into Barbados."
The Scots Magazine, Edinburgh, February 1790, *p. 73*.   [BM]
"Based on data gathered by a committee of the island Assembly" (Ragatz, *p. 410*). See *Report of a Committee of the General Assembly* (1790).

Report of a Committee of the General Assembly upon the several heads of enquiry, etc. relative to the slave trade.
London, 1790. *8 pp.*   [BM]
This report was sent in response to requests by John Brathwaite, agent for Barbados in London, in order to provide information for his testimony before the House of Lords committee investigating the slave trade. Produced by Assembly members Samuel Hinds, Ben. Babb, D. Maycock, John Bishop, Samuel Forte, and John Eastmond, the report primarily deals with conditions in the late 1780s, and ranges over a variety of matters relating to slavery and slaves in Barbados; also included is some statistical information not presented in Brathwaite's testimony. The report was also published in the *Parliamentary Papers* (*Accounts and Papers*, vol. 26, 1789), along with the testimonies of Brathwaite and Governor Parry. Brathwaite's testimony is also published in the *Jl. BMHS* (18, 1950–51, *24–38*).

Perch's Pocket Almanac, calculated by Mr. Thomas Donohue, teacher of the mathematics. For the Year of Our Lord, 1790. Being the second after Bissextile, or Leap-Year.
Barbados, 1790.
This citation was provided by Michael Chandler (personal communication); the almanac contains a calendar, the names of the Barbados Council members and public officers, astronomical information, and holidays on the island.

A short journey in the West Indies, in which are interspersed curious anecdotes and characters.
London, 1790. 2 vols.　[BM, IJ, H]
During the 1780s, the author stopped at Barbados on his way to Jamaica, but all he records of his visit is an incident he witnessed in which a house slave was mistreated by his master (vol. 1, *pp. 10–12*). Translated in *Kortze Reize in de West-Indien* (Utrecht, 1799, *136 pp.* [NYPL]).

UNITED BRETHREN
Periodical accounts relating to the Missions of the Church of the United Brethren established among the heathen.
London, 1790–1836. 13 vols.　[BM]
The Moravian mission in Barbados was first established to work among the island's slave population in 1765 (at Sharon, St. Thomas); a second mission was established in 1825 (Mt. Tabor, St. John); and a third in 1835 at Bridgetown. The sections in the *Periodical Accounts* relating to Barbados are largely composed of extracts, sometimes quite lengthy, of letters written by missionaries on the island. These provide little information on the life of the slaves, but report in great detail their formal relationship with the missions, e.g. attendance figures, baptism rates, problems of conversion; there is also considerable information on problems associated with maintaining the missions, the state of the buildings, finances, etc. Indexes to various volumes help locate materials specifically treating Barbados, the greatest quantity appearing for the later periods (e.g. vols. 11–13, 1829–36).
An Account of the United Brethrens' Missions Among the Heathens (London,

1788) may have materials on Barbados — cited by Sabin (50514).

An abstract of the evidence delivered before a select committee of the House of Commons in the years 1790, and 1791; on the part of the petitioners for the abolition of the slave trade.
London, 1791. *155 pp.*　[BMHS]
Compiled from *Parliamentary Papers* (*Accounts and Papers*, vol. 30; 1790). Also published in Edinburgh in 1791, with a second London edition in 1792 (Sabin 81745, 81746).

An Act for vesting the Bath Estate, situate in the island of Barbadoes, and late belonging to Edward Day, Esquire, deceased . . . in trustees, to be sold and conveyed pursuant to an agreement for that purpose; and for applying the money to arise by such sale in discharging the incumberances thereon.
[London, 1791.] *15 pp.*　[NYPL]
Day had died intestate and with no legal "issue." Bath descended to Day's three sisters, but a complex legal situation was precipitated by creditors' claims on the heavily encumbered plantation. Appended to the *Act* is a list of the personal names of the plantation's slaves.

HOLDER, HENRY EVANS
Discourses on various subjects, delivered in the island of Barbados by Rev. H. E. Holder of that place.
London, 1791–92. 4 vols.　[BM]
Contains about eighty-one sermons, mostly on purely religious subjects, and sometimes given in commemoration of a particular event, e.g. the hurricane of 1780.
Also by the same author, all in the BM: *A System of French Syntax* (London, 1783); *A Brief . . . Answer to the Philosophy of Masons* (Bristol, 1791); *A Sermon* [on Matt. 1:21] *Written for Magdelen Chapel* (London, 1792); *En Chiridion Ecclesiasticum . . . Seu Theses in Plurimos Articulos Ecclesiae Anglicanae* (Bristol, 1793). *See also* Holder (1788, 1792, 1816).

JORDAN, GIBBES WALKER
The principles by which a currency is established, a coinage formed, and the money circulations of this island may be restored and preserved.

Barbados, 1791. *28 pp.*   [BMHS]
Contents as indicated in title. Cundall (44) cites a 1791 London reprint.

*HOLDER, HENRY EVANS
  Fragments of a poem, intended to have been written in consequence of reading Major Majoribank's Slavery [J. Majoribanks, *Slavery: An Essay in Verse.* Edinburgh, 1792].
  Bath, 1792.   [BM]
Authored by a Barbadian (*see also* author, 1788, 1791–92, 1816).

  * *The humble petition of the planters and merchants of the island of Barbadoes, to the honourable the House of Commons, of Great Britain, in Parliament assembled.*
  [Bridgetown, 1792.]
"Protesting against the measures then under consideration in the lower chamber to reduce the price of sugar by removing the drawback granted on exportation and conditionally preventing all shipments from Great Britain" (Ragatz, *p. 254*).

MASSACHUSETTS HISTORICAL SOCIETY
  Collections.
  Boston, 1792–.   [SIU]
Transcripts of original documents. Indexes to the ten volumes of the first series yielded no references to Barbados. A sampling of some of the volumes in series 2–7 (1814–26) yielded an occasional reference to the island, primarily its commercial ties with New England in the seventeenth century.

COKE, THOMAS
  Extracts of the journals of the Rev. Dr. Coke's five visits to America.
  London, 1793. *195 pp.*   [BM]
The well-known Methodist visited Barbados a few times in the late eighteenth century, altogether spending about five weeks on the island. His journal entries on these visits (*pp. 75–79, 178–79, 181–83*) are brief, but contain some useful information on the status of Methodism in Barbados, and the effects of missionary work among slaves and poor whites. These materials were included in previously published works by Coke: *Extracts of the Journals of the Rev. Dr. Coke's Three Visits to America* (London, 1790); *A Journal of Dr. Coke's Third Tour through the West Indies* (London, 1791); *A Journal of the Rev. Dr. Coke's Fourth Tour on the Continent of America* (London, 1792).

EDWARDS, BRYAN
  The history, civil and commercial, of the British colonies in the West Indies.
  London, 1793. 2 vols.   [BM]
This classic in the British West Indies literature deals with Barbados in volume I (*pp. 327–55*), but Edwards does not appear to have visited the island. His account is largely devoted to its political history. There is also a delineation of governmental structure, commerce, population, etc. *See* Sabin (21901) for later editions.

*FRANKLIN, BENJAMIN
  Works of the late Doctor Franklin: consisting of his life, written by himself.
  London, 1793. 2 vols.   [BM, H]
Sabin (25600). E. M. Shilstone ("Some Notes on Early Printing Presses and Newspapers in Barbados," *Jl. BMHS,* 26, 1958–59, *21*) notes that this work contains biographical materials on David Harry and Samuel Keimer, Barbados's first printers. *See also* Ragatz (*p. 167*).

  * *Authentic news from Martinico. Pilgram* [*Government House, Barbados*], *February 10, 1794.*
  Bridgetown [1794].
One of three broadsides listed by Ragatz (*p. 151*) "reporting the progress of the expedition headed by Sir John Jervis and Sir Charles Grey." The other two, with the same titles, are dated February 17 and 22, 1794.

COKE, THOMAS
  A statement of the receipts and disbursements for the suppor of the missions established by the Methodist Society, for the instruction and conversion of the Negroes in the West Indies.
  London, 1794. *94 pp.*   [BM]
A useful source for the study of Methodism on Barbados during the years 1787–93, which contains budgetary information on the missions, how monies were disbursed, etc., and has an occasional reference to other aspects of social life. Sabin (14248) cites a 1793 edition with a slightly different title.

An epistle from Yarico to Inkle, together with their characters, as related in the Spectator.
Boston, 1794.
Cited by Sabin (105984).

*RICKETTS, GEORGE
The Governor's speech to the Council and Assembly of Barbados . . . August 31, 1794.
[Bridgetown, 1794.]
Listed, but not annotated, by Ragatz (*p. 137*).

"Sketch of a Voyage to and Description of the Island of Barbados."
The European Magazine and London Review, vol. 26, London, 1794, *pp. 185–87, 282–85.*   [BM, UL]
Transcription of a letter written by an English visitor to Barbados in 1789 in which he briefly records his impressions on topics such as Bridgetown, clothing fashions, food preferences, markets, etc. There is also a description of the island's physical geography and flora, and an account of visits to Cole's cave and the Animal-flower cave.

*SMITH, CHARLOTTE
The Wanderings of Warwick.
London, 1794.   [BM]
W. Sypher (*Guinea's Captive Kings.* Chapel Hill, 1942, *p. 291*) refers to this as an anti-slavery novel, some of whose action takes place in Barbados.

*LYNCH, DOMINIC
Tentamen medicum inaugurale de podagra.
Edinburgh, 1796. *37 pp.*   [E, BM]
Medical dissertation by a Barbadian.

WILLYAMS, REVEREND COOPER
An account of the campaign in the West Indies in the year 1794, under the command of their excellencies Lieutenant General Sir Charles Grey, and Vice Admiral Sir John Jervis, . . . with the reduction of the islands of Martinique, St. Lucia, Guadaloupe.
London, 1796. *211 pp.*   [BC]
As a chaplain aboard one of the ships involved in the above noted campaign, Willyams spent almost a month in Barbados in early 1794. Aside from a short description of a slave sale, his brief account of the island relates primarily to military matters.

YEARWOOD, SEALE
Letters — 1796–1810.
See S. Yearwood (1949).

*BOVELL, JOHN W.
Dissertatio medica inauguralis de hepatitide.
Edinburgh, 1797.   [E]
Medical dissertation by a Barbadian.

[GIBBES, PHILIP]
Instructions for the treatment of Negroes, etc. etc. etc.
London: Printed for Shepperson and Reynolds, 1797. *134 pp.*   [BM]
A reprinting "with additions" of Gibbes (1786) which is sufficiently different that it is discussed separately and in detail. This book contains no dedication page; its introduction is the same as that in the 1786 edition except for the final sentence which notes that the *Instructions* were "given many years ago to the valuable friend, who was then the manager [identified as Jacob Lewis] of Spring–Head plantation."

The book comprises six sections: *1]* "Instructions for the treatment of newly purchased African slaves. To the manager [now identified as Francis S. Bailey] of Spring–Head plantation" (*pp. 1–49*) derives from pages 5–8 of the 1786 edition, but contains some rewording and considerable additions with respect to the feeding of slaves. A number of suggestions, recipes, and calculations are given for the preparation of soups from local crops; these are based on "an essay" by Count Rumford (i.e. Sir Benjamin Thompson — see *Dictionary of National Biography* and BM catalog) which dealt with problems of feeding the English and German poor nutritiously and inexpensively. *2]* In an untitled section (*pp. 50–60*) the author discusses the slave trade, his dissatisfactions with some aspects of it, and offers some suggestions for its improvement. *3]* Pages 61–66 contain "a receipt to make an Italian composition for floors . . . a receipt to make cement," and directions for preparing Indian corn as a soup ingredient which quotes at length from Rumford's work. *4]* "Instructions for the treatment and Improvement of Negroes" (*pp. 67–127*) is of more informational value on plantation conditions than previous sections; it is based on pages 9–23 of the author's 1786 work, but comparing the two, this one omits or modifies some details and contains considerable additions or elaborations on a variety of topics, e.g. the author's philosophy on slave treatment, disciplinary measures, the use of the whip, slave trials, what can be considered as reasonable and unreasonable work demands, mealtimes and work schedules, the saying of grace at meals, child and infant care, dietary procedures and food provisions, treatment of the sick, marriage, religious and literacy instruction, baptism, and slave houses and gardens. 5] "Conclusion" (*pp. 128–32*) reproduces three of the letters to Jacob Lewis found in the 1786 edition. 6] Pages 133–34 contain two "pieces . . . written by a Lady" — one, "The Negroe's address to his fellows" is a poem ("We're children of Cham! He his father offended / Who gave him the curse, which to us descended / . . . . Mean time ev'ry slave, who his duty doth here / Shall receive his reward when God shall appear. . . ."), and the other "A Grace After Meat."

In addition, of the three copies I examined (BM, Brown University, and University of Miami at Coral Gables, Florida), those in the BM and Brown University Library have eight separately numbered pages which contain hymn lyrics and musical notations; these were apparently intended to be taught to, or sung by, slaves, and stress that compliance and performance of one's role will reap rewards in the afterlife.

Sabin (34856) cites this item as having been published in 1799, and Ragatz (*p. 433*) erroneously claims that it is a reprinting of *Instructions for the Management of a Plantation in Barbadoes. And for the Treatment of Negroes* (1786).

In all references to this item that I have seen (and the 1786 one on which it is based — *see* Gibbes, 1786) the author is not given, but he was undoubtedly Philip Gibbes, a prominent Barbadian planter. Primary evidence for this identification is contained in a letter written by William Bishop (dated Barbados, June 11, 1798) to Nathaniel

Elliot in London. Bishop, a plantation attorney, had been charged with "inordinate expenses," specifically for the purchase of new slaves, with the implication that if he had better treated the slaves and not worked them to excess, mortality rates would have been less and there would not have been a need for additional purchases. Bishop defends himself in this letter which includes the following comment: "Sir Philip Gibbes, from a little book which he has published, part of which I remember fell from his pen some years past, and part taken from the benevolent principles of Count Rumford, appears to be a man of humanity . . . [but] I have not a doubt were the question [of slave treatment] put to Mr. Bayley, the manager of Spring–Head, who is as conscientious a man and of as much probity as Sir Philip Gibbes, or myself, that he would answer, Sir Philip expected as many exertions from his Negroes as any gentleman in this island" (Archives Department of Leeds, Earl of Harewood Archives, Bundle of Letters and Papers on West Indian Estates and Affairs, 1795–1873). Equiano (1789, vol. 1, *pp. 209–11*) also mentions that "Sir Philip Gibbes, Baronet, Barbadoes . . . has written a treatise on the usage of his own slaves," but does not specify a title or publication date.

*DUMMETT, EDWARD J.
Dissertatio medica inauguralis de cholera.
Edinburgh, 1799.   [E]
Medical dissertation by a Barbadian.

"Oxen in Barbados."
Annals of Agriculture, vol. 32. London, 1799, *p. 213.*   [BM]
"Urges that oxen instead of horses be used in grinding canes because of the greater economy involved" (Ragatz, *p. 261*).

*WEEKES, NATHANIEL
Disputatio medica inauguralis de flava febre.
Edinburgh, 1799. *49 pp.*   [E, BM]
Medical dissertation by a Barbadian.

*WELCH, WILLIAM
Dissertatio medica inauguralis de audito.
Edinburgh, 1799.   [E]
Medical dissertation by a Barbadian.

1800–1839

[Clinton, J.]
[*Plantation Management in Barbados.*]
[London, ca. 1800.]
Evidence that a book on plantation management in Barbados was published in London around 1800 is contained in a letter (dated Bristol, December 6, 1801) written by John Foster Alleyne, a prominent Barbadian planter and plantation attorney, while on a visit to England. In the letter, addressed to Richard Smith (one of Alleyne's plantation managers) in Barbados, Alleyne writes: "I am not sure if you know him personally, but if not you may possibly have heard of Mr. J. Clinton, formerly the manager upon Rock Hall plantation. He came to England in the same ship with me the last time [Alleyne had arrived in England in July 1799] for the benefit of his health. Poor man! He has been wasting his time and money, and exposing himself by publishing a book upon management. I have sent you one of them. . . . I pity him [Clinton] very heartily for I believe him to be a very honest, industrious, and well meaning man. He is too, I have heard, a good planter, but, to be sure he never more mistook his talent than when he attempted to write a book" (West India Committee Library, Manuscripts, Alleyne Letters, *pp. 87–88*).

I have found no trace of this book (the above title is my construction) under the author's name, nor have I found any anonymously authored work at this period which fits Alleyne's description; the only item that comes close in subject matter and time of publication is *Directions to Young Planters* (1800) whose authorship Ragatz (*p. 314*) attributes to J. W. Orderson (*see* Orderson, 1800).

[Orderson, J. W.]
Directions to young planters for their care and management of a sugar plantation in Barbadoes.
London, 1800. *79 pp.*   [wic]

A useful work by a Barbadian, which concentrates upon technical matters such as husbandry, manures, soil preparation, sugar making and distillation. There are also a number of recipes for the preparation of sugar-derived beverages. Orderson feels that slaves should be well treated because they are human beings as well as valuable property, but he offers relatively little information on the slaves *per se*.

Author identification is given by Ragatz (*p. 314*), but *see* Orderson (1816) for comments on the author's name.

Moore, Samuel
The Public Acts in Force; passed by the Legislature of Barbados, from May 11th 1762 to April 8th, 1800, inclusive.
London, 1801. *523 pp.*   [bm]
The editor, clerk of the Barbados Assembly, has produced a valuable work which complements the volume by Richard Hall (1764). Barbados laws in force are reproduced in their entirety; there is also a fifty-two-page abridgement of them, a title list of the non-reproduced private and expired acts for the period 1762–1800, and a comprehensive eight-page subject index.

[Poyer, John]
A letter addressed to His Excellency the Right Honorable Francis Lord Seaforth. By a Barbadian.
Bridgetown, 1801. *27 pp.*   [bpl]
This pamphlet was written soon after Governor Seaforth's arrival on the island, and aimed at giving him "a faithful representation of the moral and political state of the colony under your government." The tone of the pamphlet is often sarcastic as Poyer offers a detailed critique of the Barbadian legal and judicial system, military fortifications, and militia organization (". . . an undisciplined rabble and a few convivial clubs . . . the Gentlemen who comprise these clubs are much less attentive to the manual and platoon

excercises than to that of the glass. They manage their knives and forks with infinitely more dexterity than they do their swords, and consider their bottles as enemies they have to subdue"), and the status and behavior of the free colored population. He also emphasizes that slavery is not only a natural condition of society, but that slaves in Barbados are well treated and enjoy a security unknown to Africans in Africa. "The Government of Barbados, my Lord," Poyer concludes, "may be aptly compared to an *Augean* stable, in which there is much filth to be removed, many impurities to cleanse, errors to correct, defects to supply and grievances to redress. The task is indeed an Herculean one."

The pamphlet is reproduced in the *Jl. BMHS*, 8, 1940–41, *150–65*) where the author is identified. A copy is also located in the Scottish Record Office (GD/46/7/5).

YOUNG, SIR WILLIAM
"*A tour through the several islands of Barbadoes, St. Vincent, Antigua, Tobago, and Grenada, in the years 1791 and 1792.*"
In Bryan Edwards, *An Historical Survey of the Island of Santo Domingo.*
London, 1801. [BM]
Young arrived at Barbados on December 6, 1791, but only stayed for about five hours. His journal entry (*pp. 261–64*), which is based on a stroll through Bridgetown, contains comments on the Negro population.

The Edinburgh Review; or The Critical Journal.
Edinburgh, 1802–44. 80 vols. [BM]
A quarterly journal with a liberal stance on the issue of slave emancipation. Indexes published in 1813, 1832, and 1850 cover the period 1802–44. Most of the references to Barbados (e.g., vols. 4, 7, 9, 25, 29, 40, 42, and 45), a few of which have been annotated in this *Guide*, are to reviews of books which deal with the island.

GIBBES, SIR PHILIP
Letter to John Beckles, Esq., Attorney General at Barbados, and correspondence between them on the subject of the con-

veyance of the Kendal plantation being unfairly obtained.
London, 1802. *76 pp.* [WIC]
Joshua Steele, a few hours before his death in October 1796, made out his will which left his plantation to his sister, Mary Ann Steele, and his two illegitimate children, Catherine and Edward. The children were identified as slaves in the will, and their claims on the estate were contested. A controversy arose between Steele's sister and his executor, Francis Bell, on the disposition of the estate, and she decided to sell the plantation to Philip Gibbes, much to Bell's objections. In the midst of the controversy, Mary Ann died and Bell, as the only executor, assumed control of the plantation. Gibbes carried on litigations, claiming his rights to purchase Kendal plantation according to the wishes of Steele's deceased sister. In these litigations, John Beckles was Bell's attorney.

The *Letter to John Beckles* is twenty-two pages long, the remainder of the book being taken up with appendices which reproduce various documents relating to the case. The case itself is an interesting one for a study of the island's legal and judicial system, especially so since it was perhaps the first major one in which slaves had been bequeathed property, a subject upon which the laws of Barbados were silent.

GRAINGER, DR. JAMES
The Sugar-Cane. A poem. In four books. With notes.
London, 1802. *170 pp.* [UL]
The author had considerable experience in St. Kitts. Although this work makes occasional reference to Barbados, it is doubtful if Grainger ever visited the island. Earlier editions were published in London in 1764 and 1766 [BM]. Grainger's *An Essay on the more common West-India diseases* (London, 1764 [BM]) contains no specific references to Barbados.

*HENDY, JAMES ALLEYNE
Dissertatio medica inauguralis de digitale, ejusque in quibusdam morbis usu.
Edinburgh, 1802. [E]
Medical dissertation by a Barbadian.

*Miller, Samuel
Dissertatio medica inauguralis de dysenteria.
Edinburgh, 1802.   [E]
Medical dissertation by a Barbadian.

*Orderson, J. W.
Colonial Register for 1802, being a correct list of all public officers in Barbados.
Bridgetown [1802].
Listed by Sabin (57504). I have been unable to locate this item under the above author's last name or the title. D. J. Murray, *The West Indies and the Development of Colonial Government 1801–1834* (Oxford, 1965, *p. 250*) cites a short title as *Orderson's Colonial Register for . . . Barbados*, gives the author as J. W. Orderson, and 1802 as the year of publication. See Orderson (1816) for a discussion of the author's name.

*Butcher, James
Disputatio medica inauguralis de pulsa arteriarum.
Edinburgh, 1803.   [E]
Medical dissertation by a Barbadian.

*Cheekes, William
Disputatio medica inauguralis de Gëre.
Edinburgh, 1803.   [E]
Medical dissertation by a Barbadian.

Letter from a Gentleman in Barbados to his friend in London, on the subject of manumission from slavery, granted in the City of London and in the West India colonies.
London, 1803. *35 pp.*   [UL]
Dated Barbados, December 1, 1802, this letter defends the slave system, with Barbadian materials being used to illustrate the author's argument. Focusing upon manumission, the letter critically discusses prohibitions against slavery on English soil, comments on the "liberality" of manumission procedures in Barbados, and briefly describes these procedures. In addition, laws respecting manumission and the emancipated slave in various of the West Indian islands are contrasted.

Jordan, Gibbes Walker
The claims of the British West Indian colonists to the right of obtaining necessary supplies from America, and of employing the necessary means of effectually obtaining these supplies under a limited and duly regulated intercourse.
London, 1804. *119 pp.*   [bos, lc]
The colonial agent for Barbados provides a treatise on trade problems in the West Indies in general; individual islands are rarely mentioned.

McKinnen, Daniel
A tour through the British West Indies, in the years 1802 and 1803, giving a particular account of the Bahama Islands.
London, 1804. *272 pp.*   [bmhs]
The author's comments on Barbados (*pp. 5–37*) are based upon a short visit to the island in 1802, and contain information on topics such as fishing, slave life, the free colored population, Bridgetown, etc.

Proceedings of the general court martial in the trial of Major John Gordon of the late 8th West India Regiment.
London, 1804. *298 pp.*   [bm]
Gordon was stationed in Barbados in 1802 when his alleged misconduct occurred. The trial itself was held in London, but, unless one is interested in the West India regiment, this is a valueless source for a study of the island's history.

*Hollingsworth, Arthur R.
Disputatio medica inauguralis de urethrea strictura.
Edinburgh, 1805.   [E]
Medical dissertation by a Barbadian.

The horrors of the Negro slavery existing in our West Indian islands, irrefragably demonstrated from official documents recently presented to the House of Commons.
London, 1805. *36 pp.*   [bm, bpl]
An anti-slavery pamphlet which argues against the permissiveness of colonial laws regarding the murder of slaves and the antipathy with which more stringent laws are greeted in the colonies. Contains extracts from a number of official letters, the originals of which are in the Public Record Office (London), which describe the murders of various slaves in Barbados.

*Husbands, William
Disputatio medica inauguralis de mensibus eorumque emansione.

Edinburgh, 1805.   [E]
Medical dissertation by a Barbadian.

*MALLONEY, DANIEL THOMAS
*Disputatio medica inauguralis de usu aquae
frigidae in febribus.*
Edinburgh, 1805.   [E]
Medical dissertation by a Barbadian.

SEAFORTH, FRANCIS LORD
[*Letter to the officers of the Barbados
militia.*]
Barbados, 1805. *2 pp.*
This untitled circular letter, dated
"Pilgrim, 6th June, 1805," was sent
when a French invasion of the island
was considered imminent. The letter
details the military strategy to be
employed in the island's defense, and
describes how slaves are to be used with
respect to this strategy. A copy is
located in the Scottish Record Office
(GD 46/17/27).

PINCKARD, GEORGE
*Notes on the West Indies: written during
the expedition under the command of the late
General Sir Ralph Abercromby; including
observations on the island of Barbadoes,
and the settlements captured by the British
troops upon the coast of Guiana.*
London, 1806. 3 vols.   [BPL]
The author, a medical doctor and
"liberal" on the slavery issue, spent a
little over a month in Barbados in early
1796, but records his impressions in
great detail in volume 1 (*pp. 192–448*)
and volume 2 (*pp. 1–200*). Although
Pinckard is often discursive, he provides
a considerable array of information on
the island's social life and customs,
and his inquisitiveness, relative ob-
jectivity, and capacity to vividly por-
tray his observations make his book a
much more useful and comprehensive
source than most other travelers'
accounts of Barbados.
A second, two volume, edition was
published in London in 1816 (Sabin
62894).

SEAFORTH, FRANCIS LORD
*A letter to the chairman of the joint com-
mittee appointed to report on the best plan
for a new militia bill for the island
of Barbados.*
London, 1806. *45 pp.*   [BPL]

The governor of Barbados outlines the
requirements for fortifying the island
against external attack, and suggests
the mechanisms by which this can be
accomplished.

PORTEUS, REVEREND BEILBY
*An essay towards a plan for the more
effectual civilization and conversion of the
Negroe slaves, on the trust estate in
Barbados belonging to the Society for the
Propagation of the Gospel in Foreign
Parts. First written in the year 1784, and
addressed to the Society; and considerably altered, corrected, and abridged.*
London, 1807. *52 pp.*   [BM]
A longtime advocate of the position
that slaves should be converted to
Christianity, the Bishop of London here
argues that attempts to instruct and
convert the Codrington slaves have not
been successful, and that the fault lies
in the Society's program, for the slaves
are intellectually capable of being
instructed. Porteus, who apparently
never visited Barbados, offers some relatively radical suggestions for altering
the life of the slaves within the context
of the slave system, but does not argue
for the abolition of slavery.
The first edition was published in
London in 1784 (Sabin 64326).

RENNY, ROBERT
An history of Jamaica.
London, 1807. *333 pp.*   [IJ]
In 1799, the author touched at Barbados
while on his way to Jamaica; in a footnote (*p. 190*) he describes an incident
of discrimination against a free colored
man in a Bridgetown tavern.

YOUNG, SIR WILLIAM
*The West-India Common-Place Book;
compiled from Parliamentary and official
documents; shewing the interest of Great
Britain in its sugar colonies.*
London, 1807. *256 pp.*   [BPL]
The author was a member of a Parliamentary committee charged with investigating economic conditions in the
West Indies. His book is especially
valuable as a reference for statistical
materials on topics such as commerce
and trade, plantation economics, taxation, navigation, military affairs, and
the slave trade. The book is organized

in such a way that materials on Barbados are easily accessible.

COKE, THOMAS
A history of the West Indies, containing the natural, civil and ecclesiastical history of each island: with an account of the missions instituted in those islands, from the commencement of their civilization.
Liverpool, 1808; London, 1810–11. 3 vols.   [BM]
Barbados is treated in two chapters of volume 2 (*pp. 88–164*); the first contains a civil history of the island based on earlier accounts, while the second, and more valuable one, delineates the history of Methodist and Moravian work and details the lives and difficulties of individual missionaries.

HAMDEN, ROBERT
Dissertatio medica inauguralis de glandulari morbo Barbadensi.
Edinburgh, 1808. *40 pp.*   [E]
Discusses elephantiasis, building upon James Hendy's 1784 volume. The author notes that he lacked the opportunity to "perceive with my own eyes the manifestations of the disease."

POYER, JOHN
History of Barbados from 1801 to 1803 inclusive. Comprising the first part of the administration of the Right Hon. Francis Humberstone McKenzie, Baron Seaforth. By John Poyer, Esq. author of the History of Barbados. Now in the press in London.
Bridgetown, 1808. *35 pp.*   [IJ]
In ranging over Seaforth's administration, Poyer discusses and criticizes the governor's personal qualities, and treats, often sarcastically, his involvement in a number of issues, e.g. the imprisonment of prisoners of war, the Assembly's award of his salary, his efforts to "improve" the island's militia and fortification system, and his efforts with respect to statutes concerning debtors, penalties for the wanton murder of slaves, and the prevention of free Negroes from accumulating real estate. He also discusses a case in which Seaforth had refused to pardon the island's acting provost marshall, a Mr. Mason, who was convicted of murder (as Mason dropped from the gallows the rope broke, and despite what Poyer claims were public requests for a reprieve, the governor ordered him to be hung again).

This pamphlet is rare. According to H. A. Vaughan ("Poyer's Last Work," *Jl. BMHS*, 21, 1953–54, *155–74*) it is a reprinting of an article that first appeared "in nine inconsecutive issues" of the *Barbados Chronicle* or *Caribbean Courier*, a newspaper founded by Poyer, over the period April 20–August 6, 1808. The first installment of this article was entitled "History of the Administration of the Rt. Hon. Lord Seaforth Late Governor etc. etc. etc." It has been reproduced under that title in the *Jl. BMHS* (21, 1953–54, *160–74*). Vaughan's article (which notes that only two hundred copies of the pamphlet were printed) is useful for background to the article (and pamphlet), its historical importance, and for biographical notes on Poyer.

POYER, JOHN
The history of Barbados, from the discovery of the island, in the year 1605, till the accession of Lord Seaforth, 1801.
London, 1808. *692 pp.*
     [BMHS, NYPL, IJ, BOS]
A political history written by a Barbadian. For the period up to the middle of the eighteenth century, Poyer relies upon Ligon (1657), the *Universal History* (which is based upon Oldmixon, 1708), Richard Hall's 1755 manuscript (*see* Hall, 1924), and to a considerable degree upon the records of the House of Assembly. For later periods the House of Assembly records are supplemented by the author's own observations and experiences. Slavery is primarily discussed in the preface where the author stresses that West Indian slaves are not ill-treated.

*BOXILL, WILLIAM
Dissertatio medica inauguralis de pneumonia.
Edinburgh, 1809.   [E]
Medical dissertation by a Barbadian.

*"History of Barbados."
The Quarterly Review, London, May 1809, *pp. 258 ff.*   [BM]
"Written around Poyer The History of

Barbados [1808]. The reviewer favors freeing the West India trade of the restrictions to which it was then subject as a means of improving the planters' position" (Ragatz, *p. 253*).

Authentic history of the English West Indies; with the manners and customs of the free inhabitants; including their civil and criminal laws, establishments, etc. . . . with the treatment and condition of the Negroes . . . etc.
London, 1810. *81 pp.*   [LC]
The author notes that he was born in the West Indies and lived there for about twenty years, but he does not specify on which island or islands. His relatively lengthy treatment of Jamaica seems to be based upon personal observations, but it is difficult to say, one way or the other, if the same holds true for Barbados. In his treatment of the island (*pp. 43–47*) he offers brief conventional descriptions of geography, governmental and judicial structure, demography and commerce. There are also some interesting observations on the customs and the economic life of the slaves who, the author concludes, are better off in Barbados than elsewhere in the West Indies.

Another nondated edition of this book was published in London [H, NYPL]; its pagination differs from the 1810 edition (Barbados is treated on *pp. 38–42*), but the contents are identical. *See also* Sabin (102821).

DEPREPETIT-DUFRENE, Y. A. J. M.
Coup d'oeil of the captainships of Grand Para, Rio Negro, and adjacent Guianas.
Barbados, 1810. *29 pp.*   [NYPL]
Translation of a French manuscript which, though published in Barbados, has nothing to do with the island.

MONTGOMERY, JAMES
The West Indies, and other poems.
London, 1810. *160 pp.* [BM, NYPL]
An 1814 London edition is cited by Cruickshank (98), but these poems have nothing to do with Barbados. The title poem, "written in honor of the abolition of the African slave trade by the British legislature in 1807," uses heavy imagery to depict Africa, the Africans being wrenched from their homes, the misery of slavery, and the liberation from bondage; the appended notes refer the reader to secondary sources, not the author's own observations. *See* Sabin (50146–147) for other and later editions.

SACK, BARON ALBERT VON
A narrative of a voyage to Surinam; of a residence there during 1805, 1806, and 1807; and of the author's return to Europe by the way of North America.
London, 1810. *282 pp.*   [IJ]
The author, chamberlain to "His Prussian Majesty," went to the tropics for reasons of health. He stopped at Barbados for about two weeks in March–April 1804 as the island was making preparations for an anticipated French invasion. His observations (*pp. 30–37*) include impressions on the physical layout of Speightstown, Bridgetown, and the countryside, a description of innovations he witnessed in cotton and sugar milling, brief comments on foods eaten by slaves, the use of cattle for traction and manure, butchering procedures, "Barbadoes tar" (manjack), the behavior of free Negroes. He further observes "that in all my walks which have been so frequent through many plantations and in different times of the day, I have never heard the unmerciful stripes of a whip, nor the groaning of a suffering slave."
Sabin (74749) cites a German edition.

*SANDERS, GEORGE
Dissertatio medica inauguralis de hydrocephalo acuto.
Edinburgh, 1810.   [E]
Medical dissertation by a Barbadian.

*BECKWITH, SIR GEORGE
By His Excellency Sir George Beckwith . . . a proclamation. Whereas I have received information . . . that Thomas Johnson Springer . . . was apprehended . . . For having been guilty of forgery and . . . was suffered to effect his escape . . . I do therefore . . . issue this my proclamation . . . commanding all magistrates . . . to apprehend or cause to be apprehended, the afore-named Thomas Johnson Springer . . . given under my hand and seal . . .
[*May 17, 1811*].
[Barbados, 1811.]

Listed by the National Union Catalog as a broadside, it is located at the Bancroft Library (University of California at Berkeley).

[BOVELL, JAMES?]
An essay attempting to prove the policy of granting the late petition of the free coloured people of Barbadoes.
[Barbados, 1811.] *15 pp.*
Supports the view that free men of color should be allowed equal civil status with whites, particularly with reference to testifying in legal proceedings, but offers very little substantive information on the condition of this population on the island.

R. Schomburgk (1848, *p. 381*) gives the pamphlet's publication date and describes the repercussions in Barbados after its appearance, and attempts to prosecute its publisher—identified by Schomburgk as James Bovell. The only copy of this rare tract that I could locate is in the William Smith Papers of the Manuscript Department, William R. Perkins Library, Duke University (Durham, N.C.); in this copy, a contemporary manuscript inscription reads "Howard Bovell / Mercht in Speights Town / but said to have been / written by his brother / James a Barrister."

BRIDGMAN, JOHN
An exposition of a series of unprecedented persecutions on the part of Major-General Alexander Wood, Commandant of St. Lucia . . . against John Bridgman, Esq. collector of His Majesty's customs in that island.
[Barbados], 1811. *91 pp.* [NYPL]
The preface and end page are signed by the author and dated Bridgetown, December 7, 1811, but none of the events described transpired in, or relate to, Barbados.

*COLLYMORE, SAMUEL I.
Disputatio medica inauguralis de pneumonia notha.
Edinburgh, 1811. [E]
Medical dissertation by a Barbadian.

*MAYCOCK, JAMES DOTTIN
Disputatio medica inauguralis de sensu et motu.

Edinburgh, 1811. [E]
Medical dissertation by a Barbadian.

*[SOCIETY FOR THE IMPROVEMENT OF PLANTERSHIP IN THE ISLAND OF BARBADOS]
Minutes of the Society for the Improvement of Plantership in the island of Barbados, instituted December 8th, 1804.
Liverpool, 1811. *156 pp.* [BMHS]
A rare item. The citation and following comments were provided by Michael Chandler (personal communication): "The item contains minutes of meetings from the inaugural one of 8 December 1804, until a regular monthly meeting of December 1810. Society membership was restricted to 13 members, each either managing his own estate, or taking an active part in management. The meetings were held in rotation at members' estates. At first a number of questions relating to cultivation were propounded, and the meetings would discuss these; later meetings took the form of a discussion of the state of the cultivation of the estate visited, with occasional papers on special subjects . . . there is little material on slave labour or slavery in these minutes."

Subsequent minutes of the Society were *apparently* never published, but I had a brief opportunity to scan a microfilm copy (located in the library of the University of the West Indies, Mona) of a three-hundred-ten-page manuscript volume of minutes for the period June 1, 1811 to April 6, 1816. The original is located in the Raymond Richards Collection of Miscellaneous Historical Documents in the library of the University of Keele (Staffordshire, England). The volume is titled *Minute Book of the Society for the Improvement of West India Plantership, 1811–1812 and of the Agricultural Society, 1812–1816.* In the 1811–13 minutes the Society is referred to as "Society for the Improvement of West India Plantership," "Society for the Improvement of Plantership," or "Agricultural Society," but from 1813 on by the last name only. I would suppose that all of these names refer to the same society as indicated in the printed title, for the contents of the manuscript volume are similar to those described for the printed one.

On the basis of a rapid perusal of the manuscript minutes, it appears that the Society met monthly, and each month's meeting was held at a different plantation. Each entry lists the names of the people attending, and most of the discussions appear to have been devoted to agricultural matters on particular estates, such as the acreage planted in various crops, crop yields, and so forth. The source appears to be a valuable one for early agricultural techniques and practices.

In an 1846 lecture delivered in Barbados, John Davy (1849, *pp. 136–40*) presented a historical sketch of the Society, relying upon information provided in the "minutes of its proceedings . . . from its foundation to the year 1816."

Montgomery; or, the West Indian adventurer.
Kingston, Jamaica, 1812–13. 3 vols.
[BM]
Cited by Ragatz (*p. 366*) who notes that this is "A novel of slight value, founded on Caribbean scenes and characters. The story opens in Scotland and continues in Barbados and Jamaica. . . . Interesting chiefly as a Jamaican literary and press production, and for the vivid pictures of island society which it presents."

PURDY, JOHN
Memoir descriptive and explanatory to accompany the new chart of the Atlantic Ocean.
London, 1812. *136 pp.* [BM]
Comprehensive maritime information on coast lines, winds, tides, weather, etc., for the entire Atlantic area. It includes data on Barbados.

"*A Letter of Marque*," *1813.*
See title (1913).

SCHAEFFER, D. F.
Description de l'Amerique et des Indes occidentales.
Berlin, 1813. *296 pp.* [LC]
A translation from an 1813 German edition published in Berlin [NYPL]. Offers (*pp. 25–26*) a brief, often distorted, description of Barbados geography, agriculture, etc., based upon unspecified sources.

[BROWNE, BENJAMIN]
The yarn of a Yankee privateer . . . [treating Barbados in 1814].
See B. Browne (1926).

DICKSON, WILLIAM
Mitigation of slavery in two parts. Part I: letters and papers of the late Hon. Joshua Steele. . . . Part II: letters to Thomas Clarkson.
London, 1814. *528 pp.*
[BM, BC, BOS]
Part 1 contains a variety of materials on Barbadian society in general, and especially valuable information on the working of the slave and plantation systems, including the organization of Steele's plantations and his controversial copyhold system. Included are items published previously and Steele's personal letters to Dickson written in the late eighteenth century. Part 2, of less immediate value for specific information on Barbados, is an intensive analysis of the slave system largely concerned with demonstrating that planters could make greater profits in the long run by better caring for, and rearing, their own slaves than by importing new ones.

*KING, WILLIAM J.
Disputatio medica de febre flava.
Edinburgh, 1814. [E]
Medical dissertation by a Barbadian.

COLQUHOUN, PATRICK
A treatise on the wealth, power, and resources of the British Empire . . . the second edition.
London, 1815. [BM]
In chapter 10, the author deals with the economic advantages Great Britain derives from the West Indies, and argues that greater economic benefits would accrue if the islands were more intensively and diversely cultivated by new immigrants from England. Within this chapter, Barbados is specifically treated on pages 350–54, but a review of the island's early political history takes up most of the account. The remainder provides an overview of the island's economy, economic history, agricultural production, land use, principal exports, and population. Statistics on these topics are also in-

cluded in the appendix. The first edition was published in London in 1814 [BM].

[COLEMAN, SIMEON]
A concise narrative of the barbarous treatment experienced by American prisoners in England and the West-Indies, etc. Written by a young man who was prisoner nearly six months in the island of Barbadoes, and five in England.
Danville [Vt.], 1816. *24 pp.* [LCP]
Around October, in 1814, the author (identified by Sabin, 102823) and his shipmates were imprisoned in Barbados after their schooner had been captured while trading in the Leewards. They were placed aboard a prison ship in Carlisle Bay and remained there for the duration of their stay. The author's account (*pp. 7–18*) describes living conditions and the life and treatment of prisoners on board this ship; he includes a description of an escape made by about forty men who managed to get as far as Speightstown before being captured by a civilian party, largely composed of slaves.

*HOLDER, HENRY EVANS
Dissertatio medica inauguralis de actione erysipelatosa, ab inflammatione prorsus distinguenda.
Edinburgh, 1816. [E, BM]
Medical dissertation by a Barbadian. For other works see author, 1788, 1791/92, 1792.

*HOLLINGSWORTH, DR.
Remarks on various subjects connected with the church establishment of Barbados, to which are added a fair statement of the present condition of the slaves, and some remarks with a view to their religious instruction.
[Barbados, 1816?]
Advertised, with the above title and author's name, in the *Barbados Mercury,* February 17, 1816. I have been unable to locate this item. It is referred to in *A Report of a Committee of the Council of Barbadoes* (1824, *pp. 43, 47*) in the following context: "A pamphlet [cited by short title on *p. 47*] published in this island some years ago [shows] that there are other persons in the colonies who have a concern for religion, besides 'a few

missionaries.' It was written by a proprieter [not named] at that time resident in Barbadoes, addressed to the people of Barbadoes, and its circulation confined to Barbadoes." An extract from the pamphlet, pages 44–47, stresses the obligations masters should have toward their slaves, particularly with respect to "their conversion."

JORDAN, GIBBES WALKER
Copies of a letter containing queries respecting the state of the silver and copper coins in Barbados.
London, 1816. *30 pp.* [BM, IJ]
This pamphlet gives information on the island's system of coinage, exchange rates with sterling, numbers of coins in circulation, etc., and some of the social organizational concomitants of monetary issues. *See also* Jordan (1791).

JORDAN, GIBBES WALKER
An examination of the principles of the Slave Registry Bill, and of the means of emancipation, proposed by the authors of the Bill.
London, 1816. [BM, IJ]
An elaborate defense of the colonies by the agent for Barbados. He condemns the Slave Registry Bill and argues that the islands, particularly Barbados, are not illegally importing slaves, have ample mechanisms to safeguard against such importations, and that the bill is nothing more than an infringement on local autonomy and a smoke screen to cloud the larger issue of Parliamentary control over island legislatures. Thus, much of this tract is devoted to a discussion of the legal and political relationship between Parliament and the colonies which becomes an appeal in "defence of our [i.e. colonial] freedom, our existence, our establishments." In addition, there is a lengthy defense of slavery and the proposition that the agricultural life of the colonies would be ruined if the slaves were to be emancipated.

*LEACOCK, JOHN HENRY
Tentamen Physiologicum inaugurale de haemorrhagiae effectibus.
Edinburgh, 1816. [E]
Medical dissertation by a Barbadian.

Legal condition of the slave exemplified.
London, 1816.
"No. 3 of the West Indian Sketches
series. Based on incidents in Demerara
and Barbados, drawn from Pinckard's
Notes [1806], in which wronged slaves
were related to have been unable to
secure justice" (Ragatz, *p. 434*).

LEITH, SIR JAMES
*An address to the slave population of the
island of Barbados.*
Bridgetown, April 26, 1816.
Governor Leith made this appeal for
calm and order soon after the 1816
slave revolt. A copy can be found in the
Public Record Office (C.O. 28/85); re-
productions of the address are in
Andrew Leith Hay (1817) and the
Barbados Mercury (April 30, 1816).

LEITH, SIR JAMES
Proclamation.
Bridgetown, 1816.
One common reason given for the 1816
slave revolt was that the slaves felt the
Crown had ordered emancipation, but
that the island's legislature refused to
comply. In this proclamation, Leith
expresses the Crown's negative reaction
to the revolt and denies that orders for
emancipation had been given. The proclamation has been reproduced in
Andrew Leith Hay (1817), and a copy
can be found in the Public Record
Office (C.O. 28/85).

ORDERSON, J. W.
*Cursory remarks and plain facts connected
with the question produced by the proposed
Slave Registry Bill. By J. W. Orderson,
late of Barbadoes.*
London, 1816. *35 pp.*   [NYPL]
A rare work, written in England; treats
a variety of issues relating to slavery
and emancipation, with particular
reference to Barbados. Orderson denies
that slaves are illegally imported,
delineates why there is no need for this
in Barbados, and discusses the existent
mechanisms for ascertaining the island's
slave population. However, most of the
tract discusses the treatment of slaves
(stressing that they are better off now
than formerly and, in general, have a
material existence superior to the
English "lower classes of labouring

poor"), manumission procedures, the
development and status of the island's
free colored population (including comments on sexual relations between
whites and blacks), and the author's
views on slavery and amelioration of
the island's slave codes. "I am not,"
Orderson remarks, "inimical to a liberal
extension of the rights and privileges of
the free coloured people . . . also . . . I
have feelings of consideration and
humanity towards the slaves not inferior to those of the most boastful phil-
anthropist . . . it being a persuasion in
my mind, that the only evils ever likely
to result from the general emancipation
of the slaves are those consequent upon
the precipitancy of the measure, and an
indiscreet interference of the Imperial
Parliament between the master and the
slave."
E. M. Shilstone ("Orderson Family
Records," *Jl. BMHS*, 25, 1957–58, *152–
57*) points out that the author's real
name is Issac Williamson Orderson and
comments: "It is remarkable that this
pamphlet and his later work *Creoleana*
[1842] both bear the name *J. W. Orderson* as that of the author. One wonders
why Orderson did not substitute the
initial I. for J. when correcting proofs
of the work." It is equally puzzling
why other works, evidently by the
same author, also bear the initials J. W.
rather than I. W. (*see* Orderson 1802,
1827).
Born in Barbados in the 1760s,
Orderson became editor of the *Barbados
Mercury*; he intermittently spent many
years in England, but died in Barbados
in 1847.

*Remarks on the insurrection in Barbados,
and the bill for the registration of slaves.*
London, 1816. *15 pp.*   [BM]
An emancipationist tract designed to
refute the commonly held notion that
the 1816 slave revolt was precipitated by
rumors surrounding the proposed
Registry Bill. The tract contends that
the planters overly exaggerated the
nature of the revolt, and that its immediate causes were in the ill-treatment
suffered by the slaves and the island's
repressive slave laws.

SKEY, JOSEPH
"Some Remarks upon the Structure of

Barbadoes, as connected with Specimens of its Rocks."
Transactions of the Geological Society, vol. 3, London, 1816, *pp. 236–42.*
[BM]
The author was a military doctor who had been stationed in Barbados. His paper, first read before the Geological Society of London in 1812, describes the island's physical geography and geology.

SPOONER, JOHN
Proclamations.
Bridgetown, 1816.
The president of the Barbados Council issued these two proclamations during the April 1816 slave revolt. One instructs commanders of the island's militia to move quickly by "the rules and discipline of war in trying the said slaves and carrying the sentences thereof into immediate execution," the other urges caution so that innocent persons are not implicated and offers "free pardon to all and every slave or slaves, not being a principal instigator or advisor in such insurrection who ... shall deliver themselves up or return to their respective owners and occupations." These proclamations were reproduced in the *Barbados Mercury* (April 30, 1816) and copies of the originals are located in the Public Record Office (c.o. 28/85).

*WILSON, JOSEPH
Disputatio medica inauguralis de digitali purpurea.
Edinburgh, 1816. [E]
Medical dissertation by a Barbadian.

[Barbados Almanac for 1818.]
[1817.] [BMHS]
Cited by E. M. Shilstone ("Book and Pocket Almanacs." *Jl. BMHS,* 28, 1960–61, *79–80*): "Covers missing. 36 pages of book $5\frac{3}{4} \times 3\frac{1}{2}$ ins. Originally about forty pages. Title page etc. missing. Contents—Almanac, one month to a page; January to June missing; begins at July. The almanac portion was interleaved. It gives the phases of the moon. Days of meeting of Masonic Lodges, Court days, Militia days. Feast days. Council days. A few dates of anniversaries of Barbadian interest.

... Hebrew calendar for 1818. Legislature of Barbados. Members of Council and of General Assembly. Courts, coroners, public officers. Customs House. Barrister-at-law. Attornies. Clergy. Justices of the Peace. Holidays observed at the Customs House 1818. Militia. Military establishment. Naval establishment. State of Freemasonry in Barbados. Exports for 1817. Number of windmills, quantity of land and slaves in each parish. Number of houses in Bridgetown. Sworn land surveyors. Mail boat establishment. Remarkable events 1789–1815. Principal potentates. Chronology from 1605–1816 (*11 pages*). The author of the almanac has not been identified."
Shilstone adds elsewhere (*p. 80*) that this almanac, "in contents and appearance ... resembles" the almanac by Tobias Phillips (1828).

[HAY, SIR ANDREW LEITH]
Memoirs of the late Lieutenant General Sir James Leith, G.C.B., with a precis of some of the most remarkable events of the peninsular war, by a British officer.
Barbados, 1817. *191 pp.* [BM]
In effect, a biography of James Leith who, in 1814, became Commander of the Forces in the West Indies and Captain General of the Leeward islands. Leith was intermittently in Barbados (and died on the island), but, aside from some references (*pp. 153–67*) to military matters and the 1816 slave revolt in Barbados, this is not a particularly useful source. The appendix (*pp. 16–20*) reproduces Leith's proclamation (1816) and address to the slave population of Barbados (1816) which followed upon the 1816 revolt.
The author is identified in the BM catalog. Sabin (39943) cites: *Memoirs and Services of Lieut. Gen. Leith in the West Indies,* London, 1818.

"On the Fall of Volcanic Dust in Barbados."
Blackwood's Edinburgh Magazine, Edinburgh, May 1817, *pp. 134 ff.* [BM]
"An extract from a letter describing this phenomenon accompanying the St. Vincent eruption of 1812" (Ragatz, *p. 181*).

WILLIAMSON, JOHN
*Medical and miscellaneous observations
relative to the West India islands.*
Edinburgh, 1817. 2 vols. [LC]
On his way to Jamaica during the
summer of 1798 the author, a medical
doctor, stopped at Barbados for three
days. His book (vol. 1, *pp. 25–27*) offers
brief observations on Bridgetown, poor
whites, elephantiasis, and a slave
ship.

*YOUNG, NATHAN L.
Disputatio medica inauguralis de cutis
inlalatione experimentis comprobanda.*
Edinburgh, 1817. [E]
Medical dissertation by a Barbadian.

[HOFLAND, BARBARA HOOLE]
*The Barbados Girl, a tale for young
people.*
London, 1818. *250 pp.* [BMHS, BM]
This novel relates the adventures of a
young white girl from Barbados who,
with a female slave accompanying her,
goes to reside in England with the friends
of her deceased father.
The author is identified in the BM
catalog; Sabin (32413) records an
earlier edition, *Matilda; or The Barbadoes Girl* (Philadelphia, 1817).

MARRYAT, JOSEPH
*More thoughts still on the state of the West
India colonies, and the proceedings of the
African institution.*
London, 1818. [IJ]
The agent for Grenada is highly
critical of emancipationist analyses of
the 1816 slave revolt in Barbados, and
suggests it was precipitated by persons
from outside the island (*pp. 7–21*).
The first edition was published in
London in 1817 (Sabin 44706).

[MONTLEZUN, BARON DE]
*Souvenirs des Antilles: voyage en 1815 et
1816, aux États-Unis et dans l'Archipel
Caraïbe.*
Paris, 1818. 2 vols. [BM]
Although the author visited a number of
the West Indian islands he did not stop
at Barbados. While in Guadeloupe,
however, news of the April 1816
Barbadian slave revolt reached that
island; the author records (vol. 2, *pp.
124–30*) the repercussions of this insur-

rection in Guadeloupe, where fear of
the slaves caused increased precaution-
ary measures to be taken.
The author is identified by Sabin
(50208) and in the BM catalog.

*Proposed institution of a colonial charity
school. On the system of Dr. Bell.
Under the patronage of His Excellency the
Governor [Combermere]. Barbados, 16th
November, 1818.*
[Bridgetown, 1818.] *9 pp.* [USPG]
The pamphlet notes that the Colonial
Charity School "is proposed for the
education in reading, writing, and
arithmetic, of such free and slave
children of the coloured and black
population of this island, as from
pecuniary and other local impediments
have not the means of deriving these
advantages from any other source than
that of public charity. . . . The most
prominent feature of this institution
shall be a well-digested system of
religious education in strict and un-
deviating conformity with the principles
of the established Episcopal church."
The pamphlet delineates admission
procedures, rules governing attendance, the composition and duties of
the school's Governing Board, etc.
The USPG copy is in the archives
(Fulham Papers, vol. 2, *pp. 547–59*).

*The report from a select committee of the
House of Assembly, appointed to inquire
into the origin, causes, and progress, of
the late insurrection.*
Barbados [1818]. *63 pp.*
[BM, BMHS, IJ]
On copies of this pamphlet published in
Barbados, library catalogs often give the
publication date as 1816 or 1817, but at
a meeting of the Barbados Assembly on
January 7, 1818, the committee's report
was formally presented and "250
copies . . . were directed to be printed as
soon as possible" (Public Record Office,
C.O. 31/47). This item, along with
various materials located in the Public
Record Office (e.g. C.O. 28/85), forms
the major source for a reconstruction of
the only slave revolt in Barbadian
history. It includes (*pp. 3–24*) the committee's actual report, which treats
the background to the revolt and the
sequence of events during it, and an

appendix. The latter includes: (*pp. 25–57*) the testimonies of whites, slaves, and free coloreds (twenty-one persons) relating to the revolt and its background; (*pp. 57–58*) a copy of a resolution passed by the House of Assembly on January 17, 1816 relating to the Slave Registry Bill introduced into the British Parliament; (*pp. 59–63*) a list of about one-hundred-eighty-five persons and the value of the property each lost as a result of the revolt.

According to Ragatz (*p. 138*) the report was "reprinted in Kingston, Jamaica, in 1818," and the BM catalog also lists an 1818 edition, published in London.

SOCIETY FOR PROMOTING CHRISTIAN KNOWLEDGE
> *The Barbados Society for Promoting Christian Knowledge; under the patronage of His Excellency the Right Honorable Stapleton Lord Combermere.*

Barbados [1818?]   [USPG]
A broadsheet that gives the reasons for the Society's formation, delineates its objectives (e.g. "the establishment of a more efficient system of education among the lower classes") and presents its by-laws; also it lists the members of the Society. The USPG copy is in the archives (Fulham Papers, vol. 2, *p. 757*).

*THOMAS, REYNOLDS CLARKE
> *Dissertatio inauguralis de medicinae progresso.*

Edinburgh, 1818.   [E]
Medical dissertation by a Barbadian.

> **The Alien Act, Barbados.* An act for establishing an alien office, with certain rules and regulations respecting aliens and other persons arriving in this island or resident therein: and also for the purpose of imposing certain taxes on absentee proprietors.*

[Bridgetown, 1819.]
A separately published act listed by Ragatz (*p. 45*).

> **[Barbados Almanac for 1820.]*
> [1819.]

Cited by E. M. Shilstone ("Book and Pocket Almanacs." *Jl. BMHS*, 28, 1960–61, *80*): "The following advertisement appeared in the *Barbados Mercury*

for December 28, 1819. 'The Barbados Almanac for 1820 in sheet and pocket form will be offered for sale at Mrs. Molls on Saturday next 1st January (1820).' Author not identified. (no copy known)."

The Christian Remembrancer.
London, 1819–34. 16 vols.   [BM]
An Anglican magazine containing articles on religion and church-associated activities throughout the world, including the West Indies. The indexes permit identification of Barbadian materials which include reports of missionary and educational efforts among the slaves, reports on the Society for the Education of the Poor, the status and progress of Codrington College, etc. Volume 10 (1828, *pp. 717–18*) contains "Report of the Committee. School for the Education of the Poor White Children of the Parish of St. Peter, Barbados." Some of the articles relating to Barbados are separately cited in this *Guide.*

*GARNER, JONATHAN
> *Dissertatio medica inauguralis de mania.*

Edinburgh, 1819.   [E, BM]
Medical dissertation by a Barbadian.

ORDERSON, REVEREND THOMAS H.
> *A sermon preached in St. Michael's Church, February 26, 1819. Before the Barbados Society for Promoting Christian Knowledge.*

Barbados, 1819. *14 pp.*   [BOS, USPG]
The author, a Barbadian (younger brother of I. W. Orderson), was rector of Christ Church parish. His sermon, addressed to the importance of spreading the gospel to the island's poor whites, is entirely theological, with no information on social conditions. The USPG copy is in the archives (Fulham Papers, vol. 2, *pp. 565–79*).

*AUSTIN, JAMES
> *Disputatio medica de hepatitide.*

Edinburgh, 1820.   [E]
Medical dissertation by a Barbadian.

*CHAPMAN, MATTHEW JAMES
> *Tentamen inaugurale de affectibus animi.*

Edinburgh, 1820.   [E]
Medical dissertation by a Barbadian.

*COBHAM, FRANCIS
Disputatio medica de dyspepsia.
Edinburgh, 1820.   [E]
Medical dissertation by a Barbadian.

JORDAN, GIBBES WALKER
Papers on subjects relating to the British colonies in the West Indies, by the late G. W. Jordan, Esq., . . . Colonial Agent for Barbados.
London [1820?]. *71 pp.*   [LC]
Contains four papers, written between 1808 and 1819, which largely relate to commercial matters of the West Indies in general. Only one paper (*pp. 46–71*), "The Case of Barbados for Indemnification of Losses in the Late Insurrection" (1819), deals specifically with the island. In it the author argues that the Crown should compensate Barbadian whites for property loss and damage as a result of the 1816 slave revolt, and he offers a plan as to how this compensation should take place.
Sabin (3263) also lists this paper as a separate item of six pages published at Westminster in 1819.

SOCIETY FOR THE EDUCATION OF THE POOR IN THE PRINCIPLES OF THE ESTABLISHED CHURCH
[Annual reports of the Barbados Society for the Education of the Poor in the Principles of the Established Church.]
Barbados [1820]–1835.   [USPG]
In 1819, the Society founded the Central School in Bridgetown at which poor white children learned reading, writing, and arithmetic, and were prepared for various trades and "employments as appear to be best suited to their inclinations and capacities." The Society's reports seem to largely deal with the progress of this school, but only the sixteenth annual report, published in Barbados in 1835, was located and consulted [USPG]. The National Union Catalog locates numbers 9–12 (1828–31), all published in Barbados, at the Providence Public Library (Rhode Island).

WALLER, JOHN AUGUSTINE
A voyage in the West Indies: containing various observations made during a residence in Barbadoes, and several of the Leeward Islands; with some notices and illustrations relative to the city of Paramarabo, in Surinam.
London, 1820. *106 pp.*   [BMHS, BPL]
The author, a surgeon in the Royal Navy, was stationed in Barbados for "a whole year" in 1807–8, and returned for ten days in June 1808 (*p. 55*). His main account of the island (*pp. 1–28*) offers valuable details on various aspects of society and culture, especially the behavior and customs of the white creoles; his negative appraisal of their behavior was specifically rebutted by John Husbands (1831). There is also information on slaves and slavery, weather, and the island's flora and fauna, etc. One of the engravings (*following p. 20*), "Slaves in Barbados," shows various aspects of slave life, including a cross-section of the interior of a slave house. Additional comments on Barbados are offered in Waller's discussion of other territories.

PAYTON, T.
Admiralty Chart. A survey of Carlisle Bay in the island of Barbadoes. From A.M.S. in the hydrographical office.
[London], 1821.   [BM]
Shows in detail the coastal areas, to below Needham's point; reproduced in Tony Campbell (1965).

*STRAGHAN, HARBOURNE G.
Disputatio medica inauguralis de tetano.
Edinburgh, 1821.   [E]
Medical dissertation by a Barbadian.

*ALLEYNE, JAMES HOLDER
Disputatio medica inauguralis de inflammatione longa cerebri.
Edinburgh, 1822.   [E]
Medical dissertation by a Barbadian.

BUTTERWORTH, WILLIAM
Three years adventures of a minor in England, Africa, the West Indies, South Carolina, and Georgia.
Leeds [1822]. *492 pp.*   [BM, RCS]
In the early 1780s, the author arrived at Barbados on a slaver which had come directly from Africa. A market glut prevented the sale of the ship's complement of slaves, and it sailed about three hours after anchoring in Carlisle Bay. The author (who was a crew member) did

not go ashore and thus "was unable to make any remarks on this valuable island" other than a short description (*pp. 128–30*) of activities in Carlisle Bay and the reactions of the African slaves to seeing land after an arduous two-month passage across the Atlantic. However, the author offers an extensive description of slaving practices on the African coast and a vivid account of the middle passage, thus conveying what many other Africans must have experienced before they landed on Barbadian shores.

The BM catalog notes the author's name is a pseudonym for Henry Schroeder. Sabin (9670) gives the date of publication as [1823].

DOWNES, JAMES J.
    An Almanack for the island of Barbadoes for the year . . . 1822.
    London, 1822. *46 pp.* [WIC]
This traditional almanac lists the names of legislature members and court judges as well as the various holidays observed on the island.

*DRAYTON, WILLIAM
    Dissertatio medica inauguralis de phthisi pulmonali.
    Edinburgh, 1822. [E]
Medical dissertation by a Barbadian.

*RUSSELL, JAMES
    Tentamen inaugurale de mania.
    Edinburgh, 1822. [E]
Medical dissertation by a Barbadian.

*STRAKER, CAROL D.
    Dissertatio medica inauguralis de phthisi pulmonali.
    Edinburgh, 1822. [E]
Medical dissertation by a Barbadian.

CAREY, HENRY CHARLES AND LEA, J.
    The geography, history, and statistics of America and the West Indies. . . . to the year 1822.
    London, 1823. [BC]
A reference work compiled for the United States Government. An overview of Barbados is on pages 385–86.

CLARKE, FORSTER
    Plan of treatment of the Negroes on the estates in Barbados, 1823.
    [Barbados? 1823.]

The title is taken from a publication of this item in the *Jl. BMHS* (2, 1934–35, 29–31) where it is noted that it "is reprinted from a broad sheet in the possession of Mr. John Chandler. . . . The sheet is signed by F. Clarke who is understood to have been Mr. Forster Clarke." Clarke briefly reviews slave work-schedules, their food, clothing, and medical provisions, and the treatment of women, children, and infants. Implicit is a defense of the planters against criticisms made by English emancipationists.

Clarke owned a plantation and was the attorney for nineteen others owned by absentees "on which there is a population of 4589 slaves . . ." (testimony in *A Report of a Committee of the Council.* 1824, p. 105).

CLARKSON, THOMAS
    Thoughts on the necessity of improving the condition of the slaves in the British colonies, with a view to their ultimate emancipation.
    London, 1823. *60 pp.* [BM]
This celebrated emancipationist tract makes occasional specific references to Barbados largely, if not entirely, drawn from William Dickson (1814); included is a detailed discussion (*pp. 34–41, 43–48*) of the management and innovations (e.g. copyhold system) on Joshua Steele's plantations, substantive data coming from Steele's letters published in Dickson's book. Later editions are cited in the BM catalog.

Great and signal triumph over Methodism, and total destruction of the chapel.
Bridgetown, October 21, 1823.
                                      [USPG]
A broadsheet notifying Barbadians that the Methodist chapel in Bridgetown had been destroyed the previous night and that Shrewsbury, the missionary, had escaped from the island. The sheet appeals to "True Lovers of Religion" in the West Indies to "follow the laudable example of the BARBADIANS, in putting an end to Methodism and Methodist Chapels throughout the West Indies." The USPG copy is in the archives (Fulham Papers, vol. 2, *p. 649*).

The late insurrection in Demarara, and riot in Barbadoes.

London [1823]. *4 pp.*

Printed on folio-size sheets, two columns to a page, this item, according to its prefatory remarks, was originally "prepared for insertion in *The Missionary Notices* [a Methodist magazine published in London] for January 1824 . . . and [is] given in this form for the greater convenience of circulation among Gentlemen connected with the West Indies."

The item largely deals with the difficulties of the Methodist mission in Barbados. Reproduced is a lengthy letter from the missionary William Shrewsbury (dated October 1823) describing attacks against himself and the chapel in Bridgetown, and one from Shrewsbury and W. Larcum, another missionary (dated March 28, 1820), which describes the religious and moral state of the island's population and the work of the Methodist mission (the original of this letter is in the Methodist Missionary Society archives, Box 1817–20, no. 120); also included are other materials and commentaries relating to the mission and the destruction of the chapel in October 1823.

A copy of this item, the only one I know of, is located among the William Smith Papers in the Manuscript Department of the Duke University Library (Durham, N.C.). See *Riot in Barbadoes* (ca. 1824) for a related item.

"Religious Establishment in Barbadoes." *The Christian Rembrancer*, vol. 5, London, 1823, *pp. 473–75.*   [BM]

A review of the distribution of Anglican churches, organizations, and schools.

Report of a debate in council on a despatch from Lord Bathurst to His Excellency Sir Henry Warde, Governor of Barbados.

Bridgetown, 1823. *41 pp.*   [NYPL]

Bathurst, secretary of state for the Colonies, had made a number of suggestions for the amelioration of the slaves' condition and for changes in the island's slave laws. In a meeting of the Council on September 3, 1823, R. Hamden, an influential member of that body, spoke against Bathurst's suggestions and this item is a printing of that speech. Hamden is "alarmed" at Bathurst's veiled threat to have ameliorative legislation enacted in England unless Barbados enacts this legislation itself, and argues that the colonists themselves are the ones who are in the best position to judge what is right and best for the slaves. His proslavery speech is an articulate, well-argued (if not eloquent) defense of the colonial planter.

A copy is located in the Public Record Office (C.O. 28/92); reprints were published in 1823 in London [BMHS] and Jamaica [BOS].

"Treatment of Slaves in Barbadoes." *The Christian Remembrancer*, vol. 5, London, 1823, *pp. 406–8.*   [BM]

Written in Barbados, this account of the Codrington plantations, according to the editor of the *Christian Remembrancer*, "exempts [The Society for the Propagation of the Gospel in Foreign Parts] from any charge of permitting the exercise of cruelty towards their slaves, or of neglecting their personal comfort and spiritual interests."

Whereas a proclamation having appeared in the Barbadian newspaper of yesterday, issued by order of His Excellency the Governor, offering a reward of one hundred pounds for the conviction of any person or persons concerned in the said-to-be riotous proceedings of the 19th and 20th instant . . . Bridgetown, October 23, 1823.

Bridgetown [1823].   [USPG]

A broadsheet. The reward was offered in connection with the destruction of the Methodist chapel in Bridgetown. This item threatens persons who would give information to the authorities concerning the participants in that affair, and warns other Methodist missionaries against coming to Barbados. Copies are located in the Public Record Office (C.O. 28/92, item 59), and USPG archives (Fulham Papers, vol. 2, *p. 647*).

*Examination of statements respecting Barbados, made by Messrs. Wilberforce, Stephen, etc.

London, 1824. *7 pp.*

Listed by Sabin (3268); I was unable to trace this item under the above title.

It may be based on *A Report of a Committee of the Council of Barbadoes* (1824).

HARTE, REVEREND WILLIAM MARSHALL
Lectures on the gospel of St. Matthew.
Vol. 1. 2nd ed. London, 1824. *192 pp.*
[IJ]
The author, rector of St. Lucy parish, delivered these lectures "to a congregation of Negroes in the island of Barbadoes. . . . The object proposed was to make the Gospel history and the principal truths of Christianity intelligible and interesting to hearers, who had neither intellectual culture, nor previous acquaintance with religion." The lectures rarely afford insights into secular life, but their tone and ideological thrust are well reflected in the concluding paragraph of the volume (*pp. 191–92*): "You see, my friends how poor your saviour was, who was obliged to work a miracle in order to pay a small tax. Poverty, therefore, is no proof, that God does not care for us. . . . You see also, how obedient your saviour was to those who were in authority over him. He submitted himself to all who had rule and power in the country . . . he yet did his duty as a man, and led a peaceable and quiet life, humbly yielding his obedience, where obedience was due. And you must follow his example. You must be obedient to all who are over you . . . as a matter of duty, as a thing in which you will please God. We are all of us placed in different stations of life, and we must do the duties of those stations, whether they be high or low. In the next world, we shall receive reward or punishment according as we behave here. . . . Be it your care . . . to honour and obey the King, and all that are put in authority under him, to submit yourselves to all your governors, and spiritual pastors, and masters, to order yourselves lowly and reverently to all your betters."

The lectures were well received by the religious and civil authorities. Sent to the Society for the Conversion and Religious Instruction and Education of the Negro Slaves in the British West India Islands, which caused their publication, they "were recommended to their missionaries as models of that simple and earnest instruction which . . . finds its way to the hearts of the ignorant. . . . They may be placed without scruple in the hands of the convert for his private readings." In the Report of the Society for July–December 1823 (London, 1824, *pp. 31–32*), it is implied that the first edition was published in 1823 (I have come across no copy of it) and is pointed out that Harte's book "is in considerable demand, and numerous applications have been made for it . . . the Governour of Barbadoes having proposed to circulate it in the adjacent islands."

This is a rare work. The 1824 edition, although listed in the BM catalog, was destroyed during the Second World War. *See also* Harte (1826).

INCORPORATED SOCIETY FOR THE CONVERSION AND RELIGIOUS INSTRUCTION AND EDUCATION OF THE NEGRO SLAVES IN THE BRITISH WEST INDIA ISLANDS
[*Annual Reports.*]
London, 1824–34. [BM, RCS]
The Barbados branch of this society was formally organized in August 1825, although minimal work was conducted under its aegis during the few preceding years. Based upon letters and other information from clergymen, the Annual Reports are useful for information on the relationship between the Anglican church in Barbados and the island's slave population.

*JORDAN, GIBBES WALKER
A statement of the condition and treatment of Negro slaves in the island of Barbados.
London [ca. 1824].
Cited by Ragatz (*p. 517*) who notes that this undated item is "Based on A Report of a Committee of the Council of Barbadoes, Appointed to Inquire into the Actual Condition of the Slaves in This Island" (1824). I have been unable to trace this item under the above author or title.

[JORDAN, J. W.]
An account of the management of certain estates in the island of Barbados.
London, 1824. *16 pp.* [H]
To counter emancipationist criticisms, the author submits this account (addressed to an unidentified person) as "a statement of the real condition

of the slave population." He had "resided nearly five years in that Island and upon these estates . . . but, in addition . . . wrote to my agent there in order to obtain more particular details," and, together with what "my memory could serve me," he describes three Barbadian plantations. For each, he delineates the total and cultivated acreage, the amount of sugar-cane acreage annually planted and harvested, and the number and categories of livestock and slaves. Information on slaves include, the number of houses on each estate and their construction; gardening activities, livestock keeping, and marketing patterns; daily work schedules and types of work performed during the agricultural cycle (including information on plantation agricultural practices); clothing, food, and medical provisions, and the care of infants and young children; and disciplinary measures.

This item is listed by Sabin (36646) who erroneously identifies the author as Gibbes Walker Jordan and locates a copy at Harvard. In the Harvard copy (the only one I was able to locate anywhere) the title page (as well as the final two pages) is missing. The title, place, and date of publication have been inscribed in manuscript, apparently by an early bibliographer, on page i of the preface. On page ii, under the final printed lines, "I have the honour to remain, your very obedient servant," there is a manuscript signature and date, in an apparently contemporary hand (but different from the one on p. i), of "J. W. [*not* G. W.] Jordan, February 1824."

J. W. Jordan was one of the signatories of a resolution condemning the destruction of the Methodist chapel in Bridgetown; he is listed as the proprietor of Walkers, Burnthouse, and Farley-Hill plantations (see *A Declaration of Inhabitants of Barbados*, 1826). Gibbes W. Jordan, a former member of the Barbados legislature and later the island's colonial agent in London, died on February 16, 1823 (Schomburgk, 1848, *pp. 415–16*).

"*Letter to the Editor on Religious Instruction in Barbados.*"

The Christian Remembrancer, vol. 6, London, 1824, *pp. 22–24*. [BM] Reports on an 1823 meeting which convened all of Barbados's Anglican ministers. At this meeting a resolution (reproduced in this letter) was unanimously passed which called for a clerical committee to form an association with planters which would establish guidelines for missionary work among Barbadian slaves. The author of this letter complains that by concerning themselves with slaves, the parish ministers will neglect the whites. What is really needed, he suggests, is for the Society for Conversion of Negro Slaves to send missionaries who would concern themselves solely with that population.

M'QUEEN, JAMES
The West India Colonies. The calumnies and misrepresentations circulated against them by the Edinburgh Review, Mr. Clarkson, Mr. Crupper, etc. etc. examined and refuted by James M'Queen.
London, 1824. *427 pp.* [BM] A detailed defense of the West India planters with occasional references to Barbados, and a critique of Joshua Steele's copyhold system. By a special act of the Barbados legislature the author was awarded five hundred pounds sterling in appreciation for his "unremitting and disinterested . . . defence of the West Indies as expressed in his pamphlet" (Public Record Office, C.O. 30/21, Act no. 469).

Another edition was published in London in 1825 (Sabin 43643).

[PHILIPS, GEORGE]
Travels in North America.
Dublin, 1824. *180 pp.* [BM] On his way from Ireland to the United States, the author stopped at Barbados for "a short stay" in February ca. 1820. He lived on board ship, but made "daily excursions" to different parts of the island. His impressions (*pp. 13–23*) offer brief information on a variety of sociocultural topics; the description given of a slave funeral combines direct quoting and paraphrasing of G. Pinckard's description in 1796 (1806, vol. 1, *pp. 270–71*).

Sabin (62456) lists three other Dublin editions.

PINDER, JOHN HOTHERSALL
Advice to Servants. Five family lectures delivered to domestic slaves in the island of Barbadoes, in the year [1822].
London, 1824. *36 pp.* [BOS]
Sunday talks, delivered by the chaplain of the Codrington plantations, on the following topics: "To Servants," which treats the obligations between masters and servants; "On Stealing," which stresses that the "principle duty of a servant to his master [is] honesty"; a lecture on the importance of being truthful with one's master; and two others dealing with "idleness" and "sobriety." In the BOS copy pages 9–16 are missing (these cover parts of the lectures on stealing and lying). Throughout the lectures there is occasional mention of specific types of behavior in which domestic slaves purportedly engage, the main emphasis being that if slaves perform their roles properly they will be rewarded in the afterlife.

A report of a committee of the Council of Barbadoes, appointed to inquire into the actual condition of the slaves in this island, with a view to refute certain calumnies respecting their treatment; and also to take into consideration certain measures affecting the West Indies, which have been lately agitated in the House of Commons.
London, 1824. *127 pp.* [BM, BOS]
The report was submitted to the council in July 1823, by the committee's chairman, R. Hamden. It contains an eighty-eight-page discussion of slavery in general but with specific reference to Barbados, and is oriented toward a rebuttal of Wilberforce's criticisms. A thirty-nine-page appendix summarizes the testimonies of persons called before the committee, as they replied to specific queries on slavery and slave life on the island. Witnesses include British military officers stationed in Barbados, planters (Reynold A. Alleyne, Forster Clarke, and William Sharp), medical doctors treating plantation slaves, and the Reverend Samuel Hinds, principal of Codrington College and the first Anglican clergyman appointed as missionary to Barbados slaves (in 1821). All of these persons are more or less favorable to the planters' cause.

Riot in Barbadoes, and destruction of the Wesleyan Chapel and Mission House.
[London, ca. 1824.] *4 pp.*
A follow-up paper, with the same format as an earlier one dealing with the same events (see *The Late Insurrection in Demarara*, 1823). It reproduces a lengthy letter (dated St. Vincent, October 29, 1823) by William Shrewsbury, the Methodist missionary who had been forced to leave Barbados; this letter describes in considerable detail the events leading up to the destruction of the Bridgetown chapel, the way in which it was destroyed, and the manner in which he escaped from the island. A pastoral letter he wrote from St. Vincent to the Methodist congregation in Barbados, and other materials related to the affair are also included.
The only copy of this paper I know of is located among the William Smith Papers in the Manuscript Department of the Duke University Library (Durham, N.C.).

STEPHEN, JAMES
The slavery of the British West India colonies delineated, as it exists both in law and practice.
London, 1824–30. 2 vols.
[BPL, IJ]
This classic and impressive study by a leading emancipationist makes occasional specific references to Barbados throughout the two volumes. Volume 1 is devoted to the slaves' legal status and an examination of slave codes; volume 2, to an examination of the work schedules, conditions and treatment of the field slave in particular. Substantive materials on Barbados (with one major exception) are derived from printed sources, largely the island's laws and testimonies contained in various volumes of the Parliamentary Papers. But much of Stephen's discussions, even though not specifically devoted to Barbados, have direct bearing on an understanding of the island's slave system.
Stephen had gone to the West Indies as a young man in the latter half of the eighteenth century, eventually practicing law in St. Kitts for eleven years.

In December 1783, on a voyage from England, he stopped at Barbados where he spent about three days. He witnessed part of the trial of four slaves (who had been accused of murdering a white medical doctor) two of whom were convicted and burned alive. The trial proceedings and judgment, and his reactions to them, are detailed in the preface to volume 2 (*pp. xvii–xxiv*), the only part of his work in which his own experience in Barbados is described. This event, as Stephen records in these pages, had a profound impact on his subsequent career and participation in the emancipationist movement.

Stephen's *The Crisis of the Sugar Colonies* (London, 1802) contains no specific materials on Barbados. In his posthumously published autobiography (*The Memoirs of James Stephen*, London, 1954), the only reference to the island is the editor's summary of the Barbados experience described above in volume 2.

"*West India Slavery.*"
The Gentleman's Magazine, vol. 94, London, 1824, *pp. 420–21*.
[BM, UL]
A letter to the editor which argues against the view that free labor can be profitable in the West Indies. As support for his position, the writer reproduces a letter (dated February 26, 1824) from Henry Sealey, a Barbados planter. Sealey's plantation had adjoined that of Joshua Steele, and he offers a critique and evaluation of Steele's copyhold system.

An authentic report of the debate in the House of Commons, June 23, 1825, on Mr. Buxton's motion relative to the demolition of the Methodist Chapel and Mission House in Barbadoes, and the expulsion of Mr. Shrewsbury, a Wesleyan missionary, from that island.
London, 1825. *119 pp.* [BM, BOS, H]
Buxton's speech, which is an interesting and valuable account of the events surrounding the destruction of the chapel and William Shrewsbury's departure, is reproduced verbatim on pages 1–50. This speech is directly rebutted in *A Declaration of Inhabitants of Barbados* (1826). Buxton's motion itself requests a condemnation of the above acts, and

calls for the King to pressure Barbados to rebuild the chapel out of public funds. Pages 50–118 comprise the transcripts of other speeches relative to Buxton's motion and Buxton's reply to these. Also included is the motion ultimately passed by the House which, though milder than Buxton's, is in substantial agreement with his sentiments. Although the value of this source is primarily in the direction of the Methodist incident itself, it is also useful for an examination of the functioning of the island's judicial and legal system.

*CARRINGTON, JOHN WILLIAM WORRELL
Dissertatio medica inauguralis de tetano.*
Edinburgh, 1825. [E]
Medical dissertation by a Barbadian.

Extracts from the Royal Gazette . . . Jamaica . . . from Saturday, June 11, to Saturday, June 18, 1825.
London [1825]. [IJ]
The lead article reproduces proceedings of the Barbados Assembly meeting of April 5, 1825, and other items relevant to Methodist missionary activities in Barbados.

*REED, BAYNES
Dissertatio medica inauguralis de febre flava.*
Edinburgh, 1825. [E]
Medical dissertation by a Barbadian.

SHREWSBURY, WILLIAM J.
Sermons preached on several occasions in the island of Barbados.
London, 1825. *426 pp.* [BM]
The author, a Methodist missionary, lived in Barbados from 1820 to 1823 and had become the focus of a *cause célèbre* which involved the destruction of the Methodist chapel in Bridgetown by a mob, and his departure from the island under threat of violence. As a defense against what he considered to be false accusations against Methodist teaching and doctrine, Shrewsbury later published these fourteen sermons "in order that the world may judge of the character and tendency of those doctrines which the Wesleyan missionaries preach in the West Indies." Although most of these sermons deal with

Methodist theology, some are valuable for a history of Methodism on the island, particularly sermon 8 which offers a concise history of the mission. This sermon also offers information about the way in which Methodists viewed the issue of conversion of Negroes to Christianity and their attitudes regarding the Negro, themes which are also, and better, reflected in sermons 13 and 14 which were delivered to slaves on two plantations in Barbados.

The slave colonies of Great Britain; or a picture of Negro slavery drawn by the colonists themselves; being an abstract of the various papers recently laid before Parliament on that subject.
London, 1825. *164 pp.*   [BM]
Printed for "The Society for the Mitigation and Gradual Abolition of Slavery Throughout the British Dominions," this volume offers (*pp. 15–26*) a summary and critique of Barbados's slave laws, and evaluates attempts made by the island's legislature to change these laws.

*"Spirit of West India Society — Outrage at Barbados."
The Edinburgh Review, Edinburgh, August 1825, *pp. 479 ff.*   [BM]
"Written around Anonymous, An Authentic Report of the Debate in the House of Commons, June 23, 1825. . . . The reviewer denounces the islanders for their destruction of the Methodist chapel in Barbados and for the expulsion of the missionary, Shrewsbury" (Ragatz, *p. 344*).

Substance of the debate in the House of Commons, June 23, 1825, on Mr. Buxton's motion, respecting the destruction of the Methodist chapel in Barbadoes.
London, 1825. *20 pp.*   [BOS]
This pamphlet was reprinted from an article that first appeared in the Methodist magazine *Missionary Notices* (no. 117); comment on the chapel's destruction is contained in a few pages of introduction and the remaining pages cover materials presented at greater length in *An Authentic Report of the Debate in the House of Commons, June 23, 1825* (1825).

WATERTON, CHARLES
Wanderings in South America, the northwest of the United States, and the Antilles in the years 1812, 1816, 1820, and 1824.
London, 1825.   [BM]
The author, a naturalist, touched at Barbados in 1825, and his general impressions are very briefly recorded on pages 279–81. For other editions *see* Sabin (102094).

A declaration of inhabitants of Barbados, respecting the demolition of the Methodist Chapel. With an appendix.
Barbados, 1826. *20 pp.*   [BM]
At a public meeting in Bridgetown, Barbadian whites passed a resolution expressing their disapproval of the destruction of the Methodist chapel. The resolution is reproduced on pages 1–2, while pages 3–5 contain the names of the 105 signatories, prominent landholders and other personages, together with the names of the plantations they owned or for which they were attorneys. The appendix (*pp. 6–20*) rebuts Buxton's speech before the House of Commons (*An Authentic Report of the Debate in the House of Commons*, 1825) and generally defends the Barbadian white position on the treatment of slaves against the criticisms of the emancipationists in England. These latter remarks, written from a very defensive position, were made because "it seems to be the maxim in present day [England] to *presume* guilt in all questions in which West Indians are concerned, and . . . to throw the *onus probandi* on the negative side of the question." A useful document for a concrete statement by a Barbadian elite on the anti-slavery controversy.

[HAMDEN, RENN?]
Some remarks in reference to recent proceedings of the legislature of Barbadoes, etc. etc. etc.
London, 1826. *43 pp.*   [RCS]
Attempts to refute criticisms made against West Indian planters by anti-slavery forces in the United Kingdom; specifically, those criticisms which maintain that the planters have passed no ameliorative measures governing slave life and have resisted all attempts to modify their slave codes. "The object

of the present inquiry," notes the author, "has been to bring to notice what has been accomplished in one island" and he does this by discussing ameliorative legislation in Barbados and the recently passed "Consolidation Act" which modified many of the island's slave laws (for a printed copy of this act see *Parliamentary Papers*, vol. 25, 1826/27, *pp. 197–287*).

An Act passed in Barbados on March 14, 1827 (Public Record Office, c.o. 30/21, no. 496) awarded Renn Hamden, a member of Council, the sum of thirty-five pounds sterling. The Act notes that he, "activated by a laudable zeal for the honor and character of this island," had recently incurred expenses in printing and having distributed in England a pamphlet he had written "in defence of the colony . . . touching the state of slavery in this island." An exhaustive search failed to yield any item published in this period under the stated authorship of Hamden. *Some Remarks* seems to fit, and for this reason I provisionally identify Hamden as its author.

Sabin gives an incomplete title entry (3279) as *On Recent Proceedings in the Legislature of Barbados*, and a complete one (86734); the latter citation locates a copy at Columbia University.

*HARPER, BARCLAY
   Disputatio medica inauguralis de phthisi pulmonali.
   Edinburgh, 1826.   [E]
Medical dissertation by a Barbadian.

HARTE, REVEREND WILLIAM MARSHALL
   Lectures on the gospel of St. Matthew. Among which are introduced eleven lectures on the early parts of the Bible, and on the Ten Commandments.
   Vol. 2, 2nd ed. London, 1826. *223 pp.*
                    [IJ]
In the IJ, this item is bound in with volume 1 (Harte, 1824), but has its own title page, imprint, and collation. In substance and orientation it is similar to his first volume, and was equally well received. In the 1824 *Report* of the Incorporated Society for the Conversion and Religious Instruction . . . of the Negro Slaves (London, 1825, *pp. 9–10*), it is noted that the first

edition of the second volume had been printed "and sent to the colonies for circulation." I have come across no copy of the first edition.

*SKEETE, EDWARD
   Disputatio medica inauguralis de podagra.
   Edinburgh, 1826.   [E]
Medical dissertation by a Barbadian.

*SOCIETY FOR PROMOTING CHRISTIAN KNOWLEDGE
   Report of the Barbados Society for Promoting Christian Knowledge.
   Barbados, 1826.
Listed in the National Union Catalog which locates a copy at the Providence Public Library (Rhode Island).

*"*West Indies — Slavery.*"
   The Retrospective Review, vol. 14, pt. 2, London, 1826, *pp. 226 ff.*   [BM]
"Written around Richard Ligon's A True and Exact History . . . [1657]. This article, from page 247 on, holds that no product but sugar could be grown in the West Indies and that, if the slaves were to be freed, nothing but a rate of wages which no planter could afford to pay could induce them to work. The emancipationists' plans would be fatal to both the estate owners and the Negroes" (Ragatz, *p. 474*).

*BISHOP, HENRY
   Disputatio medica inauguralis de vasis absorbentibus.
   Edinburgh, 1827.   [E]
Medical dissertation by a Barbadian.

DWARRIS, SIR FORTUNATUS
   Substance of three reports of the Commission of Inquiry into the Administration of Civil and Criminal Justice in the West Indies. Extracted from the Parliamentary Papers.
   London, 1827. *475 pp.*   [BM]
The Commission arrived at Barbados in 1823, the full results of its investigations later being published in *Parliamentary Papers* (1825, vol. 15, Report 517, *pp. 5–68*). In the *Substance* Barbados is dealt with on pages 1–124, and these afford an excellent source for a description and understanding of the island's legal and judicial system. Described and systematically discussed

are topics such as the slave laws, the various courts, the manner in which different types of disputes are adjudicated, etc., and there is an especially detailed examination of the ways in which Barbados's judicial processes differ "from the useages of England."

*"*History of Barbados.*"
The Museum of Foreign Literature and Science, Philadelphia, June 1827, *pp. 509 ff.*   [BM]
"A reprint of Anon., 'West Indies— Slavery,' in The Retrospective Review XIV, part 2 (1826)" (Ragatz, *p. 431*).

HOWARD, JOHN HENRY
   The laws of the British colonies in the West Indies and other parts of America, concerning real and personal property and manumission of slaves.
   London, 1827. 2 vols.   [RCS]
Barbados is treated in volume 1 (*pp. 95–149*). While the materials are drawn from official sources (e.g. Dwarris, 1827), this is nonetheless a convenient source for the topics it covers. Pages 95–101 provide a useful sketch of the island's courts, and pages 103–49 reproduce, sometimes as extracts, thirty Barbados laws (from the seventeenth through the nineteenth century) relating to property and slaves.

ORDERSON, J. W.
   Leisure Hours at the Pier; or, a treatise on the education of the poor of Barbados.
   Liverpool, 1827. *56 pp.*   [BPL]
The author outlines how he feels the class structure of society should be ordered so that society can run smoothly. Also he argues for an effective program of vocational education for lower-class white children because he feels that Barbadian free coloreds are beginning to monopolize a variety of the island's trades and crafts. *See* Orderson (1816) for a discussion of the author's name.

SOUTHEY, CAPTAIN THOMAS
   Chronological history of the West Indies.
   London, 1827. 3 vols.   [BMHS]
Largely a political history written by a Commander in the Royal Navy whose information on Barbados is based upon sources such as Edwards (1793), Pinck-

ard (1806), Ligon (1657), etc. On this work in general, Ragatz (*p. 178*) comments: "It is useful because of the year-by-year treatment given material, and because of the hundreds of dispatches, colonial and parliamentary acts, and treaties which it includes and thus makes readily accessible. The adaptation of material and the copying of documents was faithfully and accurately done."

BENSON, JOHN
   A short account of the voyages, travels and adventures of John Benson; comprising seven voyages to different parts of the world, interspersed with anecdotes and observations upon men and manners.
   N.p. [1828?] *120 pp.*   [JCB, LC]
The author was an American sailor who, in the early 1760s, at the age of about eighteen or nineteen, spent a short time in Barbados while his merchantman from Rhode Island unloaded its cargo and took on a new one. His account offers but a brief paragraph (*p. 42*) about this visit: "We arrived at Barbadoes, where we disposed of our cargo for slaves, cash and rum, with which we cleared out for the Bay of Honduras. The planters at Barbadoes are cruel to their unhappy slaves, who are condemned to servile labour and scanty fare. I have seen at high water mark, the heads of slaves, fixed upon sharp pointed stakes, while their unburied carcases were exposed to be torn by dogs and vultures on the sandy beach. Much might be written on the affliction of those wretched slaves, subjected to unjust bondage, and every species of insult and injury."

*IFILL, WILLIAM
   Dissertatio medica inauguralis de malis icto capite oriundis.
   Edinburgh, 1828.   [E]
Medical dissertation by a Barbadian.

   Memoirs of the late William Wright, M.D. with extracts from his correspondence and a selection of his papers on medical and botanical subjects.
   Edinburgh and London, 1828. *456 pp.*   [BM]
Wright was director of military hospitals in Barbados from late 1795 to April

1798, but this volume offers very little information regarding his stay on the island. Pages 103–9 treat these years and briefly delineate his activities and the medical problems he faced with soldiers. There are also occasional references to Barbados scattered in other parts of the volume.

Papers relative to Codrington College, Barbados.
London, 1828. *43 pp.*   [USPG]
An alternate title to this item is *Extracts from the Annual Reports of the S.P.G.F.P., Relative to Codrington College in the Island of Barbados.* The text is drawn from the S.P.G.'s Annual Reports from 1710 to 1825, and thus it affords a convenient, chronologically arranged overview of the development of the Codrington plantations and college for a period of over one hundred years. Appended are sketch plans of the college.

PARRY, THOMAS
Parochial sermons preached in the West Indies. To which are added three occasional sermons.
Oxford, 1828. *352 pp.*   [BM]
These sermons, some of which were delivered in Barbados, are theological in substance and generally useless for information on island society.

[PHILLIPS, TOBIAS]
The Barbados Almanack, for the year 1829 . . . calculated by a native.
Liverpool [1828]. *76 pp.*   [IJ, BMHS]
Contains standard monthly almanac information. Page 27 and the following contain names of Barbados Council members, members and officers of the General Assembly, court judges, public officers, coroners, commissioners of peace, customs house officers, clergy, land surveyors, militia officers, barristers and attorneys, holidays observed at the customs house in 1829. Also lists of the names of the commanders in chief of Barbados from the seventeenth century, a table for converting Barbados currency into sterling, and pages 49–76 offer "A Barbados Chronology" listing major political, social, legal, etc., events from the seventeenth century up to 1828.
For authorship see quote in Phillips, 1832.

RILAND, REVEREND JOHN
Two letters, severally addressed to the editor of the Christian Observer and the editor of the Christian Remembrancer, relative to the slave-cultured estates of the Society for the Propagation of the Gospel.
London, 1828. *15 pp.*   [BM]
Riland never visited Barbados, but with information derived from official reports and private letters he forcefully attacks the fact that a Christian society maintains a slave plantation, and questions whether the Codrington slaves are in a qualitatively different position from other slaves in Barbados.

Sketches and recollections of the West Indies.
London, 1828. *330 pp.*   [BM]
The author, a colonial official stationed in Dominica, visited Barbados in the late 1790s and early 1800s (prior to 1805). Superficial impressions based on a stroll through Bridgetown during his first, one-day, visit are recorded (*pp. 22–24*), as are even sparser materials based on his second visit of about a month's duration (*pp. 134–38*).

"Values in Barbados in 1828."
See title (1911).

BELL, WILLIAM
[*Journal in 1829–1830.*]
See J. Boromé (1962).

COLERIDGE, WILLIAM HART
An address delivered to the candidates for holy orders in the diocese of Barbados and the Leeward Islands; and other addresses.
London, 1829. *207 pp.*   [BMHS]
Addresses by the Bishop of Barbados on theological subjects, exhortations to young people to be good Christians, etc., which reflect religious orthodoxy of the period.

PHILLIPS, TOBIAS
The Barbados Almanack, for the year 1830.
Liverpool [1829]. *79 pp.*   [IJ]
Similar information to that in the author's almanac for the previous year; adds the "rate of passage money, per mail boat" between Barbados and other areas of the Caribbean.

A statement relative to Codrington College; extracted from the reports of the Society for the Propagation of the Gospel in Foreign Parts.
London, 1829. *30 pp.*   [USPG]
Extracts from the S.P.G.'s Annual Reports for the years 1819 to 1828 which deal with slave life on the Codrington Plantations and attempt to show how humanely the slaves are treated. A variety of topics is covered, e.g. instruction in Christianity, houses, work schedules, care and welfare, which make this a useful source for information on a "liberally" run plantation, especially if access to the Annual Reports themselves is not possible.

MAYCOCK, JAMES DOTTIN
Flora Barbadensis: a catalogue of plants, indigenous, naturalized, and cultivated in Barbados, to which is prefixed a geological description of the island.
London, 1830. *449 pp.*   [BMHS, BM]
The author, a Barbadian medical doctor, is critical of the floral descriptions and taxonomy given by Griffith Hughes (1750). This work contains a valuable appendix which lists vernacular names for plants next to their names according to the Linnean system; yet, the plant descriptions offer little to no information on domestic uses and the lore associated with plants, information which can often be found in Hughes's volume.

[NAISH, WILLIAM?]
"Notes on Slavery, Made During a Recent Visit to Barbadoes."
The Negro's Friend, no. 18. London [1830]. *12 pp.*   [BOS]
"The important information," notes the editor of this emancipationist tract, "contained in the following pages [*pp. 4–10*] was communicated by a gentleman, who visited Barbadoes in the early part of the present year, 1830." The "gentleman" provides a miscellany of observations on the treatment and disciplining of slaves; their religious, mating, and marital patterns; gardens; marketing; funerals; infant care; houses; and educational opportunities. There are also comments on the island's free colored population, prisons, and the Colonial Charity School. *See* Sabin (51733) for probable editorship.

PHILLIPS, TOBIAS
The Barbados Almanack, for the year 1831.
Liverpool [1830]. *86 pp.*   [IJ]
Similar information to that in the author's almanac for the previous year; also, list of porters' fares for various points and streets in Bridgetown, boatmen's fares, names of commissioners of fire companies. Pages *75–83* contain a "list of the names of the inhabitants of Barbados in the year 1638, who then possessed more than ten acres of land," and page *84* contains a table, "Heights from Captain Barallier's Map of Barbados." (*See* Tony Campbell, 1965, *p. 22* and E. M. Shilstone, 1937–38, for references to this map.) The "Barbados Chronology" is continued from the previous year.

RILAND, REVEREND JOHN
On the Codrington estates; a letter to . . . [the] Archbishop of Canterbury, president of the Society for the Propagation of the Gospel in Foreign Parts, on the connection of that institution with Codrington College.
London, 1830. *12 pp.*   [BM, BOS]
Supports a planned investigation by the archbishop into the "social and moral claims of the Negroes on the Codrington Estates." Riland argues against slavery in general, the system on the Codrington plantations in particular, and questions the morality of a Church body owning a plantation based on slave labor.

Brief observations on the West India question in the Quarterly Review for April 1831; with remarks on the continuation of the slave trade . . .; by a West India Proprietor.
London, 1831. *16 pp.*   [BM]
An anti-emancipationist tract which quotes from an 1831 letter sent from Barbados by Samuel Hinkson. He relates how the slaves on his plantation "are all well clothed, their houses are comfortable, and form a very pretty village, which is surrounded by a neat fence; and their own pieces of ground, around each of their cottages, are cultivated in the highest manner, and afford them so many provisions, etc., in addition to their other allowances."

Dreadful hurricane at Barbados, Thursday, August 11, 1831.
Antigua, 1831.
Cruickshank (114) notes that this is "A broadside news sheet [published at] St. John's, Antigua."

HALLAM, GEORGE
Narrative of a voyage from Montego Bay, in the island of Jamaica, to England . . . performed in the autumn, 1809. Also of a voyage from England to Barbados by Cadiz, Teneriffe, and Guadeloupe, in 1810.
London, 1831. 112 pp.   [LC, IJ]
Hallam went to Barbados to assume the governmental post of collector of customs. Part 2 of the book (*pp. 79–108*), entitled "Expedition to Barbados," describes the voyage, but ends with his arrival at the island and offers no information on Barbados itself.

"Hurricane at Barbados."
The Christian Remembrancer, vol. 13, London, 1831, *pp. 767–70.*   [BM]
A vivid eyewitness account of the devastating 1831 hurricane.

HUSBANDS, JOSEPH DOTTIN
An answer to the charge of immorality against the inhabitants of Barbadoes, which has recently been exhibited in a newspaper called the Albany Daily Advertiser.
Cooperstown: Printed for the author, 1831. 30 pp.   [NYPL]
The author was born in Barbados, and spent his childhood and "many of the first years of manhood" on the island. His pamphlet is a response to a couple of articles written by the editor of the Albany paper in which it was asserted that the "morals of the Barbadians are of a very low grade." "I was convinced," Husbands writes, "that the editor's sweeping accusation was unfounded, and I considered it to be an act of justice to myself, my family, and the inhabitants of Barbados to enter my solemn protest . . . against it." The editor had derived his information on Barbados from the account of J. A. Waller (1820) and much of Husbands's angry reaction is devoted to refuting Waller. In so doing, comments are offered on a variety of topics, e.g. sexual relations between the races,

taverns, prostitution, sexual and social behavior of whites, the effects of slavery on white behavior; also presented are some details on the physical features of Bridgetown and on the ceremonies in thanksgiving for deliverance from the 1780 hurricane.

[HYDE, SAMUEL]
Account of the fatal hurricane by which Barbados suffered in August 1831; . . . by the editor of the "West Indian."
Bridgetown, 1831. 152 pp.   [BMHS]
A lengthy account of one of Barbados's most devastating hurricanes in which the damage to the Bridgetown and Garrison areas is described in considerable detail, and the effects in each parish are reported in three to five-page summaries. Also included are an index of casualties; value of property destroyed; weather charts, etc. Contains a variety of useful information on the architecture of principal buildings, topography of Bridgetown and the Garrison area, social reactions to disaster, etc. Author attribution is given by the Barbados Department of Archives (Michael Chandler, personal communication).

LUCKOCK, BENJAMIN
The terrors of the storm practically remembered. A sermon preached at the parish church of St. Johns, Antigua, on Friday the 16th of September 1831; being a day of general thanksgiving and humiliation for the preservation of the island from the hurricane which had recently desolated Barbados.
Walsall [1831]. 31 pp.   [NYPL, BC]
The preface (*pp. v–vii*) contains extracts, of no particular value, from two eyewitness accounts of the hurricane. Although Luckock implies in his sermon that he was in Barbados during the storm, his references to the experience are very general.
Sabin (42634) cites a title with slightly different wording.

LYON, SIR JAMES
A proclamation.
[Bridgetown, 1831.]
Listed as a separately published proclamation by Ragatz (*p. 45*). See *Parliamentary Papers* (1831–32, vol. 31, Report 197).

ORDERSON, I. W.

Spare minutes at the pier; or, a short discussion on the equality of rights that may be granted to the free coloured inhabitants of this island.

Barbados, 1831. *16 pp.*

In considering a more liberal attitude "towards the Free Coloured People," Orderson argues that a distinction should be made between "free-born subjects" and "emancipated slaves." To the former "we would concede, *without restriction or impediment,* every political right and privilege of citizenship which the constitution and laws of the country confer on ourselves," while the latter should not enjoy such "privileges" until they had been emancipated for at least five years. However, he also argues that "there are . . . *other* privileges, that we denominate *social* or *domestic,* to the concession of which there are obstacles that lie deeper than any law can reach . . . [and] the Free Coloured members of our community, will yet, notwithstanding their extended *political* rights, be as far from participating in as ever." That is, among other things, he cannot entertain the notion of free coloreds serving in leading capacities in the island's political, judicial, religious, or military institutions.

This is a rare pamphlet; the only copy I know of is located in the Foreign and Commonwealth Office (formerly Colonial Office) Library in London. *See* Orderson (1816) for a discussion of the author's name.

PHILLIPS, TOBIAS

The Barbados Almanack, for the year 1832.

Liverpool [1831]. *62 pp.* [IJ]

Information similar to that presented in the author's previous almanacs.

*The present state of the British sugar colonies. [By?] a Gentleman of Barbados to his friend in London.

London, 1831.

"The planters were all but ruined due to oppressive fiscal legislation and the competition of East India sugar in both home and continental European markets. Emancipation would complete their bankruptcy" (Ragatz, *p. 263*).

*Public meeting of planters, merchants, etc.

[Kingstown, St. Vincent, 1831.]

"It was agreed to send two delegates to a proposed meeting of representatives of the Caribbean colonies in Barbados to commence on March 1, 1831 for the purpose of impressing the urgent necessity for immediate relief on the home Government" (Ragatz, *p. 264*).

*Recapitulation of the number of persons killed, wounded, those who have died of wounds, and those missing in consequence of the hurricane of August, 1831.

Bridgetown [1831?].

"A broadside. The number of deaths is given as about 2,500 and of wounded at least 5,000" (Ragatz, *p. 181*).

Report from the Committee of the Codrington Trust, to the Society for the Propagation of the Gospel in Foreign Parts, adopted at a general meeting of the Society, Friday, 21st Jan. 1831.

London, 1831. *12 pp.* [USPG, BOS]

This report originally appeared in the Society's Annual Report for 1830 (*pp. 162–69*). It is directed to the issue of a Christian body owning a slave plantation, and proposes a series of measures to prepare the way for gradual emancipation.

*SOCIETY FOR THE PROPAGATION OF THE GOSPEL IN FOREIGN PARTS

Report of the Society . . . on the condition of the Negro population on the Codrington Estate in the island of Barbados [January 21, 1831].

Winchester [1831]. [BM]

*[YEARWOOD, SAMUEL]

A pocket-book containing an Almanack for the island of Barbados for Bissextile or Leap Year [1832]. Also other useful information of a local nature. Original poetry, speeches, miscellaneous compositions, charades, etc. etc. Collected and compiled by a Barbadian.

[London? 1831.] [BMHS]

Cited by E. M. Shilstone ("Book and Pocket Almanacs." *Jl. BMHS,* 28, 1960–61, *80–81*): "Contents — A map of Barbados and frontispiece. Advertisement by compiler in relation to the publication, inviting correspondence.

A pocket-book with flap, size 4¾ × 3¼ ins. . . . Evidently this Almanac was continued annually at least as late as 1836; since the following advertisement appeared in *The Barbadian Newspaper* for 21 October 1835 – 'A Barbadian offers his Pocket Almanacks for 1836, both exceedingly improved in arrangement; price increased. Souvenirs $2 ½ and sheet almanack 35 cents. Containing a print of the Cathedral, with accommodation and names of occupants. Sold at Mr. Gill's and Mr. Armstrong's, Druggists, Broad Street.'" This quote, and those in S. Yearwood (1837) and T. Phillips (1832), indicate authorship. In addition, the author notes in the "advertisement" to his 1833 almanac (1832) that he had published one for 1832.

BAYLEY, F. W. N.
Four years residence in the West Indies, during the years 1826, 7, 8, and 9. A new edition adding an account of the hurricane of 1831.
London, 1832. *742 pp.* [BPL]
Bayley, a flamboyant, subjective, and pompous writer, spent four months in Barbados at the age of twenty-three. Many of his comments on island life, pages 88–152, refer to the slaves whom he felt to be well off and comfortable although he considers himself as an opponent of slavery *per se*. The first edition appeared in 1830 (Sabin 4051).

COLERIDGE, HENRY NELSON
Six months in the West Indies in 1825. Third edition with additions.
London, 1832. *311 pp.* [BM]
The author's four- to five-month visit to Barbados is reported in pages 37–56, 123–27, and 265–86. Despite the length of his stay, the information he provides on various aspects of social conditions is disappointingly brief. Although not an emancipationist, he nonetheless appeals for a liberalization of the slave system.
 The first edition was published in London in 1826; a fourth appeared in 1848 (Sabin 14318, 14319).

*COLERIDGE, WILLIAM HART
On the right hearing of God's work, a sermon.
Barbados, 1832. *26 pp.* [BOS]

PHILLIPS, TOBIAS
The Barbados Almanack, for the year 1833.
Liverpool [1832]. *69 pp.* [IJ]
Similar information to that presented in the author's previous almanacs. An advertisement in the *Barbadian*, November 17, 1832, indicates that this almanac series appeared in more than simply a pocket-book form: "The subscriber informs his friends and the Public in general that his ALMANACKS for 1833 have arrived, and are now for sale. . . . Pocket Almanack in roan covers . . . pocket almanack, in paper covers . . . sheet almanack. . . . The subscriber . . . being the Native who first calculated and compiled an Almanack . . . and laid the foundation for the one compiled by a Barbadian [*see* S. Yearwood, 1831, etc.], Tobias Phillips." (Quoted in E. M. Shilstone, "Book and Pocket Almanacs," *Jl. BMHS*, 28, 1960–61, *81*.)

The seaman's practical guide, for Barbadoes and the Leeward Islands, . . . all taken from actual observations by a captain in the Royal Navy.
London, 1832. *76 pp.* [BM]
Detailed information (*pp. 9–10, 17–19*) on how to approach Barbados, where to anchor, location of shoals, etc.

SIMMONS, HENRY PETER
A letter to the Right Honourable Earl Grey, First Lord of the Treasury, etc. On the subject of West Indian property.
London, 1832. *8 pp.* [BM]
Simmons, an absentee planter residing in Lymington, England, had owned property in Barbados for about thirty years. This letter was written prior to his departure from the island after conducting an inspection of his plantation. He argues against emancipation and claims that the West Indian slave receives better treatment and has greater material security than the poor in England. However, the major emphasis of the letter is to "solemnly protest against any interference with my colonial property without receiving ample compensation."

*Statement made by the Agent of Barbados

on the provisions of the colony as to the slave population.

London, 1832.

Listed in the Boston College catalog of its Williams Collection (Chestnut Hill, 1932, no. 1265); however, it is not recorded in the library's main catalog and a search of the stacks in August 1969 failed to produce it. Quite possibly this title refers to J. P. Mayers's report (see *Parliamentary Papers*, 1831–32, vol. 47, Report 739).

[YEARWOOD, SAMUEL]
  The Barbados Pocket-Book; or, lady's and gentleman's souvenir; containing an almanack for Barbados for the year of our Lord God [1833] . . . also, other useful information, poetry, charades, etc. etc. . . . By a Barbadian.
  [London? 1832.] *96 pp.*   [BOS]
Standard information is given in addition to the personal names of all members of the Barbados Council, House of Assembly, judges of the various courts, public officers, commissioners of peace, barristers, coroners, attorneys, fire company commissioners, British army officers and Barbados militia officers (the latter classified by rank and parish regiment), custom house officers, surveyors, etc. Also included, information on imports, exports, fees paid on clearing vessels, duties paid by vessels coming into the careenage; itemized duties on various imports and a list of duty-free items; information on the postal service, boatmens' and porters' fares (containing a detailed itemization of the streets of Bridgetown); lists of coins in circulation and their value in sterling. There is also a lengthy description of the 1831 hurricane.
  For authorship, *see* S. Yearwood (1831, 1837) and T. Phillips (1832).

ALEXANDER, CAPTAIN J. E.
  Transatlantic sketches, comprising visits to the most interesting scenes in North and South America and the West Indies, with notes on Negro slavery and Canadian emigration.
  London, 1833. 2 vols.   [BPL]
General and often cursory observations on Barbados where the author spent two weeks in 1831 (vol. 1, *pp. 140–80*). Reprinted in Philadelphia in 1833 (Sabin 735).

"Barbadoes, a Poem."
Blackwood's Edinburgh Magazine, vol. 34, Edinburgh, 1833, *pp. 503–28*
                                        [UL]
The author admits to not being a West Indian planter (one wonders if he had ever visited the West Indies at all), but his article defends their interests and stresses that the condition of the slave has vastly improved since the abolition of the slave trade. Much of the article is written around a review of Chapman's *Barbadoes and Other Poems* (1833), with whose point of view the author heartily agrees.

CHAPMAN, MATTHEW JAMES
  Barbadoes, and other poems.
  London, 1833. *210 pp.*   [BM]
Written by a Barbadian. The lengthy title poem extols the virtues of Barbados, its geography, history, people, etc., and reflects a point of view with respect to slavery which was not uncommon among Barbadian whites of the period, i.e. that the slave was content with his situation and generally happy with life, that those who cried out against the mistreatment of Barbados's slaves were ill-informed, and that emancipation would serve the interests of no one. The poem and the notes appended to it offer occasional useful pieces of information on the island's social life and customs.
  For biographical notes on Chapman, *see* F. A. Hoyos "Dr. M. J. Chapman" (*Jl. BMHS*, 16, 1948–49, *14–20*).

COLERIDGE, WILLIAM HART
  A letter addressed to . . . Sir Lionel Smith . . . relative to the distribution of the parliamentary grant for the relief of the sufferers from the hurricane of August 11th, 1831.
  [Barbados?], 1833. *16 pp.*   [BM]
Dated July 22, 1833, the letter offers an interesting account of the effects of a particularly devasting hurricane and the local social mechanisms employed for dealing with the resultant damage. The bickering and disputes in Barbados concerning the distribution of relief funds are also described.

Consecration Service. Used at the Jew's

Synagogue Nidchi Israel, Bridgetown, Barbadoes. In the year 5593.
[Barbados, 1833.] *25 pp.*   [NYPL]
Performed in moving into a new synagogue; the old one having been destroyed during the 1831 hurricane.

ELIOT, EDWARD
Christianity and slavery; in a course of lectures preached at the cathedral and parish church of St. Michael, Barbados.
London, 1833. *232 pp.*   [BM]
Six sermons delivered in 1832 to white congregations by the Archdeacon of Barbados. A moderately useful source for information on the institutional aspects of slavery, reflecting a relatively liberal churchman's thoughts on the subject. Eliot's objectives are, in his words, "to impress on the community the necessity of attending to the moral and religious welfare of the slave population." He stresses that he is not immediately concerned with the slaves' temporal life, but feels their condition has improved in recent years. These lectures cover the following topics: a discussion of the case for permitting slaves to be introduced to Christianity; a series of practical suggestions to be employed in disseminating Christianity to the slaves; "the causes of the infrequency of marriage among the slaves"; the kinds of obligations masters should have toward their slaves, e.g. treating them well, permitting their manumission when slaves have the money to pay for it, keeping the slave families intact, etc. These lectures were greeted adversely by some Barbadian planters.

*Extract from a Barbadian paper [The Barbadian] containing a report of the proceedings of the revival and re-establishment of Codrington College, in the island of Barbados.
London, 1833. *11 pp.*   [BOS]
Listed in the National Union Catalog.

Lieutenant-General Sir James Lyon . . . the subjoined report of the proceedings at a public meeting of the inhabitants of Barbadoes, held on the 10th of April, 1833, in consequence of the removal of General Sir James Lyon, K.C.B. . . . from the governorship of the island, is extracted from the Barbadian of the 13th of April.

[Winchester?], 1833. *4 pp.* [NYPL]
A two-page reprint of an article which first appeared in the *Barbadian*. It contains an address, delivered by Renn Hamden, lauding Governor Lyon, and comments by other Barbadians — all praising his conduct.

The other two pages of this reprint are blank, and were apparently left that way so it could be addressed and mailed. On the copy examined there is a handwritten note from George Coxe (postmarked Winchester, England, and dated June 16, 1833), addressed to his brother Peter Coxe in London, which explains the origin of this reprint. Coxe remarks "I have had a few copies struck off from the paper, The Barbadian, for the purpose of circulating them to my private friends. But totally unknown to Sir J. Lyon who in real modesty would dislike anything of the kind."

SIMMONS, HENRY PETER
A letter to the Right Hon. Earl Grey, on the West India question.
Liverpool, 1833. *37 pp.*   [BM]
The major theme of this absentee proprietor's second "letter" (*see also* Simmons, 1832) is that "the Negro is not yet fitted for his freedom" because he is morally and intellectually "defective"; "evidence" for this contention takes up most of this pamphlet.

*SMITH, SIR LIONEL
Copy of [Governor] Sir Lionel's speech on opening the legislature of Barbados, May 7, 1833.
[Barbados, 1833.]
Listed, but not annotated, by Ragatz (*p. 138*).

SOCIETY FOR THE PROPAGATION OF THE GOSPEL IN FOREIGN PARTS
Report of the Society for Propagating the Gospel in Foreign Parts on the condition of the Negro population on the Codrington Estate in the island of Barbados.
London, 1833. *11 pp.*   [BOS]
This tract addresses itself to criticisms levelled against the SPG for owning a slave plantation. "But surely," the tract notes, "the acceptance of a trust, which took place more than a century ago, when the great question of Negro

slavery had excited but little attention even in the more religious part of the community, is hardly to be brought forward as a charge against the present conductors of the institution, who, finding themselves in the character of trustees of West Indian property for a specific object . . . cannot feel themselves at liberty to abandon that trust, but are bound to make the wisest, best and most Christian use of it." The SPG had considered three plans for their estates: giving them up, immediate emancipation of the slaves, and making provisions for the slaves' gradual emancipation. The last course was decided upon, and the tract concentrates on the rationale behind this decision, pointing out that "to emancipate the [slaves] suddenly and indiscriminately would only be to injure the objects of our just and charitable solicitude." Preparing slaves for "gradual" emancipation includes religious education and encouragements to marry. Reproduced are eleven resolutions passed by the Society to serve as incentives for the slaves to marry, and an extract from a letter by the Bishop of Barbados, dated June 1830, reporting on his visit to the Codrington plantations and the favorable condition of the slaves.

[YEARWOOD, SAMUEL]
The Barbados Pocket-Book; or, lady's and gentleman's souvenir; containing an Almanack for Barbados for the year of our Lord God [1834]. . . . By a Barbadian.
[London? 1833.] *96 pp.* [BOS]
Contains information similar to that given in the author's almanac for the previous year. For authorship, *see* S. Yearwood (1831, 1837) and T. Phillips (1832).

*CLARK, CHARLES
A summary of colonial law, the practice of the Court of Appeals from the plantations, and of the laws and their administration in all the colonies; with charters of justice, orders in council, etc.
London, 1834. *746 pp.* [BM]
"An invaluable legal work. Considers the laws applying to the British Colonies in general, peculiarities of the system then prevailing in each, such acts of Parliament as imposed regula-

tions on the outlying possessions, and miscellaneous points of English law upon matters relating to the latter" (Ragatz, *p. 377*). Barbados is treated on pages 175–96.

MARRYAT, CAPTAIN FREDERICK
Peter Simple.
London, 1834. [BM]
Marryat, as an officer in the Royal Navy, visited Barbados around 1813. In this novel, Peter Simple also visits the island, and he briefly describes shipping and marketing activities in Carlisle Bay; a slave ship; and various characteristics and verbal expressions of the Negro population (chaper 30). In chapter 31, there is a detailed and unique description of a "Dignity Ball" held by Bridgetown's free colored population; Marryat himself had attended such a ball (*see* Oliver Warner, *Captain Marryat: A Rediscovery*, London, 1953). Simple returns to Barbados on a second trip and gives (chapter 50) a lengthy description of a Methodist service in Bridgetown conducted by a Negro preacher.

MARTIN, R. MONTGOMERY
History of the British colonies.
London, 1834–35. 5 vols. [BMHS]
The section on Barbados (vol. 2, *pp. 312–28*) is primarily a political and economic history based on written sources. The same materials are contained in the author's *History of the West Indies* (London, 1836–37, vol. 2, *pp. 185–211* [BMHS]). Martin "did not visit the West Indies until 1851, when official business took him to Jamaica" (Ragatz, *p. 172*).

PHILLIPS, TOBIAS
The Barbados Almanack, for the year 1835.
Liverpool [1834]. *76 pp.* [IJ]
Information similar to that included in the author's previous almanacs; also list of agricultural exports for 1833, and a short article (*pp. 61–62*) "The following is a specific cure for the disease called the Rose (vulgarly termed fever and ague) published by Dr. Abel Stewart, of Barbados."

ST. CLAIR, THOMAS STAUNTON
A residence in the West Indies and

America, with a narrative of the expedition to the island of Walcheren.
London, 1834. 2 vols.   [NYPL]
The author, an army officer, first visited Barbados in late 1806 or sometime in 1807 and stayed for a few months. The few details offered about his visit (vol. 1, *pp. 373–77*) include brief comments on the tavern in which he stayed in Bridgetown, his opinions on the effects of climate on health, and his noting that the "15th Regiment of Foot with the York Chasseurs, and the 7th West India Regiment constituted the force at this time quartered at Barbados" (the names of some officers are also given). Another visit of a month's duration was made in December 1808–January 1809 (vol. 2, *p. 233*), but the time was spent on board ship in Carlisle Bay, and no description of this visit is given.

This work was also published under the title *A Soldier's Recollections of the West Indies and America With a Narrative of the Expedition to the Island of Walcheren* (London, 1834 [BMHS]).

SIMMONS, HENRY PETER
 Third letter to the Right Hon. Earl Grey, First Lord of the Treasury, etc. On the question of Negro emancipation.
London, 1834. *15 pp.*   [BM]
This "letter" by an absentee proprietor with holdings in Barbados, treats various questions surrounding the issue of compensation to planters upon emancipation of the slaves. He reiterates some points made previously (*see* Simmons, 1832, 1833), and notes that his former reluctance to accept emancipation was not because he wanted slavery to continue but because he felt that with the Negro "character, a precipitant emancipation would bode no good for anyone."

SOCIETY FOR THE PROPAGATION OF THE GOSPEL IN FOREIGN PARTS
 Report respecting the Negroes on the Codrington Estates.
London, 1834.   [USPG]
Extracts from letters written in 1833 by the Bishop of Barbados and the Rev. Thomas Watts.

WENTWORTH, TRELAWNEY
 The West India Sketch Book.
London, 1834. 2 vols.
          [NYPL, BPL, LC]
The author lived in the West Indies for "several years" during the 1820s. Although he records something of his visit to Barbados (vol. 2, *pp. 278–99*) he does not say when and how long he was on the island. His observations are generally superficial, but brief comments are offered on speech patterns of the slave, physical aspects of Bridgetown and the countryside, and cooking; there are also extensive quotes from Richard Ligon (1657), and the transcription of a two-verse song, with musical notations, he heard sung by a "pretty mulatto wench." The author's name is given in volume 2 (*p. 385*). A second edition was published in London in 1835 (Sabin 102635).

COLERIDGE, WILLIAM HART
 An address privately delivered to candidates for the holy order of deacon, on the day previous to their ordination, May 27, 1835.
Barbados, 1835. *19 pp.*   [BOS]
A lecture which begins with advice on how to care for horses, keep personal accounts, dress, spend leisure time, and concludes with general comments on the moral and religious obligations of the deacon's role.

COLERIDGE, WILLIAM HART
 Charges delivered to the clergy of the diocese of Barbadoes and the Leeward Islands; together with prayers on certain public occasions and addresses to candidates for holy orders.
London, 1835. *324 pp.*   [BMHS]
An occasional reference within the text might be of use for a history of the Anglican church in Barbados, but this source is generally similar to the author's 1829 volume. The appendix presents various statistical and other information on the Barbados diocese.

MADDEN, R. R.
 A twelvemonth's residence in the West Indies during the transition from slavery to apprenticeship.
London, 1835. 2 vols.   [BMHS]
The author, a medical doctor, briefly

visited Barbados in late 1833 and records, often superficially, his impressions (vol. 1, *pp. 14–43*) on miscellaneous topics, e.g. Bridgetown taverns, slaves, population characteristics.

Sabin (43697) cites an 1835 Philadelphia edition.

PHILLIPS, TOBIAS
The Barbados Almanack, for the year 1836.
Liverpool [1835]. *78 pp.* [IJ]
Information similar to that published in the author's almanacs for previous years; also information on the police establishment, magistrates' fees, constables' fees, coins in circulation and their values. Also presented are the names of members of various standing committees, e.g. molehead committee, committee of correspondence, public accounts, town hall, market.

ROWLAND, THOMAS
Memoirs of the late Rev. Isaac Bradnack, Wesleyan Minister, and formerly a missionary in the West Indies.
London, 1835. *158 pp.* [IJ]
Bradnack arrived at Barbados in March 1804 and left for Jamaica at the end of that year. The pages devoted to his stay (*38–44*) sometimes contain brief extracts from his journal, and offer superficial comments on his missionary activities.

BROWN, WILLIAM HENRY
Journal of a voyage from London to Barbadoes.
Alnwick, 1836. *97 pp.* [IJ]
The author went to Barbados as an Anglican minister (missionary?), arriving in early 1835 after a "35 day passage." His journal (*pp. 1–57*) is primarily an account of the voyage itself, his impressions of Barbados (*pp. 54–56*) being confined to a description of the scene in Carlisle Bay as the ship's passengers disembarked. The remainder of the book (*pp. 59–97*) is comprised of poems written by the author.

CARTER, JOHN MONEY
Views in the island of Barbados, West Indies, on stone from drawings taken in the early part of the year 1835 by Lieut. J. M. Carter. The Royal Regt.
London [1836?]. [BMHS, BOS]

An apparently rare set of ten oblong folio sheets which may have been bound into a volume or contained in a folder. Each drawing has its own caption: *1*] The title page with a drawing "Chapel and School on the Society's Estate" [i.e. Codrington]; *2*] "Trafalgar Square, Bridgetown"; *3*] "Pilgrim, the Governor's Residence"; *4*] "Main Guard, St. Ann's Garrison"; *5*] "Bridgetown"; *6*] "St. Ann's Garrison"; *7*] "The Brick Barracks, St. Ann's Garrison"; *8*] "Codrington College"; *9*] "Near Worthing, Hastings in the Distance"; *10*] "Monument Near the Military Hospital."

The Barbados Museum and Historical Society has all but number 5, and the rare books room of the Boston Public Library has numbers 1, 3, 7, and 10.

*ELIOT, EDWARD
Christian responsibilities arising out of the recent change in our West Indies colonies, in five discourses.
London, 1836. [BM]
Eliot was Archdeacon of Barbados.

PHILLIPS, TOBIAS
The Barbados Almanack, for the year 1837.
Liverpool [1836]. *87 pp.* [IJ]
Information similar to that presented in the author's almanacs for previous years. Phillips's almanac series apparently continued through 1858 (E. M. Shilstone, "Book and Pocket Almanacs," *Jl. BMHS*, 28, 1960–61, *82*).

The Public Acts in force passed by the Legislature of Barbados from the first of William IV.
Bridgetown, 1836. *317 pp.*
Cited by Chandler (*A Guide to Records in Barbados*, Oxford, 1965, *p. 167*) who notes that a copy is located in the Colonial Office Library, England (now the library of the Foreign and Commonwealth Office).

ROLPH, DR. THOMAS
A brief account, together with observations, made during a visit in the West Indies, and a tour through the United States of America, in parts of the years 1832–3.
Dundas, U[pper] C[anada], 1836. *293 pp.* [BM, IJ]

Rolph is interested in showing that although slavery *per se* is bad, slaves are nonetheless happy, loyal, and materially secure. In 1833, he stayed about three months in Barbados, spending some time at Vaucluse plantation in St. Thomas, and his observations (*pp. 18–58*) provide information on the planters, poor whites, slaves, and Barbadian society in general. Reprinted in London in 1842 under the title *A Descriptive and Statistical Account of Canada* (Sabin 72877).

*SOCIETY FOR ADVANCING THE CHRISTIAN FAITH
    The two charters of the Society for Advancing the Christian Faith in the British West India Islands, and elsewhere, within the diocese of Jamaica and of Barbadoes, and the Leeward Islands.*
London, 1836. *32 pp.*
Sabin (85883) locates a copy at Columbia University.

HALLIDAY, SIR ANDREW
    The West Indies: the natural and physical history of the Windward and Leeward colonies; with some account of the moral, social, and political condition of their inhabitants, immediately before and after the abolition of Negro slavery.
London, 1837. *408 pp.* [BPL]
Pages 8–95 deal with Barbados where Halliday, the Deputy Inspector General of Army Hospitals, spent a little over three months in late 1833 and early 1834. Much of his account is devoted to a discussion of the physical condition and health problems of soldiers stationed on the island. Also included is an extensive geological description of Barbados, a description of the 1831 hurricane, and some minor details on religion, but virtually nothing on slave life.
    Sabin (29899, 29900) notes that "In some copies the title reads: The West Indies . . . with the History of the Past and Present State of British Guiana: A Geological Map of the Barbadoes, and a catalogue of Plants, by J. D. Maycock, M.D. London. 1837."

LLOYD, WILLIAM
    Letters from the West Indies during a visit

in the autumn of 1836 and the spring of 1837.
London [1837?]. *263 pp.*
[BMHS, NYPL]
An emancipationist's perspectives, primarily on the status of the Negro, during the apprenticeship period. Two short visits to Barbados are the basis for the brief and often superficial impressions recorded on pages 1–19, 80–119.
    Reprinted in Birmingham in 1839 [BM].

    The present condition of the Negro population in the British colonies; particularly in relation to the working of the apprenticeship system established under the "Act for the Abolition of Slavery."
London, 1837. *28 pp.* [BM]
Published by the London Anti-Slavery Society, this is based upon the reports of four of the Society's members who visited the West Indies (*see* Joseph Sturge and Thomas Harvey, 1838). There are occasional references to Barbados which are used as part of a general critique of the apprenticeship system, an indictment of the mistreatment and discrimination against apprentices, etc.

*YEARWOOD, SAMUEL
    The Barbados Pocket Book; or lady's and gentleman's souvenir containing an almanack for Barbados for the year of our Lord [1838]. Also, other useful information, poetry, charades, etc. . . . By Samuel Yearwood. Native of St. Lucy's Parish.*
[London, 1837.] [BMHS]
Cited by E. M. Shilstone ("Book and Pocket Almanacs." *Jl. BMHS*, 28, 1960–61, *81–82*): "Facing the title-page, a prospect of Codrington College. . . . It seems that this 'Souvenir' commenced to be published in 1832 [sic]. Page 2 [of the above almanac] 'On hand, a few copies of the Souvenir for 1832–33, 35–36. Persons wishing to have the series complete from the first publication, may do so at half price.'"

COLERIDGE, WILLIAM HART
    A charge delivered in the Cathedral Church of Barbados, July 25, 1838.
London, 1838. *145 pp.* [BOS]
The sermon (*pp. 3–33*) was delivered a few days before the end of the appren-

ticeship period and stresses the moral and religious obligations of the clergy. While much of it is devoted to theological topics *per se*, there is occasional information on the Barbados church establishment and the religious behavior of the apprentice with respect to the Anglican church. The appendix (*pp. 44–145*) contains a variety of other addresses Coleridge delivered since 1835 including those given between 1835 and 1838 at cornerstone-laying ceremonies for the reconstruction of parish churches destroyed during the 1831 hurricane.

HODGSON, CAPTAIN STUDHOLME
Truths from the West Indies. Including a sketch of Madeira in 1833.
London, 1838. *372 pp.* [BM, BMHS]
The author was in the West Indies from late December 1833 to the end of 1836. It is clearly implied in a number of places in the book that he visited Barbados, although he appears to have spent most of his time in Trinidad. Hodgson discusses a wide variety of social conditions, customs, and institutional behavior and is particularly critical of the planters and their treatment of slaves. Although there are occasionally specific references to Barbados, whatever value the book might have is largely minimized by the author's general failure to identify specific islands in his discussions of particular topics.

HOVEY, SYLVESTER
Letters from the West Indies: relating especially to the Danish island St. Croix, and to the British islands Antigua, Barbadoes and Jamaica.
New York, 1838. *212 pp.* [BPL]
The author, an American professor, was sent to the West Indies by the American Union for the Relief and Improvement of the Colored Race, specifically "to collect and diffuse facts in respect to the condition of slavery and of the Africa Race." He visited Barbados sometime between 1835 and 1837. Although his observations are immediately relevant to the Apprenticeship period, there are a variety of useful materials (*pp. 94–120 passim*) pertaining to social life which are applicable to the pre-1834 period.

KELLY, JAMES
Jamaica in 1831: being a narrative of seventeen years' residence in that island.
Belfast, 1838. *60 pp.* [IJ]
In April 1814, the author stopped at Barbados for "a few hours" while on his way to Jamaica. A paragraph (*p. 1*) describes his impressions of Bridgetown's black and white population (e.g., "I was disgusted with the appearance of the white creoles I saw. The contrast between our rosy-cheeked selves and them produced an extempore feeling of exultation. . . . I was struck with the shining faces of the Negroes . . . [and] was astonished to learn that they were the slaves of the same haggard-looking creoles I had been so shocked with . . .").

STURGE, JOSEPH AND HARVEY, THOMAS
The West Indies in 1837; being the journal of a visit to Antigua, Montserrat, Dominica, St. Lucia, Barbadoes, and Jamaica; undertaken for the purpose of ascertaining the actual condition of the Negro population of those islands.
2nd ed., rev. London, 1838. *476 pp.* [BPL]
The authors feel that despite emancipation the apprenticeship system contains many elements of the slave system. They spent a little over two weeks in Barbados in 1836–37, and their treatment of the island (*pp. 1–7, 117–43*), although concentrating upon the life of the apprentice, contains materials relevant to the pre-1834 period. Information, largely derived from conversations with whites, is provided on topics such as schools, churches, free colored, color prejudice, and the Bridgetown jail.

The first edition was also published in 1838 (Sabin 93264); *see* Sabin (93259–61) for other works by Sturge relating to the West Indies.

THOME, J. A. AND KIMBALL, J. H.
Emancipation in the West Indies. A six months' tour in Antigua, Barbados, and Jamaica in the year 1837.
New York, 1838. *128 pp.* [BC]
The authors, representatives of the American Anti-Slavery Society, spent about two months in Barbados where they were concerned with observing and describing the operation of the apprenticeship system. Their account

(*pp. 53–84*) is an extremely valuable source for social conditions at this time, and includes as well a variety of useful materials comparing the apprenticeship with the slave period.

The second edition was published in New York in 1839 (Sabin 95460).

CUST, SIR EDWARD
Reflections on West India affairs, after a recent visit to the colonies. Addressed to the consideration of the Colonial Office.
London, 1839. *88 pp.*   [NYPL, LC]
The author visited Barbados sometime after emancipation, but specific references to the island are few and very brief. Some opinions are offered on the life of the emancipated slave (*pp. 8–9*); the landscape is described by noting "In Little England . . . the roads (not so good as they might be) are stirring with a busy population on foot, on horseback, and in carriages. The land is one uninterrupted field of sugar cane and guinea corn, for there are few trees and no woods. . . . The cottages

are here devoted each to a single family; they are surrounded very frequently with a little garden for cassava, ginger, aloes, peppers etc.; in some cases . . . a pretty flower bower decorates the door of the Negro dwelling" (*p. 18*); additional brief comments are offered on white females and the island's future (*pp. 48, 83*).

NUGENT, LADY MARIA
A journal of a voyage to, and residence in the island of Jamaica, from 1801 to 1805.
London, 1839. 2 vols.   [BM]
On her way to Jamaica, the author stopped at Barbados for barely two days in July. Her experiences in the Bridgetown area are recorded in a page or two, and include brief comments on the scene in Carlisle Bay, Governor Seaforth, living accommodations, etc. Reprinted, with notes by Frank Cundall, under the title *Lady Nugent's Journal* in 1907, 1934, and 1939. A 1966 edition is edited by Philip Wright.

1840–1968

EASEL, THEODORE
Desultory sketches and tales of Barbados.
London, 1840. *264 pp.*   [BMHS]
Easel wrote this book *en route* to England after having spent a few weeks in Barbados sometime after the apprenticeship period. His experiences on the island are related in random fashion and largely in anecdotal form; they range over a variety of topics, such as, island society, geography, etc. Included are discussions of the behavior and customs of the plantocracy; comments on the Negro population since emancipation; and a story, "The Obiah-man, or a tale of St. Philips," which had been told to Easel and which deals with the behavior of a particular slave during the 1816 insurrection. The author identifies himself on pages 8–9, but the name may be a pseudonym.

A letter to the Right Hon. Lord Stanley, M.P., Principal Secretary of State for the Colonies, on the sugar question, with some

account of the anomalous position of Barbados . . . by a late member of the House of Assembly.
London, 1842. *60 pp.*   [BM]
Pages 1–44 of this pamphlet are devoted to an exposition of labor and economic problems of Barbados in the immediate postemancipation years, especially that of labor migrations to Guiana. Pages 45–60 (the appendix) include case materials on laborers who had been induced to leave Barbados to work on plantations in that country.

ORDERSON, J. W.
Creoleana: or, social and domestic scenes and incidents in Barbados in days of yore.
London, 1842. *246 pp.*   [BMHS, IJ]
Set against the background of Barbadian society in the last quarter of the eighteenth century, this novel (apparently written in the late 1830s) focuses upon the amorous relationship between the children of two planter families. Although occasional information is

provided on Barbados and the customs and mores of the plantocracy, the author, a Barbadian, is less concerned with societal context than with the personality and behavior of his characters. *See* Orderson (1816) for discussion of the author's name.

* The Public Acts in force, passed by the Legislature of Barbados, in the first, second, third and fourth years of the reign of Her Majesty Queen Victoria.
Bridgetown, 1842. *316 pp.*
Cited by Chandler (*A Guide to Records in Barbados*, Oxford, 1965, *p. 167*) who notes that a copy is located in the Colonial Office Library, England (now the library of the Foreign and Commonwealth Office).

Letters from the Virgin Islands, illustrating life and manners in the West Indies.
London, 1843. *286 pp.* [IJ, LC, BM]
The author, a colonial official, stopped at Barbados for about a month, sometime between 1820 and 1830. Remaining in Bridgetown, his impressions (*pp. 1–6*) are confined to a brief description of the daily scene he viewed from the veranda of Betsey Austin's "hotel," a brief sarcastic commentary on the Barbados militia which he observed training one day, and comments on a "half-caste," Sidney Smith, who would stand by Nelson's statue and harangue passersby with comments on the state of Barbados and its womenfolk. While in Tortola, the author met William Chaderton "a native of Barbados [who] like many other young creoles of limited fortune, first directed his attention to medicine . . ." but who later became a clergyman. While in the Virgins, Chaderton "by death of his father in Barbados [inherited] a property in domestic slaves. . . . They were not liberated immediately for, as the rector would justly argue, freedom brings with it duties in the social body, and without some training for those, it often degenerates into sheer indolence and apathy" (*pp. 128–30*).

[FLANNIGAN, MRS.]
Antigua and the Antiguan: a full account of the colony and its inhabitants.
London, 1844. 2 vols. [BM]

The author makes a few passing references to Barbados where she paid "a short visit" sometime in the 1830s; she describes the island's poor white inhabitants ("I never saw so truly wretched a class") and offers a brief comment on clothes-washing by the seaside (vol. 2, *pp. 100–102, 144*). *See* Ragatz (*p. 224*) for authorship.

* The Public Acts in force, passed by the Legislature of Barbados between the 8th April 1800, and the 1st year of the reign of King William the Fourth.
Bridgetown, 1844. *230 pp.*
Cited by Chandler (*A Guide to Records in Barbados*, Oxford, 1965, *p. 167*) who notes that a copy is located in the Colonial Office Library, England (now the library of the Foreign and Commonwealth Office).

TRUMAN, GEORGE; JACKSON, JOHN; AND LONGSTRETH, THOMAS
Narrative of a visit to the West Indies, in 1840 and 1841.
Philadelphia, 1844. *130 pp.* [NYPL]
The authors, American Quakers, visited Barbados for about two weeks in early 1841; their "narrative," relating to the island (*pp. 67–82*), contains useful observations on schools, churches, plantation labor, and comparisons with the slave period. Also included are summaries of conversations held with Samuel Prescod "a colored man, and editor of a paper called 'The Liberal.'"

CAPADOSE, LIEUTENANT COLONEL [HENRY]
Sixteen years in the West Indies.
London, 1845. 2 vols. [BM]
The author arrived at Barbados in October 1840 and stayed approximately three months. The island is treated on pages 1–61 of volume 2, a little less than half of these pages being devoted to a fairly literal translation of Father Labat's (1722) description of Barbados in 1700. The remaining pages contain information on various aspects of social life and customs which could be applicable to the pre-1834 period as well.

PHILLIPS, P. LOVELL
An essay on tropical agriculture. With

some remarks on certain analyses of
Barbadian soils, etc.
3rd ed. Glasgow, 1845. *120 pp.*
                                    [WIC]
The author, a former resident of Barbados, tries to encourage planters to
adopt scientific methods of agriculture,
and devotes most of this work to a
detailed discussion of soil chemistry,
manuring, etc., with occasional brief
references to actual plantation agricultural practices. Some of the latter
information may be applicable to pre-
1834.

GARRISON, WILLIAM LLOYD (ed.)
  *"Extracts from the journal of Major John
  B. Colthurst [in 1835–1838]."*
  The Liberator, Boston, July 23, 1847–
  January 14, 1848.   [NYPL]
See Manuscripts, Boston Public Library
(Ms. U.1.2).

PARRY, THOMAS
  *Codrington College, in the island of
  Barbados.*
  London, 1847. *64 pp.*   [BM]
A chronologically arranged history, by
the Bishop of Barbados, which heavily
relies upon, and extensively quotes
from, official reports of the Society for
the Propagation of the Gospel in
Foreign Parts. The pamphlet also
contains a brief section on the religious
instruction of slaves.

SCHOMBURGK, SIR ROBERT H.
  The History of Barbados.
  London, 1848. *722 pp.*   [BM]
Ragatz's (*p. 183*) evaluation of this
volume is quite apt: "This book is a
classic in West Indian history. It is a
scholarly study . . . based largely on
research done in the British Museum
Library and that of the Literary
Society of Barbados. Much use has been
made of official publications, local
newspapers, and information gained
by personal experiences . . . there are
many footnotes and references to
sources." The work is an especially
useful guide to, and reference for, the
island's pre-1834 history as Schomburgk's discussion follows a more or less
annual chronology.
  Also by Schomburgk: *A Topographical
Map of the Island of Barbados based upon*

Mayo's [1722] *Original Survey in 1721
and Corrected to the Year 1846* (London,
1847 [BM]).

DAVY, JOHN
  *Lectures on the study of chemistry . . . and
  discourses on agriculture; with introductions
  on the present state of the West Indies, and
  on the agricultural societies of Barbados.*
  London, 1849. *291 pp.*   [BM, IJ]
The author, a medical doctor, was
stationed in Barbados for a few years;
he arrived on the island in July 1845.
Although these five lectures are primarily concerned with various aspects of
the physical sciences, they contain some
valuable materials on agricultural practices and sugar making in Barbados
which can easily refer to the pre-1834
period as well. In addition, the
author's introduction contains some
useful short histories of agricultural
societies on the island.

DAY, CHARLES WILLIAM
  Five years residence in the West Indies.
  London, 1852. 2 vols.   [BPL]
The strongly ethnocentric and prejudicial account of Barbadian society
and culture (vol. 1, *pp. 1–64*) is based
upon the author's visit to the island in
late 1846.

BRUCE, JOHN (ed.)
  *Letters and papers of the Verney family
  down to the end of the year 1639.
  Printed from the original mss.*
  London, 1853. *308 pp.*   [BMHS]
Only one of the letters reproduced in
this volume (pp. 192–95) deals with
Barbados. Written in 1638 by Thomas
Verney, it is largely devoted to a description and discussion of the island's
food and commercial crops. For more
on the Verney family, with occasional
references to Barbados, *see* F. P.
Verney, *Memoirs of the Verney Family
During the Civil War* (London, 1892, 2
vols.), and M. M. Verney, *Memoirs of
the Verney Family During the Commonwealth,
1650 to 1660* (London, 1894).

SHURTLEFF, NATHANIEL B. (ed.)
  *Records of the Governor and company of
  the Massachusetts Bay in New England.*
  Boston, 1853–54. 5 vols.   [SIU, BM]
Indexes to the volumes, which contain

verbatim transcriptions of records from 1628 to 1686, occasionally mention Barbados, but the very brief textual references, mainly relating to trade relationships with New England, have very limited informational value.

DAVY, JOHN
The West Indies, before and since slave emancipation . . . founded on notes and observations collected during a three year's residence.
London, 1854 *551 pp.* [BM, LC]
The lengthy section of Davy's book devoted to Barbados (chaps. 2–4, *pp. 33–162*) is based upon written materials and his own observations during the late 1840s. He ranges over a variety of social patterns and agricultural practices and makes frequent comparisons with the preemancipation period based upon his reading and discussions with informants. His description of sugar production and plantation agricultural practices is especially detailed, and there are, as well, lengthy discussions of the island's lower-class whites and the social life of the former slave population.

SHURTLEFF, NATHANIEL B. (ed.)
Records of the colony of New Plymouth in New England . . . [1623–1692].
Boston, 1855–61. 12 vols. [BM]
A search of the detailed indexes at the end of each volume yielded only two minor references to Barbados (vol. 9, *pp. 197, 199*).

*TAYLOR, GEORGE N. AND PACKER, CHARLES (eds.)
Laws of Barbados [1646–1854].
Vol. 1. London, 1855. [BM]

REECE, ROBERT
Hints to young Barbados planters.
London, 1857. *214 pp.* [BM]
Apparently an absentee proprietor at the time of writing, the author devotes a considerable amount of this work to the use of fertilizers, but there is also information on sugar making, and a detailing of the kinds of activities which should be performed throughout the agricultural year. Some of the information presented may be applicable to the pre-1834 period.

COGGESHALL, GEORGE
Thirty-six voyages to various parts of the world, made between the years 1799 and 1841.
3rd ed. New York, 1858. *583 pp.*
[NYPL, LC]
The author, an American sailor, spent some of his seafaring days traveling between New England and the West Indies; yet, on return voyages from Brazil in 1838, 1839, and 1841 his ship passed by Barbados without stopping. Earlier editions of this work (1851, 1852–53) do not mention the island.

MOISTER, REVEREND WILLIAM
Memorials of missionary labours in Western Africa, the West Indies, and at the Cape of Good Hope.
3rd ed., rev. and enl. London, 1866.
[BC]
Moister lived in Barbados for almost two years, 1835–37. The account of his stay (*pp. 276–302*) is primarily concerned with Methodist activities and the history of Methodism on the island. The BM catalog lists an 1850 London edition.

SHREWSBURY, JOHN V. B.
Memorials of W. J. Shrewsbury.
London, 1868. *528 pp.* [BM]
A biography in which William Shrewsbury's residence in Barbados during the early 1820s is treated on pages 89–204. This is a valuable source for a history of Methodism in Barbados as it reproduces lengthy extracts from Shrewsbury's own letters and journals, only some of which are available in manuscript form in the archives of the Methodist Missionary Society in London.

WINTHROP, ROBERT C. (ed.)
Life and letters of John Winthrop, Governor of the Massachusetts Bay Company, at their emigration to New England, 1630.
2nd ed. Boston, 1869. [SIU]
The volume contains occasional, very brief, references to Henry Winthrop, John's second son, who had been a member of Barbados's first colonizing party in 1627. None of the letters in which Henry is referred to were written from the island.

WHITE, FATHER ANDREW
"Narrative of a Voyage to Maryland [in 1633–1634]."
Maryland Historical Society, Fund Publication, no. 7.
Baltimore, 1874. *43 pp.* [BM]
In 1634, the author, an English Jesuit accompanying Lord Baltimore, spent three weeks in Barbados while his ship was being provisioned. His account (*pp. 23–27*) offers a few sparse comments on island society and a planned uprising of indentured servants, but most of the few pages are devoted to the island's plant life. White's account was written in Latin, and in this volume the English translation is given next to the transcription of the Latin manuscript. Another translated version of the manuscript is available in Peter Force, ed., *Tracts and Other Papers*, vol. 4 (Washington, 1846), *pp. 1–47*.
For details on these translations, etc., *see* Sabin (103352–353).

LAWRENCE-ARCHER, CAPTAIN J. H.
Monumental inscriptions of the British West Indies.
London, 1875. *442 pp.* [NYPL]
Contains (*pp. 345–501*) transcriptions of seventeenth- and eighteenth-century markings on tombstones in the burial grounds of Barbados parish churches (*see also* Manuscripts, BM, Additional 23608 and 27969).

Laws of Barbados [1648–1858]. Vol. I.
London, 1875. [BM]

DAVIS, N. DARNELL
The Cavaliers and Roundheads of Barbados, 1650–1652, with some account of the early history of Barbados.
Georgetown, British Guiana, 1887. *261 pp.* [BM]
Focusing upon political history, this well-known study is based upon research into primary sources and occasionally provides transcriptions of seventeenth-century documents, letters, etc.

STEVENS, B. F. (ed.)
Facsimiles of manuscripts in European archives relating to America 1773–1783, with descriptions, editorial notes, collations, references and translations.
London, 1889–95. 25 vols.
[NYPL, LC]
The index (vol. 25) indicates that Barbados is mentioned in a handful of letters in various volumes.

MOREAU, EMILE (ed.)
Voyages de Daniel le Hirbec de Laval aux Antilles, aux Pays-Bas, et en Italie, 1642–1644.
Laval, 1890. *92 pp.* [BM]
A transcription of a manuscript written by Le Hirbec. Pages 19–20 include a description of Barbados (primarily relating to agricultural products) where the author spent about one-and-a-half days in June 1642.

BOVELL, HENRY A. AND GREAVES, W. HERBERT
Laws of Barbados, 1667–1894.
Bridgetown, 1893. 3 vols. INDEX.
Bridgetown, 1894. [BM]
Volume 1, covering the period 1667–1886, includes one seventeenth-century and six eighteenth-century laws, but none from the nineteenth century prior to 1834.

GREAVES, W. HERBERT AND CLARKE, C. P. (eds.)
Report of cases relating to Barbados to be found in the English law reports [1694–1893] and of certain cases argued and determined by the local courts.
Bridgetown, 1897. *210 pp.* [LC]
Only two cases in this volume (*pp. 1–3*) are relevant to the pre-1840 period. One treats a 1694 case involving the extension of English laws into the colonies, the other an 1831 case relating to mortgages and foreclosures.

TOPPAN, ROBERT N. (ed.)
Edward Randolph; including his letters and official papers from the New England ... 1676–1703.
The Prince Society, Boston, 1898–99. 5 vols. [BM]
Randolph apparently never visited Barbados, but these volumes (*see* indexes) occasionally contain very brief references to the island and its trade relations with North America.

*DANIELS, EDWARD S.
Extracts from various records regarding the settlement of the Jews in the island of Barbados.
Bridgetown, 1899. *8 pp.*
A rare work. Listed by an abbreviated title in Cruickshank (187) and Cundall (101b). The National Union Catalog locates a copy at Harvard University. *See* Edward S. Daniels (1918).

FIRTH, C. H. (ed.)
The narrative of General Venables, with an appendix of papers relating to the expedition to the West Indies and the conquest of Jamaica, 1654–1685.
Camden Society Publications, N.S. 60, London, 1900. [BM]
Extracts from the 1655 journal of Henry Whistler are reproduced (*see* BM, Sloane Mss. 3926, *fols. 7–10*); other information on Barbados is largely relevant to military matters.

JEFFERY, REGINALD W. (ed.)
Dyott's diary, 1781–1845, a selection from the journal of William Dyott, sometime general in the British Army and Aide-de-Camp to his Majesty King George III.
London, 1907. 2 vols. [BM]
Dyott visited Barbados for a few weeks in early 1796, and his impressions, mainly on the Bridgetown area, are recorded in volume 1 (*pp. 90–95*). Although his comments are cursory, they contain some useful information on various aspects of social life, military matters, and slavery.

HOSMER, JAMES KENDALL (ed.)
[John] Winthrop's journal, "History of New England," 1630–1649.
New York, 1908. 2 vols. [BM]
Volume 2 contains an occasional brief and superficial reference to Barbados's contacts with New England.

DAVIS, N. DARNELL
"Notes on the History of the Jews in Barbados."
American Jewish Historical Society Publications, no. 18, Baltimore, 1909, *pp. 129–148.* [BM]
A potpourri of materials transcribed from various printed sources, e.g. W. Dickson (1789), Chapman (1833),

and manuscripts, covering the period from the seventeenth through early twentieth centuries.

DAVIS, N. DARNELL
"Glimpses of the Past."
Reprinted from the *Barbados Advocate*, May 12 and 17, 1910. [BM]
Includes a brief introduction by Davis and transcriptions of miscellaneous seventeenth-century letters, e.g. a 1649 letter from the Rev. James Parker, after his arrival in Barbados, to Governor Winthrop in Massachusetts.

OLIVER, VERE LANGFORD (ed.)
Caribbeana: being miscellaneous papers relating to the history, genealogy, topography and antiquities of the British West Indies.
London, 1910–20. 6 vols. [BM]
Having ceased publication with its sixth volume, this quarterly journal largely reproduced items such as old wills, deeds, parish records, newspaper extracts, and similar materials. Although these materials were selected to illuminate family histories and genealogies, they often contained information on broader sociocultural topics. A detailed name index and table of contents in each volume facilitates the location of information relevant to Barbados.

DOW, G. F. (ed.)
Records and files of the quarterly courts of Essex County, Massachusetts.
Boston, 1911–21. 8 vols. [BM]
Each volume of these seventeenth-century records (which start in 1636) is copiously indexed. References to Barbados are generally very brief and largely relate to the island's trade relations with New England.

"Values in Barbados in 1828.
The West India Committee Circular*, vol. 26, London, 1911, *pp. 396–97.*
[WIC]
Reproduces part of the original inventory and valuation of Clapham, Nathan Lucas's plantation in St. Michael and Christ Church parishes.

GOODMAN, G. AUBREY, AND CLARKE, C. P. (eds.)

Laws of Barbados [*1667–1891*].
  Vol. 1. Barbados, 1912.   [BM]
Contains five pre-1834 laws: 1667, 1713,
1745, 1754, 1762.

*"A Letter of Marque, 1813."
West India Committee Circular, London,
  March 25, 1913, *p. 132*   [WIC]
"Issued by the Governor of Barbados,
authorizing privateering against Ameri-
can shipping" (Ragatz, *p. 255*).

OPPENHEIM, SAMUEL
  "*The Jews in Barbados in 1739. An
  Attack Upon Their Synagogue. Their
  Long Oath."*
  *American Jewish Historical Society Pub-
  lications*, vol. 22, Baltimore, 1914, *pp.
  197–98.*   [RCS, NYPL]
A transcription of a brief article which
first appeared in Bradford's *New York
Gazette* (no. 725, October 1–8, 1739).
The article is based upon a letter,
received from Barbados by the editor,
which describes the reasons why a mob
set fire to the Speightstown synagogue;
also reproduced is the oath used by
Jews in Barbadian courts.

OLIVER, VERE LANGFORD
  *The monumental inscriptions in the
  churches and churchyards of the island
  of Barbados, British West Indies.*
  London, 1915. *223 pp.*   [NYPL, LC]
These approximately fifteen hundred
inscriptions, many of which date prior
to 1834, were copied during the winter
of 1913–14; "they comprise all those in
churches and churchyards, but not
those in dissenting chapels or modern
cemeteries. About 100 of the oldest
Jewish inscriptions [from the Jewish
burial ground] have also been included." Oliver adds that some of the
inscriptions recorded by J. H. Lawrence-
Archer (1875) are "no longer to be seen
so that his collection is still invaluable
and is in no way depreciated by the
appearance of the present volume."

DANIELS, EDWARD S.
  "*Extracts from various records of the
  early settlement of the Jews in the island
  of Barbados."*
  *American Jewish Historical Society Pub-
  lications*, vol. 26, Baltimore, 1918, *pp.
  250–56.*   [NYPL]

In a footnote to this article it is pointed
out that "this material [is] drawn from
an eight-page folio leaflet, printed for
private distribution in a limited edition" (*see* Daniels, 1899). The extracts
include, "Levy of taxes in pounds of
Muscovado sugar on the Hebrew nation
inhabitants in and about Bridgetown
towards defraying the charges of this
parish . . ." February 13, 1679/80 (*pp.
250–51*); a list of some of the members
of the seventeenth-century congregation "Kaal Kadosh Nidhi Israel" (*p.
251*); "Extracts from old minute books
of the Hebrew congregation" covering
the period 1752–1841 (*pp. 251–55*);
"Extracts from Schomburgk's *History
of Barbados*" dealing with the island's
Jewish community and synagogue (*pp.
255–56*); comments by Daniels, a
leading member of the island's Jewish
community, on the state of the community in the late nineteenth century
(*p. 256*).

GANDY, WALLACE (ed.)
  *The association oath rolls of the British
  plantations . . . A.D. 1696. Being a
  contribution to political history.*
  London, 1922. *86 pp.*   [NYPL, LC]
From the originals in the Public
Record Office (London), the editor
had published one hundred copies of
this item for distribution. The oath of
association, signed by persons in England and the colonies, was drawn up
after the discovery of a plot to assassinate
William III. The sixty signatories from
Barbados included the governor, army
officers, members of the House of
Assembly, Council, and the island's
clergy.

HALL, RICHARD
  *A general account of the first settlement
  and of the trade and Constitution of the
  island of Barbados, written in the year
  1755; with a foreward by E. M.
  Shilstone.*
  Barbados, 1924. *65 pp.*   [BMHS]
This volume derives from a "verbatim
copy of the original ms" made by
Shilstone. Hall's account contains a
knowledgeable delineation of the
island's tax system, commerce, administrative and legal machinery, as well as
a list of the island's governors. Also

included is a brief historical sketch based upon Ligon (1657) and a few other sources, but the book is most useful as an introduction to Barbados's administrative structure in the mid-eighteenth century.

STOCK, LEO FRANCIS (ed.)
Proceedings and debates of the British Parliaments respecting North America.
Washington D.C., 1924–41. 5 vols.
[SIU]
This series covers the period 1542–1754. Each volume is copiously footnoted and contains a very detailed index which permits rapid location of materials pertaining to Barbados. The types of information available generally complement those provided in the *Calendar of State Papers* (*see* Manuscripts, Public Record Office); thus the series is an especially valuable source for matters pertaining to the island's commercial, political, legal, and military history.

COLT, HENRY
"*The Voyage of Sr. Henrye Colte Knight to ye islands of ye Antilleas in ye ship called ye Alexander . . . [1631].*"
In V. T. Harlow, ed. *Colonizing Expeditions to the West Indies and Guiana, 1623–1667.* Hakluyt Society, London, 1925. [BMHS, BM]
Transcript of a Cambridge University manuscript (Mm. 3, 9). In July 1631, Colt spent two weeks in Barbados while the effects of the Courteen–Carlisle controversy on proprietorship were still being felt. His description of the island's flora is of special value, and his occasional comments on various aspects of social life are of importance given the rarity of descriptive accounts of Barbados at this early period.

The Barbados section of Colt's account is also reproduced, with notes by Guy Barton, in the *Jl. BMHS* (21, 1953–54, 5–12).

[BROWNE, BENJAMIN]
The yarn of a yankee privateer. Edited by Nathaniel Hawthorne, introduction by Clifford Smyth.
New York and London, 1926. *308 pp.*
[LC, BMHS, NYPL]
The author had served as a clerk on an American privateer cruising in the

West Indies. Captured by the English, he was imprisoned in Barbados for six months during 1814. Only one week was actually spent in jail, and for the remainder of his stay, Browne was free to wander from sunrise to sunset. Thus, he spent virtually all of his time in Bridgetown and vicinity, but the relatively lengthy record of his stay (*pp. 75–142*) provides information on miscellaneous customs and aspects of social life. *See* Ragatz (*p. 226*) for author identification.

RAGATZ, L. J.
Statistics for the study of British Caribbean economic history, 1763–1833.
London, 1928. *25 pp.* [BM]
Contains a series of tables which include Barbadian statistics. The author regards his work as a supplement to William Young's *The West-India Common Place Book* (1807).

SANFORD, PELEG
The letter book of Peleg Sanford of Newport, merchant (later Governour of Rhode Island) in 1666–1668. Transcribed from the original manuscript in the Massachusetts Archives by Howard W. Preston, with an introduction and notes by Howard M. Chapin, and additional notes by G. Andrews Moriarty, Jr.
Providence, R.I., 1928. *84 pp.* [LC]
About eighty-five letter copies written by a native Rhode Islander who had been a merchant in Barbados during the years 1663–64. Upon return to Rhode Island, Sanford continued his commercial ties with Barbados, largely through his brothers William and Elisha who remained on the island. The letters, a number of which are addressed to William (other addressees include John King and Thomas Butcher), largely treat of business matters and shipping problems. Sandford was actively engaged in exporting Rhode Island provisions and horses to Barbados from which he imported agricultural products.

DONNAN, ELIZABETH (ed.)
Documents illustrative of the history of the slave trade to America.
Washington, D.C., 1930–35. 4 vols.
[SIU, IJ, LC]

A valuable source in which original documents are tied together by the editor's useful introductory summaries. Barbadian materials are easily identified by the detailed indexes at the end of each volume. Volumes 1 and 2 cover the period 1441–1807, and volumes 3 and 4 treat the northern colonies (with a number of references to Barbados) from the 1630s to the early nineteenth century. As a matter of interest, the editor notes (vol. 1, *p. vi*) "Our records of the slave trade shed little light upon the manner of people enslaved, their origins, and the differences among them, save when such points were translated into pounds sterling. This fact leaves us in ignorance of much which would today be of inestimable value in studying the African origins of the American Negro population."

MARTIN, EVELINE (ed.)
Journal of a slave dealer. "A view of some Remarkable Axcedents in the Life of Nics. Owen on the Coast of Africa and America from the Year 1746 to the Year 1757." Edited with an introduction.
London, 1930. *117 pp.* [BM]
Transcription of a privately held manuscript. Contains extensive descriptions of slaving in Africa — although Owens had deposited slaves in Barbados, his journal offers no details about the island.

CRACKNELL, EVERIL M. W. (ed.)
The Barbadian diary of Gen. Robert Haynes, 1787–1836.
Medstead, Hampshire, 1934. *70 pp.* [WIC, BM]
Pages 12–40 comprise the diary of a prominent planter and onetime speaker of the House of Assembly. The editor notes that the manuscript from which this was transcribed is fragmented, with many gaps in the entries. Aside from autobiographical materials, it contains a variety of information on social and economic conditions and customs of the period; it also includes comments on slaves and the introduction of sugar varieties and other plants. Pages 42–70 are the editor's notes. Only fifty copies of this item were printed.
Another edition of the manuscript

was published under the editorship of Edmund C. Haynes, A. Percy Haynes, and Edmund S. P. Haynes (*Notes by General Robert Haynes of New Castle, and Clifton Hall Plantations, Barbados, and Other Documents of Family Interest,* London [1912], *32 pp.* [BM]).

SENHOUSE, WILLIAM
"The Autobiographical Manuscript of William Senhouse."
Journal of the Barbados Museum and Historical Society, vol. 2, Bridgetown, 1934–35, *pp. 61–79, 115–34, 191–209;* vol. 3, Bridgetown, 1935–36, *pp. 3–19, 87–99.*
In 1771, Senhouse arrived at Barbados to become Surveyor General of Customs, a post he held until 1787; in 1784 he acquired Grove plantation in St. Philip. The account of his years in Barbados was written around 1791 (he died on the island shortly thereafter) and largely relates to family matters and personal affairs, plantation business, and duties connected with his office; there are also occasional references to social life, frequent mention of personalities, and a lengthy description of the 1780 hurricane and its effects.
Senhouse's "autobiographical manuscript" is longer than the section published in the *Jl. BMHS,* the unpublished portion treating his pre-Barbados years. The manuscript today forms part of the Senhouse Mss. in the Cumberland County Record Office (England). From this collection a few letters, written by Senhouse from Barbados in the 1770s and 1780s, are reproduced in Edward Hughes's *North Country Life in the Eighteenth Century: Volume II, Cumberland and Westmorland 1700–1830* (London, Oxford University Press, 1965).

SAMUEL, WILFRED S.
"A Review of the Jewish Colonists in Barbados in the year 1680."
Transactions of the Jewish Historical Society of England.
Vol. 12. London, 1936. *125 pp.* [BM]
Following page 47, there are various documents reproduced, e.g. wills and deeds, relating to the island's pre-1834 Jewish population.

SHILSTONE, E. M.
"A Descriptive List of Maps of Barbados" [*1657–1936*].
Journal of the Barbados Museum and Historical Society, vol. 5, Bridgetown, 1937–38, *pp. 57–84.*
References to about sixty-four maps, approximately two-thirds of which were done in the pre-1834 period. In many ways, this is a more valuable reference work than Tony Campbell's *The Printed Maps of Barbados* (1965) which owes a great deal to Shilstone's work, for it includes manuscript maps, often lengthy annotations, and the location of each item cited. Some of the maps are indicated as being in the author's own collection. Mr. Shilstone, a prolific contributor to Barbadian history, died in July 1969, much of his library going to the Barbados Museum and the Barbados Archives. Only some of the items cited in his list are referred to in this *Guide*. For additions to Shilstone's list and more details: *see* M. J. Chandler, *A Guide to the Records of Barbados* (Oxford, 1965, *p. 174*).

CADBURY, HENRY (ed.)
"An Account of Barbados 200 Years Ago."
Journal of the Barbados Museum and Historical Society, vol. 9, Bridgetown, 1941–42, *pp. 81–83.*
John Smith, a nineteen-year-old Quaker, visited the island for fourteen weeks in early 1742. He provides brief comments on climate, plants, towns, Carlisle Bay, beverages, water supplies, slaves, the Quaker and Jewish communities, and the Anglican church. Smith's manuscript is located in the Library Company of Philadelphia.

ARCHER, C. V. H. AND FERGUSSON, W. K. (eds.)
Laws of Barbados [*1667–1894*].
Vol. 1. Barbados, 1943. [BM]
Contains the same pre-1834 laws as Goodman and Clark (1912).

YEARWOOD, SEALE
"Letters — 1796–1810."
Journal of the Barbados Museum and Historical Society, vol. 16, Bridgetown, 1948–49, *pp. 113–17.*
The transcription of three letters in a private collection. Yearwood, the manager and attorney of Lower Estate and Moonshine plantations in Barbados, reports to Applewhaite Frere, the absentee owner, and provides a variety of useful information on plantation activities and the condition of the slaves. Frere was one of the founding members of the Barbados Society for the Encouragement of Arts, Manufactures and Commerce.

NICKALLS, JOHN L. (ed.)
The journals of George Fox.
London, 1952. *789 pp.* [F]
The most recent and intensively edited volume of George Fox's writings. It contains some very useful materials, based on Fox's visit to Barbados in 1671, on Quaker relationships with Negro slaves. Includes (*pp. 596–99*) a "Letter from Barbados to Edward Mann in London, November 1, 1671," written by John Hull who had accompanied Fox. Hull is primarily concerned with describing Fox's religious activities, but he also makes some comments on slaves.

"Quaker Records. At a Meeting of the Midwives in Barbadoes . . . [1677–1679]."
Journal of the Barbados Museum and Historical Society, vol. 24, Bridgetown, 1956–57, *pp. 133–34.*
Reproduces manuscript transcripts that were originally published in the *Journal of the Friends Historical Society* (38, 22–24); contains extracts from some of the meetings held in 1677, 1678, and 1679 in which the midwives state the procedures and philosophy they follow in offering their services to the island's free and slave population.

SHILSTONE, E. M.
Monumental inscriptions in the burial ground of the Jewish Synagogue at Bridgetown, Barbados.
The Jewish Historical Society of England. London [1956]. *205 pp.*
[RCS]
Hebrew, Spanish, Portuguese, and English transcriptions of three-hundred seventy-four tombstones, and a name index compiled from the Barbados Registry Office. A preface by W. S.

Samuel and introduction by Shilstone present an historical sketch of the island's Jewish community. Also published by the American Jewish Historical Society (New York, 1956 [NYPL]).

DERING, JAMES
"A letter from Barbados in 1640."
Journal of the Barbados Museum and Historical Society, vol. 27, Bridgetown, 1959–60, *pp. 124–25.*
A transcription of a privately owned manuscript, part of a collection discovered in 1953, that originally belonged to Sir Edward Dering (1598–1644). James's letter to Sir Edward, his cousin, is dated Barbados, July 20, 1640. He discusses his past failures in tobacco farming and his future hopes for himself and the crop. He requests Edward to help with the sum of £150 "for which I have the half of one hundred acres of land, nine servants and a good stock, which is . . . a very good bargain. . . . I doubt not but in a few years time it will bring in the money again three or four fold."

BOROMÉ, JOSEPH (ed.)
"William Bell and His Second Visit to Barbados, 1829–1830."
Journal of the Barbados Museum and Historical Society, vol. 30, Bridgetown, 1962–63, *pp. 20–36.*
Bell, a British army officer, provides a variety of useful information on various aspects of Barbadian society. His full manuscript journal is located in the Clements Library at the University of Michigan, but Professor Boromé, in a personal communication, assured me that he reproduced "all the material Bell gave on Barbados."

HOTTEN, JOHN CAMDEN (ed.)
The original lists of persons of quality; emigrants; religious exiles; political rebels . . . who went from Great Britain to the American plantations 1600–1700.
2nd ed. New York, 1880. Reprinted, Baltimore, 1962.   [SIU]
Transcriptions of manuscripts located in the Public Record Office (London). The following sections deal with Barbados: "Monmouth Rebellion of 1685: — Lists of Convicted Rebels Sent to the Barbadoes and Other Plantations in

America" (*pp. 315–44*); "Tickets Granted to Emigrants from Barbadoes to New England, Carolina, Virginia, New York, Antigua, Jamaica, New Foundland, and Other Places, 1678–9" (*pp. 345–418*; also printed in *Jl. BMHS*, 1, 1933–34, *155–80*); "Barbadoes: — Parish Registers — Births and Deaths — Lists of Inhabitants — Landed Proprietors — Servants, etc., 1678–9" (*pp. 419–508*).
All of the above are valuable for genealogical purposes, but the final item reproduces some of the comprehensive census of 1679 (*see* Public Record Office, C.O. 1/44) and offers valuable quantitative materials for the parishes of St. Michael, St. George, St. Andrew, Christ Church, and St. James, e.g. the names, sex, and number of persons in each white household; the amount of acreage held by each household; and the number of indentured servants and slaves attached to each.

KAMINKOW, JACK AND MARION
A list of emigrants from England to America 1718–1759.
Baltimore, 1964. *288 pp.*   [SIU]
"Transcribed from microfilms of the original records at the Guildhall, London." This list of servants who signed their indentures in London, includes the names of approximately forty-five persons who were destined for Barbados, with their parishes and counties of origin, occupations, years of indenture, ages, and dates of indenture.

CAMPBELL, TONY
The printed maps of Barbados, from the earliest times to 1873.
Map Collectors' Series, no. 21. The Map Collectors' Circle, London, 1965.   [SIU, BM]
A preface briefly discusses sixteenth-century maps in which Barbados is mentioned, and sixteen pages of text describe about sixty-four maps (most published before 1834), twenty-four of which are photographically reproduced. Only some of the maps cited by Campbell are referred to in this *Guide* (*See also* E. M. Shilstone, 1937–38).

KAMINKOW, MARION AND JACK
Original lists of emigrants in bondage

*from London to the American colonies
1719–1744.*

Baltimore, 1967. *211 pp.* [SIU]
Transcribed from the Treasury Money
Books in the Public Record Office
(London); includes the names of about
eight convicts shipped to Barbados over
the period 1719–29.

GHIRELLI, MICHAEL
*A list of emigrants from England to
America 1682–1692.*

Baltimore, 1968. *106 pp.* [SIU]
"Transcribed from the original records
at the City of London Record Office."
Contains the names of approximately
one-hundred twenty-six indentured servants destined for Barbados; includes
information on place of origin, age,
parentage, date of indenture, occupa-
tion, and the name of the person to
whom indentured.

2

Parliamentary Papers

In compiling this list of the House of Commons Sessional Papers or Parliamentary Papers, a systematic search was conducted of the eleven volumes of indexes covering the period 1696 (the earliest date) to 1852.[1] Not only were references to the more obvious categories such as "West India Colonies," "Slavery," and "Colonial Trade," extracted from these indexes, but, on the chance that materials might be located elsewhere, references to materials in other categories were also extracted. The hundreds of references obtained by this procedure were further examined to eliminate those which seemed to have low probability of yielding information on Barbados. All remaining references were read, and are cited only if they contain information which *specifically* mentions or refers to the island.[2]

The greatest number of materials were read on the microcard or microprint series edited by Professor Edgar L. Erickson; this series contains the only complete existing set of Parliamentary Papers. Within the following annotations, the microcard page number at which a given report begins is placed within brackets [ ]; all other page numbers, including those within parentheses ( ), refer to the pagination of the individual report itself.

Accounts and Papers

1789. Vol. 24. Slave trade
Paper 627 gives population figures; 629 includes the number of slave ships that arrived from 1785 through 1788; and 630 lists foodstuffs imported in 1785, 1786, and 1787.

1789. Vol. 26. Slave trade
Pages 13–24 include an "Extract of a letter from Governor Parry to the Right Honourable Lord Sydney, dated August 18, 1788; with eight enclosures on the subject of Negroe slaves in the said island." Pages 24–36 include "Queries from his excellency Governor Parry, answered by a planter of 1068 acres in the Parishes of St. John, St. Philip, and St. George, in the island of Barbados" which deals with the condition and life of slaves. William Dickson (1814, *pp. 143 ff.*) reproduces this item and notes that it was originally

separately published "in a very thin folio of only thirteen sheets . . . under the name of the Supplement to the Privy Council's Report," and identifies the planter as Joshua Steele.

---

1 This chapter was researched and written with the collaboration of Mrs. Sharon Hunt.

2 Excluding bills passed by Parliament. For materials relating to the West Indies in general, the researcher is advised to consult L. J. Ragatz, *A Check List of House of Commons Sessional Papers Relating to the British West Indies and to the West Indian Slave Trade and Slavery: 1763–1834* (London, 1923) and *A Check List of House of Lords Sessional Papers Relating to the British West Indies and to the West Indian Slave Trade and Slavery: 1763–1834* (London, 1931).

This volume also contains the entire, but nonpaginated, "Report of the Lords of the Committee of Council . . . concerning the present state of the trade to Africa . . . and the effects and consequences of this trade . . . in Africa and the West Indies." Part 3 of this report includes an extremely valuable section on a variety of matters pertaining to slaves and slavery in Barbados. Part 4 contains data on items exported to and imported from Great Britain from 1783 to 1787.

1790. Vol. 29. Slave trade
Contains the six-hundred-forty-page "Minutes of the Evidence taken before a Committee of the House of Commons . . . for the purpose of taking the examination of . . . witnesses . . . on the part of . . . petitioners who have petitioned . . . against the abolition of the slave trade."

Only two witnesses indicate that they had had direct experience in Barbados: David Parry, for seven years governor of the island, and Lord Admiral Rodney; their testimonies on the condition of slaves in Barbados appear in pages 463–76.

1790. Vol. 30. Slave trade
Continuation of volume 29, but containing testimonies of persons for the abolition of the slave trade. The testimonies of Rev. Thomas Gwynn Rees (*pp. 247–64*) and Rev. Robert Boucher Nicholls (*pp. 325–60*), deal directly with the condition and life of slaves in Barbados, the latter's lengthy testimony being an especially valuable source of information.

1790. Vol. 31. Miscellaneous
Paper 705 contains a table of slaves imported in 1787 and 1788.

1791. Vol. 34. Miscellaneous
Papers 745–48 (*pp. 1–281*) are a continuation of the "Minutes of the Evidence taken before a Committee of the House of Commons . . . appointed to take the examination of witnesses respecting the African slave trade." The testimonies of James Towne (*pp. 14–32*),

Maj.-Gen. Tottenham (*pp. 125–28*), Rev. Davies, George Woodward, and a Capt. Cook derive in part from their own observations on slavery in Barbados.

1792. Vol. 35. Miscellaneous
Paper 766 is a table which includes information on the number of slaves imported into Barbados from Africa in 1789, 1790, and 1791, distinguishing the names of the slaving vessels, their tonnage and crew number, total number of slaves in each shipload, the total number reexported and retained.

Paper 767 includes the total number of slaves imported, exported, and retained in 1789, 1790, and 1791.

1795–1796. Vol. 42. Miscellaneous
Paper 840 deals with "The Expedition to the West Indies, under the command of Sir Charles Grey and Sir John Jervis." Materials specifically relating to Barbados include a list of "hospital tents, bedding and stores" shipped to the island in 1794 (*pp. 23–25*), and extracts of letters from the director of the military hospital relating to medical conditions (*pp. 36–37*).

1799. Vol. 48. Miscellaneous
Paper 966, "Minutes of Evidence . . . Respecting the Shipping and Carrying of Slaves," contains the brief evidence of James Gyles, the captain of slaving ships, who offers details on the middle passage between Africa and Barbados.

Paper 967a, "Further Correspondence between the Secretary of State . . . and the . . . West Indies . . . respecting the Negroes in the West Indies," includes a copy of a letter from Gov. Ricketts to the Duke of Portland (May 31, 1798) relative to improving the condition of Barbadian slaves.

Paper 970, "An Account of the Quantity of British Plantation Sugar and Rum Imported into and Exported from Great Britain . . .," contains a list, by island, for 1798 and 1799, and includes the amount of duties, drawbacks, and bounties.

Reports

1803. Vol. 13. Finance reports...with proceedings and measures of government thereon, 1798–1803

Pages 30 and 116 list various governmental positions in 1797 and 1798, e.g. collector of customs, the names of officeholders, and miscellaneous information pertaining to each office.

1803. Vol. 14. Miscellaneous reports ... 1793–1802

Page 388 gives annual figures on sugar and rum imported from Barbados into the Port of London from 1756 to 1796, including the number of ships involved each year. Page 403 presents figures on the quantity of sugar and rum imported into the Port of London for each of the following years: 1750, 1760, 1770, 1780, 1790, 1791–95.

1803–4. Vol. 10. Papers ... respecting the slave trade

Report 119 [m.c., *p. 1*], section C, contains extracts and/or copies of eight letters relating to modifications in the island's slave laws. The letters were written between 1797 and 1802 by Govs. Ricketts and Seaforth and were addressed to the Duke of Portland and Lord Hobart.

1805. Vol. 10. Papers ... respecting the slave trade

Report 39 [m.c., *p. 623*] includes an extract of a letter from Lord Seaforth to the Earl of Camden (November 13, 1804) and four statements relating to the murders of slaves by whites.

1806. Vol. 13. Accounts ... relating to the African slave trade

In Report 265 [m.c., *p. 777*], tables 1 and 6 give the number of slaves imported into Barbados in 1802, 1803, and 1804 with the names of the ships, their tonnage and size, date of entry, and the number of slaves in each shipload.

1812. Vol. 10. Reports of the commissioners of revenue inquiry

Report 46 [m.c., *p. 327*], dated Barbados, March 6, 1812, presents a table of fees for customs; a series of cases of past discrepancies in customs duties are presented to justify new rates.

1814–1815. Vol. 7. Papers relating to the West Indies

Report 478 [m.c., *p. 431*] treats Barbados on pages 1–24. A cover letter from Gov. Beckwith to the Earl of Liverpool (January 13, 1812) primarily discusses the island's church organization, clergy, and slave manumission. Copies of reports by the rectors of each of the island's parishes follow; these include miscellaneous information on the parish and glebe, e.g. geographical size, value, minister's salary; also brief discussions and statistics concerning population size, numbers of baptisms and burials, starting around 1802, which distinguish white, free colored, and slave. A table on page 12 lists the population of each parish in 1801, distinguished by sex, white, free colored, and slave. Pages 16–19 contain a table of Africans taken as prizes and sold in Barbados from 1807–11, giving names of persons and vessels, etc. Page 20 is a table of the slave population of each parish for 1809, 1810, 1811. Pages 22–23 contain a table listing each parish, the name of its rector and the value of the rectory in 1812; the number of acres in the parish and its white, free colored, and slave population in 1809, 1810, 1811; the number of baptisms in each parish in 1810 and 1811, with the population distinguished by sex and white or free colored.

1816. Vol. 19. Colonial laws respecting slaves

Report 226 [m.c., *p. 259*] reproduces four Barbadian laws: "An Act to increase the sum made payable by former laws on the manumission of a slave, and for their better support when manumitted" (May 1801); "An Act for the better protection of the slaves of this island" (April 1805); "An Act for the punishment of such slaves as shall be found practising Obeah" (November 1806); "An Act to remove doubts concerning the trial of slaves manumitted after the commission of felonies of which they may stand accused" (March 1809).

1817. Vol. 17. Additional colonial laws respecting slaves

Report 338 [m.c., *p. 149*] reproduces one Barbadian law: "An Act for more fully ascertaining the slave population of the island of Barbados" (January 1817).

1820. Vol. 11. Colonial acts for granting four-and-half per cent duties of customs, in the island of Barbadoes and in the West Indies

Report 20 [m.c., *p. 343*] reproduces "An Act for settling an impost on the commodities of the growth of this island" (September 1663).

1820. Vol. 11. An account of the total net produce of the 4½ per cent Barbadoes and Leeward Island duties

Report 22 [m.c., *p. 358*] includes a list, and the annual salaries, of the sixteen persons who were, as of 1820, collectors and comptrollers of customs in Bridgetown, Holetown, Oistins, and Speightstown.

1820. Vol. 11. An account of the total net produce of the 4½ per cent Barbadoes and Leeward Island duties . . . so far as relates to the exchequer

Report 23 [m.c., *p. 363*] gives the names of Barbados's governors, and the sums of money they received out of the 4½ percent duty each year from 1809 through 1818.

1821. Vol. 23. Negroes

Report 61 [m.c., *p. 119*], based upon returns made by the collectors of customs in the West Indies, deals with Africans captured by British ships and apprenticed in various of the islands. Section 3 treats such cases in Barbados from 1807 to 1811 by listing the Africans, their names and sex, the vessels from which they were seized, court tried in, to whom and when apprenticed, and similar information.

1822. Vol. 20. A return of persons holding the office of governor and lieutenant governor, chief justice, attorney, and solicitor general of the . . . West India Islands

Report 178 [m.c., *pp. 528–29*] lists the names of the Barbados officeholders and the amounts and sources (the crown out of the 4½ percent duty, fees, acts of legislature) of their annual salaries.

1823. Vol. 18. Acts of colonial legislatures for registry of slaves

Report 68 [m.c., *p. 1*] includes a copy of "A supplemental Act to an Act intitled, 'An Act for more fully ascertaining the slave population of the island of Barbados'" (December 1820).

1823. Vol. 18. Slave population

Report 80 [m.c., *p. 62*] includes a variety of information on Barbados slaves in section 4 (with a cover letter from Gov. Warde, dated November 9, 1821): tables showing the number of slaves imported from 1808 to 1821, distinguished by age, sex, and point of origin; number of slaves exported from 1808 to 1821, their destination and vessel name; slaves escheated to the crown, 1808–21, by sex, name, purchaser's name, and sale price at auction; number of manumitted slaves, 1808–21; number of slaves sold for debts, 1818–21, by sex; returns of baptisms, burials, marriages, and population size for each parish, distinguishing population by sex and whether white, free colored, or slave.

1824. Vol. 23. Papers relating to the treatment of slaves

Report 160 [m.c., *p. 596*] contains copies of two Barbados laws: "An Act for the better prevention of the practice of Obeah" (July 1818), and "An Act to repeal and amend certain Acts made for the government and protection of slaves" (July 1818).

1824. Vol. 24. Slave population

Report 424 [m.c., *p. 79*] includes figures on the number of slaves in Barbados in 1817 and 1820, distinguished by sex.

1824. Vol. 24. Papers . . . in explanation of the condition of the slave population in . . . the West Indies

The report is not numbered [m.c., *p. 427*]. It contains a few items from Barbados relative to amelioration in the island's slave laws, and a letter from Gov. Henry Warde (June 11, 1823) commenting on rumors concerning emancipation and a slave insurrection; enclosed is a proclamation he issued to dispel such rumors.

1825. Vol. 15. First report of the Commissioner of Inquiry into the administration of civil and criminal justice in the West Indies

Report 517 [m.c., *p. 233*] includes a section on Barbados (*pp. 5–68*). This is a detailed description and evaluation of the island's judicial and legal system, and is an important source for the study of these subjects. The appendix to the report contains examinations and documents relating to Barbados judicial processes and the administration of justice. The examinations include questions and answers about slave courts and the judicial treatment of slaves (*see also* F. Dwarris, 1827).

1825. Vol. 25. Further papers relating to slaves in the West Indies: (demolition of the Methodist chapel in Barbadoes)
Reports 113 [m.c., *p. 169*] and 127 [m.c., *p. 177*] contain copies or extracts of sixteen communications written between October 1823 and January 1824 concerning an incident which took place in late 1823 and forced the departure of William Shrewsbury, a Methodist missionary.

1826. Vol. 26. Titles of all acts passed by the legislatures of the slave colonies since the 15th of May, 1823
Report 214 [m.c., *p. 395*], section 2, records the title of the "Slave Consolidation Act," "An Act to repeal several acts and clauses of acts respecting slaves and for consolidating and bringing into one act the several laws relating thereto" (March 1825), and notes the absence of provisions in this law with respect to marriage, manumissions, religious instruction, etc.

1826. Vol. 26. Colonial population
Report 350 [m.c., *p. 377*] includes figures on the white, free colored, and slave population in each parish for the years 1812 to 1820.

1826. Vol. 28. Slave population
Report 353 [m.c., *p. 1*] includes information on number of slaves imported and exported, 1821–25, giving sex, date, vessel name, point of origin, and name of importer and exporter; number of manumissions effected by purchase, 1821–25, giving date, sex of slave, and name of manumitter; parish returns on slave marriages, 1821–25; number of slaves eschcated to the crown, 1822–23, dates escheated and sold, from whom escheated, name, sex, and age of slaves, to whom sold, price, and miscellaneous remarks concerning individual cases; number of slaves sold for execution of debts, 1821–25, with the name and sex of the slave, the dates levied on and sold, the owner's and purchaser's names, and the price; sums of money appropriated for the poor, 1821–25, and annual lists of white and free colored pensioners, by sex, age, residence, and amount of pension; slave population in 1823 by sex and number of births and deaths; sums of money for the support of the poor, 1822–23, by parish, with names and sex of those supported.

1826. Vol. 29. Papers containing an abstract of acts passed by the legislatures of the West India colonies, since the 15th May, 1823, for improving the condition of slaves
This report is not numbered [m.c., *p. 607*]. For Barbados, the title of the "Slave Consolidation Act" (*see* 1826, vol. 26, report 214) is given in full, along with lengthy abstracts of its provisions respecting the admissibility of slave evidence, manumission, regulating of punishment by masters, acquisition of property by slaves, and "the office of guardian and protector of slaves."

1826–1827. Vol. 15. Estimates, etc. miscellaneous services; for the year 1827
Report 159 [m.c., *p. 233*] includes a table which gives the number of churches, public and private chapels, parsonage houses, white and colored schools, clergymen, lay catechists, school masters and mistresses in Barbados; also the minutes of a public meeting held in May 1825 addressed to the issue of constructing a second church in Bridgetown, and an item discussing the sum raised by public subscription for this church.

1826–1827. Vol. 22. Slaves manumitted
Report 128 [m.c., *p. 43*] includes the number of slaves manumitted in Barbados, 1821–25, noting the date of manumission, sex of the manumitted slave, the name of the manumitter, and miscellaneous remarks concerning individual cases.

1826–1827. Vol. 25. Papers . . . in explanation of the measures adopted . . . for the melioration of the condition of the slave population in . . . the West Indies
The report is not numbered [m.c., *p.*

53]; the Barbados section is found in pages 197–287 [m.c., *pp. 255–345*]. This section is introduced by copies and extracts of letters from Gov. Warde and others to the Earl of Bathurst in 1826 relative to the major "Slave Consolidation Bill." This bill, "An Act to repeal several acts and clauses of acts respecting slaves, and for consolidating and bringing into one act, the several laws relating thereto . . ." (October 1826), is reproduced in full and is followed by copies of a number of island slave laws affected by it: "An Act for the governing of Negroes" (August 1668); "An Act for the encouragement of all Negroes and slaves that shall discover any conspiracy" (October 1692); "An additional Act to an Act entitled 'An Act for the governing of Negroes'" (October 1692); "An Act for prohibiting the selling of rum or other strong liquors to any Negro or slave" (October 1692); "An Act for the encouragement of such Negroes or other slaves that shall behave themselves courageously against the enemy in time of invasion" (November 1707); "An Act to prohibit the inhabitants of this island from employing their Negroes or other slaves in selling and bartering" (January 1708); "An Act to secure the peaceable possession of Negroes and other slaves . . . and to prevent and punish the clandestine and illegal détenue of them" (June 1709); "An Act for the punishment of runaway slaves and of slaves who shall wilfully entertain, harbour, and conceal any runaway slaves" (November 1731); "An Act for the better governing of Negroes, and the more effectual preventing the inhabitants of this island from employing their Negroes or other slaves in selling or bartering" (May 1733); "An Act for rendering more effectual, and for supplying many defects in the several laws of this island for the governing of Negroes" (August 1749). (The preceding laws are also printed in R. Hall, *Acts, passed in the Island of Barbados*, 1764, numbers 84, 91, 92, 93, 112, 116, 117, 161, 164, 196.) "An Act to amend an act entitled 'An Act for the governing of Negroes'" (April 1766); "An Act to prevent distempered, maimed and worn out

Negroes from infesting the towns, streets, and highways of this island" (January 1785); "An Act to remove doubts concerning the trial of slaves manumitted after the commission of felonies of which they may stand accused" (February 1809). (The preceding laws are also printed in S. Moore, *The Public Acts in Force*, 1801, numbers 5 and 32.) "An Act to repeal part of an act entitled 'An Act for the governing of Negroes and for rebuilding and regulating a new cage'" (November 1817); "An Act for the prevention of the practice of Obeah" (June 1818); "An Act to repeal and amend certain Acts made for the government and protection of slaves" (July 1818); "An Act for the better prevention of the practice of Obeah" (May 1819).

Following these acts is a copy of a letter from Robert Haynes, speaker of the House of Assembly, to Gov. Warde (dated October 23, 1826) in which Haynes discusses at length the reasons why certain liberal provisions, recommended by the Imperial government, were not incorporated into the "Consolidated Slave Bill." Also included is a copy of a liberal "Supplemental Act" to the "Consolidated Slave Bill" (passed by the Council in October 1826, but rejected by the Assembly) and a copy of the Council minutes of October 17, 1826 in which matters relating to the amelioration of the island's slave laws are discussed.

Copies of the following acts are then included: "An Act for the encouragement of baptisms and marriages amongst the slaves, and for the due observance of the Lord's Day, commonly called Sunday, Christmas Day, and Good Friday" (October 1826); "An Act to remove pecuniary impediments to the manumission of slaves and to extend the benefit of testimony to free persons manumitted not according to the laws of this island, and to repeal certain acts and parts of acts relating thereto" (October 1826) — attached to the latter act are copies of acts passed in 1739, 1783, and 1817 to which it refers. The report terminates with correspondence and miscellaneous items relating to modifications in the island's slave laws.

*1826–1827. Vol. 26. Papers . . .
relating to the slave population in the
West Indies*
Report not numbered [m.c., *p. 1*];
materials on Barbados are located
in pages 297–302 [m.c., *pp. 109–14*].
These include extracts of letters from
the Bishop of Barbados to the Earl of
Bathurst, written in 1826 and dealing
with slave acts passed by the island's
legislature, and church and educational
matters; also miscellaneous items relating to the construction of a new church
in Bridgetown.
1828. Vol. 25. Slave population
Report 570 [m.c., *p. 567*] notes that in
1826 Barbados had 36,995 male, and
43,556 female, slaves.
*1828. Vol. 27. Papers in explanation
of the measures adopted . . . for the
melioration of the condition of the slave
population . . . in the West Indies*
Report not numbered [m.c., *p. 89*];
Barbados materials (*pp. 37–45*) [m.c.,
pp. 133–41] relate to those in volume 28
(1826–27). Included are a long letter
from the Imperial government (October
1827) commenting on the Barbados
"Slave Consolidation Act" and "Sunday Act" (*see* 1826–27, vol. 25) and
other subjects relating to the amelioration of the island's slave laws; extracts
of letters written from Barbados relating to the above acts; a copy of a petition, signed by five-hundred-twenty-six
free colored and black persons, requesting modifications in the "Slave Consolidation Act"; and a copy of "An Act
to extend the benefits enjoyed by white
persons under certain clauses of the
Consolidated Slave Act of this island
to all free coloured and free black
persons" (January 1828).
*1829. Vol. 25. Papers . . . in
explanation of the measures adopted . . .
for the melioration of the condition of the
slave population in the West Indies*
Report 333 [m.c., *p. 153*] contains a
long letter (September 1828) from the
Imperial government relating to more
liberal measures affecting the condition
and legal status of the island's slaves; a
letter from the House of Assembly
(November 1828) which discusses slave
amelioration and the workings of the
"Slave Consolidation Act," passed a
year earlier.

*1830. Vol. 21. Slave population in
the colonies*
Report 674 [m.c., *p. 619*] includes a
yearly return on the white, free colored,
free black, and slave population of
Barbados from 1825 to 1829, by sex
and the numbers of births and deaths
in each category.
*1830. Vol. 27. Four and a half
percent duties*
Report 273 [m.c., *p. 325*] includes
returns on the annual gross and net
proceeds derived from paying the 4½
percent duty on Barbados sugar and
ginger, 1820–30.
*1830–1831. Vol. 16. Papers . . . in
explanation of the measures adopted . . .
for the melioration of the condition of the
slave population in . . . the West Indies*
Report 230 [m.c., *p. 1*] contains a copy
of "An Act to remove certain restrictions
affecting the testimony of slaves" (June
1831), and an explanatory cover letter
from Gov. Lyon.
*1831. Vol. 19. Colonies: population,
trade, etc.*
Report 260 [m.c., *p. 171*] contains, in
tabular form, the following information
on each West Indian colony: Its settlement date; the nature of its governmental structure; the number of whites,
free coloreds, and slaves in 1829; the
value of imports and exports to and
from the United Kingdom in 1829; and
the number and tonnage of vessels going
to and coming from the United Kingdom in 1829.
*1831. Vol. 19. Slave emancipation:
crown slaves*
Report 305 [m.c., *p. 303*] contains
copies of orders sent to the colonies for
emancipating slaves belonging to the
crown, and includes a brief letter from
Gov. Lyon of Barbados (June 1, 1831)
relative to such slaves.
1831–1832. Vol. 4. A bill
Report 371 [m.c., *p. 659*] is a copy of a
bill passed by Parliament permitting
Barbados to import lumber, fish, and
provisions duty-free until the end of
1832 – to help alleviate the hardship
caused by the 1831 hurricane.
*1831–1832. Vol. 20. Report from
select committee on the extinction of
slavery throughout the British dominions:
with the minutes of evidence, appendix and
index*

Report 721 [m.c., *p. 1*] includes the detailed evidence of Barbados-born Rev. Wiltshire Stanton Austin (*pp. 178–83*), relating to the life and condition of the island's slave population; pages 519–20 include statistical data on slaves, based upon returns from the Barbados registry — the number in 1817, distinguished by age-group, the number of Africans and creoles in 1817 and 1820, population in 1817 and 1820, number of males and females and births in 1820, 1826, and 1829.

1831–1832. Vol. 31. West Indies
Report 197 [m.c., *p. 369*] contains copies of letters from Gov. Lyon to the Secretary of State, Viscount Goderich, describing the catastrophic hurricane of August 11, 1831, the ways in which the people responded, the nature of the damage, the problems involved in the aftermath, etc.; a copy of a proclamation issued by Lyon on August 15, 1831 which warns plunderers and exhorts the population not to deal in stolen goods; a list of British military personnel killed and wounded; and a brief extract from a letter by the Bishop of Barbados, commenting on the damage caused to his house.

1831–1832. Vol. 31. West Indies — toleration laws
Report 363 [m.c., *p. 287*] contains copies of the following Barbados laws: "An Act to extend the benefits enjoyed by white persons under certain clauses of the Consolidated Slave Act of this island, to all free coloured and free black persons" (January 1828); "An Act to repeal part of an act or statute of this island, intitled 'An Act allowing the testimony of free Negroes and free people of colour to be taken in all cases', and to extend the benefit of testimony to such free coloured and free black persons who have not yet been admitted to that privilege" (October 1830); "An Act for the relief of His Majesty's subjects in this island who profess the Hebrew religion" (May 1831); "An Act to remove certain restraints and disabilities imposed by law on His Majesty's free coloured and free black subjects in this island" (June 1831).

1831–1832. Vol. 46. Papers . . . in explanation of the measures adopted for

the melioration of the condition of the slave population in . . . the West Indies
Report 733 [m.c., *p. 297*] contains copies of two Barbados laws: "An Act to remove certain restrictions affecting the testimony of slaves" (June 1831); and "An Act for removing pecuniary deposits on the manumission of slaves" (June 1831). Also included are copies of various dispatches written from July 1831 to June 1832 between Government House in Barbados and Downing Street, plus extracts from Assembly and Council proceedings relative to modifications in the island's slave laws.

1831–1832. Vol. 47. West India colonies: Slave insurrection
Report 285 [m.c., *p. 259*] includes a copy of a dispatch from Gov. James Lyon to Visc. Goderich (July 23, 1831) referring to a slave insurrection in Jamaica and noting that all is well in Barbados.

1831–1832. Vol. 47. Slave population. Extracts from returns
Report 660 [m.c., *p. 1*] contains, on pages 21–31, the following materials on Barbados: Tables showing the number of slaves imported and exported from 1825 to 1830, giving the names of the slaves, their origin or destination, the vessel and its owner's or master's name; a list of slaves escheated to the crown, 1822–30, by name, age, and sex of slave, date and from whose estate escheated, and miscellaneous remarks pertaining to individual cases; detailed returns from each parish rector on marriages performed between 1825 and 1830, the educational establishment in his parish, e.g. types of schools, attendance figures, teachers' salaries, and the church establishment, e.g. baptisms performed, attendance figures — the population is distinguished in all informational categories by white, free colored, and slave.

1831–1832. Vol. 47. Slave laws, Barbadoes
Report 739 [m.c., *p. 177*] includes a statement by the colonial agent for Barbados, J. P. Mayers, on the condition, treatment, and legal status of slaves, changes in the island's slave laws, and the relation of such changes to suggestions which came from the Imperial government.

1833. Vol. 26. Slave registration
Report 539 [m.c., *p. 473*] includes
figures on the number and sex of
Barbadian slaves for the years 1817,
1820, 1823, 1826, and 1829; also,
figures for each year on slave births,
deaths, and manumissions, by sex.

1833. Vol. 26. Captured Negroes and crown slaves
Report 542 [m.c., *p. 453*] contains an
abstract of an 1829 case in the court of
Vice-Admiralty in Barbados of a slave
escheated to the crown; a schedule of
slaves escheated to the crown, 1823–34,
who were subsequently manumitted,
giving the date of escheat, from whose
estate escheated, and the number of
slaves involved; a return of all Africans
taken as prizes and sold in Barbados
from 1807 to 1811 giving, where possible, their names and sex, the name of
the vessel they came on, when and to
whom delivered or apprenticed, and
other miscellaneous information.

1833. Vol. 26. Slave population (slave registries)
Report 700 [m.c., *p. 427*] contains
information on the number and sex
of Barbados's slave population in 1832,
and the total number of births, deaths,
and manumissions since the previous
return; also an explanatory comment
on how Barbadian slaves are manumitted in England.

1834. Vol. 6. Copy of return of offices of registrar in chancery and clerk of the crown in Barbados
Report 519 [m.c., *p. 562*] gives mis-
cellaneous information on the post held
by George Disbrowe.

1834. Vol. 49. Customs, colonies
Report 564 [m.c., *p. 333*] lists the types
of customs offices in Barbados as of
January 1834, the salary and con-
tingency sums for such offices, and how
these sums are paid.

1835. Vol. 50. Papers . . . in explanation of the measures adopted . . . for giving effect to the act for the abolition of slavery
Report 278, part 1 [m.c., *p. 121*]
includes copies and extracts of thirty-
nine official dispatches between Barbados and London, dating from June 1,
1833 to June 20, 1835; also items such
as extracts from proceedings of the
House of Assembly, proclamations,

copies of laws. All deal with issues surrounding slave emancipation and the
apprenticeship system.

1835. Vol. 51. Slavery abolition proceedings
Report 420 [m.c., *p. 289*] includes a
figure of 82,807 slaves in Barbados in
1834.

1836. Vol. 15. Report from the select committee on Negro apprenticeship in the colonies; together with the minutes of evidence
In Report 560, the appendix [m.c., *p. 438*] reproduces "An Act to repeal
certain clauses of an Act, intitled 'An
Act for the abolition of slavery, for the
government of apprenticed labourers'"
(August 1835), and "An Act for continuing in force and amending an Act,
intitled 'An Act for the temporary
establishment of a rural police for this
island'" (August 1835).

1836. Vol. 31. Negro education
Report 211 [m.c., *p. 569*] includes
miscellaneous information on church-
administered schools in Barbados for
the emancipated slave.

1836. Vol. 49. Papers . . . in explanation of the measures adopted . . . for giving effect to the act for the abolition of slavery throughout the British colonies
Report 166, part 2 [m.c., *p. 43*] (*pp. 5–23*) includes copies or extracts of
letters written between the Barbados
and British governments in 1835 and
1836, and various enclosures; all relate
to the status and condition of apprentices and the working of the apprenticeship system.

1837–1838. Vol. 48. Accounts of slave compensation claims
Report 215 [m.c., *p. 331*] includes a
section on uncontested claims in Barbados (*pp. 171–202*) [m.c., *pp. 505–36*]
in which are listed the date of compensation, the name of each compensated
slaveowner, the number of slaves for
which the owner is compensated, and
the total sum of money awarded to each
owner; pages 325–27 [m.c., *pp. 659–61*]
list contested claims and provide the
same types of information as above; on
page 334 [m.c., *p. 668*] it is noted that,
as of 1837, over £62,000 were still
claimed, but "no award has been
made"; pages 339–40 [m.c., *pp. 675–76*]
list the names of the commissioners,

appraisers and other personnel responsible for carrying out slave compensation in Barbados, their period of service, and the sums paid for this service; page 351 [m.c., *p. 685*] includes a list of various slave classes or categories, the average appraised value, in sterling, of each class, and the average compensation actually awarded.

1838. Vol. 3. Papers relating to the West Indies
Report 270 contains the second part of Capt. J. W. Pringle's report on prisons in the West Indies. Pages 3–19 deal with Barbados, which the author visited in late 1837, and contain a detailed examination of the physical layout, operations, treatment of prisoners, etc., in the Bridgetown jail, the "lock-ups" in Speightstown and Holetown, and the island's six "houses of correction." Appended are two plans,

one of the jail and jail yard at Bridgetown, and the other a floor plan of the jail.

1840. Vol. 8. Quantities of sugar and rum imported into England from . . . the West Indies
Report 527 [m.c., *p. 602*] includes Barbadian statistics from 1814 through 1838.

1847. Vol. 37. Lighthouse (Barbadoes)
Report 715 [m.c., *p. 69*] includes copies of letters written by Barbadian governors in the mid-1830s, explaining the need for, and problems surrounding, the construction of a lighthouse on the windward coast; also miscellaneous related documents.

1849. Vol. 32. Army
Report 56 [m.c., *p. 93*] includes a table (*p. 4*) which gives the number and type of British troops stationed in Barbados in 1820 and 1835.

IMPORT–EXPORT STATISTICS: BARBADOS–UNITED KINGDOM

The following table lists those additional reports which contain import–export statistics on trade between the United Kingdom and Barbados. These statistics generally refer to agricultural products, primarily rum, sugar, and molasses. Some tables report the quantity and/or value of specific items; others simply present general figures for all items from Barbados in a given year.

Year of Volume	Volume Number	Report Number	Microcard Page Number	Year Referred To
1808	11	—	230	1804–1806
1822	21	218	364	1821
1823	13	63	579	1822
1824	21	251, 253	649, 653	1823
1825	21	187	207, 217	1824
1826	22	222	264, 265 271, 272 274, 277 281	1825
1826/27	18	267	340	1826
1828	19	245	527	1827
1829	17	222, 223	362, 373	1828
1831	17	253	300	1829
1831/32	34	690	206	1830
1831/32	34	457, 459 651	576, 473 583	1831
1833	33	319, 320	544, 463	1832
1834	49	9	1	1833
1836	45	298	249	1834

3

Newspapers

The following list and information on Barbados newspapers depends to a considerable degree upon materials derived from the following sources: M. J. Chandler, *A Guide to Records in Barbados* (Oxford, Basil Blackwell, 1965, *pp. 172–73*); L. J. Ragatz, *A Guide for the Study of British Caribbean History, 1763–1834* (Washington, D.C., 1932, *pp. 391–400*); E. M. Shilstone, "Some Notes on Early Printing Presses and Newspapers in Barbados" (*Jl. BMHS*, 26, 1958–59, *19–33*); and D. M. McMurtrie's pamphlet, *Early Printing in Barbados* (London, 1933). Shilstone's informative article treats in some detail two newspapers, the *Barbados Gazette* and the *Barbados Mercury*.

The location of newspapers, especially significant runs of them, presents a difficulty, although a preliminary attempt has been made here. With respect to the problem of locating West Indian newspapers in general, Ragatz's comments are pertinent: "No complete files, nor any nearly so, of any of the [newspapers] are in existence. Occasional single copies are to be found in the correspondence of the governors with the Secretary of State in the Public Record Office, London [c.o. 28 for Barbados], and in various libraries throughout Great Britain and the United States. The best collection of Caribbean newspapers has been formed by the American Antiquarian Society, Worcester, Mass." (*p. 391*).

An early list of West Indian newspaper holdings in the American Antiquarian Society shows only two copies of the *Barbados Mercury* for the period treated in this *Guide* (*see* Waldo Lincoln, "List of Newspapers of the West Indies and Bermuda in the

Library of the American Antiquarian Society," *Proceedings of the American Antiquarian Society*, 36, Worcester, 1926, *134–35*), but the Society may have added others in more recent years.

In May 1969, the superintendent of the British Museum Newspaper Library (Colindale) wrote that "apart from a single issue of the Barbados Globe for 4 September 1837 we have no Barbados newspapers prior to 1838." However, occasional copies of various papers are located in the British Museum itself.

In addition, over the years, the *Jl. BMHS* has published extracts from newspapers located in the Barbados Museum and the Barbados Public Library.

BARBADIAN
"Founded in 1822. Published twice a week in Bridgetown at least as late as November 24, 1858" (Ragatz, *p. 391*).

Issues from 1822 onwards are located in Barbados (Chandler, *p. 172*), and the Public Record Office contains some issues from 1833 and 1836 (c.o. 33/4). Microfilm copies from December 14, 1822 through 1861 are located in the Library of the University of Florida at Gainsville.

BARBADOS CHRONICLE OR CARIBBEAN COURIER
Founded by John Poyer in 1807 (H. A. Vaughan, "Poyer's Last Work," *Jl. BMHS*, 21, 1953–54, *155*). Copies from 1807 to 1809 are located in Barbados (Chandler, *p. 172*).

BARBADOS GAZETTE
The earliest Barbadian newspaper, founded in 1731 by Samuel Keimer. It was "published at first [starting October

9, 1731] weekly on Saturdays and from the following year twice weekly on Wednesdays and Saturdays" (Shilstone, *p. 21*). In 1783, the paper's name was changed to the *Barbados Gazette or General Intelligencer*, and continued publication until "at least as late as February 18, 1792" (Ragatz, *p. 392*).

The earliest known preserved copy of the *Barbados Gazette*, dated April 14–18, 1733, is in the New York Public Library, although many articles from it, for the period 1731–38, were published in two volumes in London in 1741 (*see* Samuel Keimer's *Caribbeana*). The Lambeth Palace Library (Fulham Papers, vol. 16, no. 64) has an issue of April 30–May 3, 1735. The Public Record Office contains "Ten numbers . . . for scattered dates in 1742, 1745, 1746, and 1747," and "several numbers" from 1746 and 1747 in c.o. 28/27 and c.o. 28/46 (Herbert C. Bell, David W. Parker *et al.*, *Guide to British West Indian Archive Materials in London and the Islands, for the History of the United States*, Washington, D.C., 1926, *pp. 53, 61*). One issue, May 30, 1753, is in the British Museum, and the John Carter Brown Library has one dated August 2, 1755; copies from October–December 1761 are in the Public Record Office (c.o. 28/50; Bell, Parker *et al.*, *p. 62*). In Barbados, there are copies from June 30, 1787 to February 14, 1789 (Chandler, *pp. 172, 177*), and the New York Public Library has an issue dated January 20, 1790. *See* Chandler (*p. 177*) for microfilms of this paper.

BARBADOS GLOBE AND COLONIAL ADVOCATE
The Public Record Office contains some issues from 1830 to 1832, 1833 to 1836, 1837 to 1838 (c.o. 33/1, 33/2, 33/4); and various issues from 1835, 1837 to 1838 are in Barbados (Chandler, *p. 172*).

BARBADOS GLOBE AND DEMERARA ADVOCATE
Copies from 1827 to 1828 are located in Barbados (Chandler, *p. 172*) and some issues from 1829 and 1830 are in the Public Record Office (c.o. 33/1).

BARBADOS GLOBE, OFFICIAL GAZETTE AND COLONIAL ADVOCATE

"Founded in 1817. Published twice a week in Bridgetown . . ." (Ragatz, *p. 392*). The earliest copies located in Barbados date from 1842 (Chandler, *p. 173*).

BARBADOS MERCURY
The *Barbados Mercury* commenced publication in 1762, appearing first as a weekly. On January 1, 1805 the paper's name was changed to the *Barbados Mercury and Bridgetown Gazette*, later coming out twice a week, and finally ceasing publication sometime after 1847 (Shilstone, *pp. 27–33*).

The American Antiquarian Society holds an issue for February 1, 1766, (Lincoln, *p. 135*), the Public Record Office holds some issues from March 1766 in c.o. 28/32 and c.o. 28/50 (Bell, Parker *et al.*, *pp. 56, 62*), and the Library Company of Philadelphia holds one for April 19, 1766. A copy dated February 2, 1775, is in the American Antiquarian Society (Lincoln, *p. 135*) and the British Museum holds issues from October 28, 1780 and October 27, 1781; the Royal Commonwealth Society has one for January 18, 1783. The Barbados Museum holds a September 6, 1803 copy (see *Jl. BMHS*, 2, 1934–35, *210*). Other issues located in Barbados are from April 5, 1783 through December 11, 1784, and July 21, 1787 through April 11, 1789; January 8, 1805 through 1818, and occasional numbers from 1819, 1820, 1821, 1822; 1823 through January 1825, and 1835 (Chandler, *pp. 172, 177*). The Institute of Jamaica has issues dated January 1, 19, and February 5, 1822. Various issues from 1833 and 1836 are located in the Public Record Office (c.o. 33/4), and a copy, dated October 3, 1815, is located in the Boston Public Library. *See* Chandler (*p. 177*) for microfilms of this paper.

IMPARTIAL EXPOSITOR
H. A. Vaughan ("Poyer's Last Work," *Jl. BMHS*, 21, 1953–54, *157*) refers to this little-known paper as follows: "William Williams . . . had . . . been the editor, from 1797 to 1806, of the *Impartial Expositor* . . . to which [John] Poyer is said to have contributed. It is therefore not surprising that when the

Impartial Expositor went out of circulation Williams and Poyer should have agreed to start the [*Barbados*] *Chronicle* together."

I know of only one copy of the *Impartial Expositor*, an issue from October 3, 1804, located in the library of the Barbados Museum; its imprint notes that the paper was "Printed Wednesday and Saturday by Edward Allshorn" (Michael Chandler, personal communication).

LIBERAL
A biweekly which commenced publication on June 28, 1837. Issues from 1837 through 1859 are located in Barbados while the Public Record Office has "some issues of 1838–1856, in c.o. 33/5–12" (Chandler, *p. 172*).

NEW TIMES
A weekly which commenced publication on April 23, 1836 (*see* advertisement in the *Barbadian* April 23, 1836). This paper, whose first editor was Samuel Prescod, was "devoted chiefly to the interests of the coloured community. It was the first periodical and the only one which advocated the rights of the coloured people.... It boldly exposed oppression, whether emanating from the government house or originating in the colonial assembly" (J. Thome and J. H. Kimball, 1838, *p. 74*).

The paper continued publication until at least March 8, 1839; a copy of this issue is located in the BM newspaper library at Colindale [C. Misc. 382 (11)] (Michael Chandler, personal communication).

WEST INDIAN
A semi-weekly which started publication on November 4, 1833 and was edited by Samuel Hyde until 1836 (*see* news items and advertisements in the *Barbadian*, October 26 and November 6, 1833, and July 20, 1836).

The Public Record Office holds issues from November and December 1833 (c.o. 33/4). Some numbers from 1835 are located in Barbados (Chandler, *p. 173*), and the Library of Congress has numbers from January 1 to December 31, 1835.

WESTERN STAR
Started publication around June or July 1836, but ceased shortly thereafter with the death of its editor, Samuel Hyde, on September 22, 1836 (*see* advertisement and news item in the *Barbadian*, July 20 and September 24, 1836).

I know of no copies of this paper.

4

Prints

Although some Barbados prints have been mentioned separately in the preceding sections (e.g. Allard [1680?], Copens 1695, Carter [1836?], Waller 1820, *The Royal African* [1749]), no effort was made, especially in early phases of the research described in the preface, to compile a complete list of all prints, drawings, etc., relating to the island. It can be noted, however, that illustrations depicting social scenes for the time period covered in this *Guide* are relatively rare when compared to illustrations of the island's physical geography, buildings, etc.

The following list,[1] then, supplements items cited above; all of these items, except number 5, are located in the BMHS.

1. The Honble. Dudley Woodbridge, Esq., Director General of The Assiento Company of England in Barbados.
Portrait engraved in mezzotint by John Smith, after Sir Godfrey Kneller. 1718. For details on Woodbridge's involvement with the Royal Assiento Company, *see* John Bennett 1734.

2. Christopher Codrington.
Copperplate engraving, from an original painting by Sir James Thornhill in All Souls College, Oxford. Published by S. and E. Harding, London. November 1, 1776.

3. The Barbados Mulatto Girl.
By Augustine Brunias, colored lithograph. ca. 1790. The central character is flanked on either side by two Negro

1 Provided by Neville Connell in personal communications (August 15, October 20, 1969).

fruit sellers, one of whom is offering her wares; in the distance is a house with three coconut trees.

4. Francis, Lord Willoughby of Parham.
Copperplate engraving by Sanvoort. Painter unknown. Published by Edward Harding, London. March 7, 1798.

5. Rachel Pringle of Barbados.
Colored engraving. Published by William Holland, London. 1796. Published in the *Jl. BMHS* (9, 1941–42, between pages 116 and 117).

6. A West India Sportsman.
By J. F. Hand-colored engraving, caricature. 1807.

7. H.E. Lieutenant-General Sir George Beckwith, K.B., Governor of Barbados, Commander of H.M. Forces in the West Indies.
Engraved by S. W. Reynolds after painting of J. Eckstein. Portrait. 1808.

8. A View of Carlisle Bay, Barbados, taken from Ricketts Battery.
Colored aquatint, after painting by W. J. Lord. 1822.

9. Barbados, Newcombe and Mrs. Sambo.
By C. Williams. Colored engraving, caricature. ca. 1820. Depicts a sailing boat, with two sailors and two other men, flying the Union Jack. An officer lifting a black woman into the boat at the end of the jetty. A white man, with raised stick and umbrella, is in pursuit followed by two Negroes; in distance, hill with houses, and ships at sea.

10. Sir Evan John Murray MacGregor, Bart.
Mezzotint from the original painting

by George Watson. ca. 1820. Mac-Gregor became the island's governor in 1836.

11. St. Paul's Chapel.
Lithographed from an original drawing by a lady to aid in the erection of a Free Chapel School on Rebitt's Land. Uncolored lithograph. ca. 1835.

12. Viscount Combermere in Cavalry Dress, Standing Beside his Horse.
Combermere became governor of Barbados in 1817.

13. Long Bay Castle, Barbados, From a Sketch by Fanny Trollope.
Uncolored lithograph. Engraved by P. Ganci. ca. 1840.

14. Bridgetown, Barbados. From Brittons Hill. . . . During the late Epidemic, 1846.
After a painting by W. Hedges; T. S. Templeton, lithographer.

15. Codrington College, Barbados. View of the Church and Schools.
Colored lithograph. By P. Ganci. 1850.

16–19.
Four lithographs made after daguerreotypes by W. H. Freeman, M.D. 1853. Depicting St. Ann's Garrison and Savannah; Needhams Point, Garrison, Burial Ground, and the town and Harbor of Bridgetown; Chapel of St. Matthias with the graves of officers of H.M.S. *Dauntless* and list of officers buried at St. Matthias.

5

Manuscripts

BARBADOS

Archives in Barbados[1] date back to about 1647, some twenty years after its first settlement, but the surviving records are by no means complete from that date. Until 1964 there were limited facilities for the care of archives and their use for research purposes, although the Barbados Public Library and the Barbados Museum and Historical Society had small collections of manuscripts. Records were generally kept by departments responsible for their creation or custody, but they were seldom kept in suitable conditions or organized for use. In 1960 and 1961 a survey was carried out by the University (then University College) of the West Indies. The results of the survey were published in *A Guide to Records in Barbados* by M. J. Chandler (Oxford, Basil Blackwell, 1965).[2]

The Department of Archives

Largely as a result of the impetus given by the survey, the government of Barbados established a Department of Archives in 1964 and the present writer took up his duties as the first archivist on July 1, 1964, on which date the department came into being. The department occupies premises at the Lazaretto Building, Black Rock, St. Michael, in close proximity to the University of the West Indies' Cave Hill campus, and its associated institutes. Normal reading facilities are available at the department, but at present there

[1] This chapter was specially written for this *Guide* by Michael J. Chandler, Barbados Government Archivist, in July 1969 and updated in July 1970. [J.S.H.]

[2] Chandler's *Guide*, of course, makes obsolete the discussion of manuscripts in Barbados published in Bell, Parker et al., *Guide to British West Indian Archive Materials* (Washington, D.C., 1926), *pp. 334–40*. In the early 1960s many manuscripts in Barbados were microfilmed by the University of the West Indies and a UNESCO microfilm unit. The manuscripts microfilmed by University of the West Indies are listed in the *mistitled* mimeographed guide "Barbados: Guia de los Documentos Microfotografiados por la Unidad Movil de Microfilm de la UNESCO," Instituto Panamericana de Geografia e Historia, Comision de Historia (Mexico, 1965). The materials filmed by UNESCO, under the direction of Dr. Francisco Sevillano-Colom, are actually listed in "List of Microfilmed Materials at the Barbados Public Library," mimeographed (Barbados, 1960). The University of the West Indies microfilms are located at the University library and, with some exceptions, at the Barbados Public Library. [J.S.H.]

are no facilities for photocopying or microfilm reading.

As a generalization it can be said that for political and constitutional studies prior to 1834, it would be necessary to use the archives at the Public Record Office, London, for the political records surviving in Barbados are by no means complete. On the other hand, the major demographic and topographical material is only to be found in Barbados.[3] There is a curious dearth of material about the slave population, and of other records just about the time of emancipation.

The Archives

The Department of Archives is still transferring records from departments of government and local government organizations, and is receiving deposits of records from churches, business organizations, and a few private individuals. This is a continuing process, and it may be some years before the majority of the records listed in the published [Chandler] *Guide* have been received by the department. In addition there will be accruals of more recent records which were not listed at the time of the survey. In the meantime the *Guide* serves as a guide to the archives as well as to records not yet in the department's custody. Many of the latter are, however, kept under the eye of the department, and can be made available if required. The Department of Archives is always ready to advise on the whereabouts and availability of any records listed in the *Guide*.

Major classes of records prior to 1834 already transferred to the Department of Archives are those of the House of Assembly (*Guide, pp. 2–3*); and the Registration Office Secretariat (*pp. 4–12*), Courts (*pp. 14–17*), Record Branch (*pp. 30–35*),[4] and Population (*pp. 35–38*) sections. The local government records of all parishes have already been transferred, and the records of the City of Bridgetown will be transferred in the near future.[5] Few records of the Anglican diocese and parish churches are yet in the care of the department, but the registers of the churches (virtually the only pre-1834 records) are represented in the copies (indexed) in the Registration Office population section. Records of the Moravian church have been transferred, but those of the Methodist church have not. The records from Sharon Moravian church are more extensive than those listed in the *Guide* (*pp. 135–36*) and include some diaries of 1789–94, 1800–14, 1834–82.

The bulk of transfers to the department have been government and local government records. In addition to the pre-1834 material mentioned above, the department now houses records of Government House (*Guide, p. 1*), Accountant General (*pp. 44–46*), the Department of Education (*p. 49*), the Barbados General Hospital (*pp. 53–55*), the Mental Hospital (*pp. 55–56*), the Lazaretto (*p. 56*), the Waterworks (*pp. 68–71*), and the Department of Medical Services (dating from 1925). Of private

---

[3] See Chandler's *Guide*, pages 35–36, for details on the 1679/80 census; also for the 1715 census of the island's white population, which enumerates over sixteen thousand persons, gives first and last names, ages and sex, often notes kin relationships of persons in the same household, and household servants. [J.S.H.]

[4] Complete transcriptions, or extracts, of wills, deeds, etc., are often found in genealogical studies published in the *Jl. BMHS* and in sources such as V. L. Oliver's *Caribbeana* (1910–20). These sometimes contain materials on island life which are useful to the social historian. Seventeenth-century items relating to the Hawtayne, or Hawton, family, were also published in at least two articles by G. H. Hawtayne in *Timehri: Journal of the Royal Agricultural Society of British Guiana*, 7 (1893), *16–43*, and 10 (1896), *93–118*. [J.S.H.]

[5] For publication of various early vestry records in the *Jl. BMHS* see Chandler's *Guide, pp. 72, 95, 162*. [J.S.H.]

records listed in the *Guide* only those of the Barbados Chamber of Commerce (*pp. 141–42*), and the Barbados Union Oil Co. (from the Barbados Public Library, *pp. 145–46*), and Messrs. Carter and Co. (*p. 154*) have been deposited in the department. The records from Messrs. Bovell and Skeete (*pp. 149–53*) are also held by the department in temporary safekeeping.

Manuscript Collections and Private Manuscripts

The Lucas transcripts[6] are still held by the Barbados Public Library, and all the manuscripts listed at the Barbados Museum and Historical Society are still to be found at the museum. Accessions to the museum collection are noted in the society's periodical *Journal*.

There have been no significant additions of early manuscripts to the museum's collection since the compilation of the *Guide*, nor have any important private collections of manuscripts come to light. They are, of course, difficult to locate, but in an island as small as Barbados, I believe that they would be known by now, if any existed. Some plantation and private houses may have an early map or two, a rainfall record, a few deeds or commissions; but it seems unlikely that any large collection of business (or plantation) accounts, or of diaries or correspondence, is lying hidden or unknown in private hands.

Finding Aids

In the Department of Archives a set of the detailed lists of records which were summarized to form the *Guide* is available for reference; and detailed lists of records transferred are prepared for reference in the department. Detailed calendaring and indexing have not yet been carried out, but a catalog of all known Act titles and texts has been typed for 1642–1912; and there is a catalog of Chancery case papers ca. 1820–1910, with a corresponding index to estates. There are numerous finding aids to various series of the archives, but these are largely nominal indexes (to population registers, record books of deeds, wills, etc.). There is very little in the way of subject indexing to any of the archives.

WEST INDIES

(*other than Barbados*)

Manuscript materials relating to Barbados may be located in various West Indian territories, but, at present, the extent of such collections is difficult to ascertain. It may be surmised, however, that they would not be particularly extensive for a variety of reasons stemming from colonial history and preservation difficulties.

The indexes to E. C. Baker's *A Guide to Records in the Windward Islands* (Oxford, Basil Blackwell, 1968) and *A Guide to Records in the Leeward Islands* (Oxford,

---

[6] Made between 1818 and 1828 by Judge Nathaniel Lucas; these include early Council minutes and a variety of other items. Some of the transcripts have been published in the *Jl. BMHS*. For details see Chandler's *Guide, pp. 157–59*. [J.S.H.]

Basil Blackwell, 1965) contain no references to Barbados for the time period considered here, although it is possible that a detailed scrutiny of various collections Baker mentions would yield Barbadian materials.

Two repositories in Jamaica were surveyed in November, 1969; The Institute of Jamaica's West India Reference Library, and the library of the University of the West Indies at Mona.

Institute of Jamaica

Manuscripts relating to Barbados were identified through a typescript list, and a card catalog arranged by subject; only the first item described here was personally examined.

MS 101. [Major Hort] "For the United Service Journal. Barbados in 1840 . . ." *27 folio pages.*
The author was apparently stationed on the island; his description ranges over a variety of topics including the island's military establishment and the life of soldiers, climate and flora, hospitality of the planters and merchants, and the types of food and drink consumed by them at meals, problems of health and disease, shipping and mail boats; there is even a description of the local bathtubs and bath taking. Included with the manuscript are a number of sketches, in both black and white and water color. According to the Institute's cataloger, the artist is unknown and "the sketches were found filed with the MS (September 1965) and presumably they were acquired together. There may or may not be an intrinsic connection between them." Some of the sketches are of English Harbor in Antigua, and about a dozen or so present various Barbadian scenes, dated 1842 and 1843, e.g. views of Joes River, plantation scenery, Porry's Spring, views of the countryside around Bridgetown. Few of the sketches show people and social settings.

MS 13. "Report of the Committee of Council for hearing appeals from the plantations . . . petition of appeal of Susanah Brome of Barbados; counsel's opinion, at Barbados, on Sir Joseph Eyle's case." 1741.
"Attorney General's opinion: case in the matter of Brome." 1746.

MSS FILE. "An Account of the ordinance of other stores of war demanded for Barbados with estimates of the value and annual charge of sending an engineer and storekeeper." May 9, 1702.

"Warrant for supplies for Barbados chapel." May 15, 1721.

"An account of the arms to be sent to Barbados, with the value of cost and charges." May 20, 1702.

"Appointment of Andrew Stone as clerk of the courts of Barbados." 1749.

"Account of the amount of all ships and vessels or cargoes or part of cargoes condemned as prize in the name of H.M. in the Vice Admiralty courts of Jamaica, New Foundland, Bermuda, Nova Scotia, Bombay, Bahamas, Barbados." 1812.

MSS BOX D. List of clergy and schoolmasters who went to Barbados [from England, Anglican]. n.d.

University of the West Indies

The University of the West Indies library contains both original and machine copies of Barbados manuscripts. Some of these were identified with the aid of K. E. Ingram's "A List of Manuscripts and of Photocopies of Manuscripts in the U.W.I. Library" (typescript, ca. 1965).[7] Some of the photocopies have been listed elsewhere in this *Guide*, under the repositories in which the originals are located, but the library has others which I was unable to survey. Similarly, there may be other original manuscripts which did not come to my attention. None of the manuscripts bear catalog numbers, they are arranged in files, by date; all the items mentioned below, except the final one, were personally examined.

1. Thomas S. Dalby, personal business accounts, 1786–90; *20 folio pages*, containing an occasional reference to estates in Barbados, but with very little detail.

2. Sir John Thomas Duckworth, vice-admiral; a collection of letters received, statements, invoices, etc., 1800–15. Only three items appear to have been written from Barbados:

Copies of two short letters from Charles Coleman to Duckworth, dated September 30 and November 5, 1801. These deal with prisoners of war in Barbados, particularly a Frenchman, Monsieur Moulon. Appended is a brief table, "Report of the number of prisoners of war in Barbados the 5th November 1801," that lists a total of 385 prisoners, 363 French and 22 Spanish, 289 of whom were in the prison, the remainder in the hospital.

---

[7] This is a preliminary list prepared for internal use in the University of the West Indies library. In the case of photocopies, until they are cataloged descriptions have been derived from lists provided by the repositories holding the originals or from sources such as the National Register of Archives, London.

Copy of a letter written by Alex Cochrane, dated Carlisle Bay, April 16, 1806, relating to naval battles with the French at St. Domingo and sailing to Tobago. This letter is copied in one written by James Rutherford to Duckworth, dated Plymouth, July 20, 1807.

3.] "Return of the Number of Slaves and Estimated Value thereof, in each class . . . on the 1st day of August 1834." Eighteen sheets, each printed on both sides, with information provided in manuscript giving the name of the estate or "domicile of the slaves," owner's name, total number of slaves in possession, the number of slaves in each class, e.g. head people, tradesmen, inferior tradesmen, field laborers, and the total value of slaves in each class.

The following slave owners are mentioned: Sir Reynold Abel Alleyne, Rev. William Als, John Alleyne Beckles, J. Rycroft Best, Charles K. Bishop, Edward Blades, Christopher M. Brathwaite, Margaret Ann Brathwaite, Miles Brathwaite, Rev. John Brathwaite, John Briggs, George P. Culpeper, Richard H. Chase, James R. Chasman, Charles Cudogan, Charles Evelyn, Joseph Evelyn, Edward Lake Hinds, Thomas W. Hinds, Rev. Edward Lovell, Joseph R. McCormey, James D. Maycock, John Martin Morris, Conrad Nile, Joseph M. Piggott, Richard P. Pile, Robert Reece, William Sharpe, John Simpson, Thomas W. White.

Their plantations include: Baxters, Bay, Breedys, Brewsters, Brighton, Cabbage Tree, Charity Hall, Colleton, Fair View, The Garden, Grange Hill, Haggatts, Haymans, Hope, Lower Grays, Mallards, Mount Pleasant, Risk, Springfield, Stewart Hill, Three Houses, Vaughns, Waterford, Westmoreland, Wildy, Woodland.

4. Nine counterclaims, "Commission of Compensation," in respect of certain slaves, with numbers of slaves and "estimated value in sterling." 1834. Nine printed forms, each of four folio pages. Information, provided in manuscript, includes the name of the estate, slaveowner, and counterclaimant, number of slaves in each class, value, and "particulars of the counter-claim." All of the claims are dated October 16, 1834 and are against Baxters plantation in St. Andrew, forming part of the estate of John Alleyne Beckles, deceased.

The "particulars" focus on estate encumbrances, outstanding debts of the owner, etc., and often delineate the estate's ownership and financial history —all in justification for claims upon the compensation paid the estate for the emancipation of its slaves. Persons making these claims are: Thomas Busby, Thomas Joshua Cummins, Thomas Dayrell, Michael Deane, Mary Husbands, John William Spencer, John Wood, Bryan Taylor Young.

5. J. Maister letter to R. Bruce, dated Barbados, December 21, 1840.

Describes efforts to record Bruce, Barwick, and Walrond family histories, but is mainly concerned with health and disease problems of British troops stationed on the island. He concludes by noting: "This place must be much altered since you were here. The emancipation and the hurricane of 1831 seems to have driven away nearly all the inhabitants worth knowing. No civility whatever is shewn generally to the military and there are not half a dozen houses we have been asked to."

6. Ingram's list records a photocopy of Gladstone Robertson's "Journal of a Voyage . . . through the West India Islands . . . October 15, 1828– August 1829." This includes a brief account of Barbados. The original is in the Library of the Athenaeum, Liverpool.

ENGLAND

The manuscript collections listed in the following pages cannot be considered a definitive compilation of Barbadian manuscripts in England; such a task would be monumental even in the unlikely event that all relevant collections have already been located. However, included below are most, if not all, of the major known collections as well as some of the minor ones. It was not possible to personally visit certain of the repositories; in such cases, the sources of my information are given in the discussion of these places. Under the address of each repository visited, I have given the date of the visit; such dates can aid in determining changes in the repository or its collection.

A valuable introduction for the researcher unacquainted with archival work in the United Kingdom is the pamphlet *Record Repositories in Great Britain*, published by the Historical Manuscripts Commission (HMSO, 2nd ed. London, 1966; 3rd ed. 1968). This pamphlet aids in establishing "where the record material available in this country may be found, and what organizations will help [the student] to approach and use it" (*p. v*). The list of repositories is selective but it nonethe-

less includes the major ones containing state and local records, the major libraries and museums with manuscript collections, and the repositories of the Church of England and other religious denominations. Miscellaneous information is given for each repository, e.g. address, name of archivist or librarian, days and hours open, and the availability of microfilm readers and ultraviolet lamps. In addition, the pamphlet offers useful background information on record collections in general and the agencies concerned with them.

I personally contacted only a handful of county record offices (see *Record Repositories* for a complete listing of offices). From all indications, quite a few of them may have Barbadian-related manuscripts, especially offices in which are kept papers of families that had holdings or other interests in the West Indies; such classes of private papers are also sometimes located in the family residences themselves. Private manuscripts of this nature can be important but they are often difficult to locate despite the efforts of the Historical Manuscripts Commission and the National Register of Archives

(Quality House, Quality Court, Chancery Lane, London, W.C.2).

The National Register of Archives is a valuable aid in locating private and other collections not in state archives, but because the NRA's subject catalog is limited, relevant manuscripts can often best be found by looking up personal names.

Charles Andrews's and Frances Davenport's *Guide to the Manuscript Materials for the History of the United States to 1783, in the British Museum, in Minor London Archives, and in the Libraries of Oxford and Cambridge* (Washington, D.C., 1908) proved useful, and parts are cited below. The *Guide* itself should be consulted for papers of the Privy Council (*pp. 170–87*), the House of Lords (*pp. 189–272; see also* L. S. Stock, 1924–41, under published works), the Royal Society (*pp. 355–68*), and manuscripts in the library of Cambridge University (*pp. 424–30*).

B. R. Crick's and A. Miriam Alman's *A Guide to Manuscripts Relating to America in Great Britain and Ireland* (London, Oxford University Press, 1961) contains a handful of references to manuscripts which mention Barbados (*see* the *Guide*'s index), but in their introduction the authors note that "material *exclusively* West Indian" has not been included in their *Guide*, and refer the reader to Herbert C. Bell, David W. Parker *et al.* (*Guide to British West Indian Archive Materials, in London and in the Islands, for the History of the United States*, Washington, D.C., 1926).

In the preface to Bell, Parker, *et al.*, it is noted that the volume "undertakes to provide special guidance to a body of widely scattered archival materials, for the history of the British colonial empire in America and of the United States in the period before 1815. It may be denoted by the general term 'British West Indian'." The major value of this *Guide* lies in its listing (*pp. 45–86*) of some of the contents of various volumes in the Public Record Office, London (*see* section on the PRO, below); the *Guide*'s discussion of manuscripts located in Barbados (*pp. 334–40*) has been superseded by the publication of Michael Chandler's *A Guide to the Records in Barbados* (Oxford, Basil Blackwell, 1965; *see* section on Manuscripts, Barbados).

Charles O. Paullin's and Frederic L. Paxson's *Guide to the Materials in London Archives for the History of the United States since 1783* (Washington, D.C., 1914) is of limited value for the location of Barbadian manuscripts; aside from the references in this *Guide* noted below (*see* section on the PRO) there are some references to papers of the Privy Council and the House of Lords.

Among the papers presented at the Caribbean Archives Conference (Caribbean Archives Conference, University of the West Indies, 1965. *Report*. Kingston, Jamaica, 1967) are three by D. B. Wardle, the Records Administration Officer at the Public Record Office, London. Two of these can be noted here: "The Location and Availability of Records Relating to the Caribbean in the State Archives in England" (*pp. 120–29*) which gives a general and useful introduction to the records of the Public Record Office, Parliament, the Hydrographer of the Navy, the Post Office, National Maritime Museum, and the British Museum; and "List of Records Relating to Caribbean Countries not in State Archives (or in the British Museum or National Maritime Museum) in England and Wales" (*pp. 504–10*) which briefly records a variety of manuscript collections, some of which are noted in the following pages, and seems to be based upon the catalogs of the National Register of Archives. The other paper presented at this conference by Wardle is mentioned below (section on PRO).

Parts of some English manuscript collections have been reproduced for the Library of Congress. *See* G. G. Griffin's *A Guide to Manuscripts Relating to American History in British Depositories Reproduced for the Division of Manuscripts of the Library of Congress* (Washington, D.C., 1946) for a guide to Barbados materials taken from the Public Record Office, British Museum, House of Lords, the Royal Society, United Society for the Propagation of the Gospel, Lambeth Palace Library, and the Greater London Record Office.

Other guides, lists, etc., which are useful for specific repositories, are noted in relevant sections of the following pages.

Baptist Missionary Society Archives
93–97 Gloucester Place, London, W.1

Although the Baptists founded missions in various of the islands, e.g. Jamaica, Trinidad, the Bahamas, prior to 1834, none were established in Barbados. In August 1968 the BMSA list, "Papers relating to the West Indies 1813–1914" (mimeo., 1964, *26 pp.*), was searched and it appeared to contain no materials which dealt with the island.

Berkshire Record Office
Shire Hall, Reading
(January 1967)

The BRO contains a variety of manuscripts relating to various of the West Indian islands; the Barbadian materials form part of the "Stuart Papers." The background to these manuscripts is given in the catalog prepared by W. J. Smith, the county archivist: "By her father's will, Mary Stuart, wife of Mark Stewart Pleydell, inherited a moiety of his personal estate. This was confirmed by a decree in Chancery, 8 July, 1717: as a result, the papers of Col. Robert Stuart, who returned to England from Barbados, where he had a sugar plantation, in 1705, have come into this collection and form a separate section." Robert Stuart died in England in 1714.

Only some of the bundles in this manuscript collection relate to Barbados and the operation of the Stuart sugar plantations. In general, the manuscripts cover the period 1696–1739, and the information contained in the Barbadian-related manuscript bundles, which are briefly described below, are of primary interest with respect to economic matters, specifically plantation affairs.

D/EPb E73 "Colonel Stuart's Debt Book." Contains miscellaneous papers, 1699–1706, some of which relate to Barbados, including a letter from Stuart to his estate attorney, Mr. Cleland, in Barbados on how the sugar plantation should be managed.

D/EPb E76 "Barbados Ledger." A bound volume of approximately two hundred pages treating the period 1700–27. This includes a variety of items relating to plantation business and legal affairs, e.g. instructions to attorneys, securities, list of judgments by courts.

D/EPb E78
A bundle containing ninety-eight letters, covering the period 1704–20, most of which were written to Robert Stuart and, after his death, to his wife, by Stuart's plantation manager and attorneys in Barbados. The letters largely relate to economic and legal matters.

D/EPb E87
A bundle of fifteen bills of lading for cargoes of sugar sent from the Stuart plantation, 1700–1706.

D/EPb E91
Approximately forty-three miscellaneous items, covering the period 1696–1721 and dealing with plantation economic and legal affairs.

D/EPb E94
A thin bundle, 1706–26, containing miscellaneous correspondence, only some of which relate to Col. Stuart's business affairs in Barbados.

In addition to the Stuart materials, the BRO contains an anonymously authored manuscript "A Short Account of the English Plantations in America," May 1695 (Trumbull Additional Mss. no. 13) which includes a brief conventional description of the government, economy, agricultural products, etc., of Barbados.

British Museum
Great Russell Street, London, W.C.1
(July 1966–January 1967)

The numerous materials relating to Barbados in the Department of Manuscripts of the BM were located with the aid of Andrews's and Davenport's *Guide* (1908, *pp. 1–170*) and various of the BM's manuscript catalogs (*see* T. C. Skeat, *The Catalogues of the Manuscript Collections in the British Museum*, British Museum, rev. ed., London, 1962), particularly those of the Egerton and Additional Manuscripts up to 1960 (the most recent available) and the Sloane and Stowe Manuscripts. Some of the following manuscripts were not personally examined.

ADDITIONAL MANUSCRIPTS

4435 *fols. 13–14*
Letter from B. Hothersall to Philip Miller, dated Barbados, July 12, 1737, in which the author describes his attempts to plant grapevines, and some of his experiments with wine making.

8133C *fols. 204–17*
Memorial of merchants and planters, interested in and trading with Barbados and the Leeward Islands, to the Lords of the Treasury.

9764 *fol. 3*
Debts of Lord Francis Willoughby, July 23, 1677.

10119 *fol. 166b*
Account of character and history of the 4½ percent duty of Barbados, seventeenth century.

11411
A ninety-eight-folio volume entitled "Book of Entrie of Forraigne Letters" presumably collected by Thomas Povey. The volume contains a variety of letters and other items written between 1665 and 1661. Most of the letters were written by Thomas Povey from Barbados; other authors are Martin Noell and Lord Willoughby; addressees include: Richard Povey, Daniel Searle, William Povey, Lord Willoughby, Gen. Brayne, Gen. Doyley, Edward Digges, Col. Osborn, Col. Russell, etc.; *fols. 9–11*, a

petition, drafted in 1655, in which "the planters of Barbados humbly insist that . . . they may pay no customs for ye exportation of necessaries for their subsistence," and request a reduction in duties on ginger and white sugar; also given are the reasons for these requests; *fols. 13–14*, Instructions to the Governor and Council of Barbados to observe the Navigation Act of 1651; *fols. 95–97*, text of the "Articles of Surrender," January 11, 1651/52.

14034
Fols. 1–29 "Ground plats of all the forts, batteries and magazines in Barbados, with their names and number of guns. Received from thence in September, 1696." A plan of twenty-two forts; *fols. 170–73*, a manuscript copy of the Barbados law "An Act for limitation of actions and avoiding of suits, and for the better securing of their estates," June 6, 1732.

15556 *fol. 109*
Abstract of title, etc., with opinion of counsel W. Norton regarding estate in Barbados, with pedigree of Rawdon, 1765 (*see also* 33845).

15741
"Observations of the Master of the St. Ann in a voyage to the West Indies in 1762," includes brief materials on navigation, provisioning, wood and watering possibilities in various of the islands. The Barbados entry, dated September 30, 1762 (*fols. 4–5*) also contains a detailed colored plan of Carlisle Bay, dated October 30, 1762.

15898 *fols. 127–49*
Commission and instructions to Sir Richard Dutton, Barbados, seventeenth century.

18986 *fol. 205*
Letter from Thomas Modyford and others to the Commissioners of the Admiralty, concerning a prize court at Barbados, August 9, 1655.

21134 *fol. 42*
Barbados and Irish trade, ca. 1730.

22617
Fol. 141, copy of a report concerning the naval office in Barbados, sent from the London Custom House (February 16, 1694), and giving a brief history of the office; *fol. 149*, Memorial of the clerks of the Navy Office in various of the islands, including Barbados.

23608
Fols. 1–8, J. H. Lawrence-Archer, "A collection of all the monumental inscriptions prior to 1750 in Barbados," 1857–58. The manuscript to his published work (1875); transcriptions from tombstones in parish church burial grounds; *fols. 35–44*, "Extracts from the older entries in the parish registers of Barbados." *See also* 27969.

24516
"A Register of the names of all the passengers that passed through the port of London, in one year, 1635"; includes the names of some who went to Barbados.

25120
Contains copies of the 1674–79 official correspondence of Secretary of State Henry Coventry, including eighteen letters, largely dealing with political matters, addressed to Gov. Jonathan Atkins of Barbados (*fols. 41, 42, 67, 68, 90, 96, 112, 120, 124, 127, 129, 130, 132, 135, 141, 142, 143, 150*).

27382 *fols. 191–95*
Contains the anonymously authored "The present state of justice in the American plantations, and particularly in the island of Barbados, with some thoughts how the same may (in great measure) be amended for the future." No date is given, but the latest date mentioned in this item is 1661.

27969
J. H. Lawrence-Archer's extracts from various parish and public records in Jamaica and Barbados, with copies of monument and tombstone inscriptions 1643–1750, also some up to 1800; complements 23608 with some additional items.

28076 *fols. 111, 125*
Warrant to Maj. Edmund Andros for pay of arrears due the officers and soldiers of the Barbados regiment, June 22, 1674.

28089 *fols. 41–46*
Papers relating to the 4½ percent duty

in Barbados, late seventeenth century.

28103 *fol. 117*
Letter from Admiral Rodney aboard the H.M.S. *Sandwich*, Barbados, June 30, 1781, dealing with military matters and conflicts with the French.

29863
"Journal of Captain J. Johnson, 1822–1825." Johnson arrived at Barbados on June 17, 1824 and left four days later; his two-page journal entry (*fol. 75*) contains sparse comments of interest to navigators.

30307
"Voyage of Prince Rupert to the West Indies, 1649 to 1650." Although it was intended to visit Barbados, trouble developed on board the ship as it approached the island and "thus being in confusion wee over runn our reckoning and passed the Barbados in the night without seeing it."

32687 *fols. 451–62*
Letters from Governor Howe to the Duke of Newcastle, 1732.

32691–32693
Newcastle papers, containing an occasional item relating to Barbados, eighteenth century.

32695
Same as above.

32705
Fol. 157, letter from the Assembly of Barbados to J. Sharpe, 1745; *fol. 296*, petition from the Assembly to the King, 1745; *fol. 454*, Letter from Barbados Attorney General Jonathan Blenman to J. Sharpe, 1745.

32706 *fols. 69, 131*
Letters from Blenman to Sharpe, 1746.

32707
Fol. 121, minutes of the Barbados Assembly, 1746; *fol. 397*, Copy of correspondence between the governor and speaker of the Barbados Assembly, 1746.

32718 *fols. 43–44*
"Copy of the letter from the Committee of Correspondence in Barbadoes to Mr. Sharpe relating to Tobago," January 25, 1748, which also deals with military and defense matters in Barbados.

32720
Newcastle papers, containing an occasional item relating to Barbados, eighteenth century.

32770 *fol. 32*

Letter from Governor Worsley of Barbados to the Duke of Newcastle, 1730.

32782 *fol. 261*

Letter from Governor Howe to the Duke of Newcastle, 1733.

32867 *fol. 446*

Letter from Governor Pinfold to the Duke of Newcastle, 1756.

32921 *fol. 27*

Letter from J. Blenman to J. Sharpe, 1746.

32938 *fols. 356–63*

A cover letter from Governor Pinfold to the Duke of Newcastle and a manuscript entitled "Reflections on the true interest of Great Britain, with respect to the Caribee Islands . . . in which the importance of Martinique is particularly considered. By a planter at Barbados, 1762." Most of the "Reflections" is taken up with making a case for Britain's taking Martinique and establishing a colony there. There are also comments on various of the islands, including Barbados, primarily relating to economic matters.

33028

Fol. 379, "Copy of a letter from several planters in Barbados to Edward Lascelles, Esq., Collector of [Customs at] Bridgetown, 20 January, 1743." Signed by one-hundred-sixteen of the island's planters, the letter deals with the $4\frac{1}{2}$ percent export duty on sugar and discusses the types of sugar manufactured in Barbados; *fol. 380*, "Copy of a letter from several merchants, Barbados, 1737," in which these persons discuss what they consider to be fair duties on sugar; *fol. 382*, "Letter from the Commissioners of Customs, 1733," deals with sugar duties.

33029

Fols. 5–7, letter from the Attorney General, J. Blenman, to Gov. Thomas Robinson (Barbados, November 15, 1744) which deals with the accidental firing upon a ship that was believed to have not been cleared for departure from the island; *fol. 8*, extracts of the minutes of the Assembly, December 1744, relating to the above incident; *fols. 9–12*, a petition to the King from the speaker and members of the House of Assembly in which fifteen charges are leveled against Gov. Robinson, [1745]; *fols. 13–18*,

letters from J. Blenman to Gov. Robinson (October 21, November 14, and December 5, 1745) relating to political difficulties with the island's legislature; *fols. 19–20*, "Additional complaints against Thomas Robinson"; *fols. 32–33* deal with a case in the Barbados Court of Chancery, 1746; *fols. 37–39*, letter in French, signed by J. Frere, T. Applewhaite, and J. Gollop, addressed to the King and dated February 26, 1746, relating to Governor Robinson's behavior.

33231 *fols. 2–5*

Plans of forts in Carlisle Bay, eighteenth century.

33845

"History of Barbados and leases of Colonel Rawdon's land, taken from the Secretary's office in Barbados, ca. 1750." A manuscript volume containing extracts from *Some Memoirs of the First Settlement of the Island of Barbados* (*see* W. Duke, 1741) as well as a variety of legal rulings and land documents relating to Rawdon. *See also* 15556, *fol. 109*.

35251 *fols. 39–40*

"The protestation of one Tho. Modiford presented . . . by ye hands of . . . Major Thomas Nowell," Barbados, March 20, 1656, deals with political matters.

35655

A volume containing the "Correspondence of Walter Pollard, 1771–1788." The letters in this volume are by and between W. Pollard, his brother Thomas, and his father Dr. Thomas Pollard of Barbados. Walter had left Barbados for England and subsequently settled in the United States; though many of these letters were written from Barbados, virtually all deal solely with family matters.

35865 *fol. 247*

"Tobaccoes entered in the porte of London in fower years from Lady Day, 1637 [to 1640]"; includes figures on Barbados produce.

35907

Fols. 50–59, a published pamphlet (see *Representation of the Board of Trade relating to the Laws made, Manufactures set up, and Trade carried on, in His Majesty's Plantations in America*, London, 1733); *fols. 60–69*, another pamphlet (see *Representation from the Commissioners for Trade and*

Plantations, to the ... Lords ... in Parliament, in pursuance of their Lordships to His Majesty ..., relating to the state of the British Islands in America, London, 1734).

36216

Hardwicke Papers, Privy Council Cases, 1722–43. The following relate to Barbados: *fol. 8,* Isaac and Abraham Mendez, July 25, 1722; *fol. 19,* William Moore, Francis Ford, George Barry, March 11, 1724; *fol. 24,* Richard Morris, 1730.

36217

Hardwicke Papers, Privy Council Cases, 1744–58. *Fols. 172–81,* a printed item "Samuel Adams, esq. et al. – Appellants vs. William Sturge, respondent. The appellants case to be heard before ... the Privy Council for hearing appeals from the plantations ... at Whitehall ... on the 8th day of July 1757." An appeal from a decision by the Barbados Court of Chancery in 1755 relating to a case of disputed lands between various heirs of the Adams family; reviews a considerable amount of information on the Adams family in Barbados since 1666.

36218

Hardwicke Papers, Privy Council Cases, 1759–63. *Fols. 90–91,* appeal to the Privy Council (February 1761) between George A. Selwyn, appellant and John Murray, respondent, concerning a dispute over an administrative office in the Barbados Court of Chancery; *fols. 154–80,* include other Barbados cases in 1762.

36219

Hardwicke Papers, Privy Council Cases, 1764–65. *Fols. 140–63,* the appeal of a case first dealt with at the Barbados Court of Chancery, September 1762, between Thomas Suleven et al., appellants, and Reynold Skeete et al., respondents.

36220

Hardwicke Papers, Privy Council Cases, 1766–69. *Fol. 135,* case involving the seizure of a vessel in Barbados by Admiral Tyrrell; *fols. 183–92,* case to be heard before the appeals court of London, January 1769, the original litigation occurring in Barbados between John Carter, appellant and Catherine Sims, respondent.

37067

"Index of the names of testators whose wills are preserved among the records of the island of Barbados, 1776–1800." Compiled by E. Fitzpatrick (*see* R. V. Taylor's article in the *Jl. BMHS,* 27, 1959–60, *104*); also compiled by him are Add. 38650, 38825.

38331 *fol. 97*

"Calculations of sugar made in the different isles, between 1743 and 1747."

38338 *fols. 193–94*

"The Expense of the Negroes sent from Barbados on the expedition against Martinique, under the command of Admiral Rodney and General Monckton" [1762?].

38650

"Index of the names of testators whose wills are preserved among the records of the island of Barbados, 1647–1796." n.d. *See* Add. 37067.

38714

"Barbados Papers, 1664 to 1706." A volume of one-hundred-eleven folios containing letters and miscellaneous papers, authored by various persons, most of which relate to business, trade, and legal matters.

38825

"Index of marriages from Parish Registers, 1643–1700." *See* Add. 37067.

39946

A volume of thirty-two folio pages describing a "Voyage to Guinea, Antigoe, Bay of Campeachy, Cuba, Barbados, etc.," by an anonymous author who addresses the account to Mrs. Penelope Hill of Leicester, his sister. The author was in Barbados during August and September 1716, and returned again in December of that year, but his account offers virtually no descriptive materials on the island.

43507

Fols. 1–5, "The Barbadoes Plantation – Accompts belonging to Sir James Lowther, Baronet of London. Commencing January the 1st 1756 and ending December 31st 1756." Useful plantation account containing a list of slaves and their occupations, expenses, etc.; *fols. 7–30* "An abstract of the accounts of Lowther's plantation in Barbados, 1825, 1827, 1828, 1829, 1833, and 1835." Lowther's plantation, located in Christ Church, was owned during the period

1825–35 by the Duke of Cleland and Lord William Powlett.

45124

James Francis Grant, midshipman, "Logbook of H.M.S. St. Albans, 1780–1783." The ship arrived at Barbados on November 25, 1781, left on January 14, 1782, returned on December 16, 1782, and left again about January 12, 1783. The brief entries in the logbook relating to the ship's stay at Barbados (*fols. 62–64, 98–101*) are mainly concerned with weather conditions, nautical matters, daily activities on ship, and stores taken aboard.

46545

Lexington Papers. "Letters and Documents concerning the Council of Trade and Plantations of which he was a member, 1699–1702." An occasional item in this volume touches on legal and economic matters in Barbados.

EGERTON MANUSCRIPTS

2395

Fols. 48–53, a published pamphlet (see *A Brief Relation of the Beginning and Ending of the Troubles of the Barbadoes*, 1653); *fol. 84*, petition of the Carlisles to the Protector, concerning Barbados, n.d.; *fol. 105*, proposition and queries regarding the West Indies, notably Barbados, n.d.; *fols. 114–22*, copy of the Commission for Daniel Searle to be Governor of Barbados; *fol. 131*, grant to William Povey the provost-marshal's office at Barbados, September 16, 1657; *fols. 148–51*, reports of committees on revenues of Barbados and insurance of ships, n.d.; *fol. 155*, extracts from R. Ligon's *History of Barbados*; *fol. 175*, address of the Assembly of Barbados to Oliver Cromwell, appealing for his protection, September 1653; *fol. 176*, letter from Thomas Povey to Daniel Searle, governor of Barbados, October 20, 1659; *fol. 182*, petition of the Assembly of Barbados, "for and in behalf of the inhabitants thereof, addressed to . . . the Parliament of the Commonwealth of England," requesting various measures to preserve their internal political autonomy; *fol. 184*, "A Reply to the Exceptions taken to the Waie of Proceedings and the desires of the Cheife Merchants and Planters in relation to

the Barbadoes," n.d.; *fol. 238*, Declaration and act of Governor, Council, and Assembly [of Barbados] for continuance of the peace of the island, January 12, 1659; *fol. 239*, copy of power of attorney given by Thomas Povey to Edward Bradbourn of Barbados to demand of his brother, William Povey, provost-marshal of Barbados, certain goods and money, February 9, 1659; *fol. 240*, "Desires by waie of instruction to Tho: Noell, Esq. concerning the settling some matters of difference between Mr. Tho: Povey and Mr. Wm. Povey," n.d.; *fols. 245–52*, commissions for Col. Thomas Modyford to be governor of Barbados, April 24, 1660; *fols. 279–80*, "Reasons offered by the Lord Willoughby why he ought not to be confined in his settlement upon Surinam," 1652; *fol. 287*, "Humble demands of Governor, Council and Assembly to Governor Willoughby of Barbadoes for confirmation of certain rights and liberties belonging to the inhabitants of the island," Barbados, 1660; *fol. 305*, letter from the Council of Barbados to the King, July 10, 1661; *fols. 329–33*, various items relating to political matters in the 1660s; *fol. 383*, letter from William Povey to his brother Thomas Povey, Barbados, September 9, 1663; *fols. 444–45*, "A relation of some passages in the Barbadoes," (ca. 1660s) deals largely with political matters; *fol. 465*, "The heads of addresses which we desire your excellency to present to his Majesty," presented to the governor and treating subjects such as the 4½ percent duty, military defense, etc.; *fol. 477*, "Lord Willoughby's proposals concerning the West Indies," April 8, 1672, is largely political and economic and contains brief mention of food supplies in Barbados; *fols. 483–84*, letters from Lord Willoughby to Thomas Povey, 1672; *fol. 490*, "Concerning the plantations," March 17, 1672, is a statement on the economic value of Barbados to Great Britain; *fols. 501–2*, "Considerations about the Spaniards buying Negroes of the English Royal Company and receiving 2/3 at Jamaica and 1/3 at Barbados." February 2, 1675; *fol. 584*, report read at the meeting of the Lords of Trade, June 26, 1679, concerning the laws of Barbados;

fol. 587, consideration touching council to be appointed by the governor of Barbados, received from Capt. Langford, n.d.; *fol. 602*, a published broadsheet (see *A true state of the case between the heires . . . of . . . Courteen . . . and . . . Carlisle and planters in the island of Barbadoes* . . .[London, ca. 1644]); *fols. 625–27*, "An estimate of the Barbadoes and of the now inhabitants there," n.d. A brief account of the island is followed by a two-sheet "census" which lists the parishes and acreage in each, the number of free whites, the number of christenings and burials, and the number of indentured servants and slaves; *fol. 642*, letter from the Council for Foreign Plantations to the Governor, Council and Assembly of Barbadoes concerning manufacture of sugar (ca. 1661).

2543 *fol. 123*
"A State of Yor Mats Interest in the West Indies," ca. 1660s, deals chiefly with Barbados political and economic issues.

2597 *fols. 188–89*
Two letters from James, 2nd Earl of Carlisle, concerning Barbados (these letters are published in V. L. Oliver, ed., *Caribbeana*, vol. 3, 1914, *pp. 316–19*).

3020 *fols. 61–62*
Solomon Eccles "to ye Governor and Council of Barbados," April 1678. The author, a Quaker, defends himself against various charges (reproduced here) including "discouraging ye Kings subjects from fighting against ye French."

HARLEY MANUSCRIPTS

1510 *fols. 704, 791*
Letters from Commissioners of Prizes to Lord Willoughby, regarding a Dutch ship taken into Barbados as a prize, May 8, 1667.

1511 *fol. 34*
Establishment of prize offices at various places, including Barbados, May 1672.

6845 *fol. 198*
"An extract out of several letters from Barbados dated 12 and 14 March . . . written by several persons aboard Penn's fleet to their friends in London . . ." May 1655. Deals with military issues relative to the expedition to Jamaica.

7310 *fols. 149–50*
Letter from Edwyn Stede, deputy-governor, to the Royal African Company, February 28, 1694, relative to the slave trade to Barbados, numbers supplied, prices, etc.

KING'S MANUSCRIPTS

123 *fol. 116*
"Plan de la Barbade," 1702, shows the location of various forts on the island.

133 *fol. 118*
"A Plan of Fort George on Mount Charity in Barbados . . . by Thomas Walker," 1762. A detailed colored sketch.

205 *fols. 456–73*
Copy of "Answers of Charles Pinfold, Governor of Barbados, to the queries proposed by the Lords of Trade and Plantations," June 1, 1762. A useful source which surveys the island's military posture, trade, population, governmental problems, economy, etc.

SLOANE MANUSCRIPTS

793
"A Briefe Journall, or a succint and true relation of the most remarkable passages observed in ye voyage undertaken by Captaine William Jackson to the Western Indies or continent of America. Anno Domini 1642." A lengthy description of a military expedition launched from Barbados against Spanish settlements. The author was in Barbados from September to November 1642, but, other than mentioning the names of some of the hundreds of Barbadians who participated in this venture (*fols. 3–4*), the journal is of no informational value on the island *per se*. This item has been published in installments in the *West India Committee Circular* (vols. 26 and 27, 1911–12) and also in the *Camden Miscellany* (V. T. Harlow, ed., vol. 13, London, 1923).

1831A *fols. 35–42*
"Part of a voyage made to the West Indies in the Gilliflower bound with the rest of the fleet from Stoaks Bay, Dec. 19, under Rear Admiral Deakens in . . . 1654; this containing only some passages among the Caribe Islands."

The log of a ship that stopped at Barbados from January 18 to March 31; the three brief entries written while at Barbados relate only to wind and weather conditions.

2302

A twenty-eight-folio volume which contains the letters of J. Walduck, in Barbados, to James Petiver in London, written between November 1710 and September 1712. The overall aim of these often lengthy letters is to convey to Petiver what Barbados is like. In so doing, Walduck ranges over a wide variety of subjects, some at greater length than others, e.g. laws and the working of the island's legal system, aspects of its church and governmental organization, miscellaneous customs of the Europeans and the African slaves, foods and beverages prepared and eaten, holidays, fauna and flora. All of the Sloane Mss. letters are reproduced in their entirety in the *Jl. BMHS* (15, 1947-48, *27-51, 84-88, 137-49*), but there is confusion in the sequence of printing which has resulted from the way in which the last letter (dated September 17, 1712) has been bound in the British Museum volume. The transcription of this letter in the *Jl. BMHS* should read as follows: from the last sentence on page 144 (". . . and we distillate it for Rum."), one should go to the fourth paragraph on page 145 (starting with "There is a sort of Drink . . ."), continue reading until the final sentence on page 149 (ending with ". . . Catalogue of what I send you, But . . ."), and then return to the first line on page 145 ("But if my wife or servants . . ."). For other letters by Walduck *see* Sloane Mss. 3338.

2441

A twenty-two-folio volume entitled "An Account of Barbados and the Government Thereof," 1683/84. Prepared during the administration of Gov. Richard Dutton, the account offers brief summaries of the island's political history up to 1670/71, administrative, legislative, and judicial organization, population (including statistics), forts, shipping, imports, exports, public revenues, and religion. Attached is a survey of the island, 1683/84, which includes parish statistics under the headings of

families and housekeepers, free persons, unfree persons and servants, slaves, men able to bear arms, acres of land useful and possessed, sugar works, marriages, christenings, burials. Also included are a variety of data on military fortifications and the militia (including the names of officers), the names of Council members, officials of the courts of Common Pleas, Court of Exchequer, justices of the peace, and various colonial officials. In addition, statistics on the number of persons (slave and free) who left and entered the island during 1682-83, shipping, revenues, and liquors imported. There is also an artistically drawn map of the island which shows plantations, forts, and churches along the coastal areas. The manuscript has been published in the *Jl. BMHS* (3, 1935-36, *44-57*).

2902

Fol. 20, a personal letter from Abraham Hill, member of the Board of Trade, to Joseph Barton who is on his way to Barbados, December 10, 1697; *fol. 80*, a series of brief note jottings, probably written by Abraham Hill around 1701-2, and treating various aspects of Barbados economics, e.g. plantation profits, tax sources, servants' clothing allowances; *fols. 81-84*, "Act for better securing the liberties of His Majesty's subjects within the island of Barbados," November 3, 1697; *fol. 87*, a brief summary of a resolution by the Barbados Council, July 1696, on the slave trade.

3338 *fols. 74-77*

Letters from J. Walduck to John Searle, dated Barbados, October 29 and November 24, 1710. Walduck signs himself as Searle's uncle. These lengthy letters are largely devoted to Walduck's "discourse of the New World," primarily the Spanish Empire; there are no materials on Barbados. *See also* Sloane Mss. 2302.

3662 *fols. 54-62*

John Scott, "The Description of Barbados" [1668?]. Scott's well-known account of Barbados is based not only upon his own observations but upon those of informants and documentary materials. In his "description" he reviews the island's early history and colonization, the political turmoils of the early years as the proprietorship battle raged between Courteen and Carlisle, the introduction of sugar and its economic advantages and consequences, and the major political, military, and economic events up to around 1668, the latest date mentioned. A useful transcription of the Scott manuscript has been published in the *Bulletin of the Barbados Museum and Historical Society* (nos. 11 and 12, November 1967 and February 1968) with notes (including biographical materials) and an introduction by Neville Connell. Another publication of the manuscript appeared in the *Weekly Argosy of British Guiana* (August 17, 1907).

3926

Henry Whistler, "A journall of a voardge from Stokes Bay, and intended by God's assistant for the West Inga: and performed by the Right Honourable Generall Penn, Admiral." 1655. Whistler was a member of the expedition sent by Cromwell to engage the Spanish in the West Indies. For two months, in early 1655 (modern reckoning), he was in Barbados, and his description of the island and its inhabitants, though brief (*fols. 7–10*), is of interest. In it, he remarks on various commercial and subsistence crops, the slaves, and makes various comments on the European population, including his now classic remark: "This Illand is the Dunghill wharone England doth cast forth its rubidg: Rodgs and hors and such like peopel are those which are generally Broght heare. A rodge in England will hardly make a cheater heare; a Baud brought ouer puts one a demuor comportement, a whore if hansume makes a wife for sume rich planter." The Barbados section of Whistler's journal is published in Frank W. Pitman, *The Development of the British West Indies* (New Haven, 1917, *pp. 5–7*), C. H. Firth, *The Narrative of General Venebles* (London, 1900, *pp. 144–46*), and Neville Connell transcribed the account for the *Jl. BMHS* (5, 1937–38, *184–85*).

3984 *fol. 214*

"A moderate calculation of the annual charge and produce of a plantation in Barbados containing one hundred acres of land built and stoct as followeth . . . presented unto your . . . Majestyes view by us . . . inhabitants and planters in this your Majestyes island." A 1685 petition, signed by deputy-governor Stede and the Council and Assembly of Barbados, requesting release from the obligation to pay the 4½ percent duty on exports, and showing the financial burden the duty imposes. Published under the title "Groans of the Plantations" in the *Jl. BMHS* (16, 1948–49, *25–32*).

4052 *fol. 105*

Letter from Richard Towne to Hans Sloane, Barbados, April 30, 1732. A very brief note requesting a copy of Sloane's "History of Jamaica," enclosing some specimens of undescribed materials, and notifying Sloane that he is preparing "a second edition of my treatise on the diseases in these parts" (*see* Richard Towne, 1726).

In addition to the above materials, the Sloane Mss. contain a number of lists of plants sent from Barbados to England, or of plants growing on the island; these lists, dating between 1683 and 1697, occasionally offer ethnobotanical information. They are located in the following volumes: 1963 *fols. 182–83*; 2346, *fols. 29, 180, 197b*; 3332 *fol. 20*; 3343 *fols. 5–7, 48, 249–50, 263–66, 276, 283*; 4070 *fols. 17–21*; 4072 *fol. 299*. All of these lists are published in David Watts's *Man's Influence on the Vegetation of Barbados, 1627 to 1800* (Occasional Papers in Geography, no. 4, University of Hull, 1966).

STOWE MANUSCRIPTS

184 *fols. 124–27*

Letters from Robert Rich (Earl of Warwick) to Col. Drax, Gov. Bell, the Council of Barbados, etc., 1646–48, dealing with political matters.

201 *fol. 145*

Letter from Lord Willoughby, February 8, 1673, describing the capture of Tobago from the Dutch.

324 *fol. 4*

Account of the English sugar plantations in Barbados in the 1660s, relating chiefly to commercial topics.

755 *fol. 19*

Letter from Lord William Willoughby,

Governor of Barbados, July 26, 1667, requesting the home government to supply Scot servants to Barbados on four-year indentures.

In addition to the above, Charles O. Paullin and Frederic L. Paxson (*Guide to the Materials in London Archives for the History of the United States since 1783,* Washington, D.C., 1914) list the following items: *Additional Mss.* 4157, no. 172, Report of the Council of Barbados between Robert Crowley and John Johnson, October 16, 1665; 5414 roll 15, Map of the island of Barbados (Paullin and Paxson note "this is apparently by the same hand as Sloane 2441"); 9843, General orders to the English army in Barbados, 1817–19. *Lansdowne Mss.* 1197 *fol. 119,* Notes respecting the Natural History of Barbados, 1737. *Sloane Mss.* 2903, no. 19, "Observations out of Ligon's History of Barbados with queries thereon, by Dr. Goddard."

Church Missionary Society

157 Waterloo Road, London, S.E.1
(July 1968)

The CMS did not establish a mission station in Barbados but its archives contain a number of manuscripts relating to the island. The CMS catalog, "Papers of the West Indies Mission, 1819–1861," facilitates location of such materials which are primarily of value for Anglican Church affairs as well as the Colonial Charity School, an Anglican-related school for slave and free colored children.

MISSION BOOKS, *1820–1858* (M) *8 vols.*
The mission books contain copies of original letters, minutes, papers, etc., arranged chronologically. Each volume is indexed by name of correspondent and selected subjects. Volume 1 (M1) 1820–27 contains a number of materials relating to the origin, development, organization, etc., of the Colonial Charity School; similar types of materials, as well as information on the Anglican Church in Barbados, are contained in volume 2 (M2) 1827–34, and volume 3 (M3) 1834–37. Some of the above materials are also found in items recorded below.

CORRESPONDENCE WITH BISHOPS RE ADMINISTRATIVE MATTERS IN THE DIOCESE, *1824–1855* (O2).
Contains (1–14) letters from W. H. Coleridge, the Bishop of Barbados, written between 1832 and 1838.

REPORTS AND PAPERS RE SCHOOLS AND EDUCATION, *1820–1855* (O4).
Barbadian materials (1–11) include various items on the Colonial Charity School during 1820, 1821, 1823, and 1825; rules of the school [ca. 1822]; returns of the diocese giving population, clergy, churches, etc., 1841; a letter, written in 1825, by Charles Phipps, schoolmaster of the Colonial Charity School.

CORRESPONDENCE AND PAPERS RE CHURCH MISSIONARY SOCIETY PROPERTY (O8).
Contains a letter (1) from Charles Phipps, to Mr. Jackson, dated Barbados, August 15, 1831. The schoolmaster of the Colonial Charity School gives an eyewitness account of the hurricane of 1831 and the devastation caused by it, and requests financial aid for reconstruction of the school.

LETTERS AND PAPERS OF INDIVIDUAL MISSIONARIES, CATECHISTS AND OTHERS.
Two letters written from Barbados in 1836 by John Armstrong, a missionary from British Guiana, dealing with personal matters (O14/35–45); letters from Thomas Harris, secretary of the Colonial Charity School Society, to various persons, written in 1820–23, 1825 and relating primarily to school matters. The Armstrong letters are copied in M3, the Harris ones in M1.

The indexes of the Society's annual publication, *Church Missionary Record* (London, 1830–34, 5 vols.) contain no references to Barbados or the Colonial Charity School.

Congregational Council for World Missions
11 Carteret St., London, S.W.1
(July 1968)

The CCWM (formerly London Missionary Society) never established a station at Barbados, but had an important one in Tobago. The missionaries who went to that island sometimes first stopped at Barbados. However, the ten-page typescript list of manuscript materials dealing with the West Indies in the CCWM archives only refers to a handful of items relative to Barbados. These were written by Richard Elliot, a missionary, who spent about ten days on the island in early 1808 on his way to Tobago, and then returned for another few weeks in August 1809. The items are located in the box labeled *Tobago.*

FOLDER NO. 1, JACKET A
Letter from R. Elliot to George Barder, dated Barbados, April 2, 1808, in which he describes his trip from England, but says nothing about the island; letter from R. Elliot to G. Barder, dated Tobago, June 28, 1808, offering a more detailed account of his trip, but only briefly commenting on Methodist and Moravian missionaries in Barbados.

FOLDER NO. 1, RICHARD ELLIOT'S JOURNAL
There are nine very brief entries written in Barbados (March 31–April 9, 1808) while Elliot was waiting to go to Tobago; these entries largely deal with the prayer meetings he attended. The ten entries written in Barbados during his second visit (August 10–31, 1809) all relate to the church services and prayer meetings he attended, and note the size of the audiences to which he preached.

Dr. Williams's Library
14 Gordon Square, London, W.C.1
(July 1968)

"This library, primarily theological but including many historical and other works, originated in a bequest of Dr. Daniel Williams (1643[?]–1716), a Presbyterian clergyman of London, and a friend of the celebrated Rev. Richard Baxter (1615–1691), whose Mss. are preserved in the library" (Andrews and Davenport, 1908, *p. 343*). Although the librarian of the DWL was doubtful if the library contained any materials relevant to Barbados, Andrews and Davenport (*pp. 344–45*) list three items. In addition, the library's manuscript catalog was consulted, but it largely records personal names and was thus only minimally used.

59. 4. 60
A letter from Ephraim Bendall to R. Baxter, dated Deale, January 20, 1674, stating that he is going to Barbados and New England.

59. 5. 195–196
John Bushel and others to Richard Butler, dated Barbados, April 3, 1666, referring to the sad news of the silencing of great numbers of ministers, requesting that Butler inquire if some minister would like to come out from England, and stating the qualifications for the job as well as mentioning Gov. Willoughby's chaplain.

59. 6. 131
A brief letter from Thomas Jackman to Richard Baxter, dated Worcester, May 6, 1659. Jackman had heard about a fire which had destroyed much of Bridgetown. He attributes it to "divine displeasure" caused by the refusal of white Barbadians to permit "their slaves and Negroes to be instructed in the faith and to become Christians . . ." There are only two other references to T. Jackman in the DWL catalog, neither of these having anything to do with Barbados.

East Sussex Record Office

Pelham House, Lewes

The following is derived from Francis W. Steer, *The Shiffner Archives. A Catalogue* (Lewes, n.d.).

2721–2727

Papers relating to shipping ventures of "The Lewes Merchants" or "John Bridger and Co." Includes letters of John Gascoigne of Barbados, and John Hutchinson of London concerning sugar bought for shipment, and giving recent news of Boscawen's fleet off Newfoundland; account with John Gascoigne; insurance policy for goods in ship *Lewis* for voyage Newhaven–Madeira–Barbados. 1755–57.

2811

Insurance policy at five guineas percent premium, by the trustees of Henry and John Shiffner, on a cargo of wine on the ship *Bridgetown* (master, John Fowler) sailing from Madeira to Barbados and thence to London. n.d.

Essex Record Office

County Hall, Chelmsford

Information on Barbados manuscripts is derived from the National Register of Archives (report 6803, *p. 104*), F. G. Emmison, *Guide to the Essex Record Office* (Chelmsford, 1946–48, 2 pts.), and K. E. Ingram, "A List of Manuscripts and of Photocopies of Manuscripts in the U.W.I. Library" (typescript, ca. 1965).

D/DRY (095)

Correspondence of Lord Ralph Grey, Governor of Barbados, including letters written from the island after Grey had left. Includes a congratulatory letter from William Penn of Philadelphia on the termination of Grey's term of office. 1700–1706.

D/DRg (1/148–158)

Various papers of the Nightingale family of Barbados, e.g. will, legal papers, bills of sale for slaves. Includes the will of Granado Nightingale with bequest of two slaves, April 22, 1680; bills of sale to Edward Nightingale, Barbados merchant, for two slaves, 1662, 1663; deed of sale from Roger Punnett of St. Phillip's parish to Edward Nightingale for a female slave, her daughter, and "one Breedeing sowe," sold for 3885 pounds of muscovado sugar, October 4, 1662 (transscribed in full in Emmison, *pp. 132–33*). 1654–80.

D/DHC (F1)

Will of Thomas Root, Secretary of Barbados. 1660.

Gloucester County Records Office

Shire Hall, Gloucester

Through the National Register of Archives the following item was located in August 1968, and a Xerox copy of it obtained: "A Song of the Negro Slaves at Barbados," n.d. (GCRO list *p. 29*, box 58). This is a one-page manuscript of "An African Song or Chant, taken down in notes by G. S. [Granville Sharp] from the information of Dr. William Dickson" (*see* William Dickson, 1789). This valuable manuscript records the musical notation and verses of a chant, sung by "A single Negro (while at work with the rest of the gang)

[who] leads the song, and the others join in chorus at the end of every verse."

This item belongs to the Hardwicke Court papers and arrangement must be made through the GCRO to see it. Hardwicke Court contains many items of Granville Sharp, and it may well contain other manuscripts relevant to Barbados.

Greater London Record Office
Dartmouth Street, London, S.W.1
(*January 1967*)

The GLRO (formerly the Middlesex County Record Office) has only a handful of wills and deeds relating to Barbados; there is a typescript list of these items from which the following notes have been taken. References are given in parentheses.

DEEDS

1. Relating to the White River plantation, parish of St. Philip, 1765 (MCRO, *Acc.* 621, Box 1, F.L. 1).
2. Relating to Haymans sugar plantation, 1751–58 (MCRO, *Acc.* 621, Box 4, original bundle 15).
3. Relating to the parish of Christ Church, 1684–1767 (MCRO, *Acc.* 621, Box 4, original bundle 18).

4. Belonging to Sir John Gibbons, 1697–1767 (MCRO, *Acc.* 621, Box 5, F.L. 3).

WILLS

1. Of Sir John Gibbons, 1768; property includes Haymans, Coopers Hill, and Mullins plantations (MCRO, *Acc.* 621, Box 4, original bundle 15).
2. Copies of wills of Sir William Gibbons, 1759 and 1772; property includes Mullins, Borrowfield, Bishops, Morgan Lewis and Cooper Hill plantations (MCRO, *Acc.* 621, Box 5, F.L. 2).
3. The original of the 1772 will noted above (MCRO, *Acc.* 621, Box 5, original bundle 7).

Guildford: Museum and Muniment Room
Castle Arch, Guildford, Surrey

This repository was not visited, but the National Register of Archives and correspondence with the archivist helped identify some manuscripts related to Barbados (although there may be more): *Loseley Mss.* 778/21/1–2, a lease and release of Congre Road and Foull Bay plantations, August 30–31, 1695, from John Hilton to Henry Molineux; 778/21/3 is a draft certification of the above by the Lord Mayor and Aldermen of the City of London. *Unclassified Documents*, no. 2022, an estimate of cost of buying one-hundred-fifty acres in Barbados for a plantation and stocking it with slaves, oxen, etc.; also a note on climate and crops; no date, but of the seventeenth century and possibly related to *Loseley Mss.* 778/21/1–2.

Hampshire Record Office
The Castle, Winchester

This repository was not visited, but through the National Register of Archives a manuscript was located and a copy of it obtained through correspondence with the HRO archivist: *Blachford Mss.* 8M57/7, a brief note from T. Griffin to Robert Blachford (Barbados, November 7, 1726) in which he notes that on the middle passage from Africa fifty-eight out of two-hundred-nine slaves died, that his ship stopped at Barbados for provisions, and is "under saile for Jamaica." There may be more materials related to Barbados in the HRO.

Imperial War Museum
Lambeth Road, London, S.E.1

A personal communication from the archivist in January 1969 states that "although some of our records date back to the late nineteenth century, they do not go back as far as 1834. We certainly have nothing relating to the island of Barbados for the period 1627–1834."

Kent County Archives Office
Maidstone

The following is derived from Felix Hull, *Guide to the Kent County Archives Office* (Maidstone, 1958) and K. E. Ingram, "A List of Manuscripts and of Photocopies of Manuscripts in the U.W.I. Library" (typescript, ca. 1965).

SACKVILLE OF KNOLE MSS. (U269) Agreement between Francis Whitworth as clerk of H.M. Courts in the Island of Barbados, and George Newport of London, merchant, for a term of seven years; Francis Whitworth will continue in office, Samuel Wadeson of Barbados, as his deputy, or will appoint whoever George Newport directs. 1731.

A brief for Francis Whitworth and others against an Act passed in the Barbados Assembly for the better regulating of the fees of the courts in that island. 1735.

Lambeth Palace Library
London, S.E.1
(April 1967)

Working with the manuscripts in the LPL is greatly facilitated by the extremely useful and detailed calendar and index written by William Wilson Manross (*The Fulham Papers in the Lambeth Palace Library*. Oxford, Clarendon Press, 1965). His work is an indispensable tool for any researcher interested in the Fulham Papers. The LPL librarian doubted if any manuscripts in the library, other than those in the Fulham Papers, related to Barbados for the time period considered; all of the following, then, relate solely to these papers.

In general, the papers form a valuable source of information for the history of the Anglican Church in Barbados, but the volumes of correspondence also contain valuable information on miscellaneous subjects of interest to one concerned with broader social and cultural topics. Barbadian materials are contained in the following:

GENERAL CORRESPONDENCE
Volume 15 (nos. 125–295) covers the years 1703–30 and includes letters and other items written by various persons, e.g. clergymen, in Barbados and treating, in one form or another, many different subjects; volume 16 (nos. 1–215) covers the period 1731–1827, and

also includes (nos. 216–30) a variety of undated manuscripts relating to Barbados. All of the items in these volumes are calendared by Manross, and thirteen letters from Arthur Holt to the Bishop of London are reproduced by John A. Schutz and Maud O'Neil in their article "Arthur Holt, Anglican Clergyman, Reports on Barbados, 1725–1733" (*Journal of Negro History*, 31, 1946, *444–69*).

DIOCESAN BOOK FOR THE PLANTATIONS

Volume 37, pages 1–8 deal with Barbados; these pages are not calendared by Manross. They comprise a summarization of information provided by each of the eleven parish rectors in response to seventeen queries sent by the Bishop of London; the information deals with a variety of topics related to the church establishment in each parish, e.g. how long each minister had been in his parish, number of white families in it, when the youth of the parish are catechized, number of schools, number of "infidels" (full answers to these queries were returned between February and May 1724; these are to be found in vol. 15 of the General Correspondence, *pp. 203–14*). Also included here are notes on the names and dates of service of var-

ious rectors of the parishes, going back to the seventeenth century.

ORDINATION PAPERS

According to Manross (*p. 297*) these "are testimonials and other documents presented to the Bishop of London by candidates for ordination, or by ordained clergymen seeking licenses for the colonies." The Barbados papers are in volume 27 (*pp. 39–315*) treating the years 1750–90, and volume 28 (*pp. 1–269*) which covers 1793–1819. Manross's calendar lists the names of all persons from Barbados covered by the above periods, as well as biographical data on them.

MISSIONARY BONDS

Barbados materials are in volume 35 (nos. 59–129) which covers the period 1750–1810. According to Manross (*p. 323*) "These are bonds that were posted by ministers receiving the King's bounty for emigration to the colonies." He lists (*pp. 332–33*) the names of persons for whom bonds were posted.

ENTRIES OF CLERGY LICENSED FOR THE PLANTATIONS

Volumes 38 (*pp. 58, 90–91*) and 39 (*pp. 34, 42–43*) contain the names of persons who were ordained and licensed for work in the plantations by the Bishops of London.

Leeds Archives Department
Sheepscar Library, Chapelton Road, Leeds 7
(July 1968)

All of the West Indian manuscripts at Leeds are from the Earl of Harewood's archives. The typescript list of these archives, dated 1963 (no West Indian materials had been added subsequently) has the following introduction to the West India section: "The Lascelles family owned or own estates in Barbados, Jamaica and Tobago. The late Earl of Harewood left the West Indies estates to his younger son, the Hon. Gerald Lascelles. There are remarkably few W. India papers at Harewood [because] the estates were for a time administered as a business partnership under the name Lascelles and Maxwell. ... The records of Lascelles and Max-

well descended to the firm of Messrs. Wilkinson and Gaviller, a West India merchant house ... [in London]. All the records were destroyed [in 1940] in an air raid. Some transcripts are in the Pares collection in Rhodes House library, Oxford."

The Harewood plantations in Barbados were Belle (St. Michael), Thicket (St. Philip), Fortescue (St. Michael), Mount (St. George), Cooperhill, and possibly one other; most of the items which deal with these plantations in the preemancipation period are concerned with business affairs. The West Indian collection is arranged in two bundles, both of which contain some materials relative to the Barbadian plantations.

BUNDLE OF ACCOUNTS, ETC.
Includes "abstracts of produce of the estates and other property in the West Indies belonging to Lord Harewood, 1805–1839"; "Quarterly Report on the Belle plantation, 1836."

BUNDLE OF LETTERS AND PAPERS ON WEST INDIAN ESTATES AND

AFFAIRS
Contains around one-hundred-fifty letters written between 1795 and 1873 with occasional enclosures on business affairs. Not many of these letters deal with the Barbadian plantations in the preemancipation period, but, unfortunately, my detailed notes on these were lost, thus preventing identification of the relevant letters in this bundle.

Leeds Central Library

The following information is derived from K. E. Ingram, "A List of Manuscripts and of Photocopies of Manuscripts in the U.W.I. Library" (typescript, ca. 1965).

TEMPLE NEWSAM RECORDS

TN/po 2 CII
Twenty-three personal accounts of Lord Richard Irwin as governor of Barbados and governor of Hull (England). 1719–21.

TN/po 2 CIII
Bills and receipts chiefly relating to

Lord Richard Irwin and his army career. Other bills relate to the transport of goods to and from the Barbados where Irwin was appointed governor on March 16, 1720/21. He died shortly before setting out April 10, 1721.

TN/po 5A
Letters patent approving Irwin as governor of Barbados. n.d.

TN/c 12/159
Letter to Lady Irwin from Robert Warren in Barbados about getting coach and horses there. October 11, 1721.

Liverpool Record Office
William Brown Street, Liverpool, 3

The LRO was not visited, but in a personal communication, January 1968, the archivist noted: "Most of the Ms. material relating to the West Indies, available in the Record Office and Local History Department of this library deals with the island of Jamaica. There are however three letters among the collection of Norris family papers deposited in the Record Office, relating to the trade with Barbados of Richard Norris (1670–1731), Liverpool merchant, in the years 1703, 1705. Robert Gladstone (1805–75), also a Liverpool merchant, describes his visit to Barbados

on pages 25–28 of his Ms. *Journal of a Voyage and Residence in Demerara with a continuation of the same through the West India Islands, 1828–1829.*"

In addition, David M. Matteson (*List of Manuscripts Concerning American History Preserved in European Libraries and Noted in Their Published Catalogues and Similar Printed Lists.* Washington, D.C., 1925, *p. 93*) notes that the Liverpool Public Library contains the following: "Ms. KF102. Sales Book of Thomas Case, Liverpool, 1763–69. With accounts of the sale of slaves at Barbados etc. 1767–68. In 1 Ms. volume."

Methodist Missionary Society
25 Marylebone Road, London, N.W.1
(April 1967)

The MMS has two broad categories of manuscripts relating to the West Indies: letters (and letter copies) and journal-diaries written by missionaries or ministers stationed in, or visiting, the islands. The journals or diaries, contained in four boxes, were all written during the nineteenth century and deal with most of the West India islands, but none refer to Barbados.

The letters are also kept in boxes; twenty-five of these span the years 1803 (the earliest date) to 1840. Within each box, letters are numbered consecutively and are arranged chronologically by island. For example, in the first box, which contains approximately three hundred letters written between 1803 and 1813, letters from Barbados are numbered 188 to 206, the earliest one dated April 30, 1804; in the next box, covering 1814–15, the few Barbados letters are numbered 124–29; the third

box, 1815–18, contains only one letter from Barbados (no. 86). There is no central catalog or list of letters; however, some volumes contain indexes which help to identify letters written from Barbados, but others do not and the researcher must go through the entire volume.

Although the Methodist missionaries were concerned with working among slaves, their letters are not especially useful sources of descriptive materials on the life and behavior of this population. The letters are largely devoted to the progress and setbacks of missionary activities and thus are invaluable sources for the history of Methodism on the island; occasionally the letters also afford glimpses into other areas of Barbadian society inasmuch as the wider society often directly impinged upon the progress and movements of the missionaries themselves.

National Maritime Museum
Greenwich, London, S.E.10

The archives of the NMM were not consulted, but in a March 1968 personal communication the custodian of manuscripts reported: "We have many . . . documents concerning the West Indies, but none, so far as we see, contains an

actual account of Barbados, but many ships visited the island. We were not able to make an exhaustive search, so that should you care to visit us . . . you may find something."

Northamptonshire Record Office
Delapre Abbey

The following are derived from K. E. Ingram, "A List of Manuscripts and of Photocopies of Manuscripts in the U.W.I. Library" (typescript, ca. 1965)

G2766

Bargain and sale, John, Earl of Bath and Dame Anne, Lady Willoughby of Parham, of plantation in Barbados.

1679.

G2915

Agreement, William Willoughby of Hundsen, James, Earl of Suffolk, and John, Earl of Bath, re royal grant of fines, monies, etc., issuing from estates in Barbados. 1663.

Oxford University: Bodleian Library

The manuscript collections at the Bodleian were not personally examined. The following list has been compiled from V. T. Harlow's *A History of Barbados, 1625–1685* (Oxford, 1926) and his *Colonizing Expeditions to the West Indies, 1623–1667* (London, 1925), and Andrews's and Davenport's *Guide* (1908, *pp. 372–423*). Thus, the library's catalogs should be consulted primarily for materials dating from the 1780s to 1834. Some of the Bodleian Mss. relating to Barbados have been published, and these are noted below.

In addition, the Rhodes House Library, which is a department of the Bodleian, contains a few manuscripts relating to pre-1834 Barbados. See Louis B. Frewer, comp., *Manuscript Collections (excluding Africana) in Rhodes House Library Oxford* (Bodleian Library, Oxford, 1970. Nos. 589, 590, 621, 636, 637). The papers of the British Anti-Slavery and Aborigine Protection Society (founded around 1823) are also housed in the RHL and these as well may include Barbadian materials.

ASHMOLEAN MANUSCRIPTS

240 fol. 276
"Copy of a statement regarding apparition of a man in the Barbadoes," signed by Tho. Vaughan, Jacob Luke, J. Parry, Edith Murry, July 13, 1660.
423
Fol. 244, "Description of a comet in Barbadoes, November 29, 1664," in a letter by Richard Morris from Col. Lewis Morris's plantation, January 9, 1665; *fol. 268*, letter from William Fisher to John Champante relating to a comet seen in Barbados, March 9, 1667.

CLARENDON MANUSCRIPTS

71, 72, 80, 81, 82, 84, 85
"Correspondence between the Earl of Clarendon and Lord Francis Willoughby, Lord William Willoughby, and others, 1660–1667" (Harlow, 1926, *p. xiv*).

87
"Details of Sir Richard Dutton's misgovernment, 1683" (Harlow, 1926, *p. xiv*, listed as vol. 88, *fols. 40–43* in Andrews and Davenport, *p. 416*).

RAWLINSON MANUSCRIPTS A

3 fol. 135
Copy of a license from the Governor of Barbados for a ship of Hamburgh, 1653.
20 fol. 1
Petition to Gov. Searle of Barbados from John Colleton and John Yeamans, 1654.
26 fol. 146
Proceedings at a session held at Barbados, regarding lands held by lease, May 15, 1655.
60 fol. 131
Proposals for the protection of British commerce and excluding strangers from trading with Barbados, submitted to the Protector by Simon de Casseres, n.d.
62 fol. 638
(Cited, but not identified, by Harlow, 1926, *p. xiv*.)
257 fol. 109
(Cited, but not identified, by Harlow, 1926, *p. xiv*.)
271 fols. 1–6
Copies of petition and letters from George Lillington, Michael Terrill, David Ramsay and Benjamin Cryer of Barbados, relative to their suspension by Gov. Granville, 1704.
272
Fol. 224, letter from Col. Romer to Duke of Marlborough and others regarding rumor that he is to be sent to Barbadoes and protesting against it, Boston, March 6, 1704; *fol. 307*, copy of minutes of the Barbados Council, July 4, 1660.

RAWLINSON MANUSCRIPTS B

250 fols. 55–65
Papers relating to Jamaica and Barbados, 1670–1708, dealing with such questions as powers of the governor,

disputes between the governor and assembly, privileges of the assembly and trade of the colonies, with tables of goods exported.

RAWLINSON MANUSCRIPTS C

66

Letter book of J.C., a London merchant supplying English residents in North America and the West Indies, March 3, 1710–September 6, 1717, together with a list of correspondents' names. Barbados addressees include Conrad Adams, Capt. Pitts, William Weaver, Joseph Ward, William Phyllips, George Graemes, Robert Anderson, Dr. Lucas, John Phillips, and Thomas Phillips.

94 *fol. 33, ff.*

"A collection of petitions and depositions in connexion with the Carlisle–Courteen dispute, which together with the Chancery [Public Record Office] and Trinity College, Dublin, documents are invaluable for the history of the original settlement of Barbados" (Harlow, 1926, *p. xiv*). Some of the depositions have been reproduced by Harlow (1925, *pp. 25–42*) under the title: "A brief collection of the depositions of witnesses and pleadings of Commissioners at law in a difference depending between the merchants and inhabitants of Barbados on the one part and the Earl of Carlisle, Lord Willoughby, etc. on the other part. The said depositions were taken the 15, 17, 19 and 26 of March 1647 and the 9 of April 1647." N. D. Davis ("Papers Relating to the Early History of Barbados," *Timehri* 5, 1891, *51–60*) reproduces John Powell's testimony, 1660, and Henry Powell's petition, ca. 1652.

933

Fol. 12, deposition of William Fletcher, master of ship *Barbadoes Merchant* of Liverpool, May 2, 1700; *fol. 124*, "Reasons why the Bishop of London does conceive that the copy of a letter from the Lords Commissioners of Trade and Plantations, upon the petition of the agents of Barbadoes to His Majesty relating to an ecclesiastical court attempted to be erected in that island, is an unfair report," n.d.; *fol. 132*, copy of Barbados Act relating to ecclesiastical court in that island, August 15, 1719.

967

Log of ship *John* bound for Virginia and Barbados, January 31, 1701 to September 17, 1701.

TANNER MANUSCRIPTS

36 *fol. 36*

"Referring to Sir Richard Dutton's policy, 1681" (Harlow, 1926, *p. xv*).

54, 55, 56

These volumes contain "numerous letters between officials in England and the Barbadian government, particularly the Ayscue–Willoughby correspondence, during the years 1650–1660" (Harlow, 1926, *p. xv*). Some of the letters in these volumes were transcribed by N. D. Davis and are located in box 8 in the Davis Collection at the Royal Commonwealth Society. Ayscue's letters to Willoughby were also published by Davis in the *Argosy* of Georgetown, British Guiana (late nineteenth or early twentieth century), under the title "Sir George Ayscue's Account of his Expedition against Barbados in 1651–1652"; the Tanner Mss. reproduced in this article, which deals with military and political issues, are volume 55 *fols. 79, 79b, 85, 86b, 138, 141, 142b*. Harlow (1925, *pp. 48–53*) reproduces, from volume 54 (*fols. 153–54*), "A letter from Barbados by the way of Holland concerning the condition of honest men there," August 9, 1651. This letter, in Harlow's words, "is of interest and importance; for besides giving us an insight into the feelings of the Commonwealth party while under the domination of the Royalists in Barbados, it illustrates the close connection of the islanders with the traders of Holland" (Harlow, 1925, *pp. 48–53*).

Another Tanner Ms., a letter from Lord Willoughby to his wife in England, written around 1651, describes the repercussions in Barbados of the Civil War and the establishment of a Barbados-derived colony in Guiana. This letter has been published in R. Schomburgk (1848, *pp. 273–76*) and Henry Cary's *Memorials of the Great Civil War* (vol. 2, London, 1842, *pp. 312–19*).

In addition, a manuscript by George

Fox, located in the Bodleian, has been published under the title "Journal of a Voyage to America and West Indies in 1671–1673" (*Journal of the Friends Historical Society*, 9, 1912, *5–39*). Accompanied by other Quakers, Fox landed at Barbados in October 1671, and stayed for about three months. His journal entries in this edition are, however, very scant and are mainly concerned with his religious activities on the island.

N. D. Davis has published "a transcript of a broadside" (printed?)

located among the Rawlinson manuscripts ("An Early Impression of Barbados." *West India Committee Circular*, 28, no. 395, 1913, *539*). Davis dates "the document, which is unique so far as we can ascertain . . ." at post 1665, and it appears to have been written no later than the 1670s. About one-half of the one-page transcript discusses the production of sugar and other commercial crops, e.g. cotton, ginger, and the remainder gives a brief overview of the island's geography, towns, population, etc.

Public Record Office
Chancery Lane, London, W.C.2
(*May–July 1967; August 1968*)

The voluminous manuscript collections of the PRO, particularly those of the Colonial Office, or the CO group, contain materials of fundamental importance to a study of Barbadian political, commercial, and military history and, in general, the development of the island's national institutions; they are of less value for information on topics such as customs, social behavior, etc.

Materials relevant to Barbados are sometimes located in other PRO groups, but, aside from the Shaftesbury papers (see below) these were minimally consulted. For references to Barbados in the papers of the Admiralty Office, Audit Office, Board of Trade, Customs Office, Foreign Office, High Court of Admiralty, Lord Chamberlain, Treasury (see also *Calendar of Treasury Papers* published by the PRO) and War Office, the reader should consult C. O. Paullin's and F. L. Paxson's *Guide to the Materials in London Archives for the History of the United States since 1783* (Washington, D.C., 1914) and especially Charles Andrews's *Guide to the Materials for American History, to 1783, in the Public Record Office of Great Britain* (vol. 2, Washington, D.C., 1914); Andrews's *Guide* also offers useful introductions to these manuscript groups and offices, often presents at least a partial listing of the contents of various volumes in the collections, and gives

an overview of some of the PRO's special collections, e.g. Rodney papers, Shaftesbury papers. In both Andrews and Paullin and Paxson the indexes help to identify the Barbados materials. In addition, in the first volume to his *Guide* (1912), Andrews itemizes some of the materials in the State Papers, Domestic Series (*see also* the *Calendar of State Papers, Domestic Series*, published by the PRO). Also of value in identifying the years and volumes of the record groups noted above (as well as those in the CO group) is D. B. Wardle's "Records Relating to Caribbean Countries in the Public Record Office, London" (Caribbean Archives Conference, University of the West Indies, 1965. *Report.* Kingston, Jamaica, 1967, *pp. 472–98*).

A very useful history of the CO records, the departments which produced them and their organization, descriptions of the various classes of papers, etc., is provided by R. B. Pugh (*The Records of the Colonial and Dominions Offices*, Public Record Office Handbooks, no. 3, HMSO, London, 1964). Similar types of information on the CO group are given by Charles Andrews in the first volume of his *Guide* (1912). Some of the CO manuscripts are available on microfilm in the Library of Congress; for a guide to these *see* G. G. Griffin *A Guide to Manuscripts Relating to*

American History in British Depositories Reproduced for the Division of Manuscripts of the Library of Congress (Washington, D.C., 1946).

The volume of manuscripts dealing with Barbados in the CO group makes a detailed listing of them impossible at present; such a task would be a project of major proportions; however, using the CO papers of the seventeenth and part of the eighteenth centuries is considerably eased by the availability of two major series of calendars: *Calendar of State Papers, Colonial Series. America and the West Indies* (44 vols. London, 1860–1963) which covers the period 1574 to 1738; and *Journal of the Board of Trade and Plantations* (14 vols. London, 1920–38) which spans 1704–82. Each volume of these calendars contains a comprehensive name and subject index. The ideal for a researcher would be to use the calendars in conjunction with the manuscripts as the calendars are an amalgam of direct quotations and paraphrases, and, in some cases, an abbreviated version of the original manuscript might omit very specialized information. However, if one does not have access to the manuscripts, the calendars, especially those of earlier years, are more than an adequate substitute.

With respect to some of the record classes mentioned below, the cataloging system in the PRO has been changed since many of the calendars (especially the earlier volumes) were published. For example, volume 5 of the Colonial Entry Books was formerly CEB 5, volume 6, CEB 6, and so on; under the new system these volumes are CO 29/1, CO 29/2, etc. Thus, one attempting to locate the original manuscript from a reference provided in the calendar is advised to first consult the lists located in the PRO's Round Room which correlate the old and new systems; these lists have been published in Andrews's *Guide* (vol. 1, 1912, *pp. 279–307*).

Besides Charles Andrews's *Guide* (vol. 1, 1912), which also contains references to Barbados in various classes not noted below (*see* index in his *Guide*), additional aids in using the CO papers are Paullin's and Paxson's *Guide* (1914) and, especially, H. C. Bell, D. W. Parker *et al.*,

Guide to British West Indian Archive Materials, in London and in the Islands for the History of the United States (Washington, D.C., 1926). Bell, Parker *et al.* also contain references to Barbados in classes not mentioned here (*see* index to their *Guide*) as well as a listing of some of the contents of the classes discussed below. The PRO publication, *List of Colonial Office Records, Preserved in the Public Record Office* (London, 1911), provides a convenient chronological listing of the Barbados CO classes; each volume in each class is correlated with the years and subject it covers.

COLONIAL PAPERS, GENERAL SERIES (CO 1)

A miscellany of papers, e.g. official correspondence, instructions to governors, petitions, proceedings of legislative bodies, territorial descriptions, relating to both the American and West Indian colonies, including many relevant to Barbados. The period covered is 1574–1757 (sixty-nine vols.), but the majority of papers are earlier than 1688. Items in this class include:

"Some observations on the island of Barbadoes" [1667]. Contains statistics on European emigrations from the island and considers the implications of these departures, comments on indentured servants, slaves in trades and crafts, the island's defense system and military fortifications, Jews, and political history (CO 1/21, no. 170).

"An account of the English sugar plantations, January 23, 1668." Concentrates upon economic problems and the importance of the islands to Great Britain with focus on Barbados; mentions indentured servants (CO 1/22, no. 20).

"A list of the most eminent planters in Barbadoes in 1673." Over seventy names with the acreage held by each person; appended to a letter from Peter Colleton, May 28, 1673, in which he reports on population estimates made in the 1660s (CO 1/30, no. 42); *see also* Shaftesbury Papers (PRO 30/24/49).

Sir Jonathan Atkins, "An Account of His Majesty's Island of Barbadoes and the Government thereof," February 1676. Compiled in response to questions raised by the Lords of Trade; includes population figures by race, age category, and sex (co 1/36, no. 20; copy in co 29/2, *pp. 1–14*).

Sir Jonathan Atkins, "Answers to 32 queries by the Lords of Trade and Plantations," July 4, 1676. The governor systematically ranges over a variety of matters relating to the island's political, military, economic, etc., status with brief references to slaves and miscellaneous social issues.

Sir Jonathan Atkins, "Further answers to the 32 queries of the Lords of Trade and Plantations on the state of Barbados," March 26, 1680. Supplements the preceding item; encloses the 1679 census and comments on problems associated with it (co 1/44, no. 45).

"Census of Barbados, 1679. Supplied by Governor J. Atkins to the Lords of Trade and Plantations in March–April 1680." A voluminous and extremely valuable and detailed census based upon materials provided by the ministers and churchwardens of each parish; military materials are provided by the commanders of the island's regiments (co 1/44, no. 47, *fols. 141–379*). A transcript is located in the Barbados Archives. For an analysis of this census, *see* Richard S. Dunn, "The Barbados Census of 1680: Profile of the Richest Colony in English America," *William and Mary Quarterly*, 26, 1969, *3–30*.

Sir Richard Dutton, "Answers to the heads of inquiry respecting Barbados," June 11, 1681. Similar to Atkin's "answers to 32 queries . . ." above (co 1/47, no. 7).

As of July 1967 eighteen reels of microfilm of this class, covering the period 1674–97, were available for purchase from the Public Record Office.

Original Correspondence: Barbados (co 28)

Various types of official papers including census materials, sent from the island to the home government, e.g. Board of Trade, Secretary of State. Volumes 1–114 span the period 1689–1834, volumes 115–26, 1835–38. Census materials include:

"A list of Negroes, mills, cattle-mills,

and pott kilns, July 1710," arranged by parish (co 28/13, *fol. 189*).

"A list of the inhabitants . . . taken by the several church wardens," August 16, 1712. Figures for each parish (except Christ Church) under the headings of: number of plantations, white men, women, and children, white men fit to bear arms, number of Negro slaves and slaves fit to bear arms (co 28/14, *fol. 21*).

"A Census of the Island of Barbados . . . taken in the months of October and November . . . 1715." A parish-by-parish breakdown enumerates over sixteen thousand white persons, giving first and last names, ages and sex; household units are identified and data are often provided on kin relations among household members and the names of servants attached to each. No materials on slaves (co 28/16). A full penciled transcript is located in the Barbados Archives; two articles by R. V. Taylor provide background to this transcript and relate how it was acquired (*Jl. BMHS*, 27, 1959–60, *103 ff., 135–43*). Materials for the parishes of St. Michael, Christ Church, St. George, and St. Thomas have been published by Mrs. A. St. Hill in various numbers of volumes 4–9 (1936–42) of the *Jl. BMHS*. E. B. Burley's *Memorandum Summarizing the Returns of a Census taken in the Island of Barbados, in the Year 1715* (Barbados [1913]) provides a very useful summary of parish figures with associated notes and commentary. This item originally appeared in the Barbados *Official Gazette*, November 14, 1913; a reprint, in pamphlet form, is located in the library of the Royal Commonwealth Society.

"A list of the number of planters and inhabitants . . . taken from the several lists returned into the Secretary's office," June 20, 1748. Figures for each parish, under the headings of: white men, women, and children, slaves, free Negroes (one-hundred-seven total for the island), and men fit to bear arms (co 28/29, *fol. 25*).

"An account of the number of slaves returned into the Treasurer's office . . . from the year 1780 to 1787 inclusive," May 13, 1788 (co 28/61, *fol. 204*).

"Returns of free coloured people . . .

May 1802." Island total, 2,229; figures broken down by parish and number of men, women, boys, and girls in each (CO 28/72, *fol. 62*).

"General return of the clergy of Barbados," 1817. Covers period 1812–16, and includes parish population for whites, free colored, and slaves, with baptismal and burial statistics (CO 28/86).

"An abstract of the slave population . . . October 31, 1817." Parish figures; includes detailed estimates for ten-year age-classes, and numbers of slaves born in Barbados, Africa, and other islands of the West Indies (CO 28/86).

Charles Andrews (vol. 1, 1912, *pp. 189–90*) gives a brief overview of volumes 1–60 (1689–1786), and Bell, Parker *et al.* (1926, *pp. 45–68*) provide a useful listing of some of the contents of the following volumes: 13–36, Board of Trade, Original Correspondence (1709–82); 38–42, miscellaneous papers accumulated in the offices of the Secretaries of State (1702–1803); 43–83, Secretary of State, Original Correspondence (1689–1814). L. J. Ragatz, *A Guide to the Official Correspondence of the Governors of the British West India Colonies with the Secretary of State, 1763–1833* (London, 1923), is also of some use in dealing with the items in this class, but the *Guide* contains only a partial listing of Barbadian materials, and its frugal referencing often makes it difficult to locate a given item.

As of July 1967, twenty-three microfilm reels of CO 28, treating 1689–1752, were available for purchase.

ENTRY BOOKS: BARBADOS (CO 29)

Copies of official letters, commissions, instructions to governors, etc. C. Andrews notes (vol. 1, 1912, *p. 109*) that "the earlier volumes [Entry Books] contain copies of letters received as well as of letters written, and so in part duplicate the original correspondence [CO 28]. After 1700, however, the number of in-letters entered is very small and the volumes partake more and more of the character of letter-books, containing entries of out-letters only."

Volumes 1–35 cover the period 1627–

1841. Bell, Parker *et al.* (1926, *pp. 69–74*) list some of the contents of the Board of Trade volumes (11–19, 1707–82) and the Secretary of State volumes (21–29, 1767–1813).

ACTS: BARBADOS (CO 30)

Volumes 1–21 contain copies of laws passed between 1643 and 1834; volumes 22–23, 1835–43. Volume 1 is a published copy of Richard Hall's *Acts* (London, 1764), volume 3 is a manuscript of William Rawlin's published *Laws* (London, 1699), and volume 4 is a published copy of *Acts of Assembly* printed by John Baskett (London, 1732). The remaining volumes in this class largely contain manuscript copies of the island's laws, some of which are not included (or only included by title) in the volumes published by John Jennings (1654), William Rawlin, Richard Hall, and Samuel Moore (1801). Moore's work goes up to 1800, thus the manuscript laws in the PRO are of special significance for later periods. CO 30/17 covers the period 1797–1805; CO 30/18, 1806–10; CO 30/19, 1811–14; CO 30/20, 1814–25; CO 30/21, 1825–34; CO 30/22, 1835–39. Some of the nineteenth-century laws, especially those dealing with amelioration of the island's slave codes, were published in various volumes of the House of Commons Sessional Papers (*see* Parliamentary Papers).

SESSIONAL PAPERS: BARBADOS (CO 31)

These include the minutes of the House of Assembly and Council: CO 31/1–53 cover the period 1660–1834, and CO 31/54, 1834–38.

Bell, Parker *et al.* (1926, *pp. 75–85*) list the dates of minutes included in each volume (vols. 1–43, 1660–1784). With respect to volumes 1–4 (1660–95) Charles Andrews notes: "These volumes contain also minutes of proceedings of the Council of War, Committee of Public Concern, and many supplemental papers relating to trade, war defense, etc., including letters from planters, petitions, papers on sugar industry and methods, and commissions of the governors. Often these transcripts are in part entry books of miscellaneous documents as well as of acts and of assembly and council proceedings. The earlier volumes are generally the more valuable in this respect; later volumes are apt to be meagre" (vol. 1, 1912, *p. 191*).

The PRO does not have minutes from 1804 to 1809 and from July 1814 to July 1815; some of these are available in the Barbados Department of Archives (*see* M. J. Chandler, *A Guide to the Records in Barbados*, Oxford, Basil Blackwell, 1965, *pp. 2–5*).

In addition, the PRO has two typescript volumes of Council minutes: volume 1, February 1654 to August 1656; volume 2, August 1656 to December 1658. These were presented to the PRO in 1934 by F. G. Spurdle who transcribed the minutes from the originals located in Barbados.

MISCELLANEA: BARBADOS (CO 33)

CO 33/13–26 contains shipping returns (1678–1819); C. Andrews (vol. 1, 1912, *p. 191*) gives an overview of two of the earlier volumes as well as references to other PRO groups which contain related Barbadian statistics. Bell, Parker *et al.* (1926, *pp. 85–87*) provide more detailed information on CO 33/13–19 as well as shipping returns in the Treasury papers.

CO 33/27–29 include materials relating to the Courts of Chancery, Escheats, Grand Sessions, and Common Pleas (1722–31); CO 33/30 contains Treasurer's accounts from 1726 to 1737 (*see* C. Andrews, vol. 1, 1912, *pp. 191–92*).

The Blue Books of Statistics from 1821 (the earliest date) to 1834 are in CO 33/33–46; for 1836–38, in CO 33/47–49.[8] CO 33 also contains copies of various Barbados newspapers (*see* Newspapers). The remaining volumes in this class (about one-hundred-fifty volumes cover the period 1678–1941) largely, if not entirely, relate to the post-1838 period.

---

[8] The books for 1831 and 1835 are missing (M. J. Chandler, *A Guide to Records in Barbados* [Oxford, 1965], *p. 171*).

SHAFTESBURY PAPERS (PRO 30/24)

A detailed index and supplementary report to these papers is located in the Round Room. The following items dealing with Barbados were located and consulted.

PRO 30/24/48

Ten letters and one "proclamation," written between November 8, 1669 and December 26, 1670, which relate to the relationship between Barbados and South Carolina, e.g. problems associated with immigration to the mainland colony, maintenance of economic and social ties between the two territories. All of the letters (nos. 18, 45–52, 54) were written from Barbados; authors include Joseph West, Henry Brayne, John Yeamans, N. Carteret, and Thomas Colleton; addressees are Lord Ashley, Peter Colleton, G. Carteret, and the Lords Proprietors of Carolina. Number 44 is the "Barbados Proclamation" which contains "the grants of the Lords Proprietors of Carolina to those that settle therein," November 4, 1670.

PRO 30/24/49

Miscellaneous items which principally deal with economic and political conditions on the island: (no. 1) "Award of the arbitrators between Sir Anthony Ashley Cooper and Gerald Hawtaine, and inventory of stock, etc. on the plantation in Barbados," June 18, 1652; (no. 2) "Sir Anthony A. Cooper to Robert Hooper. Bargain and sale of a plantation in the parish of St. George," February 27, 1655; (no. 2b) "Abstract of some principal passages concerning Sir William Courteen's heirs, and their claim in and to the island of Barbados, collected by John Darell from Capt. Henry Powell, John Powell, and others," 1660; (no. 3) a miscellany from the 1670s, e.g. "List of the most eminent planters in Barbadoes," various materials on Gov. Willoughby, "An accompt of the English sugar plantations," and a letter from Peter Colleton (August 12, 1673) to J. Locke discussing various plants he has sent to England.

In addition, V. T. Harlow (*A History of Barbados, 1625–1685*. London, 1926, *p. xiii*) notes that the following groups contain Barbados materials:

CHANCERY PROCEEDINGS

Charles I. Bundles C. 60/38, C. 58/4, "containing materials similar to those found in Trinity College (Dublin) and the Rawlinson Mss. in Oxford."

LEDGERS AND FILES OF THE
ROYAL AFRICAN COMPANY

T. 70/15, 16, 238 (letters from the company's factors at Barbados, 1679–81); T. 70/646 (statement of Negroes sold in Barbados, 1662–63); T. 70/314, 936–41 (statements of sales, 1673–84).

Michael Chandler (personal communication) provided the following references to Treasury Papers dealing with slave registration and compensation in Barbados, all in the first few decades of the nineteenth century:

T. 71/520–565 (slave registers and indexes, 1817–34); T. 71/790–803 (valuers' returns, nos. 1–5349); T. 71/895–900 (registers of claims); T. 71/940 (index to claims); T. 71/1083–1108 (claims and certificates, original, nos. 1–5349, not continuous); T. 71/1280–1287 (counterclaims, nos. 1–5343); T. 71/1306 (adjudications in contested cases); T. 71/1356–1359 (certificates for compensation and lists of awards); T. 71/1418 (Parliamentary returns of awards); T. 71/1505 (Assistant Commissioners' proceedings, reports); T. 71/1516 (Assistant Commissioners' proceedings, letters to Central Commission); T. 71/1549 (Assistant Commissioners' proceedings, exhibits: returns of sale of slaves); T. 71/1619 (Miscellanea, in-letters 1833–37).

Royal Commonwealth Society

Northumberland Avenue, London, W.C.2
(*July 1968*)

The library of the RCS (formerly Royal Empire Society, Royal Colonial Institute) contains the following manuscripts and manuscript collections dealing with Barbados.

DAVIS COLLECTION

This comprises a sizable miscellany of notes, manuscript transcriptions, articles, etc., produced over many years by the amateur historian and genealogist N. Darnell Davis (1846–1915). Davis, a prolific writer and seemingly tireless researcher of Caribbeana, presented his papers to the RCS shortly before his death. The mass of materials in this collection is difficult to categorize, but its most valuable elements are the transcriptions of deeds of sale, parochial minutes, wills, accounts, and other official documents, largely relating to the seventeenth century, some of the originals of which have been either destroyed or lost. The collection as a whole is of unequal quality, and frequently bits of information are recorded on scraps of paper, without referencing or context, and quite often the hand-writing is very difficult to decipher. However, the collection can be a rewarding one. The papers are stored in fifteen boxes, and searching through them for relevant Barbadiana is enormously facilitated by a detailed list in each box of its contents.

ESTATE PLANS

1. Estate plan of the mansion of Joseph Storey, parish of St. Michael, 1829; this plan simply delineates a land plot of twenty-three acres.

2. Estate plan (with colored illustration) of Quintynes, the plantation of Josiah Heath, parish of St. John, 1829. The plan shows the layout and dimensions of each of the plantation's fields, and notes that Quintynes is surrounded by lands owned by Richard and Robert Haynes. The "colored illustration" affords a panoramic view of Quintynes, showing the sugar mill and boiling house in the foreground, and fields in the background.

SPARKE FAMILY PAPERS (MSS. 7)

Only three of the fifty-four documents

in this collection relate to Barbados, and these primarily deal with family matters.

1. Bill of freight from Arthur Sparke in England for a trunk sent by the "Kinge of Powland" to Gabrielle Sparke in Barbados, January 5, 1649.

2. Letter from Charles Sparke in Barbados to his brother Arthur, March 29, 1655.

3. Letter from Charles Sparke in Barbados to his mother Mary Sparke in London [March 29, 1655?].

After my visit to the RCS, the library added "Crichton letters, 1832–34, from West Indies, including Barbados, with some references to anxieties of pre-emancipation period" (Michael Chandler, personal communication).

Shropshire County Record Office
Shire Hall, Shrewsbury

The following item is listed in Mary C. Hill, *A Guide to the Shropshire Records* (Shrewsbury, 1952, *p. 118*): "Apprentice-ship. John Sherman to go to Barbadoes. 1647."

Society of Friends Library
Euston Road, London, N.W.1
(March 1967)

The SFL contains an extensive collection of manuscripts written by Quakers during the seventeenth and eighteenth centuries. A fairly comprehensive name and subject card catalog facilitates identification of materials relevant to Barbados. Many of these, including some of the items mentioned below, have been published in one form or another in the *Journal of the Friends Historical Society* (*see* indexes to the various volumes) and in works such as J. Nickalls (1952).

ABRAM RAWLINSON BARCLAY COLLECTION

A collection of two-hundred-forty-nine letters, written during the seventeenth century by different persons from various locales and addressed to George Fox and others. The letters are bound into two volumes: volume 1 contains letters 1–125 and volume 2, numbers 126–249. Letters 1–157 have been calendared in sundry issues of the *Journal of the Friends Historical Society*, beginning in 1930 and up to 1964; the remainder are available only in manuscript.

Of letters 1–157, only ten were written from Barbados. Covering the period 1661–81, their authors include Josiah Coale, Oliver Hooton, John Rous, George Rose, and Ralph Fretwell (ARB Mss., nos. 44–50, 62–63, 99). The letters are calendared in volumes 33 (1936), 37 (1940), and 46 (1954) of the *Journal of the Friends Historical Society*. There may be an occasional letter from Barbados amongst numbers 158–249, but a rapid survey of these did not yield any.

The ten letters noted above are not particularly informative, and would be primarily of interest to one concerned with early Quaker personages and activities in Barbados; in this respect, the most useful letter is one from John Rous to George Fox and others, written in 1681 (ARB Mss., nos. 48–49; extracted in the *Jl. of the F.H.S.*, 33, 1936, *60–63*) in which he gives a succinct account of the status of the Quaker community in Barbados and its religious establishment. Although most of these letters are largely devoted to religious subjects, there is occasional reference to wider societal issues, but no mention of slaves or slavery.

EPISTLES RECEIVED

The epistles are mainly designed to give the London Meeting a brief account of various Quaker groups' activities during the year; but, generally speaking, the ones sent from Barbados offer relatively few concrete details. Most of the epistles are largely composed of pious and religious sentiments and expressions, although the names of individual Quakers are often mentioned and some information on Quaker activities and relations with the wider community are sometimes given. Epistles sent by Barbadian Quakers between 1689 and 1706 are in volume 1 (*pp. 87, 89, 161, 217, 229, 250, 252, 363, 369, 388, 408, 438*); 1705–37 (vol. 2, *pp. 12, 15, 205, 213, 249, 269, 299, 319, 335, 371, 391, 409, 429, 454, 465, 485, 507, 538*); 1738–58 (vol. 3, *pp. 1, 16, 30, 45, 67, 86, 118, 129, 145, 216, 237, 257, 305, 307, 326, 348, 452*); 1764 (vol. 4, *p. 142*); there are no epistles from Barbados after 1764 until 1801, last date of volume 5, the final volume.

EPISTLES SENT

These were sent by the London Meeting, and are often in the form of a lengthy reply to the ones sent from Barbados; however, they are mainly composed of "spiritual advice," and none of the items contained in volume 1 for example, which, for epistles sent to Barbados, covers the period 1690–1703 (*pp. 42, 137, 182, 200, 233, 242, 270, 313, 358, 445*), afford any information not contained in the Epistles Received.

GIBSON MANUSCRIPTS

These include two letters relevant to Barbadian Quakers: *T.S.* 438, a letter from a group of Friends in Barbados to groups in Jamaica and Antigua, 1709, which introduces Thomas Story; and *T.S.* 460, a short letter from the Barbados Meeting to the London one referring to Story's visit to Barbados in 1714 (*see* Thomas Story, 1747).

LONDON YEARLY MEETINGS

These manuscripts are bound into more than twenty volumes, starting with the year 1668. Each volume is indexed so that references to Barbados can be easily located although, it is to be noted, the indexes do not always list all references to the island in a given volume. Materials on Barbados in the Yearly Meetings are largely summaries of epistles received in London and are generally of little value. Also included are reports or excerpts from reports and journals of Quakers who traveled to the colonies. Among these, the following contain materials on Barbados:

Benjamin Holmes, "Account of his travels in America. Written from Antigua, August, 1719" (vol. 5, *pp. 446–64*). Holmes spent a month on the island in June 1719 and the very brief account of his visit (*pp. 459–60*) is largely taken up with his activities in the Quaker community.

Joshua Fielding, "Account of his travels in America," 1729 (vol. 7, *pp. 81–84*), lived on the island from November 1725 to March 1726, but only discusses (*p. 81*) the meetings he attended.

Edmund Peckover, "Journal of travels in North America and Barbados, 1742–1743" (vol. 9, *pp. 322–39*), spent "some weeks" in Barbados in 1743, and the short two-paragraph account of his visit (*pp. 338–39*) is devoted to the condition of the island's Quaker community. Peckover's journal has been published in the *Journal of the Friends Historical Society* (1, 1903–4, *95–109*).

LUKE HOWARD COLLECTION

Only one item in this collection refers to Barbados: John Haydocke's "Epistle to Friends in the island of Barbados or elsewhere . . . 8th month 1676" (vol. 150, no. 20).

PORTFOLIOS

These are bound volumes containing miscellaneous manuscripts; the materials in them relating to Barbados were identified by using the library's catalog. Generally speaking, the manuscripts in these volumes provide little information except for anyone interested in the names of Quakers who lived in or visited Barbados during the seventeenth century.

Volume 16

No. 28, a 1686 testimonial from Roger Longworth in Barbados; no. 58, a 1674 account by George Fox who relates the adventures of John Stubbs, a Quaker who had visited Barbados; no. 62, a religious epistle written in the 1680s; no. 74, George Fox's account of the life of Elizabeth Hooton in which he mentions that she had visited Barbados for a few months in the 1670s; no. 77, a brief account by John Jay, who became a Barbados planter, mentioning his visit to the mainland colonies and England.

Volume 17

No. 1, comprises brief accounts by various Quakers who traveled in the "services of the Lord"; some touched at Barbados, but no details are given about these visits; no. 2, "Visits of Ministers of the Society of Friends to the West Indies in 17th and 18th Centuries." A compilation, made from various sources sometime in the nineteenth century, which lists the names of persons, the islands they visited, and the years in which the visits were made.

Volumes 26, 27, 28

Nos. 1; 58–60, 74; and 3, 135, respectively, contain epistles sent by the Barbados Meeting, between 1744 and 1748, to London.

SWARTHMORE MANUSCRIPT TRANSCRIPTIONS

Copies of a large number of letters written by and to Quakers in the seventeenth and early eighteenth centuries (the originals are also located in the Friends Library). The transcriptions, which are all very legible, are bound into six volumes, each volume containing hundreds of letters and an index; the index names the author of each letter, the date and place of writing, and the addressee.

In the six volumes, there are only twenty-three letters written from Barbados, spanning the years 1655 to 1675. The majority of lines in all of these are devoted to the expression of religious sentiments similar to those of the epistles. Occasionally there are also general statements about the progress of Quakerism on the island, information on the relationships between the Quaker and non-Quaker community, and ample critiques of the religious and moral life of non-Quakers. There is no mention of slaves or slavery. Authors of the various letters include Henry Fell, Robert Malins, Joseph Nicholson, George Rose, John Rous, Robert Widder, Peter Evans, Mary Fisher, Lewis Morris, Peter Pearson, Richard Pinder, John Taylor, Elizabeth Trot, and George Fox. Their letters are found in volume 1 (*p. 578*); volume 2 (*pp. 101, 107, 111, 117, 121, 125, 129, 223, 943, 945*); volume 3 (*pp. 251, 261, 899*); volume 4 (*pp. 127, 151, 273, 289, 293, 369*); volume 5 (*p. 379*); volume 6 (*p. 451*).

MISCELLANEOUS

1. Philip Madin, "Account of his journey to the West Indies with Thomas Colley, 1779" (Mss. Box W); a small ninety-four-page notebook. Madin arrived at Barbados, his first port of call from England, on May 16, 1779, and left the island close to seven weeks later. During his stay he apparently traveled extensively throughout Barbados, but much of his diary account of this visit (*pp. 11–25*) is devoted to an itemization of the meetings he attended, and naming the Quakers he met and stayed with. He also lists the food plants of Barbados and briefly describes the uses to which they are put, and offers some brief, but valuable, comments on a slave funeral and the slaves' religious beliefs.

2. Thomas Colley, "Account of visit to the West Indies, etc. with Philip Madin, 1779" (Mss. Box P); a notebook with unnumbered pages. The narrative of Colley's stay in Barbados essentially follows the same lines as Madin's (see above), i.e. stress upon Quaker meetings attended and the state of the Quaker community on the island. There are also a few descriptive pages dealing with the island's plant life, a few general observations on the slaves, and mention of a Quaker meeting attended by slaves.

United Society for the Propagation of the Gospel
15 Tufton Street, London, S.W.1
(*July–August 1968*)

The USPG (formerly Society for the Propagation of the Gospel in Foreign Parts) began its long and well-known formal association with Barbados in the first decade of the eighteenth century with its acquisition of the Codrington plantations. Aside from the extensive manuscript collection relating to these plantations and the college itself, there are other materials related to clerical issues and the Anglican Church establishment on the island. Some of the manuscript collections described below are available on microfilm at the University of California at Los Angeles and some are in the Library of Congress. Two studies of Barbados which were primarily based upon research into the Codrington materials in the USPG archives are: Frank J. Klingberg, ed., *Codrington Chronicle: An Experiment in Anglican Altruism on a Barbados Plantation, 1710–1834* (University of California Publications in History, vol. 37, Berkeley and Los Angeles, 1949) and J. Harry Bennett, *Bondsmen and Bishops: Slavery and Apprenticeship on the Codrington Plantations of Barbados, 1710–1838* (University of California Publications in History, vol. 62, Berkeley and Los Angeles, 1958).

BARBADOS JOURNAL, *1710–1738* and BARBADOS COMMITTEE, *1710–1726, 1741–1742*

Two volumes containing the minutes of the SPG's London committee charged with overlooking the affairs of the Barbados plantations. The volumes complement each other in dates covered so that one must use both of them concurrently in chronologically tracing the development and problems of the plantations and college. The minutes *per se* are usually very brief, but frequently include extracts from or paraphrases of reports and letters from Barbados. A detailed name and subject index, prepared on file cards by a Miss Bankes, ca. 1962–67, is available in the USPG Archives and is an invaluable aid to the user of the volumes; in her index, X.23 refers to the Barbados Committee volume, and X.14 to the Barbados Journal. *See also* SPGFP, *Annual Reports* (1701–1839) for related materials.

FULHAM PAPERS

Four thick volumes of original letters, etc. There is no detailed index or calendar to these volumes, but the first sheet of each one contains a general summary of contents, arranged by territory. Only two of the volumes include materials from the West Indies, and only one has materials from Barbados (vol. 2, 1803–27, *pp. 535–760*). Most of these items were written by ministers and addressed to the Bishop of London; they primarily relate to the Society for the Conversion and Religious Instruction . . . of the Negro Slaves . . ., and efforts by the church in Barbados to convert the island's slave population. Most, if not all, of these materials are available on microfilm in the Library of Congress; for details on these see G. G. Griffin, *A Guide to Manuscripts relating to American History in British Depositories reproduced for the Division of Manuscripts of the Library of Congress* (Washington, D.C., 1946, *pp. 196–98*).

LETTER BOOKS

The materials in these volumes are for the most part of the type found in the General Correspondence of the Lambeth Palace Library manuscripts. *Series A* is comprised of twenty-six volumes of copies of eighteenth-century letters received in London. According to V. L. Oliver ("The Church in the West Indies," *Caribbeana*, 3, 1914, *204–10*), "most of the originals of these [letters] and many later letter books were subsequently destroyed by fire." There is a comprehensive typescript calendar of each volume's contents which is stored in the office of the USPG archivist. Of the twenty-six volumes in this series, only four contain letters written from Barbados: volume 6, 1710–11 (*pp. 28, 66–67, 76, 111–15*); volume 7, 1711–12 (*pp. 75–76*); volume 24, 1732–34 (*pp. 267, 273, 277–81, 284–85, 287 91, 297 304, 315*); volume 26, 1735–37 (*pp. 381–83*).

Series B consists of twenty-one volumes of original letters received in London; of these volumes, B.6 deals with the West Indies, including Barbados, for the period 1728–79, and volume B.8 relates solely to Barbados, 1739–42. There is also a detailed typescript

calendar of these volumes available in the archivist's office.

Series C consists of various unbound letters, documents, etc., relating to the period 1800–1850. These were not consulted; according to the archivist most deal with North America, but some with the West Indies, perhaps even including Barbados.

Michael Chandler (personal communication) adds the following items relating to Codrington College and the plantations: X 24–30 (Barbados Committee minute books, 1741–1833); X 32 (Memoranda book, copies of letters, etc., 1711–1809); X 33 (Attorney's book, 1720–ca. 1802); X 34–38a (Letter books and accounts, 1712–23, 1779–1812); X 39–43c (Plantation and College accounts, 1721–30, 1744–1811). *See also* Chandler's *A Guide to Records in Barbados* (Oxford, 1965, *pp. 105–7*).

University of Leeds

"In the Brotherton Collection, University of Leeds, there are a small number of documents and letters relating to Barbados . . . [these] fall between the years 1650 and 1657 . . ." (*Jl. BMHS*, 24, 1956–57, *175–90*). This article in the *Jl. BMHS* reproduces, with biographical and other notes, various items largely pertaining to political, military, and commercial affairs.

University of London Library

Senate House, Malet Street, London, W.C.1
(*November 1966–February 1967*)

The UL library contains two manuscript collections with materials on Barbados: the William Hewitt Papers and the Newton Estate Papers. Both collections came to the University of London in 1960–61; they have been carefully arranged by Mrs. C. E. Micklem whose description and list of each is available in the library's Paleography Room.

WILLIAM HEWITT PAPERS (MS. 522)

Hewitt went to the West Indies from

England in 1766 and apparently remained in the islands until his death in 1781, serving as "His Majesty's commissioner for the distribution of land in the southern Caribee islands," and holding other colonial appointments; he also owned land and slaves in, at least, Dominica. Mrs. Micklem judges his papers a "haphazard and mixed accumulation, from both England and the West Indies [which represent] most facets of his life," but it is difficult to judge from them how long Hewitt lived in Barbados; he was certainly on the island from November 1779 to March 1781, though he may have taken sidetrips elsewhere during this period.

The collection does not contain many items dealing with, or referring to, Barbados. Those that do, primarily treat of Hewitt's business interests elsewhere, and, in general, the papers are of little value unless one is primarily concerned with biographical data on Hewitt himself.

NEWTON ESTATE PAPERS (MS. 523)

This is an extremely valuable collection of well over one thousand items dealing with Seawell and Newton plantations in the parish of Christ Church; the period covered is from 1706 to the 1890s, although the most extensive documentation is from 1794 to 1824.

Mrs. Micklem has performed an excellent job in arranging this collection, and her detailed list of its contents enormously facilitates research. The UL is also to be credited with the handsome and effective way in which the papers have been bound into volumes.

The papers, prior to 1794 (and after 1824), are largely composed of plantation financial accounts and are of unequal quality for various years during this period. The plantation owners during the eighteenth century included John Newton (the original owner who died in 1706), his son Samuel, and Samuel's son, John Newton (d. 1783). In 1794 the plantations came into the hands of the brothers Thomas and John Lane.

John, a barrister, and Thomas, a solicitor and sometime clerk for the Goldsmith's company of London, resided in England. Thomas, in the words of Mrs. Micklem, "took over the dealings with Barbados from the beginning. He was in London and he knew the merchants, and continued to manage [the estates] even after he and his brother divided [them] in 1803, John taking Seawells, and Thomas, Newton. . . . [Thomas] kept his accounts and letters received from his managers in Barbados and from his merchants in exemplary order, as well as full copies of almost all his correspondence to

them." Thus, for a thirty-year period, from 1794 to the death of the two brothers in 1824, the Newton Estate Papers afford an extensive documentation of, and excellent view into, a fundamental institution of Barbadian society.

The papers themselves are of a varied sort, but are largely composed of business ledgers and journals as well as logs of work activities, reports on slaves, and related documents. In addition, there is the relatively voluminous correspondence, especially between Lane and Samson Wood (the plantations' manager from 1796 or 1797 to 1803), but also John Farrell (the manager who replaced Wood on Newton plantation), William and Robert Reece (who later managed Seawell and Newton, respectively), Gen. Robert Haynes (the estates' attorney in Barbados), and the major English firms with which the Lanes conducted business, Daniels in Bristol and Blackmans in London.

In sum, the Newton Estate Papers would be of considerable interest to one concerned with plantation economics, and they also provide valuable materials on topics such as the organization of plantation labor, treatment of slaves and slave life, occupational specialization, commercial and subsistence crop production, agricultural practices, soil, climate and insect problems, sugar and rum manufacture, shipment of plantation produce abroad, the relationship between absentee owners and managers, the role of the plantation manager and attorney, and customs of the plantocracy.

In 1967, sixty-six documents relating to the Newton plantations and Lane family were transferred to the University of London from the Greater London Record Office. However, these papers date from the post-1840s to the 1920s, with the following exceptions: *A.989*, Schedule of deeds of the Barbados Estate of Richard Stuart Lane, September 11, 1823–May 8, 1856; *A.990*, Copy of the will of Thomas Lane of Leyton Grange, Essex, September 11, 1823; *A.991*, Declaration of trust of £5,580, Richard Lane, August 9, 1836.

West India Committee Library
18 Grosvenor Street, London, W.1
(August 1968)

The well-known West India Committee records, including the minutes of its meetings, were not consulted, though materials relevant to Barbados are contained within them. In addition to these, and according to the librarian, the WIC contains only two volumes of manuscripts dealing with Barbados. These were searched and are described below.

ALLEYNE LETTERS

A bound volume of two-hundred-sixty-eight pages, containing copies of letters written by John Foster Alleyne, a prominent Barbadian planter and member of Council. Some of the letters were written from Barbados, but most were written from Westbury College in Bristol; the period covered in the volume is from July 5, 1799 to February 21, 1804 (Alleyne arrived in England in July 1799, returned to Barbados in June 1802, and returned again to England in June 1803).

Many of the letters written from England are addressed to Benjamin Storey, the manager of Cox and Sandy Lane plantations, and Richard Smith, the manager of Porters — all located in the parish of St. James. Alleyne's letters are replies to letters written by Storey and Smith reporting on plantation conditions; his letters contain a miscellany of information on topics such as the mechanics of shipping sugar to England, sugar manufacture, plantation management and agricultural practices, weather and crop conditions, insect problems, cotton production, the condition and treatment of slaves, etc. These letters are especially informative since Alleyne wrote frequently and at length, often recapitulating the issues raised in his managers' letters; thus one can readily follow the context and main threads of the correspondence.

In 1802, while in England, Alleyne purchased Mount Standfast plantation in St. James (owned by Stephen Walsh) which was adjacent to Porters and which, at one time, had belonged to the Alleyne family. In a number of letters, the negotiations and problems associated with acquiring and taking possession of Mount Standfast are discussed in detail.

Alleyne was also the attorney for Black Rock plantation (owned by James Holder), Turners Hall (owned by Henry Galt), and Blowers (owned by Thomas Daniel and Sons of London), and occasionally his letters from England contain references to the business affairs of these plantations.

From England, Alleyne also wrote to relatives in Barbados, e.g. Sir John Gay Alleyne, his uncle (who died in December 1801) and Abel Alleyne, his brother. These letters contain a great deal of materials on the activities and business affairs of the Alleyne family, and afford a very useful and vivid source of information on the life styles of the Barbadian plantocracy, both on the island and in England.

As noted above, Alleyne returned to Barbados in June 1802 and stayed for almost a year before returning to England. The letters he wrote on the island (July 24, 1802–April 16, 1803) are addressed to various persons, and largely treat of his business affairs and issues surrounding plantation management.

For biographical materials on the Alleyne family, *see* Louise R. Allen, "Alleyne of Barbados," *Jl. BMHS*, 3, 1935–36, *100–114 ff.*

COPIES OF SEVENTEENTH-CENTURY DOCUMENTS RE BARBADOS

A bound volume of transcriptions of miscellaneous letters and documents located in the Public Record Office (London). The transcriber is unknown and the transcriptions appear to have been made in either the late nineteenth or early twentieth centuries. The materials included in this volume range in date from 1637 to 1678, but concentrate in the 1660s. Some of these transcriptions provide useful information on island social and political conditions.

Miscellaneous Private Collections

A few manuscript collections in private residences were located. For various reasons, access to these collections was not possible; although not much can be said about them, some information was acquired through correspondence with their owners.

CAVE

Owner: Major S. F. Cave (Hill House, Bletchingly, Surrey) may have materials related to Nicholas Abbey plantation. In a letter (October 1966) the owner remarked "I have some documents. . . . They are mostly slave conveyances. . . . Several of the documents cannot be unfolded without special treatment, due to age."

DRAX

Owner: Admiral Sir R. E. E. Drax (Charborough Park, Wareham, Dorset). Applications should be made through Messrs. Preston, Redman, solicitors (Hinton House, Hinton Road, Bournemouth, Hants.). The National Register of Archives (no. 1075) mentions that there are deeds relating to Barbados, 1663–1856; the owner, in a letter (October 1966), noted that "I *may* have one book containing some of the Drax Hall accounts, lists of slaves, etc., probably of the 18th century."

FITZHERBERT

Owner: Sir John FitzHerbert (Tissington Hall, Ashbourne, Derbyshire). Applications should be made through the Historical Manuscripts Commission (Quality Court, Chancery Lane, London, W.C.2). According to the National Register of Archives, there are correspondence, accounts, etc., from agents relating to plantations in Jamaica and Barbados, ca. 1760–1850. The former owner of these papers was Sir William FitzHerbert; in a letter (January 1967) the new owner, Sir John FitzHerbert, noted his recent inheritance of the papers, "some of which may well deal with Barbados, but as they have not been sorted I am afraid it is impossible to give you any idea what there is."

GODSAL

Owner: Mr. Alan Godsal (Haines Hill, Twyford, Berkshire). In a letter (October 1966) the owner stated: "I do have certain papers [relating to pre-1834 Barbados] which might be of interest . . .," but these were in storage and the nature of the papers was not specified; the papers may relate to the Colleton family and plantations.

IRELAND

The locating of Barbados-related manuscripts in Ireland has been facilitated by the publication of the detailed multivolumed catalog, edited by Richard J. Hayes, *Manuscript Sources for the History of Irish Civilization* (Boston, G. K. Hall, 1965, 11 vols.). This catalog identifies manuscripts located in Irish repositories as well as elsewhere, e.g. the British Museum. Volumes 1–4 are indexed by personal names, volumes 5–6 by subjects, volumes 7–8 by places, volumes 9–10 by dates, and volume 11 contains lists of manuscripts. Volumes

1–4, 9–11 were not consulted, volumes 7 and 8 contain no references to Barbados, and volumes 5–6 contain Barbados entries under the subject headings "Barbados" and "Irish Abroad: West Indies."

Barbados-related manuscripts located in Irish repositories, as indicated in volumes 5–6 of the catalog, are limited in number, and are confined to the Genealogical Office, Belfast Public Record Office, and the National Library of Ireland. Neither the Genealogical Office nor the Belfast Public Record Office were visited but the catalog listings of their holdings appear below.

Belfast Public Record Office

D. 1125, letters and account book of James Blair, merchant, Barbados, concerning the slave trade, shipping of cotton, etc., 1796–99.

Genealogical Office

MS. 108, *pages 71–72*, copy of grant of arms to the descendants of Thomas Briggs of Barbados and to his son, Joseph Lyder Briggs of Barbados in the West Indies, February 28, 1855; MS. 159, *page 65*, pedigree of Augustin Morris, citizen of London, cooper, from his grandfather John Morris, late of Ferns, Co. Wexford, with reference to Nugent of Barbados, ca. 1700–ca. 1780; pedigree of Morris of Ferns, Co. Wexford, of Barbados and Rotherhithe, ca. 1650–1750; MS. 168, *page 114*, pedigree of Hall of Ards and Tully in Co. Donegal, and Barbados, ca. 1700–1810; MS. 176, *pages 524–32*, pedigree of Harte of Westmill, Hertfordshire . . . of Castleconnell, Co. Limerick, and of Barbados, ca. 1300–1845; MS. 812 (35), draft pedigrees of Lynch of Barbados, ca. 1750–1900.

National Library of Ireland
Dublin
(October 1966)

Discussions with the NLI's Keeper of Manuscripts as well as a search of the catalog *Manuscript Sources for the History of Irish Civilization* produced but one manuscript related to Barbados: *Grogan Papers Ms.* 11090, Letter from Margery Rowe to her sister (Mrs. William Morgan of Waterford?) dated Barbados, June 20, 1756; a brief note in which she says she would like to return to Ireland, but finds travel difficult at her old age.

Trinity College, Dublin

(*October 1966*)

Trinity College, Dublin, contains only one collection of manuscripts relating to the West Indies; these are bound into a one-hundred-eighty-seven-page volume titled "Of the Caribbee Islands," and identified as Mss. G. 4, 15. The items in this volume are mid-seventeenth-century copies of various documents, e.g. depositions, letters, and notes, largely relating to the proprietorship claims of William Courteen, whose syndicate first colonized Barbados, and the Earl of Carlisle, who had received a grant to various of the Caribbean islands from Charles I. Related materials are located in the Bodleian Library at Oxford (Rawlinson Mss.). Both collections are essential sources for information on the island's early colonization, particularly political events, and the introduction of Arawak Indians from Guiana. See Jerome S. Handler, "The Amerindian Slave Population of Barbados in the Seventeenth and Early Eighteenth Centuries," *Caribbean Studies*, 8, 1969, *38–64*.

G. 4, 15

Pages 5–14, "The original deed of demise from the Earl of Carlisle to the Lord Willoughby . . . of the Caribbee islands for one and twenty years," February 17, "in the 22nd year of the reign of Charles."

Pages 14–18, "Deed of revocation made by the Earl of Carlisle of all officers granted to any person whatsoever in the Caribee islands."

Pages 19–35, Lord Willoughby's letters patent as Lieutenant-General of the Caribbee Islands; Grant by Lord Willoughby to the Earl of Carlisle of a quarter of his moiety of the profits; Ordinance for the discharge from his delinquency of the Earl of Carlisle, February 13, 1645.

Pages 36–49, Letters to Capt. Charles Wolverston, Governor of Barbados, February and May 1629, relating to

Carlisle's proprietory claims to Barbados.

Pages 40–41, Power of the courts of the Bishopric of Durham.

Pages 42–56, The Earl of Carlisle's First Grant of the Caribbee islands.

Pages 57–76, The Earl of Carlisle's Second Letters Patent of the Caribee Islands.

Pages 77–118, "Breviat of the Evidence given into the Committee of the House of Commons by the Petitioners against the Earl of Carlisle's Patent for the Caribee Island" [1647]. The "Breviat" is comprised of three main sections: *1*] "The first plantings of Barbados and St. Christopher to be by them, and not by my lord of Carlisle for which they produce witnesses, viz." (*pp. 80–84* are the "first plantation of Barbados," *pp. 84–85* "first planting of St. Christopher"). The witnesses who discuss Barbados include Henry Powell (the captain of the ship that brought the first European colonizing party to Barbados in early 1627), John Tuckerman, John Cleere, and Nicholas Broune (the carpenter, boatswain, and quartermaster aboard Powell's ship), Thomas Irish (captain of a ship that landed settlers in 1628), and John Acland (boatswain aboard Irish's ship). All of the above depositions briefly describe social and political conditions. *2*] "The Fortifications of those islands to be at their charge and not at my lords" includes three brief testimonials on Barbados's military defenses (*pp. 86–87*). *3*] "Arbitrary power and tyrannical government exercised there by and under the Earl of Carlisle's authority over the goods and persons of the English inhabitants there." This section is based upon various depositions and offers information under nine major headings: taxes, fines, oaths, imprisonment, whipping, pilloring, "stigmatizings," cutting of ears, death (*pp. 87–108*); pages *109–18* of the "Breviat" include the opinions of the

House of Commons committee with respect to the testimonials offered above.

Pages 119–56, Charter of the Massachusetts Bay Company.

Pages 157–61, Henry Powell's Examination, February 25, 1657. In this deposition Powell recounts the events of the island's 1627 colonization and describes the later conflicts between the Courteen and Carlisle factions; Powell was a defender of Courteen's interests.

Pages 161–64, Thomas Parris, His Examination, March 16, 1657. Parris, a London merchant, arrived at Barbados in July 1628; here he narrates how Henry Powell and others loyal to Courteen were imprisoned by Carlisle's representatives in Barbados.

Pages 165–81, "The case concerning my Lord of Carlisle's interest in Barbados and other Caribee Islands." A lengthy legal interpretation.

Pages 182–87, "A Briefe Description of the Iland of Barbados" [ca. 1650 or 1651]. Written by an unknown author, who was apparently resident on the island, the "description" offers brief comments on weather and climate, indentured servants, slaves, customs and mores of the planters, the political system and disputes between Cavaliers and Roundheads, various subsistence and cash crops, beverages, and livestock.

Photostatic copies of Trinity Mss. G. 4, 15 are located in the Library of Congress (*see* G. G. Griffin, *A Guide to Manuscripts Relating to American History . . . Reproduced for the Division of Manuscripts of the Library of Congress*, Washington, D.C., 1946, *p. 224*).

The pages of G. 4, 15 that have been published are: 77–118, in N. D. Davis, "Papers Relating to the Early History of Barbados and St. Kitts" (*Timehri: Journal of the Royal Agricultural Society of British Guiana*, 6, 1892, 327–49); 157–64, in N. D. Davis, "Papers Relating to the Early History of Barbados" (*Timehri*, 5, 1891, 51–60); 182–87, in V. T. Harlow, *Colonizing Expeditions to the West Indies and Guiana, 1623–1667* (Hakluyt Society, London, 1925, *pp. 42–48*).

SCOTLAND

A very useful overview and general discussion of archival repositories in Scotland, with particular reference to Caribbean manuscripts, is provided by D. A. G. Waddell in his paper "Location and Availability of Non-State Archival Material Abroad Relating to the Caribbean Countries" (Caribbean Archives Conference, University of the West Indies, 1965. *Report*. Kingston, Jamaica, 1967, *pp. 184–93*). In this paper, Waddell notes that the following repositories contain Caribbean manuscripts: National Library of Scotland in Edinburgh ("the principal non-state archive repository in Scotland . . . analogous to the Library and Manuscript departments of the British Museum"), University of Edinburgh Library, Glasgow Public Library, Aberdeen University Library, Mitchell Library in Glasgow, and the Scottish Record Office in Edinburgh. Of these, only the Scottish Record Office was personally visited, but some of the others may contain Barbados manuscripts relating to the time period considered in this *Guide*; for example, it is known for certain that the National Library fits this category.

In addition, "A more significant quantity of material remains the property of individuals, preserved in their private homes or in lawyers' offices. Many collections of documents in private hands have been surveyed and their locations and contents recorded in the National Register of Archives (Scotland) [P.O. Box 36, H.M. Register House, Edinburgh 2], the counterpart of the National Register of Archives in London. Many others have been located, but not yet surveyed and reported upon. The Register consists of the reports on the collections hitherto surveyed. These vary from detailed inventories to brief lists of categories" (Waddell, 1967). One private collection, located through the NRA, which contains Barbados manuscripts (and there are doubtless others), is the *Colville of Culross Mss.* containing letters from Admiral Colville to his father, Lord Colville, including some from Barbados, 1782–83; and letters from Gen. Charles Colville, including some from Barbados, 1808–9. Anyone seeking access to this and other private collections should first make inquiries through the NRA.

Scottish Record Office
Edinburgh 2
(*July 1968*)

The SRO contains state records, various types of local records, and some private manuscript collections. Materials related to Barbados in the SRO are fairly easy to identify by using the "Source List of Material Relating to West Indies and South America in the Scottish Record Office" (mimeo., n.d., *20 pp.*). A handful of collections contain Barbados manuscripts, the two major ones being the Hay of Haystoun muniments and the Seaforth papers.

HAY OF HAYSTOUN (GD 34)

A large collection of papers, many of which relate to Barbados and some to other of the West India islands. Barbados materials date from the 1630s and 1640s and are primarily concerned with political and commercial matters although there is also information on other topics. The Hay of Haystoun Mss. were minimally consulted; hence the following items relating to Barbados (and the notes on them) are largely drawn from the SRO's "Source List of Material Relating to the West Indies."

835

Two letters from William Powrey in London to Archibald Hay mentioning a very bad sickness in Barbados from which six thousand Christians had died since Mr. Powrey had returned home, May and June 1648.

920

Copy of a grant by Sir James Hay, Archibald Hay, and Richard Zurst to Peter Hay to be receiver of all rents, etc., out of the plantations and ports of the island of Barbados, due to them as assignees of the deceased Earl of Carlisle, June 13, 1636.

921

Instructions given by the Earl of Carlisle to Peter Hay, June 27, 1636.

922

Copies of letters sent to Peter Hay and others in Barbados, largely dealing with the sending of tobacco to Europe, 1636–40.

923

About fifty letters from Barbados, most of which were written by Peter Hay to Sir James Hay and Archibald Hay in London, 1636–46. Most of the letters treat of the difficulties Peter Hay is having in collecting dues owed the late Earl of Carlisle, but the letters also contain general information about Barbados, its system of government, taxation, and crops, especially tobacco and problems relating to its production and export.

924

Papers relating to Barbados, mostly consisting of letters from Peter Hay to Sir James Hay and Archibald Hay, and relating to a variety of matters, 1636–47.

925

Note of indentures of four people for four-year periods in Barbados, January 23, 1637.

926

Letter from Capt. William Hilliard in Southampton to Archibald Hay, December 18, 1637. Offers passage on his ship for people going to Barbados, and £30 per annum for a plantation of six hundred acres.

927

Commission to James Hay to be provost marshal of Barbados for seven years, April 1, 1638.

928

Petition from the Earl of Carlisle, Sir James Hay, and Archibald Hay, February 22, 1639, concerning the rights of government over the Carribbean islands.

930

Letter from Capt. William Hilliard in Barbados to Archibald Hay in London, referring to political matters.

936

Contains an item dealing with cotton shipments from Barbados in 1641.

940

Nine letters from P. Bell, Governor of Barbados, and Capt. James Brown, to James and Archibald Hay, 1641–48, giving details on the spread of political and economic discontent in Barbados and other matters.

949

Indenture in favor of Thomas Hutchin, carpenter, to serve as a carpenter in Barbados for five years, and a note of the carpenter's tools sent with him, May 1649.

951

Note of clothing and commodities sent to Barbados by Capt. Liston, August 1649.

955

Miscellaneous papers relating to Barbados.

In addition, the following items relate to Barbados, but no notes were recorded on them: 931–933, 941–948, 950, 952–954.

The Hay of Haystoun papers were used by J. Harry Bennett for his article "Peter Hay, Proprietary Agent in Barbados, 1636–1641" (*Jamaican Historical Review*, 5, 1965, 9–29).

SEAFORTH PAPERS (GD 46)

An extensive collection of the papers of Lord Seaforth who was governor of Barbados from 1801 to 1806. The papers cover his period of residence on the island as well as some earlier and later years, and include materials relevant to Barbados *per se*, as well as to his personal affairs in Scotland. There are volumes of copies of Seaforth's official and private correspondence, letters sent to him, and miscellaneous documents relating to Barbados. In general, a valuable collection for a variety of subjects, e.g. political events, legal issues, military and naval matters, economics, slavery, the slave trade, amelioration of the island's slave laws (particularly with respect to capital punishment for the murderer of a slave), and the will of Joshua Steele who left property to slaves, thus precipitating a legal controversy.

HAMILTON–DALRYMPLE OF NORTH BERWICK (GD 110)

894

Includes a letter from William Dalrymple to his father Sir Hew Dalrymple of North Berwick, dated Barbados, February 10, 1722.

MISCELLANEOUS PAPERS (MP 226–33)

Papers relating to a voyage to convey servants from Scotland to Barbados, 1701.

The SRO's list indicates that some manuscripts in the following collections may have Barbados materials but a search of them yielded nothing: *Dalhousie Mss.* (GD 45), *Hay of Belton Mss.* (GD 73), *Morton Mss.* (GD 150).

EUROPE

(other than England, Ireland, and Scotland)

Barbados had relations with the nationals and governments of other European countries, primarily with Holland, especially through trade during the seventeenth century; France, through political and military involvement during the seventeenth and eighteenth centuries; and, to some extent, Spain, through the slave trade in the seventeenth and early eighteenth centuries. Also German traders are known to have come to the island in the seventeenth century. One might therefore expect that manuscript materials relating to the island are located in various European countries, but my own very limited work in such areas prevents an extended discussion.

It can be conjectured that the important role played by the Dutch in stimulating the seventeenth-century "sugar revolution" may have left, as one of its legacies, relevant manuscripts in Dutch repositories, e.g. the State Archives at the Hague. Yet, perhaps for obvious linguistic reasons as well as problems of location, no scholar, so far as I know, has used Dutch archival materials with the specific intent of studying the island's early history.[9] For a rough guide to the State Archives, the following may be of some use: M. A. P. Meilink-Roelofz, "A Survey of the Archives Pertaining to the History of the Netherlands Antilles and Surinam Located in the General State Archives of the Netherlands" (Caribbean Archives Conference, University of the West Indies, 1965. *Report*. Kingston, Jamaica, 1967). Another source, which I have not seen, is M. P. H. Roessingh, *Guide to the Sources in the Netherlands for the History of Latin America* (The Hague, 1968); this contains some references to Barbadian materials (Michael Chandler, personal communication).

There is also the possibility that some manuscripts relating to Barbados are located in Spanish archives (e.g. Francisco M. Padrón, "Archival Material on the Lesser Antilles Located in the Archives of the Indies, Seville." Caribbean Archives Conference . . . *Report* 1967).

David M. Matteson (*List of Manuscripts Concerning American History Preserved in European Libraries and Noted in their Published Catalogues and Similar Printed Lists*. Washington, D.C., 1925, *p. 160*) cites the following item, located in the Biblioteca Nazionale Marciana (Venice, Italy): "Henrici Fermesii Narratio itineris an. MDCLVI. et sequenti a se confecti. Inc. Septembris 8. 1656. naviculam conscendens, etc. Londino solvit Fermesius 6. Id. Sept. 1656. et Insulam Barbados pertransiens, ad Anglorum Coloniam, juxta fluvium Saranam, qui ab ea Insula circiter centum ac sexaginta leucas distat, constitutam 6. Id. Febr. anni sequentis pervenit; inde Barbados ad 15 Cal. April remeavit." [Henrici Fermesii. The Narration of the Journey of H.F. in the year 1656 and completed by him in the following year. Fermesius departed London on September 6, 1656, and crossing the island of Barbados he arrived at the English colony located near the river Surinam, which is about one-hundred-sixty leagues from the island of Barbados, on February 6 in the following year; then he returned to Barbados on April 15].

With respect to French manuscripts, more details can be offered. Of major importance in locating West Indian manuscripts in Paris is the *Guide to Materials for American History in the Libraries and Archives of Paris*, under the general editorship of Waldo G. Leland. Volume 1 (Washington, D.C., 1932) by Leland deals with libraries, and volume 2 (Washington, D.C., 1943) by Leland, J. Meng, and Abel Doysié is concerned solely with the Archives of the Ministry of Foreign Affairs.

The index to volume 1 records only a few entries on Barbados at the Bibliothèque Nationale, some of the following of which were personally examined in late 1966.

MANUSCRITS FRANÇAIS
646, *fols. 78, 190, 219, 264, 443, 452*

"Traitté historique et politique du commerce de toutes les nations dans les divers endroits du monde, particulièrement par rapport aux Hollandois." This was not examined, but Leland (1932, *p. 3*) notes that it is of the late seventeenth century, and contains "Occasional references to commerce, with America, West Indies, Virginia, Barbados, etc."

---

[9] I. S. Emmanuel makes occasional references to seventeenth-century Barbadian Jews in his study based upon research in the Imperial Archives at the Hague and General Archives at Amsterdam ("New Light on Early American Jewry," *American Jewish Archives*, 7 [Cincinnati, 1955], *3–64*).

MANUSCRITS FRANÇAIS, NOUVELLES
ADDITIONS, COLLECTION MARGRY
9323, *fols. 30–43*

"Recit du voyage qui j'ai fait aux Indes
Occidentales avec M. de Cahueso
[Cahuzac], Général de l'armée navalle,
qui y fut par commandement du Roy
et du Monsigneur le Cardinal, l'an de
grace, 1629." This was examined; it is a
monthly journal by an anonymous
author who spent two days in Barbados
in July 1629; his journal entry on the
island (*fols. 33–34*) is very brief—a few
comments are made on plant life, and
it is noted that the island is full of woods
and has about six to seven hundred
inhabitants.

MÉLANGES DE COLBERT
48, *fols. 232–403*

Transcripts of English documents, auth-
enticated by S. Killingsworth, including
a commission to John Dawes, secretary
of Barbados, August 17, 1660. Not
examined.
176, *fols. 97–98*
Brief letter from Colbert de Terron to
Colbert, La Rochelle, April 17, 1670.
This was examined; the only reference
to Barbados is made as a concluding
remark: "Le bruit qui a couru de la
Barboude, a eu quelque fondement,
c'est a dire qu'il y eu de la disposition
parmi les noirs a se soulever, mais cela
a eu sans suite."

DEPARTEMENT DES IMPRIMES,
CARTES, ET PLANS; SECTION DES
CARTES ET PLANS

Portef. 106. No. 86
"Carte de l'Isle de la Barbade avec plan
de Bridge Town," by Nicolas (1775–
85).
Portef. 106. No. 87
"Plan de la Baye de Carlisle de la
Barbade," by Nicolas (1775–85).
Neither of these maps was examined.

There may be more manuscripts
related to Barbados in the above and
other collections of the Bibliothèque
Nationale as well as in other Paris
libraries listed in volume 1 of Leland's
Guide, e.g. Bibliothèque de l'Arsenal,
Bibliothèque de l'Institut de France,
Bibliothèque Sainte-Geneviève (*see* the
Guide's index, West Indies).

The Archives of the Ministry of
Foreign Affairs, as noted in the preface
to volume 2 of the *Guide*, "is one of the
largest of French archival collections."
Unfortunately, this massive 1078-page
volume contains no index, but a cursory
sampling of the sections "Correspond-
ance Politique" and "Memoirs et
Documents" dealing with England
and America yielded many references
to the West Indies, including some to
Barbados. Thus, these archives may
provide useful materials for the study
of the island's history.

In addition to the Parisian reposi-
tories, other libraries and archives in
France which have West Indian
materials may have an occasional
Barbados-related manuscript (*see* David
M. Matteson, 1925). One such repository
is the Muséum d'Histoire Naturelle in Le
Havre. Among its collection of Charles
Lesueur's sketchbooks are some draw-
ings he made while in the West Indies,
1815–16; Lesueur arrived at Barbados
in late December, 1815 (*see* Waldo G.
Leland, "The Lesueur Collection of
American Sketches in the Museum of
Natural History at Havre, Seine-
Inférieure," *The Mississippi Valley Historical Review*, 10, Cedar Rapids, Iowa,
1923–24, *53–78* and R. W. G. Vail,
"The American Sketchbooks of a
French Naturalist 1816–1837: A Description of the Charles Alexandre
Lesueur Collection, with a Brief Account
of the Artist," *Proceedings of the American
Antiquarian Society*, n.s., 48, pt. 1,
Worcester, 1938, *49–71*). With respect
to the Barbados drawings, the Director
of the Muséum d'Histoire Naturelle
wrote in July 1970: ". . . je ne vois aucun
sujet se rapportant à des scènes sociales.
Il s'agit de vues du littoral, prises du
large, montrant l'aspect de villages ou
la forme des côtes. On voit également
des paysages de l'intérieur. Un seul
dessin bien terminé montre un moulin
à canne à sucre à côté d'une maison. . . .
Nous n'avons pas de liste descriptive de
ces dessins qui ne présentent aucune
légende."

UNITED STATES

Some manuscript collections in the United States were personally consulted while information on others was derived from catalogs and correspondence with librarians and archivists. I have also indicated those libraries which maintained they had no Barbados-related manuscripts prior to the 1840s.

There are undoubtedly many more Barbados manuscripts in the United States than those cited in the following pages.[10] Problems of location, which were noted in the introductory section on manuscripts in England, are generally applicable to the United States as well. It might be expected that many manuscripts which have not been identified would be found along the East Coast, especially New England. G. A. Moriarty makes this point when he writes: "The records of the coastal towns and counties of New England contain many references and papers relating to Barbados in the XVII and XVIII centuries, the period when the commercial and social ties between the two places were very close" ("A Letter from Barbados, 1672," *Jl. BMHS*, 14, 1946–47, *2–4*). Records of this type have sometimes been published (e.g. G. F. Dow, 1911–21; N. Shurtleff, 1853–54; R. Toppan, 1898–99), but their location and the location of other types of manuscripts would be greatly facilitated if public and private repositories would make available to the National Union Catalog of Manuscript Collections information on their collections.

American Jewish Historical Society
2 Thornton Road, Waltham, Mass.

A visit to the AJHS in August 1969 and a search of its published catalog, *A Preliminary Survey of the Manuscript Collections* (New York, 1967), yielded a few items relating to Barbados; there may be more, however, in manuscript collections not yet fully cataloged.

ISAAC LEESER PAPERS, *1820–1866*

This collection includes "a manuscript guidebook on Jewish ritual slaughter written by Moses Julian in Barbados in 1820." Not examined.

JACQUES JUDAH LYONS
COLLECTION, *1728–1876*

"Contains materials relating to Jews in ... [among other places] the West Indies." Not examined. The collection has been calendared in the *Publications of the American Jewish Historical Society*,

---

[10] After this *Guide* went to press I had an opportunity to briefly consult the typescript of Kenneth E. Ingram's "Manuscripts Relating to Commonwealth Caribbean Countries in United States and Canadian Repositories" (London, Caribbean Universities Press, forthcoming). This detailed work includes a number of collections I have described but did not personally consult, as well as other collections of which I was unaware. Ingram's work is of considerable value and, when published, will be an essential source for anyone working in this area.

vols. 21 (1913) and 27 (1920). Volume 21 does contain occasional pieces of information on the Jews of Barbados.

In addition to the above, the AJHS has the Samuel Oppenheim collection which is comprised of about thirty-one boxes of, as yet, uncataloged materials; these include numerous transcripts and photostats of early documents relating to Jews in the West Indies and South America. A rapid sampling of some of these boxes yielded an occasional item relating to the Barbados Jews in the seventeenth and eighteenth centuries.

Boston College Library
Chestnut Hill, Boston, Mass.

The Barbados manuscript holdings in the Boston College Library are listed in its *Catalogue of Books, Manuscripts, etc. in the Caribbeana Section of the Nicholas M. Williams Memorial Ethnological Collection* (Boston, 1932). The following items, none of which have been personally examined, have been abstracted from this catalog.

723
Francis MacKenzie Humberstone (Baron Seaforth, Gov. of Barbados), Certificates of rates of exchange. Dated, Barbados, March 10, June 16, August 28, October 27, 1802.

732
F. I. G. MacLeson (Brig. Gen.), Warrant of payment to N. R. Garner for stationery. Dated, Barbados, June 27, 1805.

735
Edward Mathew, Return of a detachment of His Majesty's 75th Regt. under the command of Lieut. Fortye. Dated Barbados, June 13, 1782, and checked by Maj. Damer, August 10, 1782.

754
John Vaughan (Commander-in-Chief of Leeward and Caribbee Islands), Receipt for forage money for self and one Aide-de-Camp. Dated, Barbados, November 2, 1780.

755
John Vaughan, Warrants for payment of 87th Regiment of Foot. Dated, Barbados, July 25, 1780.

761
Count of disbursements for ye sloope *Adventure* at Barbados, December ye 18, 1704. Per Mee Thomas Andrews.

1512
William Penn, Despatch written on board H.M.S. *Swiftsure* riding in Carlisle Bay. Barbados, March 17, 1655.

1533
Rev. J. Robinson (Chaplain in the Royal Navy), Diary of voyage in 1824–25. The catalog does not indicate whether or not Barbados is treated in this item.

Boston Public Library
Copley Square, Boston, Mass.

Information on the following manuscripts, including a number of letters between Quakers, is based upon the printed list *Bibliotheca Barbadiensis: A Catalog of Materials Relating to Barbados 1650–1860 in the Boston Public Library* (Boston, 1968), and a visit to the library in August 1969.

MS. U.1.2

John Bowen Colthurst. "Journal as a special magistrate in the islands of Barbados and St. Vincent, July 1835–August 1838." In the summer of 1835, Colthurst was appointed Special Magistrate, by the Secretary for the Colonies, to the Bridgetown–St. Michael area. The emancipation act had created such magistrates who were charged with adjudicating disputes between apprentices and masters in terms of the act. Colthurst arrived at Barbados on November 25, 1835 and stayed on the island until his departure for St. Vincent on January 8, 1838. A conscientious and articulate "liberal," Colthurst had been an emancipationist and admirer of Wilberforce before coming out to the colonies. His journal is an extremely valuable and well-written source of information on the apprenticeship period (with frequent comparisons being made with the slave period). A variety of matters, sometimes discussed at length, are covered: e.g. the Barbados police force and militia; life and customs of the apprentices; character and behavior of the creole whites; summaries of cases heard; poor whites ("red-shanks"); the difficulties of his job (". . . to maintain the rights of the Negroes without irritating the planters"); the planters' reactions to the apprenticeship system and the apprentices themselves; racial prejudice; his own views on the slave system; discussions of proposals to make apprentices convicted of misdemeanors work on road gangs with chains; religious instruction of apprentices on plantations; Mr. Thorn (actually Joseph Thorne) a "coloured" licensed catechist, his work and the prejudices against him; a club of the island's Special Magistrates; Gov. Lionel Smith; visit to the Moravian mission; agricultural practices on the plantations.

The six volumes of Colthurst's journal are numbered consecutively (*pp. 1–224*). Volumes 1–5 (*pp. 10–146*) deal specifically with Barbados; there are, however, occasional comments on Barbados in the St. Vincent section of volume 5. Volume 4 (*pp. 93–140*) is missing from the Boston Public Library, but lengthy extracts from it and volumes 1, 2, and 3 were published in the American abolitionist newspaper, the *Liberator*, edited by William Lloyd Garrison (installments 1–10 in consecutive issues, July 23–September 24, 1847; 11–13, October 22, 29, and November 5, 1847; 14–15, December 24, 1847; 16, December 31, 1847; 17, January 14, 1848); apparently no materials from volumes 5 or 6 were reprinted. The *Liberator* is available on microfilm; the negatives are located in the New York Public Library.[11]

In the volumes located at the Boston Public Library, there are some water-colored sketches, but only two of these deal with Barbados: one an uncaptioned plantation scene, apparently unfinished and giving very little detail; the other, a caricature of a "red-shank," mounted on his horse and accompanied by his servant, going to his militia muster.

MS. U.1.2, vol. 2, *p. 62*

A letter from Mrs. Edey to Maj. J. B. Colthurst asking him to sell two slaves [i.e. apprentices]. [Barbados] February 4, 1836. Not examined.

MS. U.1.14, vol. 1

No. 2
Samuel Carpenter to Ralph Smith, on board the *John and Sarah*, relating to consignment of goods and transmission of invoices for goods shipped to William Penn. "Barbados 24th 12th mo., 1681."

No. 3
Samuel Carpenter to Ralph Smith at Philadelphia, regarding goods shipped for sale and announcing his intention to go to Philadelphia. "Barbados 10th 5th mo., 1682."

No. 4
Roger Longworth to Richard Richardson in London, for Second Day Meeting of Society of Friends, describing sufferings of Quakers in Barbados because of requirements to pay militia tax. "Barbados 6th 12th mo., 1686."

No. 5
Roger Longworth to Peter Hendricks and John Claves at Amsterdam (Holland), largely religious in nature, but reporting receipt of a letter from George Fox, his own visit to Ireland, arrival of R.H. at Frederikstead (St. Croix) and his intention to go to Pennsylvania. "Barbados 15th 12th mo., 1686."

No. 6
Roger Longworth to Second Day Meeting of Society of Friends in London, reporting intent to go to New England and Rhode Island, sending love to George Fox, and asking to be addressed in care of James Harrison in

---

11 John Alden, Keeper of Rare Books at the Boston Public Library, called my attention to the publication of Colthurst's journals in the *Liberator*.

Pennsylvania. "Barbados 14th 12th mo., 1686."

No. 7

Richard Forde (surveyor at Bridgetown) to James Harrison at Philadelphia, noting that he is transmitting three of George Fox's papers, and mentioning that "our sufferings on account of ye militia (especially) continues." "Barbados 13th 3rd mo., 1687."

No. 8

George Gray to James Harrison, Pennsbury, Pennsylvania, noting that since he is unable to take up land in Pennsylvania that his money be remitted to London or Barbados; also comments on trade. "Barbados 30th 6th mo., 1687."

No. 9

Andrew Dury to James Harrison at Philadelphia, requesting account of goods consigned for sale. Barbados, July 21, 1687.

No. 10

Andrew Dury to James Harrison at Philadelphia, requesting that balance of account owed him by Harrison be paid in bread, soap, flour, or lumber; expresses hope that Harrison has paid Joseph Bryer "in order to help pay for a small vessel I am building in Roades Island." Barbados, September 1, 1687.

No. 11

Samuel Chace to Benjamin Wright at Philadelphia, noting the enclosure of a bill of sale for a slave named Sandelow, to be sold in Philadelphia, the profits of the sale to be remitted in doeskin gloves and shingles; asks for Philadelphia prices on "ravill cotton," lime juice, "and other commodities of our island," and mentions a smallpox epidemic in Barbados. Barbados, April 24, 1705.

No. 12

Ellis Hughes, bill of sale conveying to Israel Pemberton of Philadelphia the Negro slave Peter, consigned to Hughes by Thomas Mogridge of Barbados. [Philadelphia?], June 4, 1712.

No. 13

John Oxley to Hannah Fishbourn; mostly a religious epistle, but also reports the death of Esther Champion from smallpox, and the arrival of Joseph Smith from Rhode Island.

"Barbados 22nd 11 mo., 1714."

MS. U.1.21

Nos. 26–28

Lease to John and Mary Ashley by Rebecca Dixon and Sarah Pothill, heirs of Samuel Pasfeild, of Pasfeild's plantation [184 acres] St. Philip's parish. Barbados, April 20, 1727.

No. 29

Connected to the above lease, the inventory of buildings, equipment, livestock, slaves, etc., of Pasfeild plantation — based upon an inventory made in 1720 (see no. 32).

No. 30

"An inventory and valuation of the Negroes, etc., on the estate of Samuel Pasfeild . . . now in the possession of John Ashley . . . taken this 20th day of April 1727."

No. 31

Lease to John and Mary Ashley by heirs of Samuel Pasfeild of Pasfeild's plantation, St. Philip's parish. [Barbados], April 23, 1725. Witnessed by Benjamin Clarke and Robert Butler; includes property inventory.

No. 32

Henry Evans, Michael Gilligan, James Thorpe, Charles Egerton, "An inventory of the plantation of the late Samuel Pasfeild . . . in the parish of St. Philip . . ., Barbados, October 29, 1720." This is substantially the basis for the inventories noted above.

MS. H.1.7.8b

John Cotton to his son Rowland, mentioning news of Scotch and English deaths in Barbados, including Dr. [Richard] Williams and wife, formerly of New Haven. [Plymouth, Mass., before September 8, 1696.] Not examined.

CH. A.6.1

John Ledyard to Jonathan Trumball, reporting, *infra alia*, that he has Barbados rum for Mrs. Alden. Windham, Connecticut, December 4, 1761. Not examined.

G. 51.7.6

No. 68

Charles Willing to Inglis and Long,

Norfolk, Virginia, reporting dissolution of partnership with Thomas Phillips. Barbados, January 6, 1773. Not examined.

Brown University: The John Carter Brown Library
Providence, Rhode Island

A visit to the JCB and consultation with its staff in August 1969 produced the manuscripts relating to Barbados that appear below.

Ms BARB

1672 Jy
"An account of Mr. [Robert] Spencer etc. farmers of the 4½ per cent there for a yeare and halfe ended at midsummer 1672." Not examined.
   1703 D16–17
Six congratulatory addresses to Sir Bevill Granville on his appointment as Captain General and Governor of Barbados. Barbados, December 16–17, 1703.
   1703/4 Ja 31
An anonymously authored letter in which the addressee is not given; concerns Manasses Gilligan, who illegally left the island, and matters concerning the wars with France. Barbados, January 31, 1703/4.
   1704 Ja 22–D 22/1 and 2
Copies of letters from the Lord Treasurer, Godolphin, to Charles Thomas, receiver of the casual revenues in Barbados, and Gov. Granville; concerns two French ships, the *Neptune* and *Marquesse*, taken as prizes off Barbados in February and August 1702, and the disposition of these ships as decreed by the Admiralty court in Barbados. Whitehall, January 22, 1704.
   1708 Ag–1709 S1
"An account of such prizes, and seizures, as have been condemned [in the] High Court of Admiralty in this island of Barbados established since [the] month of August 1708." Barbados, September 1, 1708. A negative photostat from CO 28/12 (Public Record Office, London).
   1737 D2–1755 S13
Deals with cases in the Barbados Court of Chancery, 1737 and 1755, involving the property of Robert Bishop, Samuel Adams, and others.
   1789 Ag 25
Letter from John Thomson to Rev. R. Cholmondely; four tightly written foolscap pages, presenting very detailed business and personal financial accounts.

BROWN PAPERS

This large collection contains a limited amount of materials relating to Rhode Island trading relations with Barbados in the late eighteenth century. None of these manuscripts was personally examined.

CODEX ENG

5
"Acts of Assembly passed from June 4, 1705 to September 4, 1706. Barbados, 1706." A manuscript volume of one-hundred-one folio pages reproducing the full texts of thirty-one laws passed by the island's House of Assembly. Twenty-nine of these are only listed by title in Richard Hall's (1764) section on laws "which are now become obsolete, repealed, expired, or have had their effect" (nos. 639, 645, 650–75, 677). The two other laws appear in full text in Hall (nos. 105, 106).
   38–42
Five journals or logbooks kept by Peleg Peckham, a sailor, on trading voyages between Barbados and Rhode Island. Peckham stopped at Barbados a few times during the period 1734–42, but his log entries generally do not relate to his stay on the island. The one exception is his "harbour journall for the sloop Patience . . ." (no. 39) which spans the period August 6–23, 1740. It contains brief daily entries on the manner in which his cargo, horses, sheep, barrel staves, hoops, etc., was disposed of and a new cargo of rum and sugar

acquired; comments on a Mr. Bolton, a merchant with whom he had a business relationship; weather conditions; and shipping in Carlisle Bay.

Columbia University Libraries
535 W. 114th St., New York, N.Y.

The National Union Catalog of Manuscript Collections, 1959–1961 (Ann Arbor, Mich., 1962, *p. 623*) lists the following:

BARRELL FAMILY PAPERS,
1791–1846

"Correspondence between members of the Barrell family in London, the U.S., the Barbadoes, and British Guiana, revealing the affairs, philosophy, and social practices of the day; family chronicles; diary cashbook, autograph albums; miscellaneous papers; and photos. Includes 60 letters from Walter Barrell of London to his son, Theodore, a merchant in the Americas." Two-hundred-thirty-three items.

Connecticut Historical Society
1 Elizabeth St., Hartford, Conn.

In October 1967, the manuscript cataloger of the CHS wrote: "There seems to be no material here on Barbados. We have manuscripts relating to Haiti and Santo Domingo, but that appears to be the extent of our holdings of West Indian materials."

Essex Institute: James Duncan Phillips Library
132–34 Essex St., Salem, Mass.

The National Union Catalog of Manuscript Collections, 1962 (Hamden, Conn., The Shoe String Press, 1964, *p. 306*) lists:

CLARKE FAMILY PAPERS,
1755–1839

"Family letters to the Clarkes in Salem from members of the family in Barbadoes, and a few legal papers. Persons represented include Gedney, John, Samuel and William Clarke." One portfolio.

Harvard University: Houghton Library
Cambridge, Mass.

The Houghton library was visited in August 1969, but its manuscript catalog is incomplete and is primarily arranged according to personal names; there were only two listings under the subject category "Barbados." The Hugh Hall letter book (see below) is not one of these.

MS. AM 1302
Benjamin Bartholomew, "A relation off the wonderfull mercies off God extended hunto us ye 19 off October 1660 in the ship Exchang being bound ffrom Newingland to Barbadoes. April 1661." A poem written for Thomas Riggs. Not examined.

MS. CAN 4

Alfred Francis W. Wyatt, "3½ years in the West Indies and South America and . . . in Nova Scotia and New Brunswick . . . and Lower Canada, 1829–1839." A bound manuscript volume containing a miscellaneous array of materials written at different periods; these range from personal reflections to accounts of various places visited. Barbados was visited in 1829 and 1833; the island is mentioned in a few pages (*1–3, 23, 79, 115*), but other than briefly noting the impression it made on him, no information is given.

MS. AM 1042

Hugh Hall, Letter Book, 1716–20 (*see* New York Public Library Mss).

Historical Society of Pennsylvania
1300 Locust Street, Philadelphia

Correspondence with the curator in late 1967 and a visit to the HSP in July 1969 yielded a number of manuscript collections dealing with Barbados. Some of these are briefly described in the *Guide to the Manuscript Collections of the Historical Society of Pennsylvania* (Philadelphia, 1949), but no detailed lists are available.

YEATES PAPERS, *1718–1876*

A very large collection but only some of the papers of John Yeates are relevant to Barbados. These appear to be contained only in one box, 129a, and are mainly letters written to Yeates, a Philadelphia merchant, between 1738 and 1749. Approximately two hundred letters were written from Barbados by various persons, including John Bayley, the firm of John Bayley and Paul Bedford, Charles Bolton, John Dapwell, John Devonish, Thomas Duke, Thomas Forbes, Thomas Hothersall, Susannah Hall, Patrick Johnston, Ed. Lascelles, Howard Polgreen, the firm of Sturge and Forde, Abraham Valverde, Thomas Walcott, Nicholas Wilcox, Richard Wilshire, John Woodin. The letters are primarily concerned with commerce, trade, and shipping problems, but there is occasional personal information, reports on the island's agriculture and climate, as well as market prices on sugar, rum, and other import–export commodities.

PORT OF PHILADELPHIA, BILLS OF LADING, *1716–1772*

Two bound volumes. The bills are printed forms on which such information as the ship's name, shipper, cargo, destination, etc., is filled in. Many of these deal with materials shipped to Barbados.

EDWARD C. GARDINER COLLECTIONS. MARTHA P. BOWEN ESTATE PAPERS, *1830–1855*

"These relate chiefly to estates in Jamaica." Not examined.

BENJAMIN RUSH COLLECTION

Volume 11, pp. 29–46, *Letters of Robert Marshall of Barbados.* There are seventeen letters, all written from Barbados by Marshall and addressed to Rush, a physician in Philadelphia; they cover the period of April 27, 1790 to April 1, 1798. Most of the letters relate to personal matters, e.g. Marshall's son who was sent to Philadelphia to study medicine under Rush. Marshall was a physician, and a number of letters are devoted to general descriptions of the illnesses of his white patients, the cures he employed in treating them, etc. Marshall had also referred some of his Barbadian patients to Rush, and some of his letters are little more than personal introductions of these patients to Rush. In all, these letters are of limited value in regard to medical matters on the island, and offer no descriptive materials on Barbados *per se.*

WILLIAM POLLARD LETTER BOOK, *1772–1774*

One volume of copies of letters written

by a Philadelphia merchant to his clients. Only one letter is addressed to Barbados; to W. Randle Phillips, dated 1772, relating to hoops shipped from Philadelphia.

The following collections contain no materials on Barbados: *Peter Grotgen Memories, 1774–1850*; *Abraham DuBois Papers, 1792–1809*; *Charles Barton Journals, 1828–1831*; *Elijah Brown, Jr.,*

Diary, 1801–1805; *Jacob Ritter, Jr., Autobiography, 1836*; *John Stamper's Letter Books, 1751–1770*; *Clement Humphrey's Papers, 1798–1801.*

The HSP also has three boxes of manuscripts of, and relating to, the Dutch West India Company, 1626–1834. All of these are in Dutch, and some may be relevant to early Barbadian history.

Library of Congress: Manuscript Division
Washington, D.C.

A visit to the LC in August 1969 and search of its card catalog and *Handbook of Manuscripts in the Library of Congress* (Washington, D.C., 1918) yielded the following items.

WEST INDIES, BRITISH

No. 4
Letter from [Gov.] Pinfold to Lord [Halifax], May 31, 1757. Not examined.
No. 5
Barbados Executive Council Minutes, January 3–10, 1759. Not examined.

PAPERS RELATING TO BARBADOS, *1663–1762*

"A folio volume from the Chalmers portion of the Force collection. Contains: Lord Parham's [Willoughby] Instructions as Governor of Barbados, 1663. Reports of the Attorney General on Acts passed in Barbados, 1700–1747. Report about Spanish ships trading with Barbados. Letters of Governor Pinfold to General Monckton and others, 1762. A tabular account of sums paid out of the Treasury from taxes raised, 1762. Lists of exports, etc.," (not examined). Also includes a published copy of *A True and Faithful Account of an Intire and Absolute Victory over the French Fleet in the West Indies by Two East India Ships and other Vessels at Barbadoes* (London, 1690).

PROCEEDINGS OF TRIAL OF THE MURDERERS OF REYNOLD ALLEYNE ELLOCK, BARBADOS, *1821* (Ac 2567)

A twelve-page typescript carbon presented to the LC in 1922; transcriptions of various official papers relating to a case in which four slaves were accused, tried, and convicted of the premeditated murder of the owner of Mount Wilton plantation on the night of October 2, 1821. The death sentence pronounced by the court of two justices of the peace and three freeholders reads: "That the said four Negro men shall be conveyed . . . from the gaol to some convenient place on Mount Wilton plantation by a sufficient and proper guard and be hanged by the neck until they be dead; then that their heads be severed from their bodies and stuck up on long poles in some public and convenient place or places; and their bodies be hanged in chains in some other convenient and public place or places on the said plantation by some Negro to be pressed . . . for that purpose."

An account of this murder, based on a copy of the coroner's inquest and proceedings before the justices, was published in the *Jl. BMHS* (8, 1940–41, *166–71*).

PINFOLD MANUSCRIPTS

Charles Pinfold was governor of Barbados from 1756 to 1766. The eleven bound volumes of this collection, all manuscripts unless otherwise noted, were once his property:

Minutes of the Council, October 28, 1735–July 15, 1736. Includes lengthy depositions by various persons, describing the Windward and Leeward islands and Guyana, and lists of fees collected by the Barbados courts and colonial offices.

Minutes of the Council, August 10, 1756–May 6, 1760.

Minutes of the Council, May 28, 1760–May 27, 1766.

Orders of Governor Pinfold. Contains two sets of lengthy orders issued by the King and dated March 18, 1756, copies of the Barbados Council Minutes, July 15, 1766–May 26, 1767, "Extracts from the Council books in Barbados beginning the 13th October 1641 — and ending 7 March 1688," "Extracts from Council books in Barbados beginning the 19th March 1688/9 and ending 27 November 1739."

Barbados, Journal of the Assembly 1756–1765. Minutes from August 31, 1756 (the first meeting attended by Pinfold, the day after his arrival on the island) to March 18, 1765.

Barbados, Pinfold's Letter Book, 1756–1764. Copies of official letters sent by Pinfold, August 14, 1756–January 4, 1764.

Barbados, Pinfold's Letter Book, 1764–1766. Same as above, from February 2, 1764 to May 25, 1766.

Barbados, Pinfold's Letter Book, 1756–1766. Copies of official letters and notes received by Pinfold, August 12, 1756–May 24, 1766.

Acts of Assembly, 1762–1766. The full texts of twenty-five laws passed between November 1762 and May 1766. None of these are contained in Richard Hall (1764).

Acts of Assembly, 1643–1762. The published volume of Richard Hall's *Acts* (1764). A manuscript commentary on the testimony of Jews in the courts is laid in between pages 94 and 95, and another manuscript note between pages 420 and 421, comments on Hall's law no. 221.

Acts of Assembly, 1648–1738. A published volume including *Acts of Assembly, Passed in the Island of Barbados, From 1648* to *1718* (London, Printed by John Baskett, 1732) and *Acts of Assembly Passed . . . From 1717–18 to 1738, Part II* (London, Printed by John Baskett, 1739). Following the final page of the latter item, there are forty-six manuscript pages giving the titles of Acts expired, repealed, etc., and the full texts of those in force, passed between July 10, 1739 and March 6, 1753. In the printed volumes there are also various manuscripts laid in between some pages (*pp. 36–37, 184–85, 252–53, 402–3*) which are notes and commentaries relating to some of the Acts. Two manuscript notes (laid in between *pp. 252 and 253*) present detailed information on the island's defense system, e.g. the names of the forts, the number and size of guns in each, and the number of matrosses and gunners manning them.

In addition to the above, Ragatz (*Guide, p. 25*) notes that the LC's *Papers Relating to the West Indies, 1762–1824* "includes ships outbound from St. Vincent and Barbados, 1772," and Philip Hamer's *Guide to Archives and Manuscripts in the United States* (New Haven, 1961, *p. 120*) records that the collection, *The West Indies Miscellany, 1494–1821,* contains materials relating to the British West Indies, including Barbados, 1756–67.

Copies of some Barbados-related manuscripts are also in the LC; *see* G. G. Griffin's *A Guide to Manuscripts Relating to American History in British Depositories Reproduced for the Division of Manuscripts of the Library of Congress* (Washington, D.C., 1946).

The LC also has the manuscript journal of George Washington's visit to Barbados in November–December 1751. This was not examined, but it has been published by J. M. Toner (*The Daily Journal of Major George Washington, in 1751–2, Kept While on a Tour from Virginia to the Island of Barbados,* Albany, 1892 [NYPL]) and John C. Fitzpatrick (*The Diaries of George Washington, 1748–1799.* Vol. 1. Boston and New York, 1925 [SIU]). At the age of between nineteen and twenty, Washington, in the company of his brother Lawrence, came to the island where he stayed about six or seven weeks. The journal of his stay (Fitzpatrick comments that it is the "worst mutilated of all the surviving diaries") has many gaps and the entries are generally very brief. These are largely devoted to the names of the persons he met, and the social functions he attended. There are also some sparse comments on geography, population, medicine, agriculture and agricultural productivity.

There is, in the Journal and Diaries section of the LC, a four-hundred-twenty page volume, written in 1814, "Memoirs of an Old Officer [Major Richard Augustus Wyvill]. As an officer in the British army, Wyvill visited Barbados for three days in 1796, and was stationed on the island for approximately sixteen months in 1806–07. The journal entries (*pp. 129–30, 381–94*) include brief commentaries on a variety of subjects, e.g., the military establishment and St. Ann's garrison, slaves and slavery, free colored, miscellaneous customs and attitudes of the white creoles, Jews.

Maryland Historical Society
201 W. Monument St., Baltimore

The manuscript curator, in a letter written in late 1967, remarked: "The Maryland Historical Society holds extensive collections concerning trade with the West Indies in the 17th, 18th, and 19th centuries. These collections, however, contain mainly account books and letterbooks of Baltimore merchants in the trade. How much material on Barbados is included I do not know. . . . We do have the Ridout collection (MS 367) with a typescript account of Sir Thomas Ridout's voyage to the West Indies in the mid-18th century [In another letter the manuscript curator notes that Ridout did not visit Barbados]. . . . and a letter from J. Dickey in 1803."

GEORGE LAW PAPERS, MS. 1346

J. Dickey to George Law, dated Barba-

dos, February 16, 1803. A Xerox copy of this brief letter was obtained. It is concerned with personal matters and is prefaced with the remark: "I would have written you oftener, but really in the Hum Drum manner I have been passing my life for some time past in this stupid Island, I have had nothing of any kind worth communicating."

In addition *The National Union Catalog of Manuscript Collections, 1967* (Washington, D.C., 1968, *p. 166*) lists the following:

MACKUBIN FAMILY PAPERS, *1795–1845*

Two boxes, in part, transcripts. Includes "bills of lading for voyages to and from Barbados."

Massachusetts Historical Society
1154 Boylston Street, Boston 15

In early 1968, the director of the MHS sent me "Xerox copies of the cards in our manuscript catalogue on the subject of the island of Barbados." *1*] In a draft of letters of Massachusetts General Court to Edward Winslow (1650?) (Photostat). *2*] Address to King, Nov. 13, 1668 (Photostat). *3*] Sailing in- structions to John Ware, master of "Friendship," Jan. 22, 1693/94 (Photostat). *4*] In Grey, R., June 30, 1698. *5*] Barbados commerce and churches dealt with in Edward Boylston to Edward Wigglesworth, May 26, 1723 (Misc. Bound). *6*] Barbados commerce [mentioned] in Richard Martin's petition, 1651; in vote of Massa-chusetts General Court modifying ban on trade, Oct. 17, 1651; Daniel Searle to Gov. Endecott, Nov. 5, 1653; in Matthew Armstrong's bill of lading, Jan. 28, 1659/60. All of these are photostats.

In addition, K. E. Ingram, in a November 1967 letter suggested that the following items in the MHS may contain Barbados materials: Thomas Prince's Journal of his voyages, 1709–10; Hugh Hall papers, 1723–74, twenty-one items. Ingram's "A List of Manuscripts and of Photocopies of Manuscripts in the U.W.I. Library" (typescript, ca. 1965) lists: Council of Trade to Queen Anne, advising that the petition of Thomas Pinder, merchant of London, for passes for four Spanish ships or other ships to trade for Negroes between Barbados and New Spain, may not be granted, as this would infringe on the Act of Navigation. December 3, 1708; "Reflections on the True interest of Great Britain with respect to Caribbe Islands. As well the old settlements as the neutral islands and the conquests. In which the importance of Martinique is particularly consider'd. By a Planter at Barbados," 1762 (Phillipps Ms. 34775, seventeen leaves, folio).

Moravian Church Archives
Main St. and Elizabeth Ave., Bethlehem, Pennsylvania

The National Union Catalog of Manuscript Collections, 1962 (Hamden, Conn., The Shoe String Press, 1964, *p. 126*) lists the following:

MISSION RECORDS, *1737–*
"Records from missions in Alaska, Antigua, Barbados . . . consisting of church diaries, letters, and reports; and records of the Society for Propagating the Gospel Among the Heathen and the Society for the Furtherance of the Gospel."

New York Historical Society
170 Central Park West, New York, N.Y.

The National Union Catalog of Manuscript Collections, 1965 (Washington, D.C., 1966, *p. 175*) lists:

WILLIAM KENYON LETTER BOOK, *1798–1800*

"Merchant of New York City. Letters to merchants in England, the West Indies, and various cities in the U.S., relating to matters of interest to export–import merchants, particularly the dangers to ocean commerce, troubles with the French, high insurance rates, supply and demand of various goods, and finances. Includes letters to . . . Leonard Parkinson [at] Barbados." 1 volume.

K. E. Ingram, "A List of Manuscripts and of Photocopies of Manuscripts in the U.W.I. Library" (typescript, ca. 1965) lists: Account book of general merchandise, kept by Mathias Lopez, of Barbados, 1779–89, folio, *359 pp.*

The New York Public Library

Fifth Avenue and 42nd Street

In July 1969, the items described below were found in the Manuscript Division of the NYPL.

AN ACCOUNT OF THE LATE NEGRO INSURRECTION WHICH TOOK PLACE IN THE ISLAND OF BARBADOS ON EASTER SUNDAY, *April 14, 1816*
A twenty-eight page manuscript bound into a copy of John Poyer's *The History of Barbados* (1808). The anonymous author has carefully transcribed a number of items relating to Barbados's one true slave-insurrection: The account of the revolt published in the *London Times* of June 5, 1816; an extract of a letter written from Barbados on April 22, 1816; an account "by a passenger who came by the ship 'Barton' which is now at Liverpool"; "Account of the loss in St. Philips and Christ Church parishes, with the owners' names and estates"; the report in the *Barbados Mercury* of April 30, 1816 which includes Governor Leith's address to the slave population (*see* published works); extracts from two letters by Col. John R. Best to Abel R. Dottin in London, dated Barbados, April 27 and September 28, 1816.

THEODORE BARRELL, LETTER BOOK, *1816–1817*

Contemporary copies of letters written by a merchant of Norwich, Connecticut; only two relate to Barbados, and both are addressed to William Gill on the island. One, dated Norwich, December 14, 1816, deals with trade and personal matters, and the other, December 26, 1816, notifies Gill of the death of Dr. Wilson, and asks him to apprise Wilson's "connexions" in Barbados of the event.

HUDSON COLLECTION (BOX 1)

Papers of Capt. James Hudson, mariner of Newburyport, Massachusetts. In this box one of the file folders (labeled "letters, 1743–1785") contains sailing orders and other items, dated 1743, 1749, 1758, related to trading voyages to Barbados. These are apparently the only items in the Hudson collection relating to Barbados.

MANUSCRIPTS RELATING TO BARBADOS, PRESERVED AT THE BODLEIAN LIBRARY, OXFORD

Four published sheets which reproduce about fifteen letters written between 1663 and 1667. Most were written by Lord Francis Willoughby, the island's governor, to the Earl of Clarendon, and relate to politics and the settlement of South Carolina. Judging by the print, I would guess that these letters were transcribed by N. Darnell Davis and originally published sometime in the early twentieth century in the *Argosy* of Georgetown, British Guiana. (*See* Manuscripts, England: Oxford University and Royal Commonwealth Society). These sheets are also located at the Institute of Jamaica.

REPORT OF ADMIRAL [GEORGE B.] RODNEY TO THE HON. GEORGE GRENVILLE . . . *1762*

A contemporary manuscript copy, dated Martinique, December 4, 1762, to the First Lord of the Admiralty, giving an account of the economic state, health conditions, strategic importance, and the status of the harbors of the Leeward and Windward islands. Only one brief paragraph mentions Barbados: "The inhabitants are more numerous than all the other islands and are at an extraordinary expence in raising their sugars. The whole being the produce of the dung made by their cattle, the natural earth of the island being very near the rock, has long since been worn out, and from the great expence attending cultivation, there is scarce an estate throughout the whole island unincumbered with debts, its inhabitants are eager to possess and would soon settle a new colony."

HUGH HALL, JR., DIARY IN ALMANAC FORM, OF WEATHER OBSERVATIONS, *1714–1717*

A photostatic copy made "from the original owned by Mrs. Jerome W. Coombs of Scarsdale, N.Y." and presented to the library in 1933. Contains an elaborate daily weather record from January 1714 to December 1717, but only the period November 1716 to April 1717 was recorded at Barbados. Also included are genealogical notes on the Hall family (including its Barbadian branch) and a list, apparently taken from official returns, of the number of slaves, windmills, and pot kiins in each of the island's parishes, 1715.

HUGH HALL, JR., LETTER BOOK, *1716–1720*

Photostatic copies of the originals located in the Houghton Library at Harvard University (MS Am 1042). These are copies of approximately three hundred letters written by Hall between November 26, 1716 and July 18, 1720 to persons in Boston, London, and Barbados. A large percentage of the letters were written from Barbados itself where Hall first went in 1716, after graduating from Harvard, to enter into partnership with his father, an island merchant. The letters form a valuable collection of information, primarily on commerce and trade between Barbados and North America; also, many relate strictly to personal and family matters. A branch of the Hall family had settled in Boston; appended to the volume are photostats of published genealogical information on this family.

Rhode Island Historical Society
52 Power St., Providence

Correspondence in late 1967 with the librarian elicited the following comments: "Unfortunately our West Indies logbooks are catalogued only under that description and we have only one card that mentions Barbados. We do have a large collection of commercial correspondence, for the most part from the eighteenth century, and I know that Rhode Island had business relationships with Barbados at an early date."

South Carolina Historical Society
Fireproof Building, Charleston, S.C.

In a letter, October 1967, the secretary remarked: "I do not believe we have any original Barbados material available. . . . There is correspondence with the British West Indies in the papers of Henry Laurens, . . . its contents dating from 1747."

Stonington Historical Society Library
Stonington, Conn.

The National Union Catalog of Manuscript Collections, 1962 (Hamden, Conn., The Shoe String Press, 1964, *p. 116*) lists:

MINER FAMILY PAPERS, *1672–1846*

About seventy-five items, in part photo-copies. Includes a 1761 letter "from James Miner from Barbadoes concerning his capture by a French privateer, his escape, and subsequent capture by the ship Coliquex."

University of Florida Libraries
University Station, Gainesville

The National Union Catalog of Manuscript Collections, 1959–1961 (Ann Arbor, Michigan, 1962, *p. 520*) lists the following collection:

WEST INDIAN PAPERS AND RECORDS, *1772–1828*

"Documents, chiefly British, consisting of pay warrants, receipts, abstracts of expenses, price lists, and other papers from various islands in the West Indies including Bermuda, Antigua, Barbados." Two-hundred-sixty-six items.

University of Michigan: Clements Library
Ann Arbor, Michigan

The Clements Library was not visited, but correspondence with its manuscript curator in late 1965, and a search of the library's published catalogs (Howard H. Peckham, *Guide to the Manuscript Collections in the William L. Clements Library*, Ann Arbor, 1942; William S. Ewing, *Guide to the Manuscript Collections in the William Clements Library*, 2nd ed., Ann Arbor, 1953) yielded a variety of items related to Barbados.

WILLIAM BELL, JOURNAL, *1830–1833*

See J. Boromé (1962–63).

FYFFE FAMILY PAPERS, *1756–1845*

"A collection of 57 letters of various members of the Fyffe family, from two periods: 1756–1777 and 1842–1845. . . . A descendant of the family, David Fyffe, is represented by thirty-eight letters to his mother in Dundee [Scotland], written while he was stationed at St. Vincent and in the Barbadoes. He entered the army in 1836 and rose to be a major in the 46th regiment. He died in 1855. His letters are very chatty and informative" (Peckham, *p. 82*). In a letter written in late 1965, the manuscript curator noted that David Fyffe's letters "are primarily those of a son to his mother, describing the island, the political situation, and his own activities. They were written during the 1840s."

GERMAIN PAPERS, *1683–1785*

"Political and military correspondence of Lord George Sackville (1716–1785), better known as Lord George Germain. About 2000 pieces. . . . The collection is . . . described in the Clements Library Bulletin 18: *The Papers of Lord George*

Germain (Ann Arbor, 1928), by Randolph G. Adams. . . . Names of writers of letters and authors of documents [include] Barbadoes. Governor and Council" (Peckham, *pp. 106–7*).

MILDMAY PAPERS, *1748–1756*

"Correspondence and negotiations of Sir William Mildmay, first baronet (d. 1771), and the British commissioners to France. Mildmay and William Shirley (1694–1771) were appointed joint commissioners to France in January, 1749/50, to settle matters provided for in the Treaty of Aix-la-Chapelle. These were the boundaries of Nova Scotia, the right to the islands of St. Lucia, Tobago, St. Vincent, and Dominica, and the accounts of prizes taken at sea after the signing of the preliminary articles of peace. . . . Names of writers of letters and authors of documents [include] Barbadoes. Governor, Council and Assembly" (Peckham, *pp. 189–90*).

SHELBURNE PAPERS, *1663–1797*

"Political correspondence and official papers of Sir William Petty, second Earl of Shelburne and first Marquess of Lansdowne (1737–1805). About 11,000 pieces. . . . Shelburne associated with some of the most learned men of his time, and his interests were wide. . . . The manuscripts which he had assembled, numbering 1245 volumes, were bought by the British Museum in 1807 (Lansdowne Mss.). His own papers, consisting of his voluminous official correspondence on British, American, and European affairs and other papers he appropriated, were retained by his family at Bowood until 1921. About one third of the lot is concerned intimately with American affairs. To distinguish the collection from the British Museum manuscripts it is called the Shelburne Papers. . . . Names of writers of letters and authors of documents [include] Barbadoes. Attorney General, Clergy, Merchants and Traders, Naval Office, Society for Encouragement of Arts, Manufactures and Commerce" (Peckham, *pp. 220–22*).

In a letter in late 1965, the manuscript curator stated that the "18th century materials on Barbados found in our Shelburne papers relate mainly to government administration of the island and evidence no explicit reference to slavery."

University of South Carolina Library
Columbia, S.C.

In November 1967 the librarian reported "we have no manuscript materials on the Barbados in our collection."

Virginia Historical Society
P.O. Box 7311, Richmond, Va.

The director of the VHS wrote in October 1967: "We do not hold any letters, journals, diaries, or similar materials in our library relating to the island of Barbados in the 17th, 18th, and early 19th centuries."

Abercrombie, Gen. *See*
  Abercromby, Ralph
Abercromby, Ralph, 26, 62
Abolition. *See* Slave trade
The abridged minutes: Society
  for the Encouragement of
  Arts, 48
An abridgement of the acts:
  Hall, 37–38
*Abridgement of the minutes of
  the evidence taken before a
  committee*, 52
Absenteeism. *See* Planters
An abstract of all the statutes:
  Hayne, 13
An abstract of the evidence, 55
An abstract of the proceedings:
  Society for the Propagation of
  the Gospel in Foreign Parts,
  18
Abstracts of some letters: Rich, 7
*An account of a late epidemical
  distemper*: Sandiford, 42
An account of an encrinus: Ellis,
  36
An account of Barbados:
  Cadbury, 103
*An account of Barbados and the
  government thereof*: Dutton,
  135
*An account of some of the
  labours*: Taylor, 12
An account of the campaign:
  Willyams, 57
An account of the donations, 42
*An account of the European
  settlements*: Burke, 36
An account of the expedition:
  Gardiner, 36
Account of the fatal hurricane:
  Hyde, 84
An account of the management:
  Jordan, 75–76
*An account of the number of
  Negroes delivered*, 20
*Account of the number of Negroes
  imported*, 54
*An account of the United
  Brethrens' missions*, 55
Acland, John, 162
*An act for vesting the Bath
  estate*, 55

Acts. *See* Laws
*Acts, passed in the island of
  Barbados*: Hall, 37, 111
Acts and statutes: Jennings, 4
Acts of assembly: Baskett, 23,
  26, 29, 150, 176
An act to encourage privateers,
  18–19
Adams, Conrad, 146
Adams, Samuel, 132, 172
Adams family, 132
Additional manuscripts (British
  Museum), 129–33, 137
*An address delivered to the
  candidates*: Coleridge, 82
Addresses of the grand jury,
  32–33
Address of the executors, 10
An address privately delivered:
  Coleridge, 90
*An address to the committee of
  correspondence*: Dickinson,
  38–39
Address to the publick, 38
*An address to the slave
  population*: Leith, 68
Administrative system:
  descriptions and overviews of,
  33, 41, 100, 135, 182. *See
  also* Governmental system
Admiralty chart: Payton, 72
Adventures of Jonathan Corncob, 50
Advice to servants: Pinder, 77
African company. *See* Royal
  African Company
Africans. *See* Prizes
Agricultural Society, 65
Agriculture: products and
  production, descriptions and
  overviews, 2, 4, 17, 19, 21, 22,
  44, 45, 54, 66, 96, 98, 128,
  136, 140, 155, 158, 163, 174,
  177, 179–80; cultivation
  practices, 4, 6, 11, 14, 34,
  35, 38, 44, 45, 47, 49, 59,
  64, 65–66, 76, 96, 97, 158,
  159, 170, 177; productivity,
  effects of absenteeism on, 54;
  products, export statistics,
  115. *See also* Sugar
Aisene, Georges: *Journal de ce
  qui s'est passé*, 3

Aix-la-Chapelle: treaty of, 182
Alexander, J. E.: *Transatlantic
  sketches*, 87
The alien act, 71
Alien office: law establishing, 71
Allard, Carel: *Orbis habitabilis*,
  11
Allen, James, 51
Allen, Louise B., 159
Alleyne, Abel, 159
Alleyne, James Holder:
  Disputatio medica, 72
Alleyne, John Foster, 59, 159
Alleyne, John Gay: 159; *A
  defence of the conduct*, 36;
  Remarks upon a book, 41
Alleyne, Reynold A., 77, 125
Alleyne family: biographical
  materials, 159
Allin, John, 5
Allshorn, Edward, 118
Alman, A. Miriam, 127
An almanac: Dolland, 36–37
An almanack: Downes, 73
Almanacs: Seller, 13; Grew, 34;
  Dolland, 36–37; Holst, 50;
  Orderson, 51; Perch, 51, 55;
  Phillips, 69, 82, 83, 85, 86,
  89, 91; no author identified,
  71; Downes, 73; Yearwood,
  85–86, 87, 89, 92
Alocs, 94
Als, William, 125
Amelioration. *See* Slave laws
America: N., N., 4; Ogilby, 8
American Antiquarian Society,
  42, 116
American husbandry: Young, 44
Americanische reiss-beschreibung,
  10–11
American Jewish Historical
  Society: manuscripts, 168–69
The American physitian: Hughes,
  8–9
American Union for the Relief
  and Improvement of the
  Coloured Race, 93
Anderson, Robert, 146
Andrews, Charles: *Guide to the
  materials*, 147; and Davenport,
  Frances, *Guide to the
  manuscript materials*, 127

Andrews, Thomas, 169
Andros, Edmund, 130
Anglican church: 11–12, 71, 72, 80, 82, 88, 90, 103, 108; missionaries, 71, 75, 76, 77; churches, distribution of, 74; organizations, 74; schools, distribution of, 74; cathedral, print of, 86; deacon, role of, 90; clergy, 100, 142; chapels, 110; organization and affairs of, 110, 137, 141–42, 156–57; records of, 122. *See also* Churches; Clergy; Religion
Animal-flower. *See* Caves
Animal husbandry. *See* Livestock
Animals. *See* Fauna; Livestock
Anketell, John: *Poems on several subjects*, 43; *Yarico to Inkle*, 43
Annamaboe, Prince of, 33–34
An answer to the charge of immorality: Husbands, 84
Antigua: land allotments, 2; slaves, 20, 38; plantation organization, 38; sugar and rum manufacture, 38; descriptions and overviews, 60, 93, 95; broadside, published at, 84; sermon preached at, 84; emigrants from Barbados to, 104; English Harbor, sketches of, 124; voyage to, description of, 132; Quakers in, 154; and Moravians, 178; documents relating to, University of Florida, 181
Antigua and the Antiguan: Flannigan, 95
Anti-slavery societies. *See* Society, Anti-Slavery
Applewhaite, T., 131
Apprentices, Negro: life and customs, 93, 94, 170; laws affecting, 114; sale of, 170. *See also* Apprenticeship period and system
Apprentices, white, 49, 153. *See also* Indentured servants; Poor whites
Apprenticeship period and system, 92, 93, 94, 114, 169–70. *See also* Apprentices, Negro
Arawak Indians, 162
Archer, C. V. H. and Fergusson, W. K.: *Laws of Barbados*, 103
Armstrong, John, 137
Armstrong, Matthew, 178
Armstrong, Mr., Bridgetown druggist, 86
Army, British: 26, 57, 62, 69, 90, 91, 99, 113, 124, 126, 130, 132, 134, 136, 137, 146, 169, 177; medical condition of, 82, 107; officers, names of, 87, 100; troops, number of, 115. *See also* Military; West India Regiment
Arnold, William, 30

Articles of agreements, 3. *See also* *Articles of surrender*
Articles of surrender, 129
Arts, 47
Ashley, John: 171; *The present state of the British sugar colonies*, 25; *The British empire in America*, 26–27; *Proposals offered for the sugar planters' redress*, 27; *The sugar trade, with the incumberances*, 27–28; *Some observations on a direct exportation of sugar*, 28; *Memoirs and considerations*, 30; *A supplement to the second part of the memoirs*, 32
Ashley, Lord, 151
Ashley, Mary, 171
Ashmolean manuscripts (Oxford University), 145
Assembly, House of: 26, 182; minutes and proceedings, 25, 130, 131, 148, 150–51, 176; names of members, 34, 69, 73, 82, 100; slave revolt, report on, 70–71; records of, 122; petitions, 130, 133
Assiento Company, Royal, 28
The association oath rolls: Gandy, 100
Astronomical observations: Maskelyne, 38
Athenaeum, library of the (Liverpool), 126
Atkins, John: *A voyage to Guinea, Brazil*, 28
Atkins, Jonathan, Gov., 22, 130, 148–49
Atlas Geographicus, 21
Attorney general, 42, 124, 175, 182
Attorneys. *See* Barristers; Plantations
Austin, Betsey, 95
Austin, James: *Disputatia medica*, 71
Austin, Wiltshire Stanton, 113
Authentic history, 64
Authentic news from Martinico, 56
An authentic report of the debate, 78, 79
The autobiographical manuscript: Senhouse, 102
Ayres, Philip: *The voyages and adventures of Capt. Barth. Sharp*, 12
Ayscough, Samuel, 25
Ayscue, George, 3, 146. *See also* Aisene, Georges

Babb, Benjamin, 54
Bahamas, 61, 124, 128
Bailey, Francis S. *See* Bayley, Francis S.
Baker, E. C.: *A guide to records*, 123
Baltimore, city of. *See* Maryland

Baltimore, Lord, 1, 98
Baptisms: number of, 108, 109, 113, 134, 135, 150
Baptist Missionary Society Archives, 128
Barallier, Capt., 83
Barbadian, 116
Barbadiana: A list of works, ixn8
The Barbadian diary: Cracknell, 102
Barbadoes, and other poems: Chapman, 87
Barbadoes, a poem, 87
The Barbadoes packet, 23
The Barbadoes petition, 21
Barbados: descriptions and overviews of, 1, 3, 4, 28, 79, 87, 126, 134, 148–49, 181; Department of Archives, 121–23; first colonization of, 146, 162
Barbados Almanack: Seller, 13; Grew, 34; Holst, 50; Phillips, 69, 82, 83, 85, 86, 89, 91
Barbados. A poem: Weekes, 35
Barbados Chronicle or Caribbean Courier, 63, 116, 118
Barbados Gazette: eulogies of Gov. Howe, printed in, 28–29; extracts from, in Keimer's *Caribbeana*, 31; address from Quakers, printed in, 35; *Remarks on Zenger's tryal* (Blenman), printed in, 42; *To the equity and policy of a great nation*, printed in, 54; described and copies located, 116–17
Barbados Gazette or General Intelligencer, 51, 117
The Barbados girl: Hofland, 70
Barbados Globe, Official Gazette and Colonial Advocate, 117
Barbados Globe and Colonial Advocate, 117
Barbados Globe and Demerara Advocate, 117
Barbados: guia de los documentos, 121
The Barbados managers, 26
Barbados Mercury, 51, 68, 116, 117
Barbados Mercury and Bridge-town Gazette, 117
Barbados penny, 26
The Barbados pocket-book: Yearwood, 87, 89, 92
Barbados seeds, 15
The Barbados Society for Promoting Christian Knowledge, 71. *See also* Society for Promoting Christian Knowledge, Barbados
Barbados tar. *See* Manjack
Barder, George, 138
Barney, John, 49
Barrell, Theodore, 173, 179
Barrell, Walter, 173
Barrell family: correspondence of, 173

Barristers: names of, 69, 82, 87
Barry, George, 132
Bartholomew, Benjamin, 173
Barton, Joseph, 135
Barwick family: history of, 126
Baskett, John, 23, 26, 29, 176
Bate, Richard, 20
Bath, Earl of, 144
Bathtubs, 124
Bathurst, Earl of, 74, 111, 112
Baxter, Richard, 138
Baxter, Thomas: *A letter from a gentleman*, 30
Bayley, F. W. N.: *Four years residence*, 86
Bayley, Francis, S., 57, 58
Bayley, John, 174
Bayley and Bedford, firm of, 174
B., E.: *A letter sent from Barbados*, 9
Beardmore, J.: *A narrative of facts*, 51
Beckles, John, 60
Beckles, John Alleyne, 125, 126
Beckwith, George, Gov.: 108, 119; *Proclamation*, 64–65
Bedford, Paul, 174
Beeby, William, 32
Belfast Public Record Office: manuscripts, 161
Belgrove, William: *A treatise upon husbandry*, 35
Bell, Francis, 60
Bell, Herbert C. and Parker, David W.: *Guide to British West Indian archives*, 127, 148
Bell, John: *An epistle to friends*, 30
Bell, Philip, Gov., 136, 165
Bell, William, 104, 181
Bellin, Jacques Nicolas: *Description geographique*, 36
Bendall, Ephraim, 138
Bennett, J. Harry, viii, 165
Bennett, John: *A memorial of the difficulties*, 28; *Essay for regulating and improving the trade*, 29; *Two letters and several calculations*, 29; *The national merchant*, 29
Benson, John: *A short account of the voyages*, 81
Berkshire Record Office: manuscripts, 128
Bermuda, 124, 181
Beschrijvinghe van Virginia, 2
Besse, Joseph: *A collection of the sufferings*, 34–35
Best, John Rycroft, 125, 179
Beverages: from cassava and potato, manufacture of, 6; types consumed, overviews and descriptions of, 11, 103, 124, 135, 163; Mobby, 16; from sugar, recipes for, 59. *See also* Rum; Wine
Bibliographies: of Barbados and Caribbean, discussed, ix–xi
Biblioteca Nazionale Marciana (Venice), 166
Bibliotheca Barbadiensis, ixn8, 169

Bibliothèque Nationale (Paris): manuscripts, 166–67
Biet, Antoine: *Voyage de la France equinoxiale*, 5
Birch, Thomas: *A collection of state papers*, 31
Birch, Thomas, Rev., 38
Bishop, Charles K., 125
Bishop, Henry: *Disputatio medica*, 80
Bishop, John, 54
Bishop, Robert, 172
Bishop, William, 58
Bishops of Barbados. *See* Coleridge, William Hart; Parry, Thomas
Blachford, Robert, 141
Black, Jeannette D., 9, 20
Blackmans, firm of, 158
Blades, Edward, 125
Blair, James, 161
Blanc, Gordelier du: description of Barbados, 7
Blenman, Jonathan: 23, 30, 130, 131; *Remarks on several acts*, 31–32; *Remarks on Zenger's tryal*, 42
Blome, Richard: *A description of the island of Jamaica*, 8, 9; *The present state of His Majesties isles*, 8
Bloudy newes, 3
Blue Books, 151
Blumeau, Jonathan, 32
Board of Trade, 27, 28
Bodleian library. *See* Oxford University
Bolton, Charles, 173, 174
Bolton, John: *Judas*, 7
Bond, Francis, 7
Boromé, Joseph: *William Bell*, 104
Boston College library: manuscripts, 169
Boston Public library: manuscripts, 169–72
Bovell, Henry A. and Greaves, W. Herbert: *Laws of Barbados*, 98
Bovell, Howard, 65
Bovell, James: *An essay attempting to prove the policy*, 65
Bovell, John W.: *Dissertatio medica*, 57
Bowen, Emanuel: *A complete system of geography*, 33
Bowen, Martha P.: estate papers, 174
Boxill, William: *Dissertatio medica*, 63
Boylston, Edward, 177
B., R. *See* Burton, Richard
Bradnack, Isaac, 91
Brathwaite, Christopher M., 125
Brathwaite, Edward, viii
Brathwaite, John, agent for Barbados, 49, 54
Brathwaite, John, Rev., 125
Brathwaite, Margaret Ann, 125
Brathwaite, Miles, 125

Brayne, Gen., 129
Brayne, Henry, 151
Breviat of the evidence, 162–63
Bridge, Tobias, 9
Bridger, John, firm of, 139
Bridgetown: descriptions and impressions of, 7, 57, 60, 61, 64, 70, 82, 84, 90, 99, 101, 112, 115; fires in, 7, 9, 26, 38, 39, 42, 43, 138; plans of, 24, 39, 167; heavy rains in, 26; streets in, 39, 83, 87; numbers of houses, 69; principal buildings, architecture of, 84; taverns, 90, 91; views of, 91; church, 112; jail, 115; records of, 122. *See also* Towns
Bridgman, John: *An exposition of a series*, 65
A brief account: Rolph, 91–92
Brief account of the desolation, 45
A brief account of the present declining state, 15
A brief and perfect journal: S., I., 4
A brief . . . answer to the philosophy: Holder, 55
A briefe description of the iland, 163
A briefe relation of the late horrid rebellion: Foster, 2
A brief narrative and deduction, 10, 11
Brief observations on the West India question, 83
A brief relation of the beginning and ending, 4
A brief representation of my Lord Dupplin's, 19
A brief treatise of the principal fruits: Tryon, 13
Briggs, John, 125
Briggs, Joseph Lyder, 161
Briggs, Thomas, 22, 161
The British empire in America: Oldmixon, 19–20; Ashley, 26–27
British Museum: manuscripts, 129–37
Brome, Susanah, 124
Brotherton collection (Leeds, University of), 157
Broune, Nicholas, 162
Browne, Benjamin: *The yarn of a yankee privateer*, 101
Brown, James, 165
Brown, William Henry: *Journal of a voyage*, 91
Brown University. *See* The John Carter Brown Library
Bruce, Alexander: *Dissertatio medica*, 43
Bruce, John: *Letters and papers of the Verney family*, 96
Bruce, R., 126
Bruce family: history of, 126
Brunias, Augustine, 119
Brydges, George: *Letters from Sir George Brydges*, 52. *See also* Rodney, Adm.

Bryer, Joseph, 171
Bulkly, Samuel, 30
Burials: number of, 108, 109, 134, 135, 150
Burke, Edmund: *An account of the European settlements*, 36
Burley, E. B., 149
Burnyeat, John: *Journal of the life and gospel labours*, 15; *The truth exalted*, 15
Burton, Richard: *The English empire*, 13
Busby, Thomas, 126
Bushel, Edward, 7
Bushel, John, 138
Bushel, John and Bond, Francis: *A true and perfect narrative*, 7
Bushnel, John. *See* Bushel, John
Business. *See* Commerce
Butcher, James: *Disputatio medica*, 61
Butcher, Thomas, 101
Butel-Dumont, George Marie: *Histoire et commerce*, 36
Butler, Richard, 138
Butler, Robert, 171
Butterworth, William: *Three years adventures*, 72–73
Byam, William: *An exact relation*, 5
Byng, Robert, Gov., 20, 30
By the King's authority, 38

Cadbury, Henry, 103
Cahueso, M. de. *See* Cahuzac, M. de
Cahuzac, M. de, 167
Calendar of State Papers, Colonial Series, 148
Cambridge University: manuscript collections, 127
Camden, Earl of, 108
Campbell, John: *Candid and impartial considerations*, 36
Campbell, Tony: *The printed maps*, 103, 104
Candid and impartial considerations: Campbell, 36
Candid observations on two pamphlets, 38
Capadose, Henry: *Sixteen years*, 95
Carey, Henry Charles and Lea, J.: *The geography, history, and statistics*, 73
Caribbeana: Comitas, xi; Keimer, 31; Oliver, 99
Caribbean Archives Conference: papers of, 127, 147, 166
Caribbean Courier, 63
Carlisle, James Hay, Earl of: 2, 11, 19, 134, 146, 162–63, 164; *A declaration*, 2
Carlisle Bay: 54, 73, 89, 91, 94, 103; prison ship in, 67; survey of, 72; prints of, 119, 120; plans of, 129, 131; shipping in, 173

Carlisles: petition to Cromwell, 133
Carolina. *See* South Carolina
Carpenter, Samuel, 170
Carrington, John William Worrell: *Dissertatio medica*, 78
Carter, John, 132
Carter, John Money: *Views in the island of Barbados*, 91
Carteret, G., 151
Carteret, N., 151
Case, Thomas, 143
The case of Barbados for indemnification: Jordan, 72
The case of Samuel Hanson, 12
The case of William Sharpe, 21–22
Case stated between the East India Company, 8
Cassava, 6, 94
Casseres, Simon de, 145
Castle, William: *A short discovery of the coast*, 32
A catalogue of books: Zouch, 17
Catalogus plantarum: Sloane, 19
Catholics, 5
Cattle. *See* Livestock
Cattle mills. *See* Sugar mills
Cavaliers and Roundheads: conflicts between, 2–6 passim, 98, 146, 163
The Cavaliers and Roundheads: Davis, 98
Cave, S. F., 160
Caves: Oliver's, 33; Animal-flower, 33, 57; Cole's, 57
Censuses: of 1679–80, 104, 122n3, 149; and 1715, 122n3, 149. *See also* Population statistics
Chace, Samuel, 171
Chaderton, William, 95
Chalkley, Thomas: *Youth persuaded to obedience*, 25; *Free thoughts*, 28; *A collection of the works*, 33
Champante, John, 145
Champion, Esther, 171
Chancery proceedings (Public Record Office), 152
Chandler, John, 73
Chandler, Michael J.: *A guide to records*, 121
Chapin, Howard M., 101
Chapman, Matthew James: *Tentamen inaugurale*, 71; *Barbadoes, and other poems*, 87; biographical notes, 87
A charge delivered in the cathedral: Coleridge, 92–93
Charges delivered to the clergy: Coleridge, 90
Charter of Barbados, 3
Chase, Richard H., 125
Chasman, James R., 125
Cheekes, William: *Disputatio medica*, 61
Chocolate trees, 50
Cholmondely, R., 172
Christianity and slavery: Eliot, 88

The Christian Remembrancer, 71
Christian responsibilities: Eliot, 91
Chronological history: Southey, 81
Churches: 95, 177, 110, 112; organization and establishment of, 22, 67, 93, 108, 113, 135; laws relating to, 24; attendance at, attitudes toward, 42. *See also* Anglican church; Methodists; Moravians; Religion
Churchill, A.: *A collection of voyages and travels*, 32
Church Missionary Record, 137
Church Missionary Society: manuscripts, 137
Church of England. *See* Anglican church
Civil structure. *See* Administrative system; Governmental system
C., J.: letter book of, 146
The claims of the British West Indian colonists: Jordan, 61
Clarendon, Earl of, 145, 179
Clarendon manuscripts (Oxford University), 145
Clark, Charles: *A summary of colonial law*, 89
Clarke, Benjamin, 171
Clarke, C. P., 98, 99
Clarke, Forster: 77; *Plan of treatment of the Negroes*, 73
Clarke, Gedney, 42, 173
Clarke, John, 173
Clarke, Samuel, geographer: *A true and faithful account*, 7–8; *Geographical description*, 8
Clarke, Samuel, of Barbados, 173
Clarke, William, 173
Clarkson, Thomas: 66; *Thoughts on the necessity*, 73
Claves, John, 170
Cleere, John, 162
Cleland, Duke of, 133
Cleland, William: 128; *The present state of the sugar plantations*, 22; *Some observations shewing the danger*, 22
Clements library. *See* Michigan, University of
Clergy: 108, 124; laws relating to, 24; names of, 82. *See also* Anglican church; Churches; Religion
Climate. *See* Weather
Clinton, J., 59
Clothing: 6; fashions, 57; washing of, 95; sent to Barbados, 165
Coale, Josiah, 153
Cobham, Francis: *Disputatio medica*, 72
Cochrane, Alex, 125
Cocoa, 50
Codrington, Christopher, 19, 21, 119

Codrington college: 35; status, development, and history of, 18, 71, 82, 88, 96, 156–57; plan of, 24; views of, 91, 92, 120

Codrington college: Parry, 96

Codrington plantations: agricultural practices, management, and production, 18, 23; slaves, condition and treatment of, 18, 40, 62, 74 83, 85, 88–89, 90, 156–57; status, development, and history of, 18, 82, 156–57; slaves, domestic, 77; slave owning, criticized, 83, 85; slaves, gradual emancipation of, defended, 88–89; view of, 91. *See also* Plantations

Codrington trust: *Report from the committee*, 85

Coffee, 50

Coggeshall, George: *Thirty-six voyages*, 97

Coinage. *See* Currency

Coke, Thomas: *Some account of the late missionaries*, 52; *Extracts of the journals of the Rev. Coke's five visits*, 56; *Extracts of the journals of the Rev. Dr. Coke's three visits*, 56; *A journal of Dr. Coke's third tour*, 56; *A journal of the Rev. Dr. Coke's fourth tour*, 56; *A statement of the receipts and disbursements*, 56; *A history of the West Indies*, 63

Colbert. *See* Terron, Colbert de

Coleman, Charles, 125

Coleman, Simeon: *A concise narrative of the barbarous treatment*, 67

Coleridge, Henry Nelson: *Six months*, 86

Coleridge, William Hart: 112, 113, 137; *An address delivered to the candidates*, 82; *On the right hearing*, 86; *A letter addressed*, 90; *An address privately delivered*, 90; *Charges delivered to the clergy*, 90; *A charge delivered in the cathedral*, 92–93; miscellaneous addresses, 93

A collection of original voyages: Hacke, 12

A collection of state papers: Birch, 31

A collection of the sufferings: Besse, 34–35

A collection of the works: Chalkley, 33

A collection of voyages and travels: Churchill, 32

Colleton, James, 49

Colleton, John, 145

Colleton, Peter, 148, 151

Colleton, Thomas, 151

Colleton family, 160

Colley, Thomas, 155

Collyer, J., 38

Collymore, Samuel I.: *Disputatio medica*, 65

Colman, George: *Inkle and Yarico, an opera*, 51

Colonial: officials, names of, 61, 108, 114, 135; offices, fees collected by, 176

Colonial Office library, 91, 95. *See* Public Record Office (London)

Colonial register for 1802: Orderson, 61

Colonies: value to Great Britain, 28, 30, 36; ceded, disposition of crown lands in, 38; relationship with Parliament, 67

Colquhoun, Patrick: *Treatise on the wealth*, 66–67

Colt, Henry: *The voyage of*, 101

Colthurst, John Bowen: journal of, 96, 169–70

Columbia University: manuscripts, 173

Colville, Adm., 164

Colville, Charles, Gen., 164

Colville, Lord, 164

Combermere, Gov., 70, 120

Comet: appearance described, 145

Comitas, Lambros, xi

Commanders-in-Chief: names of, 82

Commerce: 17, 26, 27, 30, 32, 37, 47, 132, 136, 147, 157, 164–65, 172, 174, 178; descriptions and overviews of, 22, 36, 45, 56, 64, 100; sources for study of, 25, 101; history of, delineated, 36; statistics on, 62. *See also* Economy; Trade

A comparison between the British sugar colonies and New England, 27

Compensation, Commission of, 125

A complete system of geography: Bowen, 33

Concerning a zoophyton: Hughes, 33

A concise narrative of the barbarous treatment: Coleman, 67

Congregational Council for World Missions: manuscripts, 138

Connecticut: trade with, 179

Connecticut Historical Society: manuscripts, 173

Connell, Neville, 136

Consecration service, 87–88

Considerations on the Negroe cause: Estwick, 42–43

Considerations on the present decline: Estwick, 46

Consolidation Act. *See* Slave laws

Constant, Peter, 9

Constitution Hill: observatory at, 38

A continuation of the state of New-England, 9

Convicts: shipped to Barbados, 105

Cook, Capt., 107

Cooking, 90

Cooper, Anthony Ashley, 151

Copens, Samuel: *A prospect of Bridge Town*, 15

Copies of a letter containing queries: Jordan, 67

Copyhold system. *See* Steele, Joshua

Copy of Sir Lionel's speech: Smith, 88

A copy of the articles exhibited by Mr. Freeman, 19

A copy of the petition of William Freeman, 19

Corncob, Jonathan, 50

Corrantee, John. *See* Corrente, John

Corrente, John, 34

Correspondence, Committee of, 38–40, 91, 130

Cosmography in four books: Heylyn, 9

Cotton: production, 6, 64, 147, 159; shipping, 161, 165

Cotton, John, 171

Cotton, Rowland, 171

Council, legislative, of Barbados: 133, 182; address to governor, 26; names of members, 34, 37, 55, 69, 73, 82, 87, 100, 135; slaves, report on, 77; minutes of, 123n6, 145, 148, 150–51, 175, 176

Coup d'oeil: Deprepetit-Dufrene, 64

Courteen, William: 1–2, 8, 10, 11, 101, 136, 162–63; heirs of, 151

Courts: 3, 100, 122, 145; meeting days, 69; officials of, 124, 135, 141; chancery, 131, 132, 151, 172; fees of, 141, 176; ecclesiastical, 146; escheats, 151; grand sessions, 151; common pleas, 151; admiralty, 172. *See also* Judicial system

Coventry, Henry, 130

Coxe, George, 88

Coxe, Peter, 88

Cracknell, Everil M. W.: *The Barbadian diary*, 102

Creoleana: Orderson, 94–95

Crichton letters (Royal Commonwealth Society), 153

Crick, B. R. and Alman, A. Miriam: *A guide to manuscripts*, 127

The crisis of the sugar colonies: Stephen, 78

Cromwell, Oliver, 3, 133

Crops. *See* Agriculture; Flora

Crouch, Nathaniel, 13

Crowe, Mitford, Gov., 20, 21

Crowley, Robert, 137

Cruickshank, J. Graham: *A bibliography of Barbados*, ix, x

Cryer, Benjamin, 145
Cuba, 132
Cudogan, Charles, 125
Culpeper, George P., 125
Cumberland County Record Office: manuscripts, 102
Cummins, Thomas Joshua, 126
Cundall, Frank: *Bibliography of the West Indies*, ix, x; *Lady Nugent's journal*, 94
Cunninghame, James, Gov., 45, 46
Currency: described, 6; pieces of eight, 16; paper, introduction of and controversy surrounding, 21–22; Barbados penny, 26; coinage, 55–56, 67, 87, 91; exchange rates, 67, 87, 91, 169
Cursory remarks and plain facts: Orderson, 68
Curwen, Alice: *A relation of the labour*, 11
Cust, Edward: *Reflections on West India affairs*, 94
Customs office: duties and fees, 108; collectors and comptrollers, 109; types of, 114

Dalby, Thomas S., 125
Dalhousie manuscripts (Scottish Record Office), 165
Dallett, F. J., 34
Dalyrymple, Hew, 165
Dalrymple, William, 165
Daniel, Thomas (and sons): firm of, 158, 159
Daniels, Edward S.: *Extracts from various records regarding the settlement*, 99; *Extracts from various records of the early settlement*, 100
Dapwell, John, 174
Darell, John, 151
Davenport, Frances, 127
Davies, J.: *The history of Barbados*, 6; *The history of the Caribby-Islands*, 6
Davies, Rev., 107
Davis, N. Darnell: 147, 179; *The Cavaliers and Roundheads*, 98; *Glimpses of the past*, 99; *Notes on the history of the Jews*, 99; papers of, Royal Commonwealth Society, 146, 152; transcriptions of manuscripts, 163
Davy, John: *Lectures on the study of chemistry*, 96; *The West Indies*, 97
Dawes, John, 167
Day, Charles William: *Five years residence*, 96
Day, Edward, 55
Dayrell, Thomas, 126
Deakens, Adm., 134
Deane, Michael, 126
De Cahuesco, M. *See* Cahuesco, M. de

De Cahuzac, M. *See* Cahuzac, M. de
De Casseres, Simon. *See* Casseres, Simon de
A declaration by James: Carlisle, 2
A declaration of inhabitants, 79
A declaration set forth by the lord lieutenant general, 2–3
Deeds: transcriptions and extracts, 99, 122n4, 152; of Jews, 102; in Barbados archives, 122; relating to Christ Church parish, 140; J. Gibbons, 140; of plantations, 140, 158, 160; R. S. Lane, 158
A defence of the conduct: Alleyne, 36
De Laet, Jean. *See* Laet, Jean de
Demerara, 74, 143
Demography. *See* Population
De Montlezun, Baron. *See* Montlezun, Baron de
Dent, Samuel, 48, 50
Deprepetit-Dufrene, Y. A. J. M.: *Coup d'oeil*, 64
Dering, Edward, 104
Dering, James: *A letter from Barbados*, 104
De Rochefort, Charles. *See* Rochefort, Charles de
De Ruyter, M.A. *See* Ruyter, M. A. de
Description de l'Amerique: Schaeffer, 66
Description geographique: Bellin, 36
Description of Barbados: Speed, 10
A description of the island of Jamaica: Blome, 8
A description of the new world: Gardyner, 3
A description of the province of New Albion: Plantagenet, 2
A description of the West Indies: Singleton, 41
A descriptive and statistical account of Canada: Rolph, 92
A descriptive list of maps: Shilstone, 103
Desultory sketches: Easel, 94
A detection of the state and situation: Robertson, 27
De Terron, Colbert. *See* Terron, Colbert de
Devonish, John, 174
Dickey, J., 177
Dickinson, John: *An address to the committee of correspondence*, 38–39, 40
Dickson, William: 106, 139; *Letters on slavery*, 52–53; *Mitigation of slavery*, 66
Die Sabbathi, 2
Diets. *See* Cooking; Foods
Digges, Edward, 129
Dignity ball. *See* Free colored
Directions to young planters: Orderson, 59

Disbrowe, George, 114
Discourse delivered at St. Paul's: Hunt, 46
A discourse of the duties on merchandize, 15, 16
Discourses on various subjects: Holder, 55
Diseases: epidemics, 2, 38, 42, 164; descriptions and overviews of, 11, 24, 31, 35, 39, 46, 51, 60, 126; treatment of, 24, 31, 39, 42, 47, 89; yellow fever, 31, 39; glandular 47, 48, 53; elephantiasis, 47, 51–52, 63, 70; rose, 89; small pox, 171. *See also* Medical
Disputatio medica: Leman, 45; Weekes, 58; Butcher, Cheekes, Hollingsworth, Husbands, 61; Malloney, 62; Collymore, Maycock, 65; King, 66; Wilson, 69; Young, 70; Austin, 71; Alleyne, Cobham, Straghan, 72; Bishop, Harper, Skeete, 80
Dissertatio inauguralis, 71
Dissertatio medica: Lashley, 39; Bruce, Goulding, 43; Hall, 46; Bovell, 57; Dummett, Welch, 58; Hendy, 60; Miller, 61; Boxill, Hamden, 63; Sanders, 64; Holder, 67; Garner, Thomas, 71; Drayton, Straker, 73; Carrington, Reed, 78; Ifill, 81
Dissertation upon earthquakes, 14
Dixon, Rebecca, 171
Dr. Williams's Library: manuscripts, 138
Documents illustrative: Donnan, 101–2
Dolland, John: *An almanac*, 36–37
Dominica, 82, 93, 157, 182
Donnan, Elizabeth: *Documents illustrative*, 101–2
Donohue, Thomas, 51, 55
Dottin, Abel, R., 179
Douglass, William: *A summary, historical and political*, 35–36
Dow, G. F.: *Records and files*, 99
Dowding, G., 32
Downes, James J.: *An almanac*, 73
Doyle, William: *Some account of the British dominions*, 42
Doyley, Gen., 129
Doysié, Abel, 166
Drawings. *See* Sketches and drawings
Drax, Col., 136
Drax, Edward, 49
Drax, Henry: *Instructions for the management of Drax-Hall and the Irish-Hope*, 35, 49
Drax, R. E. E., 160
Drayton, William: *Dissertatio medica*, 73
Dreadful effects of a hurricane, 45
Dreadful hurricane at Barbados, 84

Du Blanc, Gordelier. *See* Blanc, Gordelier du
Duckworth, John Thomas, 125
Dudley, Joseph: *A proclamation*, 19
Duffey, Willoughby, 25
Duke, Thomas, 174
Duke, William: *Memoirs of the first settlement*, 30; *Some memoirs of the first settlement*, 30
Dummett, Edward J.: *Dissertatio medica*, 58
Dunn, Richard S., 9, 149
Dury, Andrew, 171
Dutch: trade with, 3, 31; wars with, 6, 9, 52, 136; prize taken, 134. *See also* Holland
Dutch West India company: manuscripts of, 175
Du Tertre, Jean Baptiste. *See* Tertre, Jean Baptiste du
Duties. *See* Four-and-a-half percent duty; Sugar
Dutton, Richard, Gov., 12, 13, 129, 135, 145, 146, 149
Dwarris, Fortunatus: *Substance of three reports*, 80–81
Dyott, William, 99
Dyott's diary: Jeffery, 99

Early impression of Barbados, An: Davis, 147
Earthquakes, 14
Easel, Theodore: *Desultory sketches*, 94
Eastmond, John, 54
East Sussex Record Office: manuscripts, 139
Eccles, Solomon, 134
Eckstein, J., 119
Economy: descriptions and overviews of, 1, 2, 8, 14, 16, 33, 36, 41, 43, 44, 66, 128, 134, 135; effects of export duties on, 18; condition and problems of, 25, 26, 27, 44, 94, 102, 136, 148, 149, 151, 165; issues and events in, 29, 30, 131, 134, 136, 165; history of, 89. *See also* Commerce; Trade
Edey, Mrs., 170
The Edinburgh Review, 60
Edmundson, William: *A journa of the life*, 22
Education, 71, 72, 81, 112. *See also* Schools
Edward Randolph: Toppan, 98
Edwards, Bryan: *The history, civil and commercial*, 56; *An historical survey*, 60
Edwards, Paul: *Equiano's travels*, 53
Egerton, Charles, 171
Egerton manuscripts (British Museum), 133–34

Elephantiasis. *See* Diseases
Eliot, Edward: *Christianity and slavery*, 88; *Christian responsibilities*, 91
Elliot, Nathaniel, 58
Elliot, Richard, 138
Ellis, John: *An account of an encrinus*, 36
Ellock, Reynold Alleyne: murder of, 175
Emancipation. *See* Slave emancipation
Emancipation in the West Indies: Thome and Kimball, 93–94
Emigrants, 104, 135, 148
Emmanuel, I. S., 166n9
En chiridion ecclesiasticum: Holder, 55
Endecott, Gov. (Massachusetts), 178
England. *See* Great Britain
England's grandeur: Tryon, 17
England's slavery: Rivers and Foyle, 4–5
The English empire: Burton, 13
The English pilot, 45
An enquiry into the methods: Robertson, 27
Entick, John: *The present state of the British empire*, 43
Epidemics. *See* Diseases
An epistle from Yarico to Inkle, 29, 57
An epistle from Yarrico to Inkle: Seymour, 29
The epistle of Yarico to Inkle, 29
An epistle to friends: Bell, 30
The epistles of Mr. Robert Rich: Rich, 7
Equiano, Olaudah: *The interesting narrative*, 53, 58
Equiano's travels: Edwards, 53
Erickson, Edgar L., 106
An essay attempting to prove the policy: Bovell, 65
Essay for regulating and improving the trade: Bennett, 29
An essay on glandular secretion: Hendy, 43
An essay on the more common: Grainger, 60
Essay on the nature of dysenteries: Ingram, 32
An essay on the treatment and conversion: Ramsay, 47
An essay on tropical agriculture: Phillips, 95–96
An essay towards a plan: Porteus, 62
An essay towards the vindication: Morrison, 40
An essay upon plantership: Martin, 38
Essex county (Massachusetts), 99
Essex Institute, James Duncan Phillips library: manuscripts, 173
Essex Record Office (England): manuscripts, 139

Estates. *See* Plantations
Estwick, Samuel: *Considerations on the Negroe cause*, 42; *A letter to the Reverend Josiah Tucker*, 44; *To the Right Hon. Lord George Germain*, 45; *Considerations on the present decline*, 46
Evans, Henry, 171
Evans, Peter, 155
Evelyn, Charles, 125
Evelyn, Joseph, 125
The evidence delivered on the petition, 44
An exact relation of the most execrable attempts: Byam, 5
Examination of statements, 74–75
An examination of the principles: Jordan, 67
Exports: 44, 66, 69, 87, 89, 107, 128, 135; laws governing, discussed, 31; value of, 44, 112; statistics, 115, 146; prices, 174; lists of, 175. *See also* Trade
An exposition of a series: Bridgman, 65
Extract from a Barbadian paper, 88
An extract of a letter of Mr. Listers: Towns, 10
Extract of a letter to the Rev. Thomas Birch: Mason, 38
Extracts from the annual reports: Society for the Propagation of the Gospel, 82
Extracts from the journal of Major John B. Colthurst: Garrison, 96
Extracts from the Royal Gazette, 78
Extracts from the votes and proceedings, 25
Extracts from various records of the early settlement: Daniels, 100
Extracts from various records regarding the settlement: Daniels, 99
Extracts of letters received, 39
Extracts of the journals of the Rev. Dr. Coke's five visits, 56
Extracts of the journals of the Rev. Dr. Coke's three visits, 56
Eyle, Joseph, 124
Eyndhoven, Jan vans: *Journael, ofte daghe-register*, 5–6

Faber, John, 34
Facsimiles of manuscripts: Stevens, 98
Farrell, John, 158
Fauna: descriptions and overviews of, 4, 10, 11, 19, 21, 33, 34, 35–36, 38, 57, 72, 135;

Fauna (*cont.*)
  starfish, description of, 36.
  See also Livestock
Fell, Henry, 155
Fell, Lydia: *A testimony and
  warning*, 9–10
Fenning, Daniel: *A new system
  of geography*, 38
Fergusson, W. K., 103
Fermesii, Henrici, 166
*A few brief reflections upon a
  paper*, 18
Fielding, Joshua, 154
Fires. *See* Bridgetown
Fire companies: commissioners,
  names of, 83, 87
Firth, C. H.: *The narrative of
  General Venables*, 99
Fishbourn, Hannah, 171
Fisher, Mary, 155
Fisher, William, 145
Fishing, 61
FitzHerbert, John, 160
FitzHerbert, William, 160
Fitzpatrick, E., 132
Fitzpatrick, John C., 176
Five years residence: Day, 96
F., J., engraver, 119
Flannigan, Mrs.: *Antigua and
  the Antiguan*, 95
Fletcher, William, 146
Flora: descriptions and
  overviews of, 4, 7, 9, 10, 11, 13,
  19, 34, 35, 38, 57, 72, 83, 94,
  98, 101, 103, 124, 135, 155,
  167; uses of, 24, 34, 35,
  47–48, 136, 155; catalogs and
  lists of, 92, 136; varieties,
  introduction of, 102; sent to
  England, 151
Flora Barbadensis: Maycock, 83
Florida, University of:
  manuscripts, 181
Fonseca, island of, 20
Fonseca, Archbishop of Goa,
  20
Foods: types consumed, 2, 34,
  57, 124, 135; supplies of,
  133
Forbes, Thomas, 174
Ford, Francis, 49, 132
Ford, Richard: 171; *A new map
  of the island of Barbadoes*,
  9, 24
Forde, Richard. *See* Ford,
  Richard
Forstal, Richard, 8
Forte, Samuel, 54
Fortescue, William: *A short
  relation concerning the life*,
  8
*For the benefit of the West-
  India sufferers*, 45–46
For the unfortunate inhabitants,
  39
Fortifications: 7, 18, 22, 28, 38,
  59, 62, 63, 135, 148, 162, 176;
  maps and plans of, 32, 36,
  129, 131, 134. *See also*
  Military
Forts. *See* Fortifications

Fortye, Lieut., 169
Fossils: collection of, 47
Foster, Nicholas: *A briefe
  relation of the late horrid
  rebellion*, 2
Four-and-a-half percent duty:
  16, 18, 31, 112, 129, 130,
  131, 133, 136, 172; law
  establishing, 109
Four years residence: Bayley, 86
The four years voyages: Roberts,
  24
Fowle, William, 46
Fowler, John: *A general account
  of the calamities*, 46
Fowler, John, ship's master, 139
Fox, George: 8, 22, 103, 153,
  155, 170, 171; *The promise of
  God proclaimed*, 5; *To friends
  in Barbados*, 6; *To the
  ministers, teachers, and priests*,
  8, 11; *Gospel family-order*, 10;
  voyage journal, 146–47
Foyle, Oxenbridge, 4–5
Fragments of a poem: Holder,
  56
France: relations with England,
  7; archives located in, 166–
  67; wars with, 172, 182. *See
  also* French
Franklin, Benjamin: *Works of
  the late Doctor Franklin*, 56
Free and candid recollections:
  Kemeys, 46
Free colored: address to, 52;
  behavior and life of,
  comments on, 60, 62, 64, 68, 83,
  93, 95, 170, 177; legal status
  and laws concerning, 61, 65,
  68, 85, 108–9, 112, 113;
  discrimination against,
  incident of, 62; petitions, 65,
  112; real estate, holding of,
  63; schools, 70, 110, 113, 137;
  and 1816 slave revolt, 71;
  occupations, 81; dignity ball,
  89; baptisms and births,
  number of, 108, 109, 112,
  150; burials and deaths,
  number of, 108, 109, 112,
  150; population statistics, 108,
  110, 112, 149–50; marriages,
  number of, 109. *See also*
  Negroes
Freeman, W. H., 120
Freeman, William, 19
Freemasons, 37, 69, 55
Free Negroes. *See* Free colored
Free thoughts: Chalkley, 28
French: military and naval
  encounters with, 14–15, 26,
  36, 52, 56, 57, 125, 130, 132;
  difficulties with, at St. Lucia,
  24; sugar, competitive
  advantage of, 25, 26, 27;
  West Indies, trade with, 31,
  50; invasion feared, 62, 64;
  ships seized, 172; privateer,
  181. *See also* France
Frere, Applewhaite, 103
Frere, George, 41

Frere Henry: *A short history of
  Barbados from its first
  discovery*, 41
Frere, J., 131
Frere, John, 41
Fretwell, Ralph, 153
Frewer, Louis B., 145
*Friendly advice to gentlemen
  planters*: Tryon, 13
*From aboard the Rainbow in
  Carlisle Bay*, 3–4
Fulham papers: Lambeth Palace
  library, 141–42; United
  Society for the Propagation of
  the Gospel archives, 156
Fullerton, Thomas, 20
Fyffe, David, 181

Galt, Henry, 159
Ganci, P., 120
Gandy, Wallace: *The association
  oath rolls*, 100
Gardiner, Richard: *An account
  of the expedition*, 36
Gardyner, George: *A
  description of the new world*, 3
Garner, Jonathan: *Dissertatio
  medica*, 71
Garner, N. R., 169
Garrison. *See* St. Ann's garrison
Garrison, William Lloyd:
  *Extracts from the journal of
  Major John B. Colthurst*, 96,
  170
Gascoigne, John, 139
Gaviller. *See* Wilkinson and
  Gaviller
Genealogical Office, Ireland:
  manuscripts, 161
Genealogies: materials for, 99
*A general account of the
  calamities*: Fowler, 46
*A general account of the first
  settlement*: Hall, 100–101
*A general description of the
  West Indian islands*: Singleton,
  40–41
*A general history of the British
  empire*: Wynne, 42
The Gentleman's Magazine,
  25–26
*Geographical description of all
  the countries*: Clarke, 8
*The geography, history, and
  statistics*: Carey and Lea, 73
Geography, physical:
  descriptions and overviews of,
  2, 4, 8, 10, 19, 21, 33, 35, 36,
  38, 40, 43, 44, 45, 54, 57, 64,
  66, 69, 94, 147, 177
Geology, 69, 92
Georgia, 72
Germain, George: 45; papers
  of, 181–82
Germans: trade with, 6, 145,
  165

Ghirelli, Michael: *A list of emigrants*, 105
Gibbes, Philip: signs *Instructions for the management of a plantation*, 49; authors *Instructions for the treatment of Negroes*, 49–50, 57–58; and *Letter to John Beckles*, 60
Gibbons, John, 140
Gibbons, William, 140
Gibson, J.: *Plan of Bridgetown*, 39
Gill, Mr., Bridgetown druggist, 86
Gill, William, 179
Gilligan, Manasses, 172
Gilligan, Michael, 171
Ginger, 94, 112, 129, 147
Gladstone, Robert: journal, 143
Glandular disease. *See* Diseases
Glimpses of the past: Davis, 99
Gloucester County Record Office: manuscripts, 139–40
Glover, Mr., West India committee agent, 43–44
Goddard, Dr., 137
Goderich, Viscount, 113
Godolphin, Lord Treasurer, 172
Godsal, Alan, 160
Godwyn, Morgan: *The Negro's and Indians advocate*, 11–12; *A supplement to the Negro's and Indians advocate*, 12
Goldsmith's company, 158
Gollop, J., 131
Goodman, G. Aubrey and Clarke, C. P.: *Laws of Barbados*, 99–100
Gordon, John, 61
Gordon, William: *A sermon preached at the funeral*, 21; *A sermon preach'd before the governor*, 22; *A representation of the miserable state*, 22–23
Gosling, Hanbury, 51
Gosling, John Asgill, 51
Gospel family-order: Fox, 10
Goulding, Samuel: *Dissertatio medica*, 43
Governmental system: overviews and descriptions of, 10, 19, 21, 22, 35, 36, 38, 43, 56, 59–60, 64, 112, 128, 134, 135, 163, 164. *See also* Administrative system
Governors: altercations and disputes with, 12, 21, 22, 23, 25, 30, 33, 45, 131, 145, 146; office of, discussed, 16, 22, 41, 145; salaries of, 26, 63, 109; names of, listed, 30, 100, 109; address to, by Quakers, 35; correspondence of, 130, 182; instructions of, 148, 150–51, 175, 176
The governor's speech: Ricketts, 57
Graemes, George, 146
Grainger, James: *An essay on the more common*, 60; *The sugar-cane*, 60

Grand jury: address to Council and Assembly, 12
Grant, James Francis, 133
Granville, Bevill, Gov., 145, 172
Gray, George, 171
Great and signal triumph, 73
Great Britain: trade with, 2, 14, 15, 26, 27, 31, 44, 66, 107, 108, 112, 115, 133, 143, 146, 148. *See also* Exports; Imports; Trade
Greater London Record Office: manuscripts in, 140; and transferred to University of London, 158
Great newes from the Barbadoes, 10
Greaves, W. Herbert and Clarke, C. P.: *Report of cases*, 98
Grenada, 60, 70
Grenville, George, 179
Grenville, Henry, Gov., 35
Grew, Theophilus: *The Barbados almanack*, 34
Grey, Charles, 56, 57, 107
Grey, Ralph, Gov.: 139, 177; *A proclamation*, 17
Griffin, G. G.: *A guide to manuscripts*, 127
Griffin, T., 141
The groans of the plantations: Littleton, 13, 15
Groans of the plantations: Sloane manuscript, published in *Jl. BHMS*, 136
Grogan papers (National Library of Ireland), 161
Guadeloupe, 57, 70
Guiana, 62, 64, 94, 137, 146, 173, 176
Guildford: manuscripts, 140
Gyles, James, 107

Hacke, William: *A collection of original voyages*, 12
Haiti, 173
Halifax, Lord, 175
Hall, Fayrer: *The importance of the British plantations*, 26; *Remarks upon a book*, 26
Hall, Harper: *Dissertatio medica*, 46
Hall, Hugh: letter book, 174, 178, 180
Hall, Richard: *Acts, passed in the island of Barbados*, 37, 111, 150, 172, 176; *A general account of the first settlement*, 100–101
Hall, Richard, Jr: *An abridgement of the acts*, 37–38
Hall, Susannah, 174
Hallam, George: *Narrative of a voyage*, 84
Hall family, 161, 180
Halliday, Andrew: *The West Indies*, 92

Hamden, Renn: 74, 77, 88; *Some remarks in reference to recent proceedings*, 79–80
Hamden, Robert: *Dissertatio medica*, 63
Hampshire Record Office: manuscripts, 140–41
Hanson, L. W.: *Contemporary printed sources*, x
Hanson, Samuel: *The case of Samuel Hanson*, 12
Harding, Edward, 119
Harding, S., 119
Hardwick Court papers (Gloucester County Record Office), 140
Hardwicke papers (British Museum), 132
Harewood, Earl of: archives, 142–43
Harley manuscripts (British Museum), 134
Harper, Barclay: *Disputatio medica*, 80
Harris, Thomas, 137
Harrison, James, 170, 171
Harry, David, 25, 56
Harte, William Marshall. *See Lectures on the gospel*
Harte family, 161
Harvard University: Houghton library, manuscripts, 173–74
Harvey, Thomas, 93
Hawtaine. *See* Hawtayne, Gerald
Hawtayne, G. H., 122n4
Hawtayne, Gerald, 151
Hawtayne family, 122n4
Hawthorne, Nathaniel, 101
Hawton. *See* Hawtayne family
Hay, Andrew Leith: *Memoirs of the late lieutenant general*, 69
Hay, Archibald, 164–65
Hay, Edward, Gov., 52
Hay, James, 164–65
Hay, Peter, 164–65
Haydocke, John, 154
Hayne, Samuel: *An abstract of all the statutes*, 13
Haynes, A. Percy, 102
Haynes, Edmund C., et al.: *Notes by General Robert Haynes*, 102
Haynes, Edmund S. P., 102
Haynes, Richard, 152
Haynes, Robert, 102, 111, 152, 158
Hay of Belton manuscripts (Scottish Record Office), 165
Hay of Haystoun manuscripts (Scottish Record Office), 164–65
Health conditions and problems. *See* Medical
Heath, Josiah, 152
Hedges, W., 120
Hendricks, Peter, 170
Hendy, James: *An essay on glandular secretion*, 43; *Tentamen physiologicum*, 43; *A treatise on the glandular disease*, 47, 48; biographical

Hendy, James (*cont.*)
information on, 48; *A
vindication of the opinions*,
52, 53
Hendy, James Alleyne:
Dissertatio medica, 60
Hendy, James and Rollo, John:
Über die drüsenkrankheit,
51–52
Hewitt, William: papers of,
157–58
Heylyn, Peter: *Cosmography in
four books*, 8, 9
Hickeringill, Edmund: *Jamaica
viewed*, 5
The hidden things: Rich, 7
Hill, Abraham, 135
Hill, Penelope, 132
Hillary, William: *Observations on
the changes of the air*, 35,
39; *A practical essay on the
small pox*, 39
Hilliard, William, 164
Hilton, John, 140
Hinds, Edward Lake, 125
Hinds, Samuel, 54, 77
Hinds, Thomas W., 125
Hinkson, Samuel, 83
*Hints to young Barbados
planters*: Reece, 97
Hirbec, Daniel le, 98
Histoire du nouveau monde:
Laet, 1
Histoire et commerce:
Butel-Dumont, 36
Histoire générale: Tertre, 7
Histoire naturelle et morale:
Rochefort, 4
*Histoire philosophique et
politique*: Raynal, 43
An historical account: Thomas,
14
Historical Manuscripts
Commission (England), 126–27
Historical Society of
Pennsylvania: manuscripts,
174–75
An historical survey: Edwards, 60
*The history, civil and
commercial*: Edwards, 56
History of Barbados: in *The
Quarterly Review*, 63–64;
in *The Museum of Foreign
Literature*, 81
The history of Barbados:
Schomburgk, 96
*The history of Barbados, from
the discovery*: Poyer, 63
*The history of Barbados, St.
Christophers*: Davies, 6
*History of Barbados from 1801
to 1803*: Poyer, 63
An history of Jamaica: Renny,
62
*An history of Jamaica and
Barbadoes. See For the benefit
of the West-India sufferers*
*History of the administration of
the Rt. Hon. Lord Seaforth*:
Poyer, 63
History of the British colonies:

Martin, 89
*The history of the
Caribby-Islands*: Davies, 6
History of the Mango: Steele,
53
*The history of the rise, increase,
and progress*: Sewel, 24
*A history of the voyages and
travels*: Uring, 24–25
History of the West Indies:
Martin, 89
A history of the West Indies:
Coke, 63
Hobart, Lord, 108
Hodges, Thomas: *Plantation
justice*, 18
Hodgson, Studholme: *Truths
from the West Indies*, 93
Hofland, Barbara Hoole: *The
Barbados Girl*, 70; *Matilda*, 70
Hogs. *See* Livestock
Holder, Henry Evans: *A short
essay on the subject*, 52; *A
brief . . . answer to the
philosophy*, 55; *Discourses on
various subjects*, 55; *En
chiridion ecclesiasticum*, 55;
A sermon written for Magdelen,
55; *A system of French*, 55;
Fragments of a poem, 56;
Dissertatio medica, 67
Holder, James, 49, 159
Holder, William Thorpe, 49
Holetown, 115. *See also* Towns
Holidays, 37, 55, 69, 73, 82,
135
Holland: trade with, 146, 165,
166; archives in, 166. *See also*
Dutch
Holland, William, 119
Hollingsworth, Arthur R.:
Disputatio medica, 61
Hollingsworth, Dr.: *Remarks on
various subjects*, 67
Holmes, Benjamin, 154
Holst, Matthias, 37, 50
Holt, Arthur, 142
Hooper, Robert, 151
Hooton, Elizabeth, 8, 155
Hooton, Olive, 8, 153
The horrors of the Negro slavery,
61
Horses. *See* Livestock
Hort, Maj., 124
Hosmer, James Kendall:
Winthrop's journal, 99
Hotels. *See* Taverns and hotels
Hothersall, B., 129
Hothersall, Thomas, 174
Hotten, John Camden: *The
original lists*, 104
Houghton library. *See* Harvard
University
House of Lords. *See* Lords,
House of
Houses, 6, 7, 10, 94
Hovey, Sylvester: *Letters from
the West Indies*, 93
Howard, John Henry: *The laws
of the British colonies*, 81
Howe, Gov., 28–29, 130, 131

Hudson, James, 179
Hughes, Edward, 102
Hughes, Ellis, 171
Hughes, Griffith: *Concerning a
zoophyton*, 33; *Nearly
compleated, and to be publish'd*,
33; *The natural history*, 33,
34, 137; biographical
information on, 34
Hughes, William: *The American
physitian*, 8–9
Hull, John, 103
Humberstone. *See* Seaforth,
Francis
*The humble address of the
president and council*, 19
*The humble petition of the
planters*, 56
Hundsen. *See* Willoughby,
William
Hunt, Issac: *Discourse delivered*,
46
Hunt, Sharon, 106n1
Hurricane at Barbados, 84
Hurricanes: 1675, 9; 1780, 26,
45–46, 55, 84; 1786, 26; 1831,
84, 85, 87, 88, 92, 93, 112,
113, 137
Husbands, Joseph Dottin: *An
answer to the charge of
immorality*, 84
Husbands, Mary, 126
Husbands, William: *Disputatio
medica*, 61–62
Hutchin, Thomas, 165
Hutchinson, John, 139
Hyde, Samuel: *Account of the
fatal hurricane*, 84;
newspapers edited by, 118

Ibo, 53
Ifill, William: *Dissertatio
medica*, 81
Immigrants: numbers of, 135
Impartial Expositor, 117–18
Imperial War Museum:
manuscripts, 141
*The importance of the British
plantations*: Hall, 26
*The importance of the sugar
colonies*, 26
Imports: 87, 112, 135; value of,
44, 112; food, 106; statistics
on, 115; prices on, 174. *See
also* Trade
Inchbald, Elizabeth, 51
Incle and Yarico: A tragedy, 32
Incorporated Society. *See*
Society for the Conversion
Indentured servants: condition
and treatment of, 2, 5, 6, 14,
135, 148, 163; transport of,
2, 5; Royalist prisoners, 5, 6;
and law governing their status,
14; escape from island, 14;
Monmouth rebels, 14, 104;
planned uprising, 98; lists of,

Indentured servants (*cont.*)
104, 105; number of, 104, 134,
135, 149; convicts shipped,
105; Scottish, 137, 164, 165.
See also Apprentices, white;
Poor whites
Inglis and Long, firm of, 171–72
Ingram, Dale: *Essay on the
nature of dysenteries*, 32
Ingram, Kenneth E.: "A list of
manuscripts," 125;
*Manuscripts relating to
Commonwealth Caribbean
countries*, 168n10
*Ingram's essay on the nature of
dysenteries*, 32
Inkle, Thomas, 21, 51. *See also*
Yarico
Inkle and Yarico, an opera:
Colman, 51
Inkle and Yariko: Steele, 21
Institute of Jamaica:
manuscripts, 124
Institution and first proceedings:
Society for the Encouragement
of Arts, 47–48
*Instructions for the management
of a plantation*, 48–49, 58
*Instructions for the management
of Drax-Hall and the
Irish-Hope*: Drax, 35
*Instructions for the treatment of
Negroes*: Gibbes, 49–50,
57–58
The instructions of Henry Drax,
49
The interesting narrative:
Equiano, 53
Ireland: trade with, 129, 161;
National Library of, manu-
scripts, 161
Irish, Thomas, 162
*The irregular and disorderly
state*, 15
Irwin, Richard, 143
Italy: archives located in, 166

Jackman, Thomas, 138
Jackson, John, 95
Jackson, William, 134
Jails. *See* Prisons
Jamaica: slaves, slavery, and
slave trade, ix, 20, 113, 133,
141; English military
expedition against and
conquest of, 4, 99, 134;
descriptions of, 5, 8, 19, 64,
93–94; voyages to and from,
28, 55, 70, 84; trade, 44, 45,
145–46; maritime information,
45; hurricane, 45, 46; economic
conditions in, 46; history of,
46, 62; novel set in, 66;
Royal Gazette, extracts
from, 78; Methodist
missionary, 91; Barbados
emigrants, 104; Institute of,
124; Vice Admiralty courts,

prizes condemned in, 128;
parish and public records,
extracts from, 130; tombstone
inscriptions, transcriptions of,
130; source materials for
history of, 143; governor and
assembly, 145–46; Quakers in,
154; plantations in, 160, 174
Jamaica in 1831: Kelly, 93
Jamaica viewed: Hickeringill, 5
James Duncan Phillips library.
See Essex Institute
Jay, John, 155
Jeffery, Reginald W.: *Dyott's
diary*, 99
Jefferys, Thomas: *The
West-India atlas*, 43
Jennings, John: *Acts and statutes*,
4
Jerningham, Edward: *Yarico
to Inkle*, 39
Jervis, John, 56, 57, 107
Jewish Historical Society. *See*
American Jewish Historical
Society
Jews: merchants, 12, 13;
community of, descriptions
and overviews, 13, 99, 100,
102, 103–4, 148, 166n9,
168–69, 177; letter to
governor, 32; synagogue,
87–88, 100; congregation
members, list of, 100; taxes
paid by, 100; tombstone
inscriptions, 100, 103–4; and
courts, 100, 176; deeds and
wills, 102; laws relating to,
113, 176
The Jews in Barbados:
Oppenheim, 100
Joe's River: sketch of, 124
The John Carter Brown
Library: manuscripts, 172–73
Johnson, Archibald, 49
Johnson, John, 137
Johnson, J., Capt.: journal of,
130
Johnston, Patrick, 174
*A joint-letter from the most
considerable proprietors*,
20–21
Jordan, Gibbes Walker: *The
principles by which a currency
is established*, 55–56; *The
claims of the British West
Indian colonists*, 61; *Copies of
a letter containing queries*, 67;
*An examination of the
principles*, 67; *The case of
Barbados for indemnification*,
72; *Papers on subjects*, 72; *A
statement of the condition and
treatment*, 75; erroneously
identified as author, 76
Jordan, J. W.: *An account of the
management*, 75–76
Journael, ofte dagh-register:
Eyndhoven, 5–6
Journal de ce qui s'est passé:
Aisene, 3
Journal of a slave dealer:

Martin, 102
Journal of a voyage: Brown, 91
A journal of a voyage: Phillips,
32; Nugent, 94
*A journal of Dr. Coke's third
tour*: Coke, 56
*Journal of the Barbados Museum
and Historical Society*:
discussed, xi
*Journal of the Board of Trade
and Plantations*, 148
*Journal of the Friends Historical
Society*, 153
Journal of the life: Burnyeat, 15
A journal of the life:
Edmundson, 22; Story, 33
*A journal of the Rev. Dr. Coke's
fourth tour*: Coke, 56
The journals of George Fox:
Nickalls, 103
Judges, of courts: names of, 34,
37, 73, 82, 87. *See also*
Justices of the Peace
Judicial system: cases and
sources for the study of, 12,
60, 78, 101; descriptions and
commentaries on, 18, 32,
47–48, 59, 64, 80–81,
109–10, 130, 135. *See also*
Courts
Julian, Moses, 168
Justamond, J. O., 43
Justices of the Peace: names of,
37, 69

Kaminkow, Jack and Marion:
A list of emigrants, 104
Kaminkow, Marion and Jack:
Original lists of emigrants,
104–5
Keimer, Samuel: 56, 116–17;
Caribbeana, 31
Kelly, James: *Jamaica in 1831*,
93
Kemeys, John Gardner: *Free
and candid recollections*, 46
Kent County Archives Office:
manuscripts, 141
Kenyon, William, 178
Killingsworth, S., 167
Kimball, J. A., 93
King, John, 101
King, William J.: *Disputatio
medica*, 66
King's manuscripts (British
Museum), 134
Klingberg, Frank J., viii
Kneller, Godfrey, 119
*Kortze reize in de
West-Indien*, 55
Kurtze reise-beschreibung:
Uchteritz, 6

Labat, Jean Baptiste: *Nouveau
voyage*, 23

Labor: problems of,
post-Emancipation, 94;
plantation,
post-Apprenticeship, 95. *See
also* Slaves
Lady Nugent's journal: Cundall,
94
Laet, Jean (Johannes) de:
Histoire du nouveau monde, 1;
Novus orbis, 1
Lambeth Palace library:
manuscripts, 141–42, 156
Lancaster, James, 22
Land: shortage, 2, 5; value, 29;
use, 66; acreage in each parish,
69, 134.
See also Agriculture
Land owners. *See* Planters
Landsdowne manuscripts
(British Museum), 137. *See
also* Shelburne papers
Land surveyors. *See* Surveyors
Lane, John, 158
Lane, Richard Stuart, 158
Lane, Thomas, 158
Langford, Capt., 134
Larcum, William, 73
Lascelles, Ed., 174
Lascelles, Edward, 131
Lascelles, Edwin, 49
Lascelles and Maxwell, firm of,
142
Lashley, Thomas: *Dissertatio
medica*, 39
The late insurrection in Demarara,
74
Laurens, Henry, 180
Law, George, 177
Laws: full texts of, 4, 17, 23,
24, 26, 30, 37, 59, 91, 95,
97, 98, 100, 113, 114, 172,
176; discussed, 27, 37, 89,
133, 135, 176; abridged, 37,
59; repealed and expired,
titles of, 37, 59; private,
titles of, 59; English,
extended to colonies, 98; in
Public Record Office, London,
150. *See also* Slave laws
Laws of Barbados: 1648–1858,
98; Bovell and Greaves, 98;
Goodman and Clarke,
99–100; Archer and Fergusson,
103
The laws of Barbados: Rawlin,
17
The laws of the British colonies:
Howard, 81
*The laws of the British
plantations*: Trott, 24
Lawrence-Archer, J. H.:
Monumental inscriptions, 98,
100; and manuscript of, 130;
record extracts, 130
Lea, J., 73
Leacock, John Henry: *Tentamen
physiologicum*, 67
Leather processing, 47
Lectures on the gospel: Harte,
vol. 1, 75, vol. 2, 80
Lectures on the study of

chemistry: Davy, 96
Ledyard, John, 171
Leeds: Archives Department,
manuscripts, 142–43; Central
Library, manuscripts, 143;
university of, manuscripts,
157
Leewards: ix, 44, 176, 179–80;
records of, 123. *See also*
Lesser Antilles
*Legal condition of the slave
exemplified*, 68
Legal issues, 28, 31, 132, 165
Legal system. *See* Courts;
Judicial system
Legislative bodies: *See*
Assembly, House of; Council,
legislative, of Barbados
Le Hirbec, Daniel. *See* Hirbec,
Daniel le
Leisure hours at the pier:
Orderson, 81
Leith, James, Gov.: *An address
to the slave population*, 68;
Proclamation, 68; memoirs,
69
Leland, Waldo G.: *Guide to
materials*, 166
Leman, John: *Disputatio
medica*, 45
Lesser Antilles: archival
materials of, 166. *See also*
Leewards; Windwards
Lesueur, Charles Alexandre:
sketchbooks, 167
A letter addressed: Poyer,
59–60; Coleridge, 87
The letter book of Peleg Sanford,
101
*A letter from a gentleman at
Barbadoes*: Baxter, 30
*Letter from a gentleman in
Barbados*, 61
A letter from an apothecary, 23
A letter from Barbados: Dering,
104
*A letter from the committee of
correspondence*, 39–40
*A letter from the most
considerable proprietors*, 20–21
A letter of marque, 100
Letters: seventeenth century,
transcriptions of, 99
Letters: Yearwood, 103
*Letters and papers of the Verney
family*: Bruce, 96
A letter sent from Barbados:
B., E., 9
Letters from the Virgin islands,
95
Letters from the West Indies:
Lloyd, 92; Hovey, 93
Letters of Philo-Xylon: Steele,
53–54
Letters on slavery: Dickson,
52–53
Letter to John Beckles: Gibbes,
60
A letter to S[ir] C. M., 16
A letter to the chairman:
Seaforth, 62

Letter to the editor, 76
A letter to the North-American,
40
*A letter to the Reverend Josiah
Tucker*: Estwick, 44
*A letter to the Right Hon. Earl
Grey*: Simmons, 88
*A letter to the Right Honourable
Earl Grey*: Simmons, 86
*A letter to the Right Hon. Lord
Stanley*, 94
A letter to the treasurer: Nickolls
51
The Lewes merchants, 139
Lewis, Jacob, 50, 57, 58
Lexington papers (British
Museum), 133
The Liberal, 95, 118
Liberator, 170
Library Company of
Philadelphia: manuscripts, 103
Library of Congress: manuscript
copies, 147, 156, 163;
manuscripts, 175–77
*Lieutenant-General Sir James
Lyon*, 88
The life and adventures: Ramble,
42
Life and letters: Winthrop, 97
Lighthouse, 115
Ligon, Richard: *A true and
exact history*, 4; changes since
visit, 10, 19; history, extracts
from, 133; and comments on,
137
Lillington, George, 145
Lincoln, Waldo, 116
A list of emigrants: Kaminkow,
104; Ghirelli, 105
*List of microfilmed materials at
the Barbados Public Library*,
121
Liston, Capt., 165
Littleton, Edward: *The groans of
the plantations*, 13
Liverpool, Earl of, 108
Liverpool Record Office:
manuscripts, 143
Livestock: 2, 76, 163; value of,
29; care and treatment of, 38,
47, 59; cattle, oxen, 49, 58,
64; horses, 49, 58; hogs, 49;
sheep, 49; kept by slaves, 76.
See also Fauna
Lloyd, William: *Letters from the
West Indies*, 92
Locke, J., 151
Loddington, William: *Plantation
work*, 12
Logbooks, ship, 133, 146,
172–73
London: port of, emigrants
from, 130; university of,
manuscripts, 157–58
London Missionary Society, 138
London Record Office. *See*
Greater London Record
Office
Long Bay castle, 120
Longstreth, Thomas, 95
Longworth, Roger, 155, 170

Lopez, Mathias, 178
Lord, W. J., 119
Lords, House of: papers of, 127
Loseley manuscripts (Guildford), 140
Lovell, Edward, 125
Lovell, Robert: *Tentamen medicum*, 45
Love without dissimulation: Rich, 6
A loving and friendly invitation: Taylor, 12
A loving invitation: Pinder, 5
Lower classes. *See* Poor whites
Lowther, James, 132
Lowther, Robert, Gov., 22, 23
Lucas, Dr., 146
Lucas, Nathaniel, Judge: plantation inventory, 99; manuscript transcripts, 123
Luckock, Benjamin: *The terrors of the storm*, 84
Luke, Jacob, 145
Lynch, Dominic: *Tentamen medicum*, 57
Lynch family, 161
Lyon, James, Gov.: 88, 112, 113; *A proclamation*, 84

M̲cCormey, Joseph R., 125
MacGregor, Evan John Murray, Gov.: portrait of, 119–20
Mackenie, Francis. *See* Makemie, Francis
McKenzie, Francis Humberstone. *See* Seaforth, Francis
McKinnen, Daniel: *A tour through the British West Indies*, 61
Mackubin family: papers of, 177
MacLeson, F. I. G., 169
McMurtrie, D. M.: *Early printing*, 116
M'Queen, James: *The West India colonies*, 76
Madden, R. R.: *A twelvemonth's residence*, 90–91
Madin, Philip, 155
Mail, 37, 69, 82, 87
Maister, J., 126
Makemie, Francis: *Truths in a true light*, 17
Malins, Robert, 155
Malloney, Daniel Thomas: *Disputatio medica*, 62
Manager, plantation. *See* Plantations
Mango tree, 53
Manjack, 16, 64
Mann, Edward, 103
Manross, William Wilson: *The Fulham papers*, 141–42
Manufactures, 47
Manumission. *See* Slave manumissions

Manures, 59, 64
A map of the fortified part: Trail, 32
Maps of Barbados: printed, 4 (Ligon), 9 (Ford), 10 (Speed), 21 (Moll), 23–24, 43 (Mayo), 32 (Trail), 33 (Bowen), 36 (Bellin), 43 (Jefferys), 45 (*English pilot*), 72 (Payton), 85 (Yearwood), 92 (Halliday), 96 (Schomburgk); making of, encouraged, 47; lists and references to, 103, 104; manuscript, 135, 137, 167
Maritime information, 45, 62, 66, 86, 129, 130, 133
Market: impressions of, 57; committee of, names of members, 91
Marlborough, Duke of, 145
Marriages: number of, 109, 113, 135; index to, 132
Marryat, Frederick: *Peter Simple*, 89
Marryat, Joseph: *More thoughts still*, 70
Marry or do worse: Walker, 17
Marshall, Robert: letters of, 174
Martin, Eveline: *Journal of a slave dealer*, 102
Martin, R. Montgomery: *History of the British colonies*, 89; *History of the West Indies*, 89
Martin, Richard, 177–78
Martin, Samuel: *An essay upon plantership*, 38
Martinique, 57, 131, 178
Maryland: settlement of, 1, 98; trade with, 177
Maryland Historical Society: manuscripts, 177
Maskelyne, Nevil: *Astronomical observations*, 38
Mason, Abraham: *Extract of a letter to the Rev. Thomas Birch*, 38
Mason, Mr., provost marshal, 63
Massachusetts, 19, 99, 173, 177–78, 179
Massachusetts Bay, company of, 96–97, 163
Massachusetts Historical Society: *Collections*, 56; manuscripts, 177–78
Mathew, Edward, 169
Mathias, Gabriel, 34
Matilda: Hofland, 70
Maycock, D., 54
Maycock, James Dottin: 125; *Disputatio medica*, 65; *Flora Barbadensis*, 83; plant catalog, 92
Mayers, J. P., 87, 113
Mayo, William: *A new and exact map*, 23–24, 43; *A new and accurate map*, 24
Medical: practices, 34, 42, 174; dissertations, 39, 43, 45, 46,

57–73 passim, 78, 80, 81; conditions and problems, 46, 47, 82, 90, 92, 107, 124, 126, 177. *See also* Diseases
Medical and miscellaneous observations: Williamson, 70
Meilink-Roelofz, M. A. P., 166
Mein, Patrick, 20
Memoir descriptive: Purdy, 66
Memoirs: Wyvill, 177
Memoirs and considerations: Ashley, 30
Memoirs and services: Leith, 69
The memoirs of James Stephen, 78
Memoirs of the first settlement: Duke, 30
Memoirs of the late lieutenant general: Hay, 69
Memoirs of the late Rev. Isaac Bradnack: Rowland, 91
Memoirs of the late William Wright, 81–82
A memorial of the difficulties: Bennett, 28
Memorials of missionary labours: Moister, 97
Memorials of W. J. Shrewsbury, 97
Mendez, Abraham, 132
Mendez, Isaac, 132
Meng, J., 166
The merchant, citizen, and countryman's instructor: Tryon, 18
Merchants: 182; firms of, 51, 139, 142, 158, 174
Methodist Missionary Society: archives, 97, 144
Methodists: missionaries and their activities, 52, 56, 63, 73, 74, 77, 91, 97, 110, 138, 144; mission, status of, 56; and history of, 63; chapel, destruction of, 73, 74, 77, 78–79, 110; doctrines of, 77–79; Negro preacher, 89
Michigan, University of: Clements library, manuscripts, 181–82
Micklem, C. E., Mrs., 157, 158
Middle passage. *See* Slave trade
Middlesex County Record Office, 140
Midwives, 103
Mildmay, William, 182
Military: organization and defenses, 7, 16, 19, 62, 69, 130, 133, 134, 148, 149, 150, 157, 165; sources for the study of, 101, 147. *See also* Army, British; Fortifications; Militia
Militia: engages French at St. Kitts, 14–15; and Quakers, 16, 171; organization of, 22, 36, 59–60, 62, 63, 69, 95, 135, 149, 170; size of, 26, 135, 149; officers, names of, 82, 87, 135. *See also* Military
Miller, Philip, 129

Miller, Samuel: *Dissertatio medica*, 61
Mills, sugar. *See* Sugar mills
Miner, James, 181
Minute book of the Society for the Improvement of West India plantership, 65–66
Minutes of the evidence taken before a committee: 107; abridged, 52
Minutes of the Society for the Improvement of Plantership, 65
Missionaries. *See* Anglican church; Methodists; Moravians
Missionary Notices, 79
Mr. Robert Rich, his second letters from Barbadoes, 6–7
Mitigation of slavery: Dickson, 66
Mobby. *See* Beverages
Modiford, Thomas, 129, 131, 133
Modyford. *See* Modiford, Thomas
Mogridge, Thomas, 171
Moister, William: *Memorials of missionary labours*, 97
Molasses: export statistics, 115
Molehead committee: names of members, 91
Molineux, Henry, 140
Moll, Herman: map, 21
Monckton, Gen., 132, 175
Money. *See* Currency
Monmouth rebellion, 14, 104
Montgomery, 66
Montgomery, James: *The West Indies*, 64
Montlezun, Baron de: *Souvenirs des Antilles*, 70
Montserrat, 93
Monumental inscriptions: Lawrence-Archer, 98; Oliver, 100; Shilstone, 103–4
Moore, Samuel: *The public acts*, 59, 111, 150
Moore, William, 132
Moravian Church Archives: manuscripts, 178
Moravians, 55, 63, 122, 138, 170. *See also* United Brethren
Moreau, Emile: *Voyages de Daniel le Hirbec*, 98
More thoughts: Marryat, 70
Morgan, William, Mrs., 161
Moriarty, G. Andrews, 101, 168
Morris, Augustin, 161
Morris, John, 161
Morris, John Martin, 125
Morris, Lewis, 12, 145, 155
Morris, Richard, 132, 145
Morrison, Kenneth: *An essay towards the vindication*, 40
Morton manuscripts (Scottish Record Office), 165
Moseley, Benjamin: *A treatise on tropical diseases*, 51
Mulatto: lithograph of, 119. *See also* Free colored
Murders: Mason, convicted of,

63; Ellock, by slaves, 175
Murray, Edith, 145
Murray, John, 132
Museum d'Histoire Naturelle (Le Havre): sketchbooks in, 167

Naish, William: *Notes on slavery*, 83
Narrative of a visit: Truman, Jackson, and Longstreth, 95
Narrative of a voyage from Montego Bay: Hallam, 84
Narrative of a voyage to Maryland: White, 98
A narrative of a voyage to Surinam: Sack, 64
A narrative of facts: Beardmore, 51
The narrative of General Venables: Firth, 99
National Library of Ireland. *See* Ireland
National Maritime Museum: manuscripts, 144
The national merchant: Bennett, 29
National Register of Archives: England, 125n7, 126–27; Scotland, 163
The natural history: Hughes, 33, 34; and notes respecting, 137
Naval Office, 130, 182
Navigation act, 129, 178
Navigation information. *See* Maritime information
Navy, British: 69; seamen pressed into, 54
Nearly compleated: Hughes, 33
Needhams Point, 120
Negroes: 60; European beliefs concerning, 10, 88; sexual relations with whites, 84; verbal expressions, 89; racial prejudice against, 93, 170; post-Apprenticeship, life of, 94, 97. *See also* Apprentices; Free colored; Slaves
The Negro's and Indians advocate: Godwyn, 11–12
The Negro's friend: Naish, 83
Nevis, 8, 19
New Albion, 2
A new and accurate map: Mayo, 24
A new and exact map: Mayo, 23–24
New Brunswick, 174
Newcastle, Duke of, 130–31
New England: trade and contacts with, 26, 56, 97, 99, 168; importance to Great Britain, 27; emigrants to, 104. *See also* North America
New Foundland, 104, 124
Newman, John, 54
A new map: Ford, 9
New Plymouth. *See* New England

Newport, George, 141
Newspapers: extracts from, 99
A new system of geography: Fenning, 38
New Times, 118
Newton, John (d. 1706), 158
Newton, John (d. 1783), 158
Newton, Samuel, 158
Newton Estate papers (University of London), 158
New York, 104, 178
New York Gazette, 100
New York Historical Society: manuscripts, 178
The New York Public library: manuscripts, 179–80
Nicholls, F.: *Sable victims*, 53
Nicholls, Robert Boucher: *A letter to the treasurer*, 51; slaves, account of, 107
Nichols, John, 25
Nicholson, Joseph, 155
Nickalls, John: *The journals of George Fox*, 103
Nicolas, map maker, 167
Nightingale, Edward, 139
Nightingale, Granado, 139
Nile, Conrad, 125
N., N.: *America*, 4
Noell, Martin, 129
Noell, Thomas, 131, 133
Norris, Richard, 143
North America: trade with, 31, 43–44, 45, 61, 98, 173, 180; Stamp Act, controversy with, 38, 39, 40; Anglican church in, archives relating to, 157; family contacts with, 173, 180. *See also* New England
The North-American and the the West Indian gazetteer, 44
Northamptonshire Record Office: manuscripts, 144
Norton, W. 129
Notes by General Robert Haynes, 102
Notes on Slavery: Naish, 83
Notes on the history: Davis, 99
Notes on the West Indies: Pinckard, 62
Nouveau voyage: Labat, 23
Nova Scotia, 124, 174
Novels: Corncob, 50; Smith, 57; *Montgomery*, 66; Hofland, 70; Marryat, 89; Orderson, 94–95
Novus orbis: Laet, 1
Nowell. *See* Noell
Nugent, Maria: *A journal of a voyage*, 94
Nugent family, 161

Oath of association, 100
Obeah, 94, 108, 109, 111
Observations made at the Barbadoes: Towns, 10
Observations made by a curious and learned person: Stubbes, 7

Index

Observations made in a voyage:
Stubbes, 7
*Observations on the case of the
northern colonies*, 26
*Observations on the changes of
the air*: Hillary, 35, 39
Observations on the diseases:
Rollo, 46
Observations on the means:
Rollo, 46
An ode pindarick, 21
Ogilby, John: *America*, 8
Oldmixon, John: *The British
empire in America*, 19–20
Oliver, Vere Langford: 157;
Caribbeana, 99; *The
monumental inscriptions*, 100
*On recent proceedings in the
legislature*, 80
On the Codrington estates:
Riland, 83
On the fall of volcanic dust, 69
On the right hearing: Coleridge,
86
Oppenheim, Samuel: *The Jews
in Barbados*, 100; papers of,
169
Orbis habitabilis: Allard, 11
Orderson, Issac Williamson:
biographical notes on, 68,
71; *Spare minutes at the pier*,
85. See also Orderson, J. W.
Orderson, J. W.: *Directions to
young planters*, 59; *Colonial
register for 1802*, 61; *Cursory
remarks and plain facts*, 68;
Leisure hours at the pier, 81;
Creoleana, 94–95. See also
Orderson, Issac Williamson
Orderson, John, 51
Orderson, Thomas H.: *A sermon
preached*, 71
Orderson's Barbados almanac, 51
Orderson's colonial register, 61
Original lists of emigrants:
Kaminkow, 104–5
*The original lists of persons of
quality*: Hotten, 104
Osborn, Col., 129
Owen, Nicholas, 102
Oxen. See Livestock
Oxen in Barbados, 58
Oxford University: manuscripts
in Bodleian library, 145, 179;
Rhodes House library
manuscripts, 145
Oxley, John, 171

Packer, Charles, 97
Padrón, Francisco M., 166
*Papers laid before the honourable
House of Commons*, 34
Papers on subjects: Jordan, 72
*Papers relative to Codrington
college*, 82
Parham. See Willoughby,
Francis; Willoughby, William
Paris (France): manuscripts

located in, 166–67
Parish records, 99
Parker, David W., 127
Parker, James, 99
Parkinson, Leonard, 178
Parochial sermons: Parry, 82
Parris, Thomas, 163
Parry, David, Gov., 26, 54, 106,
107
Parry, J., 145
Parry, Thomas: *Parochial
sermons*, 82; *Codrington
College*, 96
Pasfeild, Samuel, 171
A pattern for governours, 28–29
Paullin, Charles O. and Paxson,
Frederic L.: *Guide to the
materials*, 127, 147, 148
Paxson, Frederic L., 127, 147,
148
Payton, T.: *Admiralty chart*, 72
Peace, commission of the:
names of members, 37
Peachie, John: *Some observations*,
15
Pearce, Mr., Methodist
missionary, 52
Pearson, Peter, 155
Peckham, Peleg, 172–73
Peckover, Edmund, 154
Pemberton, Israel, 171
Penn, William, 139, 169, 170
Penn and Venables expedition, 4
Pennsylvania: trade with,
170–71, 174–75. See also
Historical Society of
Pennsylvania
Penruddock's rising, 5
Pensioners: number of, 110
Perch, T. W., 51, 55
Perch's pocket almanac, 55
Perch's sheet and pocket almanac,
51
Perrin, William: *The present
state*, 30
Peter Simple: Marryat, 89
Petitions: on sugar prices, 56;
by Free colored, 65, 112;
from House of Assembly,
130, 133; Carlisles to
Cromwell, 133; requesting
relief from four-and-a-half
percent duty, 136; to Gov.
Searle, 145; in Sessional
papers, Public Record Office,
150
Petiver, James, 135
Petty, William. See Shelburne
papers
Philadelphia: port of, bills of
lading, 174. See also Library
Company of Philadelphia
Philips, George: *Travels in
North America*, 76
Phillips, John, 146
Phillips, P. Lovell: *An essay on
tropical agriculture*, 95–96
Phillips, Thomas, merchant, 146
172
Phillips, Thomas, slave ship
captain: *A journal of a voyage

made in the Hannibal*, 32
Phillips, Tobias: *The Barbados
almanack*, 69, 82, 85, 86, 89,
91
Phillips, W. Randle, 175
*A philosophical and political
history*: Raynal, 43
Philo-Xylon, 53
Phipps, Charles, 137
Phyllips, William, 146
Piggott, Joseph M., 125
Pile, Richard P., 125
Pilgrim (Governor's Residence),
25, 91
Pinckard, George: *Notes on the
West Indies*, 62
Pinder, John Hothersall: *Advice
to servants*, 77
Pinder, Richard: 155; *A loving
invitation*, 5
Pinder, Thomas, 178
Pinfold, Charles, Gov.: 131, 134;
papers of, 175–76
Pitman, Henry: *A relation of the
great sufferings*, 13–14
Pitts, Capt., 146
Plague. See Diseases
Plan of Bridgetown: Gibson, 39
Plan of treatment of the Negroes:
Clarke, 73
Plantagenet, Beauchamp: *A
description of the province*, 2
Plantations: economic and
business, affairs and problems,
13, 29, 56, 62, 102, 125, 128,
132, 135, 136, 142–43, 158, 159,
160; management and
organization of, 16, 35, 38,
49, 59, 65–66, 76, 103, 158,
159; manager, role of, 49, 158;
names listed on resolution, 79;
inventories of, 99, 151, 171;
legal affairs, 128; purchase,
rental, and sale, 140, 144, 151,
159, 164; plans, 152; attorney,
role of, 158, 159; produce,
mechanics and problems of
shipment, 158, 159. See also
Agriculture; Planters; Steele,
Joshua
— individual units: Balls, 53;
Bath, 55; Baxters, 125, 126;
Bay, 125; Belle, 142, 143;
Bishops, 140; Black Rock,
159; Blowers, 159;
Borrowfield, 140; Breedys,
125; Brewsters, 125; Brighton,
125; Burnt House, 76;
Cabbage Tree, 125; Charity
Hall, 125; Clapham, 99;
Clifton Hall, 102; Codrington,
18, 82, 156–57;
Colleton, 125, 160; Congre
Road, 140; Coopers Hill, 140,
142; Cox, 159; Drax-Hall,
35, 49, 160; Fair View, 125;
Farley Hill, 76; Fortescue, 142;
Foull Bay, 140; The Garden,
125; Grange Hill, 125; Grove,
102; Haggatts, 125; Haymans,
125, 140; Hope, 125; Irish-

Plantations (*cont.*)
Hope, 35, 49; Kendal, 60;
Lower Estate, 103; Lower
Greys, 125; Lowthers, 132–33;
Mallards, 125; Moonshine,
103; Morgan Lewis, 140;
Mount, 142; Mount Pleasant,
125; Mount Standfast, 159;
Mount Wilton, 175;
Mullins, 140; New Castle, 102;
Newton, 158; Nicholas Abbey,
160; Pasfeild, 171; Porry's
Spring, 124; Porters, 159;
Quintynes, 152; Risk, 125;
Rock Hall, 59; Sandy Lane,
159; Seawell, 158; Springfield,
125; Spring Head, 50, 57, 58;
Stewart Hill, 125; Taitts, 50;
Thicket, 142; Three Houses,
125; Turners Hall, 159;
Vaucluse, 92; Vaughns, 125;
Walkers, 76; Waterford
125; Westmorland, 125;
White River, 140; Wildey,
125; Woodland, 125
Plantation justice: Hodges, 18
Plantation system: organization
of, 66
Plantation work: Loddington, 12
Planters: 13, 76, 79, 85, 87, 93;
economic problems of, 15, 16;
absentee, 20, 48, 54, 86, 88,
103, 158, 159; names of, 79,
83, 104, 125, 126, 131, 148,
151; social life and customs,
92, 94, 95, 124, 158, 159, 163;
number of, 149; letters from,
150. *See also* Economy;
Social life and customs
Plants. *See* Flora
Pleydell, Mark Stewart, 128
A pocket-book: Yearwood, 85–86
Poems: on Barbados, 21, 35
(Weekes), 40–41 (Singleton),
87 (Chapman, and review of);
on slaves and slavery, 56
(Holder), 58, 64
(Montgomery); on sugar cane,
60 (Grainger); in almanacs,
85, 87, 92 (Yearwood);
authored by, Brown, 91,
Anketell, 93, Bartholomew, 173
Poems on several subjects:
Anketell, 43
Poetry. *See* Poems
Polgreen, Howard, 174
Police, 91, 114, 170
Political history: of Barbados,
reviewed and described, 2,
19, 30, 33, 36, 43, 56, 63, 66,
81, 89, 96, 98, 135–36, 148;
sources for study of, 22, 36,
41, 101, 147, 160; conditions
and events, described and
discussed, 25–26, 29, 31, 131,
133, 134, 136, 146, 149, 151,
157, 160, 162, 164–65, 181
Pollard, Thomas (brother of
Walter P.), 131
Pollard, Thomas (father of
Walter P.), 131

Pollard, Walter, 131
Pollard, William, 174–75
Ponds. *See* Water supplies
Poor whites: occupational
employment, 47–48, 81;
missionary work among, 56,
72; observations on and
descriptions of, 70, 92, 95,
97, 170; education of, 71, 81.
See also Apprentices, white;
Indentured servants
Population: descriptive
overviews, 1, 8, 19, 34, 35, 36,
38, 44, 56, 64, 91, 93,
134, 147, 177, 179; statistics,
66, 104, 108, 109, 110, 112,
134, 135, 148, 149, 150, 167.
See also Censuses
Porteus, Beilby: *An essay
towards a plan*, 62
Portland, Duke of, 107, 108
Portuguese: ship, seized by Gov.,
23
Postal. *See* Mail
Potatoes, 6
Pothill, Sarah, 171
Pot kilns: number of, 149, 180
Povey, Richard, 129
Povey, Thomas, 129, 133
Povey, William, 129, 133
Powell, Henry, 146, 151, 162, 163
Powell, John, 146, 151
Powlett, William, 133
Powrey, William, 164
Poyer, John: *A letter addressed
to his excellency*, 59–60;
*History of Barbados from 1801
to 1803*, 63; *The history of
Barbados, from the discovery*,
63; and review of, 63–64;
newspapers associated with,
117–18
Poyntz, John: *The present
prospect*, 16
*A practical essay on the small
pox*: Hillary, 39
Premium for standards: Society
for the Encouragement of
Arts, 48
Premiums for cultivation:
Society for the Encouragement
of Arts, 50
Presbyterians, 17, 138
Prescod, Samuel, 95, 118
*The present case of a Barbados
planter*, 16
*The present condition of the
Negro*, 92
The present prospect: Poyntz,
16
*The present state of His Majesties
isles*: Blome, 8
*The present state of the British
and French*: Perrin, 30
*The present state of the British
empire*: Entick, 43
*The present state of the British
sugar colonies*, 85
*The present state of the British
sugar colonies consider'd*:
Ashley, 25; and rebutted, 26

*The present state of the sugar
plantations consider'd*:
Cleland, 22
*The present state of the
West-Indies*, 45
Preston, Howard, W., 101
Prince, Thomas: journal of
voyage, 178
Prince Rupert: voyage of, 130
*The principles by which a
currency*: Jordan, 55–56
Pringle, J. W., 115
Pringle, Rachel, 119
The printed maps: Campbell, 103,
104
Printers and printing, 14, 25, 32,
56, 116
Prints, engraved, 11, 15, 34, 72,
91, 119–20
Prisoners of war: imprisonment
of, 63, 67, 101, 125
Prisons: report on, 115
Privateering: against American
shipping, 100
Privy Council: papers of, 127;
cases, 132
Prize court: case at, 129
Prize office: establishment of,
134
Prizes: Africans, 108, 109, 113,
114; condemned in Admiralty
courts, 124, 172; ship, Dutch,
134; and French, 172, 182
Proceedings and debates: Stock,
101
*Proceedings of the general court
martial*, 61
*Proceedings of the Society for the
Propagation of the Gospel*, 18
A proclamation: Lyon, 84, 113
Proclamations: prohibiting
dealing with Company of
Scotland, 17; Massachusetts
embargo on ships to Barbados,
19; ceded colonies, disposition
of crown lands in, 38; arrest
of Springer, 64–65;
condemning slave revolt, 68;
instructing militia commanders
69; pardon to slaves, 69;
concerning destruction of
Methodist chapel, 74; warning
plunderers, 84, 113; dispelling
rumors of slave revolt and
emancipation, 109
The promise of God: Fox, 5
Property: laws relating to, 81,
98, 129
*Proposals offered for the sugar
planters*: Ashley, 27
*Proposed institution of a Colonial
Charity School*, 70
A prospect of Bridge Town:
Copens, 15
*A prospect of the most famous
parts*: Speed, 10
Prostitution, 84
The public acts: Moore, 59, 111
*The public acts in force, passed
by the legislature of Barbados
between the 8th April 1800*, 95

The public acts in force passed by the legislature of Barbados from the first, 91
The public acts in force passed by the legislature of Barbados, in the first, second, third, 95
Public Concern, committee of: minutes, 150
Public meeting of planters, 85
Public Record Office (London): manuscripts, 147–52; and transcriptions of, 159–60
Pugh, R. B.: *The records of the Colonial and Dominions offices*, 147
Punnett, Roger, 139
Purdy, John: *Memoir descriptive*, 66
Pyndar, Paul, 10, 11

Quaker records, 103
Quakers: criticize Barbadian whites, 4, 5, 9–10, 12, 155; epistles and religious views of, 5, 6, 11, 22, 30, 154, 155, 170, 171; altercations with R. Rich, 7–8; meetings and community of, 7–8, 10, 11, 15, 22, 24, 33, 103, 147, 153, 154, 155; persecutions of, 9–10, 16, 34–35, 134, 170–71; relation with slaves and position on slavery, 10, 11, 16, 22, 33, 103, 155; tobacco planters, 11; encouraged to, and leave island, 12, 170, 171; and militia, 16, 134, 170, 171; debate Ramsey and Atkins, 22; merchants, 33, 170, 171; American, visit after Apprenticeship, 95; midwives, 103; manuscripts relating to, Society of Friends library, 153–55; and Boston Public library, 170–71; visiting island in 17th and 18th centuries, list of, 155. *See also Journal of the Friends Historical Society*

Ragatz, Lowell J.: *A guide for the study of British Caribbean history*, x, xi; *Statistics for the study*, 101; *A check list of House of Commons sessional papers*, 106*n*2; *A check list of House of Lords sessional papers*, 106*n*2; *A guide to the official correspondence*, 150
Ramble, James: *The life and adventures*, 42
Ramsay, David, 145
Ramsay, James: *An essay on the treatment*, 47

Ramsey, Gilbert, 22
Randolph, Edward, 98
Rawdon: pedigree of, 129
Rawdon, Col., 131
Rawlin, William: *The laws of Barbados*, 17; and manuscript of, 150
Rawlinson manuscripts (Oxford University), 145–46, 152, 162
Raynal, Guillaume Thomas: *Histoire philosophique et politique*, 43; *A philosophical and political history*, 43
Reasons humbly offered, 16
Recapitulation of the number of persons, 85
Record repositories in Great Britain: Historical Manuscripts Commission, 126
Records and files: Dow, 99
Records of the colony of New Plymouth: Shurtleff, 97
Records of the governor and company of the Massachusetts Bay: Shurtleff, 96–97
Recueil de divers voyages, 9
Red-shanks. *See* Poor whites
Reece, Robert: 125, 158; *Hints to young Barbados planters*, 97
Reece, William, 158
Reed, Baynes: *Dissertatio medica*, 78
Rees, Thomas Gwynn, 107
Reflections on West India affairs: Cust, 94
Registry Bill. *See* Slave registration
Reise nach ost-und West-Indien: Zimmerman, 42
Relation: on earthquake, 14
Relation de l'isle des Barbades: Blome, translation of, 9
A relation of the great sufferings: Pitman, 13–14
A relation of the labour: Curwen, 11
A relation of the late intended settlement: Uring, 24
A relation of the successful beginnings, 1
Religion: freedom of, established by Charter of Barbados, 3; descriptions and overviews of, 6, 92, 135, 138. *See also* Anglican church; Catholics; Churches; Jews; Methodists; Moravians; Presbyterians; Quakers
Religious establishment, 74
The remarkable occurrences: Spann, 21
Remarks on several acts: Blenman, 31–32
Remarks on the disease: Rollo, 48
Remarks on the evidence, 44–45
Remarks on the insurrection, 68
Remarks on various subjects: Hollingsworth, 67
Remarks on Zenger's tryal: Blenman, 42

Remarks upon a book: Hall, 26; Alleyne, 41
Renny, Robert: *An history of Jamaica*, 62
Report: Society for the Propagation of the Gospel, 85
The report from a select committee, 70–71
Report from the committee of the Codrington trust, 85
Report of a committee of the general assembly, 54
Report of a debate in council, 74
Report of cases: Greaves and Clarke, 98
Report of the Barbados Society for Promoting Christian Knowledge, 80
A report of the committee of the council, 77
Report of the lords of the committee of council, 107
Report of the Society for Propagating the Gospel, 88–89
Report respecting the Negroes: Society for the Propagation of the Gospel, 90
Representation from the commissioners for trade, 28
Representation of the Board of Trade, 27, 28
A representation of the miserable state: Gordon, 22–23
A residence in the West Indies: St. Clair, 89–90
Revenues. *See* Taxes
A review of the Jewish colonists: Samuel, 102
Revolts. *See* Slave revolts
Reynolds, S. W., 119
Rhode Island, 81, 101, 170, 171, 172, 180
Rhode Island Historical Society: manuscripts, 180
Rhodes House Library. *See* Oxford University
Rich, Robert, Earl of Warwick, 136
Rich, Robert, Quaker and planter: *Love without dissimulation*, 6; altercations with Quakers, 6–7; *Mr. Robert Rich, his second letters*, 6–7; *Abstracts of some letters*, 7; *The epistles of*, 7; *The hidden things*, 7; description of Barbados, 8
Richardson, Richard, 170
Ricketts, George, Gov.: 107, 108; *The governor's speech*, 57
Ridout, Thomas, 177
Riggs, Thomas, 173
Riland, John: *Two letters*, 82; *On the Codrington estates*, 83
Riot in Barbadoes, 77
Rivers, Marcellus and Foyle, Oxenbridge: *England's slavery*, 4–5
Roberts, George: *The four years*, 24
Robertson, Gladstone, 126

Robertson, Robert: *A detection of the state*, 27; *An enquiry into the methods*, 27; *A supplement to the detection*, 27
Robinson, J., 169
Robinson, Thomas, Gov., 32, 35, 131
Rochefort, Charles de: *Histoire naturelle*, 4, 6
Rodney, Adm.: 107, 130, 132, 179–80; papers of, Public Record Office, 147. *See also* Brydges, George
Rodriguez, Anthony, 12
Roessingh, M. P. H., 166
Rollo, John: *Observations on the diseases*, 46; *Observations on the means*, 46; *Remarks on the disease*, 48, 52, 53
Rolph, Thomas: *A brief account*, 91–92; *A descriptive and statistical account*, 92
Romer, Col., 145
Root, Thomas, 139
Rose, George, 153, 155
Rosenwald collection, 17
Rotheram, John: *A sketch of the one great argument*, 35
Roundheads. *See* Cavaliers and Roundheads
Rous, John: 153, 155; *A warning to the inhabitants*, 4
Rous, Thomas, 10
Rowe, Margery, 161
Rowland, Thomas: *Memoirs of the late Rev. Isaac Bradnack*, 91
The Royal African, 33
Royal African Company, 20, 21, 22, 34, 134, 152
Royal Colonial Institute. *See* Royal Commonwealth Society
Royal Commonwealth Society: manuscripts, 152–53
Royal Empire Society. *See* Royal Commonwealth Society
Royalists. *See* Cavaliers and Roundheads
Royal Society, London: papers of, 127
Rum: manufacture of, 17, 38, 49, 59, 158; duties on, 46; exports, 107; imported by Great Britain, 108, 115; prices on, 174
Rumford, Count, 57, 58
Rush, Benjamin, 39, 174
Russell, Col., 129
Russell, James: *Tentamen inaugurale*, 73
Rutherford, James, 125
Ruyter, M. A. de, 6

Sabin, Joseph: *Bibliotheca Americana*, x
Sable victims: Nicholls, 53
Sack, Albert von, Baron: *A narrative of a voyage*, 64

Sackville, George. *See* Germain, George
Sackville of Knole manuscripts (Kent County Archives Office), 141
St. Ann: observations of the ship's master, 129
St. Ann's garrison, 84, 91, 120, 177
St. Christopher: 60, 77; description of, 8, 19; military attack upon, 14–15; slavery in, 47; first settlement of, 162
St. Clair, Thomas Staunton: *A residence in the West Indies*, 89–90; *A soldier's recollections*, 90
St. Croix, 93, 170
St. Domingo, 125, 173
St. Eustatius, 42, 52
St. Hill, A., Mrs., 149
St. Kitts. *See* St. Christopher
St. Lucia: military attacks upon, 7, 57; English settlers in, 24; diseases of army in, 46; collector of customs (Bridgman), troubles of, 65; description of, 93; English rights to, 182
St. Matthias chapel, 120
St. Paul's, chapel, 120
St. Vincent: English intended settlement of, 24; volcanic ash, fall of on Barbados, 26, 69; description of, 60; meeting of planters and merchants, 85; journal of a residence in, 169–70; ships outbound, 176; letters written from, 181; English rights to, 182
Salem. *See* Massachusetts
Salisbury uprising, 5
Salmon, Mr., compiler of laws, 29, 37
Salt: production of, 47
Samuel, Wilfred S.: *A review of the Jewish colonists*, 102; historical sketch of Jews, 103–4
Sandelow, slave, 171
Sanders, George: *Dissertatio medica*, 64
Sandiford, William: *An account of a late epidemical*, 42
Sanford, Elisha, 101
Sanford, Peleg: *The letter book*, 101
Sanford, Robert: *Surinam justice*, 5
Sanford, William, 101
Sanvoort, engraver, 119
Scamler, Robert: *Several sermons*, 13
Schaeffer, D. F.: *Description de l'Amerique*, 66
Schomburgk, Robert H.: *The history of Barbados*, 96; *A topographical map*, 96
Schools: Colonial Charity, 70, 83, 137; number and types of,

71, 74, 110, 113, 142; Central, 72; during and after Apprenticeship, 93, 95, 114; school teachers, 110, 113, 124. *See also* Codrington college; Education
Schroeder, Henry, 73
Scot, Richard, 20
Scott, John: description of Barbados, 135–36
Scotland, company of, 17
Scottish Record Office: manuscripts, 164–65
Scroop. *See* Howe, Gov.
Sea: agitation of, 38
Seaforth, Francis, Gov.: 59, 63, 94, 108, 169; *A letter to the chairman*, 62; papers of (Scottish Record Office), 165
Sealey, Henry, 78
The seaman's practical guide, 86
Searle, Daniel, Gov., 129, 133, 145, 178
Searle, John, 135
The self-flatterer, 23
Seller, John: *Barbados almanack*, 13
Selwyn, George A., 132
Senhouse, William: *The autobiographical manuscript*, 102
Sermons: Scamler, 13; Gordon, 21, 22; Warburton, 40; Holder, 55; Orderson, 71; Shrewsbury, 78–79; Parry, 82; Coleridge, 82, 86, 92–93; Luckock, 84; Eliot, 88
A sermon preached at the funeral: Gordon, 21
A sermon preach'd before the governor: Gordon, 22
A sermon preached before the Incorporated Society: Warburton, 40
A sermon preached in St. Michael's: Orderson, 71
Sermons preached on several occasions: Shrewsbury, 78–79
A sermon written for Magdelen: Holder, 55
Servants. *See* Indentured servants
Sessarakoo, William Unsah, 34
Sessional papers: in Public Record Office, 150–51
Several sermons: Scamler, 13
Sevillano-Colom, Francisco, 121n2
Sewel, William: *The history of the rise*, 24
Seymour, Frances: *The story of Inkle and Yarrico*, 29
Shaftesbury papers (Public Record Office), 147, 151
Sharp, Bartholomew, 12
Sharp, Granville, 139–40
Sharp, William, 77
Sharpe, J., 130, 131
Sharpe, William, Pres. of Council: *The case of William Sharpe*, 21–22

Sharpe, William, 19th-century planter, 125
Sheep. *See* Livestock
Shelburne papers (University of Michigan), 182
Sherman, John, 153
Shiffner, Henry, 139
Shiffner, John, 139
Shilstone, E. M.: transcription of Hall manuscript, 100; biographical notes on, 103; *A descriptive list of maps*, 103; *Monumental inscriptions*, 103–4; *Some notes on early printing*, 116
Shipping: 133, 135, 174, 176; returns, 151
Shirley, William, 182
A short account of the manifest hand of God, 16
A short account of the voyages: Benson, 81
A short discovery: Castle, 32
A short essay on the subject: Holder, 52
A short history of Barbados: Frere, 41
A short journey in the West Indies, 55
A short relation concerning the life: Fortescue, 8
Shrewsbury, John V. B.: *Memorials of W. J. Shrewsbury*, 97
Shrewsbury, William J.: 73, 77, 97, 110; *Sermons preached*, 78–79
Shropshire County Record Office: manuscripts, 153
Shurtleff, Nathaniel B.: *Records of the governor and company*, 96–97; *Records of the colony of New Plymouth*, 97
S., I.: *A brief and perfect journal*, 4
Silk industry, 47
Simmons, Henry Peter: *A letter to the Right Honourable Earl Grey*, 86; *A letter to the Right Hon. Earl Grey*, 88; *Third letter to the Right Hon. Earl Grey*, 90
Simpson, John, 125
Simpson, William, 8
Sims, Catherine, 132
Singleton, John: *A general description of the West Indian islands*, 40–41; *A description of the West Indies*, 41
Six months: Coleridge, 86
Sixteen years: Capadose, 95
Skeete, Edward: *Disputatio medica*, 80
Skeete, Reynold, 132
Sketch of a voyage, 57
A sketch of the one great argument: Rotheram, 35
Sketches and drawings, 91, 124, 152, 167, 170
Sketches and recollections, 82
Skey, Joseph: *Some remarks upon the structure*, 68–69
The slave colonies of Great Britain, 79
Slave emancipation: 112, 114; gradual measures for, 85; compensation to owners, 90, 114–15, 125–26, 152; rumors concerning, 109. *See also* Slavery
Slave laws: 48, 54, 61, 63, 68, 79, 81, 108–9, 111, 113; amelioration of, 80, 109, 111, 112, 113, 150, 165; Consolidation act, 110, 112
Slave manumissions: 61, 68, 81, 108–9; number of, 109, 110, 114; law removing money deposit, 111, 113; in England, 114
Slave owners: names of, 125, 126. *See also* Planters
Slave population: natural increase, 51; mechanisms for ascertaining number, 68; statistics, 69, 104, 108–14 passim, 134, 135, 149, 150, 180; law for ascertaining number, 109. *See also* Population; Slave registration
Slave registration: 152; registry bill, 67, 68, 71
Slave revolt: plots, 9, 10, 167; in 1816, 68, 69, 70–71, 72, 94, 179; rumor of, 109
Slavery: 11–12, 13, 54, 66, 72, 88, 95, 99, 107, 165, 177; criticized, 47, 52–53, 54, 61, 66, 77, 83, 170; defended, 52, 61, 63, 67, 68, 73, 74, 77, 80, 83, 86, 87
The slavery of the British West India colonies: Stephen, 77–78
Slaves: 23, 35, 72, 102, 109, 132, 136, 137, 149, 155, 163, 177; runaways, 2, 111; condition, life and treatment, 6, 11, 13, 33, 38, 40, 47–68 passim, 73–93 passim, 103, 106, 107, 113, 158; Christian education and missionary work among, 11, 12, 18, 52, 55, 56, 58, 62, 67, 71, 75, 76, 79, 80, 83, 88, 96, 138, 144, 156; value of, monetary, 21, 22, 125; diets, 45, 49, 50, 57, 58, 64, 73, 76; houses, 49, 50, 58, 72, 76, 83; labor, organization of, 49, 50, 73, 76, 83, 125, 158; medical care, 49, 58, 73, 76; child and infant care, 49, 58, 76, 83; gardens, 49, 58, 76, 83; clothing, 49, 73, 76; sales, 53, 57, 139, 143, 152, 160, 171; names, 55, 160, 171; education, 58, 70, 71, 83; marriages, 58, 83, 89, 110, 111; baptism, 58, 111; property inherited, 60, 165; murder of, 61, 63, 108, 165; militia and military participation, 62, 132; customs, 64, 65; livestock keeping, 76; marketing, 76, 83, 111; funerals, 76, 83, 155; domestic, 77, 95; and courts, 78, 110, 112, 113; murderers of whites, 78, 175; religious patterns, 83, 155; speech patterns, 90; escheated to Crown, 109, 110, 113, 114; prohibited from buying liquor, 111; legal status of, 112, 113; church attendance statistics, 113; song, 139–40; occupational specializations, 148, 158; ages of, statistics, 150. *See also* Negroes; Quakers; Slave laws; Slave manumissions; Slave population; Slave registration; Slave revolt; Slavery; Slave trade
Slave system. *See* Slavery
Slave trade: 20–21, 22, 28, 34, 43, 57, 72, 101–2, 106, 134, 152, 161, 165; import and export statistics, 20, 54, 62, 107, 108, 109, 110, 113, 135; middle passage and slave ships, 32, 53, 70, 73, 89, 107, 141; abolition of, 51, 52, 55, 107; illegal, 67, 68; with Spanish, 133, 178
Sloane, Hans: 24, 136; *Catalogus plantarum*, 19; *A voyage to the islands*, 19
Sloane manuscripts (British Museum), 134–36, 137
Small pox. *See* Diseases
Smalridge, John, 23
Smith, Charlotte: *The wanderings of Warwick*, 57
Smith, John, Capt.: *The true travels, adventures*, 1
Smith, John, engraver, 119
Smith, John, Quaker, 103
Smith, Joseph, 171
Smith, Lionel, Gov.: 170; *Copy of Sir Lionel's speech*, 88
Smith, Ralph, 170
Smith, Richard, 59, 159
Smith, Sidney, 95
Smyth, Clifford, 101
Social life and customs: descriptions and overviews, 4, 5, 21, 23, 35, 56, 62, 72, 76, 84, 86, 87, 92–104 passim, 135, 136, 141–42, 144, 149, 154, 160, 162, 170, 173, 177. *See also* Planters; Slaves
Societies: agricultural, 65–66, 96
Society, Anti-Slavery: London, 92; American, 93; Aborigine Protection, British, 145
Society of Friends library: manuscripts, 153–55
Society for Advancing the Christian Faith: *The two charters of the Society*, 92
Society for Promoting Christian Knowledge, Barbados: *The Barbados Society*, 71; *Report*, 80

Society for Propagating the Gospel among the Heathen, 178
Society for the Conversion and Religious Instruction and Education of the Negro Slaves in the British West India Islands: 76, 156; *Annual reports*, 75
Society for the Education of the Poor in the Principles of the Established Church: 71; *Annual reports*, 72
Society for the Encouragement of Arts, Manufactures and Commerce in Barbados: 103, 182; *Institution and first proceedings*, 47–48; *The abridged minutes*, 48; *Premium for standards*, 48; *Premiums for cultivation*, 50
Society for the Furtherance of the Gospel, 178
Society for the Improvement of Plantership: *Minutes*, 65–66
Society for the Improvement of West India Plantership, 65
Society for the Mitigation and Gradual Abolition of Slavery throughout the British Dominions, 79
Society for the Propagation of the Gospel in Foreign Parts: *An abstract of the proceedings*, 18; *Annual reports*, 18; *Proceedings*, 18; *Extracts from the annual reports*, 82; extract from reports, 83; *Report of the society*, 85; *Report*, 88–89; *Report respecting the Negroes*, 90. *See also* United Society for the Propagation of the Gospel
Society Instituted for the Purpose of Effecting the Abolition of the Slave Trade, 51
A soldier's recollections: St. Clair, 90
The solemnity and order of proclaiming James, 13
Some account of the British dominions: Doyle, 42
Some account of the late missionaries: Coke, 52
Some considerations humbly offered to both houses, 18, 19
Some memoirs of the first settlement: Duke, 30
Some memoirs of the life: Tryon, 13
Some observations made upon the Barbados seeds: Peachie, 15
Some observations on a direct exportation: Ashley, 28
Some observations shewing the danger: Cleland, 22
Some remarks in reference to recent proceedings: Hamden, 79–80

Some remarks upon the structure: Skey, 68 69
Somersett case, 43
Something in answer to a book, 7
Song, 90. *See also* Slaves
South Carolina: 72, 104, 151, 179; Lords Proprietors of, 151; University of, manuscripts, 182
South Carolina Historical Society: manuscripts, 180
Southey, Thomas: *Chronological history*, 81
South Sea Company, 28
Souvenirs des Antilles: Montlezun, 70
Spain: archives in, 166. *See also* Spanish
Spanish: military expedition against, 4, 134, 136; slave trade with, 28, 133, 165, 175, 178
Spann, Jonathan: *The remarkable occurrences*, 21
Spare minutes at the pier: Orderson, 85
Sparke, Arthur, 153
Sparke, Charles, 153
Sparke, Gabrielle, 153
Sparke, Mary, 153
Speed, John: *A prospect of the most famous parts*, 10
Speightstown, 9, 64, 100, 115. *See also* Towns
Spencer, John William, 126
Spencer, Robert, 172
Spencer, Thomas: *A true and faithful relation*, 15
Spirit of West India society, 79
Spooner, John: *Proclamations*, 69
Spörri, Felix Christian: *Americanische*, 10–11
Springer, Thomas Johnson, 64
Spurdle, F. G., 151
Stamp act: controversy over, with North American colonies, 38, 39, 40
Statement made by the agent, 86–87
A statement of the condition: Jordan, 75
A statement of the receipts: Coke, 56
A statement relative to Codrington College, 83
A state of the present condition, 16
State of the trade: Whitworth, 44
Statistics for the study: Ragatz, 101
Stede, Edwyn, Gov., 134
Steele, Joshua: and Society for the Encouragement of Arts, 47–48, 50; letters of, 48, 50; *History of the Mango*, 53; *Letters of Philo-Xylon*, 53–54; contributions to English prosody, 54; slave children of, 60, 165; will of, 60, 165; copyhold system of, 66, 73, 78; *Supplement to the Privy*

Council's report, 106
Steele, Mary Ann, 60
Steele, Richard: inherits plantation, 21; *Inkle and Yariko*, 21
Stephen, James: *The slavery of the British West India colonies*, 77–78; *The crisis of the sugar colonies*, 78; *The memoirs of*, 78
Stevens, B. F.: *Facsimiles of manuscripts*, 98
Stewart, Abel, 89
Stewart, Robert, 20
Stock, Leo Francis: *Proceedings and debates*, 101
Stokes, Anthony: *A view of the constitution*, 46–47
Stone, Andrew, 124
Stonington Historical Society library: manuscripts, 181
Storey, Benjamin, 159
Storey, Joseph, 152
Story, Thomas: 154; *A journal of the life*, 33
The story of Inkle and Yarrico: Seymour, 29
Stowe manuscripts (British Museum), 136
Straghan, Harbourne G.: *Disputatio medica*, 72
Straker, Carol D.: *Dissertatio medica*, 73
Stuart, Mary, 128
Stuart, Robert, 128
Stubbes, Henry: *Observations made by a curious and learned person*, 7; *Observations made in a voyage*, 7
Stubbs, John, 22, 155
Sturge, Joseph: works on West Indies, 93; and Harvey, Thomas, *The West Indies in 1837*, 93
Sturge, William, 132
Sturge and Forde, firm of, 174
Substance of the debate in the House of Commons, 79
The substance of the evidence, 43–44, 45
Substance of three reports: Dwarris, 80–81
Sugar: manufacture and production of, 4, 6, 11, 13, 16, 17, 19, 23, 27, 35, 38, 43, 49, 59, 96, 97, 131, 132, 134, 147, 150, 158, 159; case against refining in colonies, 15; duties on, 15, 46, 129, 131; prices on, 56, 174; milling of, 58, 64. *See also* Agriculture; Four-and-a-half percent duty; Sugar mills
Sugar cane: introduction of varieties, 102; first introduction of, 136. *See also* Agriculture
The sugar-cane: Grainger, 60
Sugar industry: papers on, 150
Sugar mills: distribution on island, 9; constructional materials, 16; number of,

Sugar mills: (*cont.*)
69, 135, 149, 180; sketches of, 152, 167. *See also* Sugar
Sugar plantations. *See* Plantations
Sugar trade, 15, 16, 25, 26, 27, 28, 36, 46, 131, 139. *See also* Trade
The sugar trade: Ashley, 27–28
Suleven, Thomas, 132
A summary, historical and political: Douglass, 35–36
A summary of colonial law: Clark, 89
Summers, John, 30
A supplement to the detection: Robertson, 27
A supplement to the Negro's and Indians: Godwyn, 12
Supplement to the Privy Council's report: Steele, 106
A supplement to the second part of the memoirs: Ashley, 32
Surinam, 64, 72, 133, 166
Surinam justice: Sanford, 5
Surveyors: names of, 69, 87
Swarthmore manuscript transcriptions (Society of Friends library), 155
A system of French: Holder, 55

Tanner manuscripts (Oxford University), 146
Taverns and hotels, 62, 84, 90, 91, 95
Taxes, 3, 62, 100, 135, 164
Taylor, George N. and Packer, Charles: *Laws of Barbados*, 97
Taylor, John, 155; *An account of some of the labours*, 12; *A loving and friendly*, 12
Taylor, R. V., 149
Teachers. *See* Schools
Temple Newsam Records (Leeds Central library), 143
Templeton, T. S., 120
Tentamen inaugurale: Chapman, 71; Russell, 73
Tentamen medicum: Lovell, 45; Lynch, 57
Tentamen physiologicum: Hendy, 43; Leacock, 67
Terrill, Michael, 145
Terron, Colbert de, 167
The terrors of the storm: Luckock, 84
Tertre, Jean Baptiste du: *Histoire générale*, 7
A testimony and warning: Fell, 9–10
Third letter: Simmons, 90
Thirty-six voyages: Coggeshall, 97
Thomas, Charles, 172
Thomas, Dalby: *An historical account*, 14
Thomas, Reynolds Clarke: *Dissertatio inauguralis*, 71

Thome, J. A. and Kimball, J. H.: *Emancipation in the West Indies*, 93–94
Thompson, Benjamin, 57
Thomson, John, 172
Thorne, Joseph, 170
Thornhill, James, 119
Thorpe, James, 171
Thoughts on the necessity: Clarkson, 73
Three years adventures: Butterworth, 72–73
Thurloe, John: papers of, 31
Tobacco, 11, 104, 131, 164
Tobago: 125, 130, 182; capture from Dutch, 9, 136; description of, 16, 60; mission station at, 138
To friends in Barbadoes: Fox, 6
To Henry Grenville, 35
To His Most Excellent Majesty, 12
Tombstones: transcriptions from, 98, 100, 103–4, 130
Toner, J. M., 176
A topographical map: Schomburgk, 96
Toppan, Robert N.: *Edward Randolph*, 98
Toriano, Nathaniel, 28
Tortola, 95
To the equity and policy of a great nation, 54
To the equity and policy of Great Britain, 54
To the ministers: Fox, 8
To the Queen's most Excellent Majesty, 21
To the Right Hon. Lord George Germain: Estwick, 45
Tottenham, Maj.-Gen., 107
A tour through the British West Indies: McKinnen, 61
A tour through the several islands: Young, 60
Towne, James, 107
Towne, Richard: *A treatise of the diseases*, 24; letter to Hans Sloane, 136
Town Hall: committee of, names of members, 91
Towns, 10, 11, 103, 147. *See also* Bridgetown; Holetown; Speightstown
Towns, Thomas: *An extract of a letter*, 10; *Observations made*, 10
Trade: 2, 11, 13, 17, 21–32 passim, 41, 45, 129, 132, 134, 135, 146, 150, 171; affected by legal structure, 18; with Caribbean territories, 36; statistics on, 44, 62; proposals for excluding non-English, 145. *See also* Commerce; Connecticut; Dutch; Exports; Great Britain; Holland; Imports; Maryland; Massachusetts; New England; New York; North America; Pennsylvania; Ireland; Rhode

Island; Spanish; Sugar trade
Traders. *See* Merchants
Trafalgar Square, 91, 95
Trail, John: *A map of the fortified part*, 32
Transatlantic sketches: Alexander, 87
Travels in North America: Philips, 76
Treasurer: accounts of, 151
Treasury: sums paid from, 175
Treasury papers (Public Record Office), 151, 152
A treatise concerning the malignant fever: Warren, 31
A treatise of the diseases: Towne, 24
A treatise on the glandular: Hendy, 47
A treatise on the wealth: Colquhoun, 66 67
A treatise on tropical: Moseley, 51
A treatise upon husbandry: Belgrove, 35
Treatment of slaves, 74
Trinidad, 93, 128
Trinity College, Dublin: manuscripts, 146, 152, 162–63
Trollope, Fanny, 120
Trot, Elizabeth, 155
Trott, Nicholas: *The laws of the British plantations*, 24
A true and exact history: Ligon, 4
A true and faithful account: Clarke, 7–8
A true and faithful account of an intire and absolute, 14–15, 175
A true and faithful relation: Spencer, 6
A true and perfect narrative: Bushel and Bond, 7
A true state of the case, 1–2
The true travels: Smith, 1
Truman, George, et al.: *Narrative of a visit*, 95
Trumball, Jonathan, 171
Trumball additional manuscripts (Berkshire Record Office), 128
The truth exalted: Burnyeat, 15
Truths from the West Indies: Hodgson, 93
Truths in a true light: Makemie, 17
Tryon, Thomas: *Friendly advice*, 13; *Some memoirs of the life*, 13; *England's grandeur*, 17; *Tryon's letters*, 17–18; *The merchant, citizen, and countryman's instructor*, 18
Tryon's letters: Tryon, 17–18
Tucker, Josiah, 44
Tuckerman, John, 162
A twelvemonth's residence: Madden, 90–91
The two charters: Society for Advancing the Christian Faith, 92
Two letters: Riland, 82

Two letters and several calculations: Bennett, 29
Tyrrell, Adm. 132

Uber die drüsenkrankheit, 51–52
Uchteritz, Heinrich von: *Kurtze reise-beschreibung*, 6
United Brethren: *Periodical accounts*, 55. *See also* Moravians
United Kingdom. *See* Great Britain
United Society for the Propagation of the Gospel: archives, 156–57. *See also* Society for the Propagation of the Gospel in Foreign Parts
Universal history, 63
Uring, Nathaniel: *A relation of the late intended settlement*, 24; *A history of the voyages*, 24–25

Values in Barbados, 99
Valverde, Abraham, 174
Vans Eyndhoven, Jan. *See* Eyndhoven, Jan vans
Vassa, Gustavas, 53
Vaughan, John, 46, 169
Vaughan, Thomas, 145
Venables, Gen., 4, 99
Verney, Thomas, 96
Verney family, 96
Vestry records, 122*n*5, 152
Victorious love: Walker, 16–17
A view of the constitution: Stokes, 46–47
Views in the island of Barbados: Carter, 91
A vindication of the opinions: Hendy, 53
Virginia, 104, 146, 166, 172
Virginia Historical Society: manuscripts, 182
Volcanic ash. *See* St. Vincent
Von Sack, Albert. *See* Sack, Albert von
Von Uchteritz, Heinrich. *See* Uchteritz, Heinrich von
The votes and proceedings of the honourable the assembly, 25
Votes and proceedings of the house of assembly, 25
Voyage de la France: Biet, 5
A voyage in the West Indies: Waller, 72
The voyage of Sr. Henrye Colte, 101
A voyage to Guinea: Atkins, 28
A voyage to the islands: Sloane, 19
A voyage to the new island, 20
The voyages and adventures of Capt. Barth. Sharp: Ayres, 12
Voyages de Daniel le Hirbec: Moreau, 98
Voyages to various parts: Willock, 54

Waddell, D. A. G., 163
Wadeson, Samuel, 141
Walcott, Thomas, 174
Walduck, J.: letters of, 135
Walker, George, 44, 45
Walker, Thomas, 134
Walker, William: *Victorious love*, 16–17; *Marry or do worse*, 17
Waller, John Augustine: *A voyage in the West Indies*, 72, 84
Walrond family: history of, 126
Walsh, Stephen, 159
Walter, John, 49
Wanderings in South America: Waterton, 79
The wanderings of Warwick: Smith, 57
War, Council of: minutes, 150
Warburton, William: *A sermon preached*, 40
Ward, Joseph, 146
Warde, Henry, Gov., 109, 111
Wardle, D. B. 127, 147
Ware, John, 177
A warning to the inhabitants: Rous, 4
Warren, Henry: *A treatise concerning the malignant fever*, 31
Warren, Robert, 25, 143
Warwick, Earl of. *See* Rich, Robert
Washington, George: journal, 176–77
Washington, Lawrence, 176
Water supplies, 10, 50, 103
Waterton, Charles: *Wanderings in South America*, 79
Watson, George, 120
Watts, David, 136
Watts, Thomas, 90
Weather: observations and overviews, 7, 10, 21, 31, 39, 44, 45, 47, 51, 54, 66, 72, 103, 124, 133, 135, 140, 159, 163, 173, 174, 180
Weaver, William, 146
Weekes, Nathaniel: *Barbados. A Poem*, 35
Weekes, Nathaniel, Dr.: *Disputatio medica*, 58
Welch, William: *Dissertatio medica*, 58
Wentworth, Trelawney: *The West India sketch book*, 90
Wesleyans. *See* Methodists
West, Joseph, 151
Western Star, 118
The West-India atlas: Jefferys, 43
The West India colonies: M'Queen, 76
West India Committee library: manuscripts, 159–60
The West-India common-place book: Young, 62–63, 101
West Indian, 118
West India Reference library, 124

West India Regiment, 61, 90
The West India sketch book: Wentworth, 90
West India slavery, 78
The West Indies: Montgomery, 64; Halliday, 92; Davy, 97
West Indies, University of: manuscripts, 125–26
The West Indies in 1837: Sturge and Harvey, 93
West Indies—slavery, 80, 81
Whereas a proclamation having appeared, 74
Whistler, Henry: journal, 99, 136
White, Andrew: possible authorship, 1; *Narrative of a voyage to Maryland*, 98
White, John, 1
White, Thomas, W., 125
Whites, lower classes. *See* Poor whites
Whitworth, Charles: *State of the trade*, 44
Whitworth, Francis, 141
Widder, Robert, 22, 155
Wigglesworth, Edward, 177
Wilcox, Nicholas, 174
Wilkinson and Gaviller, firm of, 142
William Bell and his second visit: Boromé, 104
Williams, C., 119
Williams, Richard, 171
Williams, William, 118
Williamson, John: *Medical and miscellaneous observations*, 70
Willing, Charles, 171
Willock, John: *Voyages to various parts*, 54
Willoughby, Francis, Gov., 3, 5, 119, 129, 133, 145, 146, 162, 175, 179
Willoughby, Lady (of Parham), 144
Willoughby, William (of Parham), Gov., 136–37, 145, 151
Willoughby, William (of Hundsen), 144
Willoughby's fort, 38
Wills: transcriptions and extracts, 99, 122*n*4, 152; of Jews, 102; in Barbados archives, 122; testators, names of, index to, 132; of Nightingale family, 139; T. Root, 140; Gibbons family, 140; T. Lane, 158
Willyams, Cooper: *An account of the campaign*, 57
Wilshire, Richard, 174
Wilson, Dr.: death of, 179
Wilson, Joseph: *Disputatio medica*, 69
Windmills. *See* Sugar mills
Windwards: 176, 179–80; records in, 123
Wine: imports, 10, 139; making, 129. *See also* Beverages
Wing, Donald: *Short-title catalogue*, x

Winslow, Edward, 177
Winthrop, John, 97, 99
Winthrop, Robert C.: *Life and letters of John Winthrop*, 97
Winthrop's journal, 99
W., J.: biography of Robert Rich, 7
Wolverston, Charles, Gov., 1, 162
Wood, Alexander, 65
Wood, John, 126
Wood, Samson, 158
Woodbridge, Dudley, 28, 119
Woodin, John, 174
Woodward, George, 107
Workhouses, 47
Works of the late Doctor Franklin: Franklin, 56
Worsley, Henry, Gov., 131
Worthing: drawing of, 91
Wright, Benjamin, 171
Wright, Philip, 94

Wright, William: *Memoirs*, 81–82
Wyatt, Alfred Francis W., 174
Wynne, John Huddlestone: *A general history*, 42
Wyvill, Richard Augustus: memoirs, 177

Yarico, 21, 29, 32, 39, 43, 51, 57
Yarico to Inkle: 29; Jerningham, 39; Anketell, 43
The yarn of a yankee: Browne, 101
Yeamans, John, 145, 151
Yearwood, Samuel: *A pocket-book*, 85–86; *The Barbados pocket-book*, 87, 89, 92
Yearwood, Seale: *Letters*, 103
Yeates, John: papers of, 174

Yellow fever. *See* Diseases
Young, Arthur: *American husbandry*, 44
Young, Bryan Taylor, 126
Young, Nathan L.: *Disputatio medica*, 70
Young, William: *A tour through the several islands*, 60; *The West-India common-place book*, 62–63, 101
Youth persuaded to obedience: Chalkley, 25

Zenger, John Peter, 42
Zimmerman, Peter Karl: *Reise nach ost-und West-Indien*, 42
Zouch, Arthur: *A catalogue of books*, 17; laws compiled by, 23, 37
Zurst, Richard, 164